AmongUS

Essays on Identity, Belonging, and Intercultural Competence
Second Edition

Edited by

Myron W. Lustig
San Diego State University

Jolene Koester
California State University, Northridge

PEARSON

Boston • New York • San Francisco • Mexico City • Montreal • Toronto • London • Madrid • Munich • Paris • Hong Kong • Singapore • Tokyo • Cape Town • Sydney

Executive Editor: Karon Bowers
Series Editor: Brian Wheel
Series Editorial Assistant: Heather Hawkins
Senior Marketing Manager: Mandee Eckersley
Production Editor: Beth Houston
Editorial Production Service: Nesbitt Graphics
Composition Buyer: Linda Cox
Manufacturing Buyer: JoAnne Sweeney
Electronic Composition: Nesbitt Graphics
Cover Administrator: Kristina Mose-Libon

For related titles and support materials, visit our online catalog at www.ablongman.com.

Between the time website information is gathered and then published, it is not unusual for some sites to have closed. Also, the transcription of URLs can result in typographical errors. The publisher would appreciate notification where these errors occur so that they may be corrected in subsequent editions.

AmongUS: essays on identity, belonging, and intercultural competence / edited by Myron
  W. Lustig; Jolene Koester.—2nd ed.
    p. cm.
  Includes bibliographical references.
  ISBN 0-205-45353-8
    1. Pluralism (Social sciences)—United States. 2. Group identity—United States. 3.
Intercultural communication—United States. 4. United States—Ethnic relations. 5. United
States—Race relations. I. Title: Among US. II. Lustig, Myron W. III. Koester, Jolene.

E184.A1A65 2005
305.8'00973—dc22

2005048675

Printed in the United States of America

Contents

PART **THREE**

Othering: Racism and Prejudice AmongUS

PART **FOUR**

Inside/Outside: Belonging to Multiple Cultures

Preface

This book of essays, our students tell us, helps people learn about living and communicating in an intercultural world. It was created with the assistance and collaboration of colleagues and friends from many disciplines.

In the United States, we are in the midst of a great social experiment with few examples of how to proceed, much less how to succeed. The goal of this social experiment is easily articulated but difficult to achieve: to become an effective and well-functioning intercultural nation. But how do we create a single nation with many cultures? How can U.S. Americans live, thrive, and interact peacefully? How do we sustain our unique cultural identities while maintaining a common national identity?

It is easy to find the negative examples: people who are intolerant of those from other groups, people who equate "different" with "inferior" and perhaps "threatening," people who measure others only and always by standards that place themselves at the top of the hierarchy. Much harder to find are the positive examples, the useful clues, and the helpful suggestions about what it means and what is required to build something that heretofore has never existed: an intercultural United States of America, with the many cultures of the U.S. living together in harmony, living as equals, living among other U.S. Americans, living AmongUS.

For the twenty-first century inhabitants of the United States of America, this book provides examples of people whose intercultural experiences give insights and clues about how to achieve an effective and fair intercultural society. In such a society, unique cultural identities are celebrated and maintained within a common national boundary.

The essays in *AmongUS* are designed to help develop a road map toward that goal. They are written by people who themselves have struggled with the inherent tensions of living AmongUS, who have faced enormous and sometimes overwhelming challenges to their cultural identities, who have given voice to their longing for belonging, who have confronted prejudices and discrimination and have learned to survive and thrive, and who have been on the front lines of the negotiations that must be resolved peacefully if we are to live AmongUS as interculturally competent communicators.

▶ General Approach

What makes *AmongUS* different from other collections of readings in intercultural communication is the centrality of lived experiences by individuals engaged in communication with culturally different others. What is common to all of the writers is their personal and active engagement in working through the issues of cultural identity and intercultural communication in the United States. While many of the authors are scholars in their own right, their ideas on these pages are anchored primarily in their personal experiences. Thus the authors are not only informed by a deep knowledge and understanding of intercultural communication, they use their personal voices as the basis for the claims they make about intercultural relationships. The essays allow readers to feel, experience, and understand what the authors have experienced.

The impetus for creating this book came from our students. They told us that they find traditional textbooks useful but incomplete. Missing is the opportunity to understand what happens in the minds, hearts, and behaviors of people who come from culturally disparate backgrounds yet are attempting to communicate with one another. Our students challenged us to provide extended examples, not just a myriad of short vignettes, that illustrate the substantive concepts and ideas. They recognized, as we do, that those involved in intercultural communication do not always react to cultural differences with a purely detached and intellectualized response. They wanted a richer sense of the stress and distress, the passion and compassion that inevitably seems to accompany many real-world intercultural interactions. While we believe strongly that theory and research provide essential anchors for a substantive understanding of intercultural phenomena, we also agree with our students that the emotional links to these ideas come from a deep understanding of their own and others' lived experiences. The essays in this book provide that emotional link.

Each essay tells a simple and poignant story, but it also addresses many of the issues relevant to living in an intercultural nation. Thus they each have embedded within them many conceptual and theoretical ideas, which they illustrate. These ideas cut across the range of topics usually covered in more traditional textbooks in intercultural communication, cross-cultural identity, multicultural education, international business, and other disciplines. Standard textbooks have the luxury of developing conceptual ideas in a linear, straightforward, and thorough way, whereas intercultural experiences—including the lived experiences described in *AmongUS*—happen all at once, as a gestalt or an integrated whole.

▶ Changes to This Edition

Some very important and substantial changes have been made to this second edition. First, the book has been reorganized. The order of the book's four sections, and the arrangement of the essays within each section, has been restructured to provide a better depiction of the processes we typically experience when living in an intercultural world.

Second, ten new essays have been added. A new theoretical essay introduces Part II, and nine additional essays provide contemporary stories about living in a multicultural world. Included among these new essays are second essays from four of the original authors. They each describe an ongoing intercultural journey in which the author continues to learn and to live AmongUS. Taken as a whole, these new essays provide a much richer and broader range of intercultural voices and experiences.

Third, interspersed within each essay are Culture Concepts boxes. Our reviewers, adopters, and students asked for more explicit links to the theory that underlies the lived experiences that are depicted, so we added this pedagogical element. Note, however, that because intercultural communication occurs as a gestalt package of information, emotions, and experiences, each of the Culture Concepts can also be used to understand many other essays in the book.

Fourth, at the end of each essay are analytical exercises and discussion questions that we call "Learning AmongUS." These focused applications ask students to reflect on the essay, to analyze it, to link it to the Culture Concepts in that essay, and to connect it to ideas provided in other parts of the book.

Finally, for those who would like to pair this book with our other text (*Intercultural Competence: Interpersonal Communication across Cultures*), the links between the works are now more direct and straightforward, which allows them to work better in tandem.

▶ Using *AmongUS*

The book is intended for the general student reader. While grounded in a scholarly understanding of intercultural communication, the essays are presented in an easy-to-read narrative style with a minimum of footnotes and references.

The book can be used as an independent text for courses about human interactions in the intercultural United States of the twenty-first century. Because we are communication scholars, the focus of our own teaching is on the creation and interpretation of symbols, messages, and meanings. However, the essays provide a rich source of materials to teach a broad array of sociological, psychological, and interpersonal concepts that apply to education, business, and other intercultural settings.

AmongUS can also be used to complement other texts that are grounded in a more scholarly treatment of theories and constructs. Combining this anthology of essays with a more traditional textbook can provide an intellectual framework to help you understand both the experiences of those living AmongUS and the concepts that undergird them. In our own teaching of intercultural communication, we use the essays in *AmongUS* to complement the ideas in *Intercultural Competence: Interpersonal Communication across Cultures*, which we have also authored and that Allyn & Bacon also publishes.

▶ Organization

There are four major parts of the book, each with seven to nine essays. Each section begins with an overview essay that provides a substantive exposition of a major theme: identity, negotiating intercultural competence, racism and prejudice, and belonging to multiple cultures. A brief introductory paragraph to each essay helps focus your attention and puts the ideas in context.

The placement of each essay within the book is, to some extent, arbitrary. As with all human encounters, the experiences of the authors do not neatly fall into discrete categories without overlap. Thus we encourage you to read and impose your own mental frameworks on the issues exemplified by the lived experiences portrayed on these pages.

Part I, "Cultural Identity: Who Are We?" begins with a conceptual overview of how a person develops a cultural identity and its relationship to social and personal aspects of one's identity. In the six subsequent essays, the authors describe experiences that affirm or deny essential elements of their cultural identities.

Part II is titled "Crossing Cultures: Negotiating Intercultural Competence." The opening essay provides a scholarly understanding of intercultural competence, an exposition of the nature of cultural patterns, and a description of the dimensions along which cultures differ. The eight remaining essays present case studies of individuals attempting to make sense of and function both appropriately and effectively in a different cultural environment.

Part III, "Othering: Racism and Prejudice AmongUS," explores the pernicious and invidious consequences of discrimination. The introductory essay describes important background understandings about human cognitive processes that are the basis for racism, prejudice, ethnocentrism, and discrimination. The authors of the seven subsequent essays in this section speak directly about their personal experiences in reacting to and resolving the "othering" that has been directed toward them.

Part IV, the final section of the anthology, is titled "Inside/Outside: Belonging to Multiple Cultures." The introductory essay presents a theoretical perspective by which to understand the transformations that individuals experience when they interact and live within multiple cultures. Each of the seven subsequent essays tells a story about grappling with cultural identities that are anchored in multiple cultural frameworks. The authors describe their efforts to transform themselves into interculturally competent individuals.

▶ Appreciation and Assistance

Our deep appreciation goes to those who contributed the essays that form the messages of this book. The authors of the essays have been willing to present personal descriptions of their lives, which help provide models for effective and appropriate intercultural interactions with others. Their deep commitment to the celebration of cultural differences as a means of forging a well-functioning intercultural nation is evident in their work.

We would also like to thank Annegret Horsch, of San Diego State University, for her assistance with many editorial tasks. In addition, we thank the reviewers who read the essays at various stages of their inception and preparation. Specifically, we would like to acknowledge the contributions of those who provided feedback on the essays: Nanci Burk, Glendale Community College; Gary David, Bentley College; Desiree C. Duff, Cornerstone University; Anneliese Harper, Scottsdale Community College; and Ann D. Jabro, Robert Morris University. We acknowledge, as well, the important contributions to this book from our students. They continually inspire and encourage us to find ways to translate theory and research into powerful examples.

We hope you will appreciate these essays and learn from them.

Myron W. Lustig
Jolene Koester

Cultural Identity

Who Are We?

1 The Nature of Cultural Identity[1]

Myron W. Lustig and Jolene Koester

How do people come to identify themselves as belonging to a particular culture? How and when does a child begin to think of herself as a Latina, a Jewish American, or a Korean American? How are some people defined as "not members" of a culture?

Our cultural identity—the self-concept of a person who belongs to a particular cultural group—has a powerful effect on our intercultural communication. As part of the socialization process, children learn to view themselves as members of particular groups. Children in all cultures, for example, are taught to identify with their families. As a child becomes a teenager and then an adult, the development of vocational and avocational interests creates new groups with which he or she can identify. "Baseball player," "ballet dancer," or "scientist" may become important labels to describe the self.

Another feature of socialization is that people are taught about groups to which they do not belong, and they often learn that certain groups should be avoided. This tendency to identify as a member of some groups, called *ingroups*, and to distinguish these ingroups from *outgroups*, is so prevalent in human thinking that it has been described as a universal human tendency.[2]

▶ The Nature of Identity

Related to the distinction between ingroup and outgroup membership is the concept of one's *identity*, or self-concept. An individual's self-concept is built on cultural, social, and personal identities.[3]

Cultural identity refers to our sense of belonging to a particular culture or ethnic group. It is formed through a process that results from membership in a particular culture, and it involves learning about and accepting the traditions, heritage, language, religion, ancestry, aesthetics, thinking patterns, and social structures of a culture. That is, people internalize the beliefs, values, norms, and social practices of their culture and identify with that culture as part of their self-concept.

Social identity develops as a consequence of our memberships in particular groups within our culture. The characteristics and concerns common to most members of such social groups shape the way individuals view their characteristics. The types of groups with which people identify can vary widely and might include perceived similarities such as age, gender, work, religion, ideology, social class, place (neighborhood, region, and nation), and common interests. For instance, those baseball players, ballet dancers, and scientists who strongly identify with their particular professions likely view themselves as "belonging" to "their" group of professionals, with whom they share similar traits and concerns.

Finally, *personal identity* is based on individuals' unique characteristics, which frequently differ from those of others in their cultural and social groups. You may like cooking or chemistry, singing or sewing; you may play tennis or trombones, soccer or stereos; you may view yourself as studious or sociable, goofy or gracious; and most assuredly you have abilities, talents, quirks, and preferences that differ from those of others.

For ease and clarity we have chosen to present aspects of a person's identity as separate categories. A great deal of interdependence, however, exists among these three aspects of identity. Characteristics of people's social identities inevitably are linked to preferences shaped by their cultural identities. Similarly, how people enact their unique interests is heavily influenced by their cultural identities. Thus, for example, a teenage girl's identity will likely be strongly linked to her culture's preferences for gendered role behaviors, as well as to her social class and her personal characteristics and traits.

▶ The Formation of Cultural Identity

Cultural identities often develop through a process involving three stages: unexamined cultural identity, cultural identity search, and cultural identity achievement.[4] During the *unexamined cultural identity* stage our cultural characteristics are taken for granted, and consequently there is little interest in exploring cultural issues. Young children, for instance, typically lack an awareness of cultural differences and the characteristics that differentiate one culture from another. Teenagers and adults may not want to categorize themselves as belonging to any particular culture.[5] Some people may not have explored the meanings and consequences of their cultural membership but may simply have accepted preconceived ideas about it that they obtained from parents, their community, the mass media, and others. Consequently, some individuals may unquestioningly accept the prevailing stereotypes held by others and may internalize common stereotypes of their own culture and themselves. Scholars have suggested that the cultural identities of many European Americans, in particular, have remained largely unexamined, a consequence of the power, centrality, and privilege the European American cultural group has had in the United States.[6] As Judith Martin, Robert Krizek, Thomas Nakayama, and Lisa Bradford suggest,

> This lack of attention to white identity and self-labeling reflects the historical power held by Whites in the United States. That is, Whites as the privileged group take their identity as the norm or standard by which other groups are measured, and this identity is therefore invisible, even to the extent that many Whites do not consciously think about the profound effect being White has on their everyday lives.[7]

Cultural identity search is a process of exploration and questioning about our culture to learn more about it and to understand the implications of our membership in that culture. By exploring the culture we can learn about its strengths and may come to a point of acceptance of both our culture and ourselves. For some individuals a turning point or crucial event precipitates this stage, whereas for others it begins with a simple growing awareness and reinterpretation of everyday experiences. Common to this stage is an increased social and political awareness, along with an increased desire to learn more about one's culture. Such learning may be characterized by an increase in discussions with family and friends about cultural issues, independent reading of relevant sources, enrollment in appropriate courses, or attendance at cultural events such as festivals and museums. There may also be an emotional component of varying intensity to this stage involving tension, anger, and perhaps even outrage directed toward other groups. These emotions may intensify as people become aware of and wrestle with the effects of discrimination on their present and future lives and the potential difficulties in attaining educational, career, and personal objectives.

Cultural identity achievement is characterized by a clear, confident acceptance of ourselves and an internalization of our cultural identity. Such acceptance can be calmly and securely used to guide our future actions. People in this stage have developed ways of dealing with stereotypes and discrimination so they don't internalize others' negative perceptions and are clear about the personal meanings of their culture. This outcome contributes to increased self-confidence and positive psychological adjustment. Table 1 on page 6 provides sample comments from individuals in each of the three stages of cultural identity development.

▶ Characteristics of Cultural Identities

Once formed, cultural identities provide an essential framework for organizing and interpreting our experiences of others. This is so because cultural identities are central, dynamic, multifaceted components of our self-concept.

Cultural identities are central to a person's sense of self. Like gender and race, your culture is "basic" because it is broadly influential and linked to a great number of other aspects of your self-concept. These core aspects of your identity are likely to be important in the majority of your interactions with others. Most components of your identity, however, become important only when they are activated by specific circumstances. For many people the experience of living in another culture or interacting with a person from a different culture triggers a new awareness of their own cultural identities. When a component of your identity becomes important, your experiences are filtered through that portion of your identity. Because cultural identities are central, most experiences are interpreted or framed by cultural membership.

Because cultural identities are dynamic, your cultural identity—your sense of the culture to which you belong and who you are in light of it—exists

Table 1   STAGES IN THE DEVELOPMENT OF CULTURAL IDENTITY

Stage	Sample Comments	Source of Comments
Unexamined Cultural Identity	"My parents tell me about where they lived, but what do I care? I've never lived there."	Mexican American Male
	"Why do I have to learn who was the first black woman to do this or that? I'm just not too interested."	African American Female
	"I don't have a culture. I'm just an American."	European American Male
Cultural Identity Search	"I think people should know what black people had to go through to get to where we are now."	African American Female
	"There are a lot of non-Japanese people around me and it gets pretty confusing to try and decide who I am."	Japanese American Male
	"I want to know what we do and how our culture is different from others."	Mexican American Female
Cultural Identity Achievement	"My culture is important and I am proud of what I am. Japanese people have so much to offer."	Japanese American Male
	"It used to be confusing to me, but it's clear now. I'm happy being black."	African American Female

Source: Adapted from Jean S. Phinney, "A Three-Stage Model of Ethnic Identity Development in Adolescence," *Ethnic Identity: Formation and Transmission among Hispanics and Other Minorities,* ed. Martha E. Bernal and George P. Knight (Albany: State University of New York Press, 1993), 61–79.

within a changing social context. Consequently, your identity is not static, fixed, and enduring; rather, it is dynamic and changes with your ongoing life experiences. In even the briefest encounter with people whose cultural backgrounds differ from your own, your sense of who you are *at that instant* may well be altered, at least in some small ways. Over time, as you adapt to various intercultural challenges, your cultural identity may be transformed into one that is substantially different from what it used to be. The inaccurate belief that cultural identities are permanent, that "once a Chinese American, always a Chinese American," ignores the possibility of profound changes that people may experience as a result of their intercultural contacts.

Cultural identities are also multifaceted. At any given moment you have many components that make up your identity. For instance, a specific person may simultaneously view herself as a student, an employee, a friend, a woman, a southerner, a daughter, a Methodist, a baby boomer, and more. Similarly, your cultural identity typically has many facets or components.

Many people incorrectly assume that an individual could—or perhaps should—identify with only one cultural group. However, as Young Yun Kim suggests,

> If someone sees himself or herself, or is seen by others, as a Mexican American, then this person's identity is [commonly] viewed to exclude all other identities. This tendency to see cultural identity in an "all-or-none" and "either-or" manner glosses over the fact that many people's identities are not locked into a single, uncompromising category, but incorporate other identities as well.[8]

Given our increasingly multicultural world, in which people from many cultures coexist and in which the United States has become a country where individuals from many cultures live and interact, the multifaceted characteristic of cultural identity is even more important.

The cultures with which you identify affect your views about where you belong and who you consider to be "us" and "them." A good place to begin talking about your own cultural identity is to describe yourself in terms of the culture (or cultures) to which you belong. Is this relatively easy for you to do? Have you always been aware of your cultural background, or have you experienced events that lead you to search for an understanding of your cultural identity? Do you find your cultural identity primarily in one cultural group or in several cultural groups? How does your cultural identity shape your social and personal identity? Does your cultural identity result in a strong sense of others as either in or out of your cultural group? If so, were you taught to evaluate negatively those who are not part of your cultural group? Conversely, do you sometimes feel excluded from and evaluated negatively by people from cultures that differ from your own? The answers to these questions will help you understand the possible consequences, both positive and negative, of your cultural identity as you communicate interculturally.

Notes

1. Excerpted and adapted from Myron W. Lustig and Jolene Koester, *Intercultural Competence: Interpersonal Communication Across Cultures,* 5th ed. (Boston: Allyn & Bacon, 2006).

2. Marilyn Brewer and Donald T. Campbell, *Ethnocentrism and Intergroup Attitudes* (New York: Wiley, 1976).

3. Our labels are analogous to Triandis's tripartite distinction among one's collective self, public self, and private self. See Harry C. Triandis, "The Self and Social Behavior in Differing Cultural Contexts," *Psychological Review* 96 (1989): 506–520. See also Henri Tajfel, *Differentiation Between Social Groups* (London: Academic Press, 1978); Henri Tajfel, *Human Groups and Social Categories: Studies in Social Psychology* (Cambridge: Cambridge University Press, 1981).

4. Our discussion of the stages of cultural identity draws heavily on the works of Jean S. Phinney, particularly Jean S. Phinney, "A Three-Stage Model of Ethnic Identity Development in Adolescence," in *Ethnic Identity: Formation and Transmission Among Hispanics and Other Minorities,* ed. Martha E. Bernal and George P. Knight (Albany: State University of New York Press, 1993), 61–79. See also Jean S. Phinney, "Ethnic Identity

in Adolescents and Adults: Review of Research," *Psychological Bulletin* 108 (1990): 499–514; Jean S. Phinney, "Ethnic Identity and Self-Esteem: A Review and Integration," *Hispanic Journal of Behavioral Sciences* 13 (1991): 193–208.

5. Frances E. Aboud, "Interest in Ethnic Information: A Cross-Cultural Developmental Study," *Journal of Cross-Cultural Psychology* 7 (1977): 289–300; Frances E. Aboud, "The Development of Ethnic Self-Identification and Attitudes," in *Children's Ethnic Socialization*, ed. Jean S. Phinney and Mary Jane Rotheram (Newbury Park, CA: Sage, 1987), 32–55; Frances E. Aboud, *Children and Prejudice* (New York: Basil Blackwell, 1988).

6. See, for example, Richard D. Alba, *Ethnic Identity: The Transformation of White America* (New Haven, CT: Yale University Press, 1990); Theodore W. Allen, *The Invention of the White Race: Racial Oppression and Social Control* (New York: Verso, 1994); Russell Ferguson, "Introduction: Invisible Center," in *Out There: Marginalization and Contemporary Cultures*, ed. Russell Ferguson, Martha Gever, T. M. Trinh, and C. West (Cambridge: MIT Press, 1992), 9–14; Ruth Frankenburg, *White Women, Race Matters: The Social Construction of Whiteness* (Minneapolis: University of Minnesota Press, 1993); Judith N. Martin, Robert L. Krizek, Thomas K. Nakayama, and Lisa Bradford, "Exploring Whiteness: A Study of Self Labels for White Americans," *Communication Quarterly* 44 (1996): 125–144; Thomas K. Nakayama and Robert L. Krizek, "Whiteness: A Strategic Rhetoric," *Quarterly Journal of Speech* 81 (1995): 291–309.

7. Judith N. Martin, Robert L. Krizek, Thomas K. Nakayama, and Lisa Bradford, "Exploring Whiteness: A Study of Self Labels for White Americans," *Communication Quarterly* 44 (1996): 125.

8. Young Yun Kim, "Identity Development: From Cultural to Intercultural," in *Interaction & Identity*, ed. Hartmut B. Mokros (New Brunswick, NJ: Transaction, 1996), 350.

Patricia Covarrubias speaks of a sorrow arising from a sudden rupture from the only language she knew. She was just eight years old when her parents moved the family from Mexico to California. This essay describes the language of her culture and the special use of many terms of endearment (nicknames, pet names) that are so central to her identity and feelings of belonging. Patricia eloquently describes how the loss of her Spanish nicknames and the Americanization of her name to "Pat" denied her a sense of self, which she later found after a journey to reclaim "Patricia" and her return sojourn to Mexico.

2 Of Endearment and Other Terms of Address: A Mexican Perspective

Patricia Covarrubias

"This old man, he played two, he play knick-knack on my—" The singing jerked to a halt. It was my first day of school in my new country. As the school principal and I entered the third-grade classroom, Mrs. Williams ceased her piano playing and came toward me. With a hand on my shoulder, she steered me to face the children who were sitting in a large circle on small wooden chairs. "Class, this is *Pat*." With that introduction I had been rechristened. In one unexpected and infinitesimal moment, all that I was and had been was abridged into three-letter, bottom-line efficiency: *Pat*. Mrs. Williams could not have imagined that her choice of address, imposed on me in 1960, just two weeks after my mother, my brother, and I immigrated to the United States to join my father, would be a name I would revile for the rest of my life.

Yet I am not ungrateful to Mrs. Williams. She facilitated, inadvertently, an important pivotal point in my life. In calling me *Pat,* in that hair-splitting instant, she prompted what became one of my primary life themes: understanding the profound and enduring personal and social consequences of the terms people use to address one another. As a recent doctoral student in communication, I join those who suggest that address forms are unique vocabularies in and through which people strategically align themselves in reference to other people. But in that fractional childhood moment, all I could understand was that with a simple *Pat* Mrs. Williams had crammed me into a space I did not fit. I was suddenly at the mercy of a word that did not describe me. With a single syllable she invaded a private way of being and made it accessible publicly, on her terms. I knew I was not *Pat*, but I did not know enough English to defend myself.

From the moment I stepped into my new American world, the alien *Pat* separated me not only from myself but also from the classmates who would make up so much of my social life through elementary, junior high, and high school. For weeks, months, years I struggled to convey who I "really" was, using the most direct channel available to humans: speech. But I continually failed. I lacked the lexicon. I lacked the syntax. I lacked the defiance. Like a mute patient who holds the solution to a crime and wants to speak but is unable to do so, I gagged on my urge to argue for my real name, for the real me. By the time I acquired enough English and enough courage to assert my personhood, I was off by too much to catch up. Over time, the people who composed so much of my social world had formed impressions of the person they thought I was. *Pat* became a composite of my awkward utterances, their imaginations, and some destructive stereotypes.

During those early years I was in some in-between space, some hollow whose depth I did not comprehend for decades. Yet I realized from the beginning that I could not surrender to the gap that alienated me from myself and from everyone else. I sensed early on that integration and reintegration would come at a cost, but that they would come. I did not lose hope. I did not stop striving. Nor did I stop hearing my parents' admonitions for grit. Instinctively and by design, I set out to recover that which had been overtaken, without losing entirely the moment at hand.

Curiously, it was in the public sphere that the reintegration of my intimate, real self began to occur. Reintegration crystallized recently when I returned to Mexico for seven months to conduct ethnographic fieldwork for my doctoral dissertation. Since we left in December 1959 I had returned to Mexico only four or five times and only for brief visits. One absence lasted 16 years. Moreover, I had never returned alone. It was only against the backdrop of my recent stay that I have finally been able to answer my own questions: "What specifically did *Pat* take away from me?" and "Can I finally make peace with her?" For me to understand what I had lost, I first had to find out what I had possessed prior to our immigration.

My given name is Patricia Olivia Covarrubias Baillet, and I was born to a world shaped, in great measure, by what people call themselves and each other. Titles, first names, surnames, nicknames, terms of endearment, terms of estrangement—they all reflect and constitute a particular Mexican way of being. In my childhood world, people used terms of address not only to point to particular people but also to form particular relationships and to evoke complementary emotions.

As a child I was seldom called *Patricia*. To address someone by his or her first name *a secas* (literally "dryly" but connoting "alone") is perceived by most Mexicans as cold and distant. First names alone are generally reserved for reprimand or censure or to underscore formality. Therefore, in most conversations a variety of pointing terms are used to personalize one's communication with another and to affirm intimacy, friendship, esteem, and *confianza,* which is a blend of trust, respect, confidentiality, and unity.

Culture Concepts

Communication

Communication *is a symbolic, interpretive, transactional, contextual process in which people create shared meanings. Whenever people communicate, they must interpret the symbolic behaviors of others and assign significance to some of those behaviors in order to create a meaningful account of the others' actions. This idea suggests that each person in a communication transaction may not necessarily interpret the messages in exactly the same way. Indeed, during episodes involving intercultural communication, the likelihood is high that people will interpret the meaning of messages differently.*

In keeping with the Mexican penchant for avoiding formal names in favor of more personalized address when *confianza* is desired, at school and elsewhere in my world I was *Pati, Paty,* or *Patty* (the Spanish diminutives for *Patricia*). Only on formal occasions, such as at the presentation of school diplomas, are students addressed by their full names. All Mexicans have at least two last names, the first for their father's family name and the second for their mother's. As the Mexican expression goes, people have **two** parents. In the Maddox Academy annuals for 1958 and 1959, I am listed as *Covarrubias Baillet, Patricia Olivia.*

My grandmothers and great-grandmother were generous deployers of nicknames and other terms of endearment. They cajoled, hugged, bathed, dressed, played with me, took me to school, sang and read to me. They lathered me also with an abundant array of forms of address. To my paternal grandmother and great-grandmother, with whom I lived for a time, I was *Patricita, Pato* (duck), *Patita* (little duck or little foot), *la Patricita, la niña* (the girl), *la chiquita* (the little one). My mother's mother had her own selection. In addition to *Paty* and *Patricita,* she called me *mi rosita de Castilla* (my rose of Castille), *mi rosita de Jericó* (my rose of Jericho), *mi orquídea* (my orchid). I, in turn, had a term for these women who were additional mothers to me: *mamá*. My maternal grandmother was *Mamá Mary* or *Mamita Mary* (*mamita* is the diminutive for *mamá* and *Mary* is the diminutive for *María*). My paternal grandmother was *Mamá Lupe* (*Lupe* is the diminutive for *Guadalupe*).

Utterances were never spoken without the inclusion of some endearing term of address or reference, and it is those terms that anchor my memory to particular events. For instance, before leaving for work as a government secretary, Mamá Lupe, with whom I had lived for a year, always had some admonition on my behalf. "*Hay que pelarle las uvas a la Patricita,*" she'd tell her mother. My great-grandmother *Abuelita Sarita* (*abuelita* is the diminutive for *abuela,* meaning grandmother; *Sarita* is the diminutive for *Sara*) in turn responded, "*Sí Lupe.*" Once my grandmother had left, my great-grandmother was true to her word. She would sit at the wooden kitchen table and, with the sharpest corner of her longest fingernail, peel one grape at a time so the skins would not aggravate my lifelong colitis. At other times she painstakingly peeled the cooked black beans one by one so that I could eat something I especially enjoyed because of their color. Many evenings when my grandmother had returned from work she loved to tease me about getting married, or more specifically about not getting married. Sara, who was widowed before age 30 and raised three children by herself, would sweep her arm up in the air saying, "*No niña ¿para qué te casas? ¡No te cases!*" [No child, why get married? Don't get married!] Then she would laugh and gather me into her arms.

My maternal grandmother also feasted me with a glossary of nicknames. For Mamá Mary, inspiration came from the world of fragrances. Beautiful scents were her arsenal against the odors of a city that was well on its way to becoming the most populated in the world. Before donning her military nurse's uniform, her daily ritual involved anointing herself with the essence of lavender, jasmine, gardenia, or rose. "*Toma mi Rosita de Castilla, Toma mi Rosita de Jericó,*" [Here, my little rose of Castille, my little rose of Jericho] she would say, handing me a clean, folded handkerchief infused with perfume. The handkerchief was meant for me to bury my nose in as we passed sewers, exhaust fumes, or unbathed people. On lonely Saturday evenings she would blast music from the radio and invite me to dance around her tiny apartment. "*¡Ven mi orquídea, vamos a bailar!*" [Come my orchid, let's dance!] she'd exclaim, grabbing me with one hand. With the other hand she clutched a large uncapped bottle of cologne, with whose liquid orange flowers she splashed the walls as we danced to "*Las Bicicletas*" (a particularly animated Mexican song).

At home, to my mother, I was *hija* (daughter) or *mija* (contraction of *mi hija,* meaning my daughter). To my brother I was *manita* (diminutive of the term *mana,* which itself is a diminutive for *hermana,* meaning sister). My brother and I shared a bedroom; our nightly ritual involved kissing each other good night. "*Buenas noches manita*" my brother would say, pecking my cheek before climbing into his bed. Then, as we both lay in the dark, I would often say, "*Güero* (a common nickname for fair-complected people), *cuéntame un cuento*" [Güero, tell me a story]. When the tales were exhausted or when sleep weighted his eyes, *Güero* would speak into the shadowy space connecting our beds. "*Buenas noches manita, ya tengo mucho sueño*" [Good night little sister, I'm very sleepy].

In the Mexico of my early childhood, terms of address and of reference were an integral part of my history. Whether I was at school or at home, my name assured me a place in the universal continuum. I was *Patricia* because *Mamá Lupe* wanted it so; the *Mamá Lupe* who more than 20 years before my birth had left the town of Cárdenas to participate in the presidential campaign of Lázaro Cárdenas. I was *Olivia* because that was *Mamá Mary's* choice; the *Mamá Mary* whose family ranch had been confiscated by the government during the Revolution of 1910 and whose family was disbanded forever in the ensuing chaos. I had a father, *Covarrubias,* whose ancestors had come from northern Spain and settled in Mexico City. I had a mother, *Baillet,* whose fa-

Culture Concepts

Culture

Culture *is a learned set of shared interpretations about beliefs, values, norms, and social practices that affects the behaviors of a relatively large group of people. Thus culture is linked to human symbolic processes.*

ther's family emigrated from France and settled in Puebla and who had served in the Mexican military until his death.

Having a name does not grant me claims to idealism. My Mexican childhood was not perfect, but I had a secure cultural footing. In the network of rituals, myths, and traditions that has characterized many Mexicans from ancient to modern times, I held appointed office. I was daughter, granddaughter, great-granddaughter, sister, niece, cousin, pupil, Catholic, playmate. I lived in a world where public and private domains routinely exchanged places. Thus, while I had a generalized public function as defined by my status and role, I also had a differentiated intimate space. It was in this intimate space that my uniqueness was largely shaped and sustained by the banquet of terms of address that were meant exclusively for me. So it was for the first eight years of my life.

A few days before Christmas 1959 I experienced a concentrated outpouring of address forms unlike any other I had yet known. In a nervous stream, the sounds from my grandmothers' lips overflowed: *"Patricita," "Patty," "Paty," "Patita," "mi rosita," "mi orquídea," "mi niña," "mi niñita."* We had gathered at the train station for a final good-bye and it would be my last feast of spoken endearments for a long time.

I didn't know it at the time, but I was just a few days away from a pivotal moment. Two weeks after our final parting from Mexico City, I was introduced to Mrs. Williams and her third-grade class in California. "Class, this is *Pat*." I still cannot hear that phrase without my stomach cramping. With a single turn of the tongue, my mother's and my father's surnames vanished, my first name and its variations were razed, and the effect and history associated with them were dimmed. For the next eight years—in elementary, junior high, and high school—I was *Pat*. When last names were required I was *Pat C.* because others could not or would not try to pronounce *Covarrubias*.

I do not recall ever having been asked during my years in primary education how I wanted to be addressed. I did not resist. There were fiercer battles to win. There was the language barrier and the loneliness that provoked. There was the sorrow resulting from the school principal's decision to place me in classes targeted for students with learning disabilities, including mental retardation. (Thanks to my parents' intervention the placement did not last long.) And there was the frustration of the school's decision to send me to remedial speech classes, where I spent tedious hours in a closet-sized room practicing the pronunciation of words ending in *ch*: *"Catch, which, such, finch, march, fetch, cinch, conch, sandwich, catch, which, such, finch, march. . . ."* It seems some Hispanics tend to say *sh* instead of *ch*, but it took the therapist months to figure out I was not one of them. Yet there were other obstacles.

In a decision made strategically for my brother's and my benefit, only a few months after my arrival in Mrs. Williams's third-grade classroom my parents decided to move to another small California town. The new town had schools known for exceptionally high academic standards. It also had virtually no Hispanic residents. It was my parents' design for us to grow up where we would be obliged to learn English as quickly as possible and, thus, to learn to defend ourselves. But, as with Mrs. Williams, I did not know *what*—or more specifically *who*—awaited me in the new town. On a prematurely hot spring morning, Barry Hanna confronted me.

Barry remained a classmate for the next three years. His eyes were sky blue, resolute, and mean. From the moment of my arrival he made it his self-appointed duty to expose me to a prolific set of new terms of address that humiliated, confused, and hurt me. To Barry I was "spic," "beaner," "taco," "taco eater," "mex," "wetback," "green card," "stupid Mexican," and "lazy Mexican." For a long time I didn't understand what some of those expressions meant. They were in neither the textbooks nor the dictionary.

Barry was a relentless terrorist. With calculated slyness and regularity he would turn around from his school desk so only I could see him, lift the middle finger of his right hand, and point it straight at me. In predictably random attacks he approached me in the playground scowling, "Beaner, go home!" One day at recess, with his lips in a snarl exposing large yellow teeth, he reached toward my ear and tried to yank my pierced earring off my left ear. "Indian!" he scowled. (Pierced earrings were not yet fashionable in the United States but an accessory most Mexican women wear and are seldom seen without.) For weeks I wept, pleading with my mother to let me remove the earrings. Eventually she relented. I still did not know enough English to defend myself.

At the time I knew nothing about the controversial *bracero* program, rat-infested underground border tunnels, or immigration reform efforts. I knew something about injury, confusion, and disconnection. I knew that I was terrified to go to school and face the tyranny of Barry's epithets. When I finally figured out their meanings, I asked my father "*¿Por qué?*" [Why?] "*Porque son ignorantes y mediocres. Porque son ignorantes y mediocres,*" ["Because they are ignorant and mediocre,"] he repeated with infuriating calm. I would have felt consoled if he had said, "Because they're racist, prejudiced, bad." But those terms were never uttered in my parents' home.

For my father, a human being's maximum sin was to be ignorant and mediocre. Ignorance and mediocrity, he claimed, prevent people from behaving according to the highest order of integrity, honor, knowledge, and wisdom. In fact, until I reached adulthood, on more occasions than I want to remember he sanctioned me, saying, "*No seas mediocre*" [Don't be mediocre] and "*No seas ignorante*" [Don't be ignorant]. So my father's quiet response did not soothe my childhood hurt and frustration, but it did prepare me for other, larger battles.

From my father's words and examples, I learned to view ignorance and mediocrity—whether mine or someone else's—as something I could do something about. My father's approach also helped me to realize that others' failings need not become my own. As a little girl I craved for my parents to smother me with pity; as an adult, I am strengthened by their injunction: "*No te hagas la*

Culture Concepts

Culture Is Learned

People learn about their culture through interactions with parents, other family members, friends, and even strangers who are part of the culture. Culture is learned from these individuals as part of the socialization process. Culture is also taught by the explanations people receive for the natural and human events around them. Cultures exist in the minds of people, not in external or tangible objects or behaviors.

víctima. No te dejes." [Don't play the victim. Don't yield to them/it]. In my parents' eyes one was a social casualty only by choice. Whether right or wrong, that is what they said and that is how they lived. In spite of Mrs. Williams and Barry Hanna, I learned to eliminate victimization as an option for confronting life's battles. And there has never been a shortage of battlegrounds.

One such battleground came as a surprise. When I was an undergraduate major in French language and literature my struggles involved the school's Hispanic community. On multiple occasions members of various Hispanic organizations challenged my choice of academic discipline. "Why do you study French?!" one demanded to know. "You're Chicana! We're never going to win the war this way!" This second-generation compatriot did not realize I **was** trying to win a war and that **he** was adding to my challenges. Once again, my intimate "I" was appropriated publicly, this time by one from whom I least expected it. I was saddened that he, whose cultural history included the oppressive reduction of individuals to easy stereotypes, should have thought I ought to abide in **his** preferred terms and conceptualizations of personhood. For him, I seemed to be but a category of person. I was still someone who was fighting for terms that fit. Yet things were changing. Some victories lay ahead. I was about to take a crucial step in the recovery of the intimate "I," of *Patricia*. Curiously, this change occurred in the most public of contexts, the mass media.

Immediately after finishing a master's degree in French language and literature I began an internship in the newsroom of the number-one-rated television station in northern California. With less than a year of unpaid training I was hired and given the opportunity to present news stories on air. I remained there as news reporter for the next several years. But the fight for my name followed me like a crawling plague. I was tired of it, but practice and fatigue had made me bold. Besides, by now I had mastered English.

In my private life I was married to an Anglo-Saxon man who supported my use of the name *Covarrubias*. But professionally there was dissent. The senior anchor, who was especially sensitive to being embarrassed on the air, frequently tripped and stuttered in pronouncing my name when introducing my early news stories. "Patricia Co—Corr—Corva . . . ias has more on that." After a particularly problematic show, he stormed into the newsroom and decreed, "Patricia, that name has got to go! I suggest something more pronounceable." I felt hot coals in my stomach as I grabbed onto my father's words, *"Porque son ignorantes."* "Yes, ignorance is something I can do something about," I repeated mentally in an attempt to douse my own flames. So I engaged every news anchor in pronunciation drills. "Co-va-rru-bi-as, Covarrubias. See, it's very phonetic."

My battle also pertained to my first name. I was willing to accept *Patricia, Trish, Trisha, Patrish,* even *Patrisher* (someone's sense of humor). But *Pat* was no longer an option. And so, for my name to fit on the screen, it had to be typed on fonts slightly smaller than those used on other reporters' names. On every aired report *Patricia Covarrubias* stretched from one end of the television set to the other. My family and I took great pleasure in that.

After nearly 20 years, at last I had rid myself of the imposed persona. I was no longer crammed into a name that was not mine. But after so much time living in a fiction, I could no longer identify clearly the parts that would enable complete self-reintegration. The missing dimensions were indeed obvious, but I didn't see them. The search took much longer than it should have. However, self-discovery and synthesis were the unexpected dividends of my recent doctoral fieldwork in Mexico.

In the port of Veracruz, I called the construction company where I recently spent seven months collecting ethnographic data. *Chabela* (diminutive of *Isabel*), the 33-year-old secretary of the CEO, answered the phone. *"¿Hola manita? ¿Cómo estás Paty?"* she exclaimed on hearing my voice, adding, *"¡Que gusto de oir tu voz mana!"* [Hello *manita* how are you Paty? What a pleasure to hear your voice *mana*!]. *Manita, Mana, Patty,* there they are again each time I call Mexico, the sounds from my early childhood. The subjective, perhaps inefficient, soft vocabularies of María, Guadalupe, and Sara.

It is not out of ghostly nostalgia that I call as often as I can. It is more to satisfy a physical need to feel close to a world bent on re-creating the structures and emotions of family at every turn. I am fulfilled hearing and speaking the language that requires people to pay more than passing glances at each other. I am filled as I yield and am yielded to by terms with particular intimates in mind.

During my stay in Mexico, I observed and experienced hundreds of such interactions with intimates. *"¿Linda niña, que haces por aquí?"* [Pretty girl, what are you doing around here?] the company owner greeted me with a hug when we ran into each other at work one morning. *"Muñeca te sirvo un café"* [Doll, I'll serve you some coffee] offered Nieves, the dean of architecture at a local university, at our initial interaction. Subsequent interactions included the terms *mi reina* my queen, *mi amor* my love, and *corazón* [heart or dear heart].

At a reunion with a male friend I had not seen since our teenage years, he rushed to embrace me, remarking, *"¡Patita, Patita, no lo puedo creer!"* [Patita, Patita (diminutive of *Patricia*), I can't believe it!"]. A female relative christened me *Pata* (a name she made up for me). The wife of the couple with whom I lived drew me into her family by calling me *Patricha* (a name she created for me) and *hija* (daughter) or *mija* (contraction for my daughter). In the public market I was frequently called *"güera"* and *"güerita."* On a particular occasion in a public office when I was asked my name, out of habit I responded, *"Patricia Covarrubias."* Somewhat perturbed, the receptionist asked, *"¿Covarrubias qué?"* Not so indirectly I was being reminded that I have a mother as well. *"Baillet,"* I sputtered quickly.

Moreover, my age and social status had earned me some culturally traditional forms of address for which I was not prepared. For the first time in my life I was addressed as *señora,* in recognition of my marital status and perhaps my age. Although I resisted it as politely as possible, I was sometimes called *Licenciada,* in recognition of the fact that I have a college education, and *Maestra (teacher)* because of the workshops I presented. In formal situations I was systematically addressed as *Doctora* despite my efforts to explain I was not yet a "doctor." In seven months I was called *Patricia* on only a handful of occasions and almost always at initial introductions. Routinely I was *Paty or Patty.*

My fieldwork in Mexico was intended to focus on others' ways of speaking. Naively, I never imagined it would result in the rediscovery and recovery of my own speaking style. As others were generous and inventive in their use of forms of address with me, I reciprocated. Expressions came easily and naturally. We drew on a common pool of linguistic possibilities and added our own variations. We were mutually intelligible. I felt socially integrated—or rather, reintegrated. This was a new feeling for me. It was this feeling that *Pat* had displaced so many years before.

"Thanks, Pat," smiled the ticket agent in Los Angeles as I received my boarding pass. I had just cleared U.S. customs and was on my final flight home. Home? I had left "home" when the Veracruzanos and I embraced for the last time. Yes, they are my *home,* they are my history. But in a matter of hours I would rejoin another part of my history, the non-Mexican husband who understands my need for a name of my own. In a matter of days, I would again conjoin with the fellowship of intimates in whose joyous transitions and silent collapses we often partake. Soon I would reconnect with the community of mentors whose guidance and support are not contingent on my ability to fit within their slotted social restraints. They are my history as well.

"Have a good flight, Pat," said the ticket agent. I started laughing. He never knew why.

Culture Concepts

Sapir-Whorf Hypothesis of Linguistic Relativity

Sapir and Whorf presented ideas on the relationship between language and thought. In the firm, or deterministic, version of the hypothesis, language functions like a prison—once people learn a language, they are irrevocably affected by its particulars. This makes competent intercultural communication an elusive goal. The softer version takes a less causal view of the nature of the language-thought relationship. In this view, language shapes how people think and experience their world. People from different initial language systems can learn words and categories that are sufficiently similar to their own so communication can be accurate. The weight of the scholarly evidence supports the softer position that language plays a role in shaping *how people think and experience the world, but it is not all encompassing.*

▶ ▶ ▶ Learning AmongUS

1. Using the definition of communication provided, explain why there was a loss of shared meaning in the communication between Covarrubias and her first teacher in the United States.

2. How important is it for a teacher to learn what a student's name is and how to pronounce it properly? How did Covarrubias's essay affect your ideas on this issue?

3. Was Covarrubias's first U.S. teacher communicating competently with her? Explain.

4. How might a teacher with students from many cultures interact with them in a manner that avoids the negative consequences Covarrubias describes?

5. Are there parallels in your family to Covarrubias's different names? Do you have pet names, family names, or terms of endearment?

6. If you know another language, compare and contrast the naming practices of the two languages.

7. Does the Spanish language have characteristics that produce different meanings and understandings than the English that Covarrubias was forced to use outside her home?

8. Using the culture concept of formality-informality, covered in Part IV, explain what occurred with Covarrubias's first class and teacher in the United States.

Chang Hee Yoon was adopted from a Korean orphanage as an infant. Her name was changed to Mei Lin Swanson Kroll, and she was raised in Minnesota. This essay describes the evolution of her identity as a Korean and her reactions to the ignorance and stereotyping she still encounters. Her story provides a meaningful touchstone for individuals born into one culture and socialized in another.

3 My Name Is . . .

Mei Lin Kroll

My name is Yoon, Chang Hee—and my name is Mei Lin Swanson Kroll. There's obviously a story here, and also a metaphor for my life. I was born in Seoul, South Korea, and was named Yoon, Chang Hee in an orphanage. I was then transracially adopted at the age of five months, and my parents changed my name to Mei Lin Swanson Kroll.

Mei Lin is actually a Chinese name, but my parents thought it sounded Asian and would be easy for non-Asians to say; they didn't realize that Koreans wouldn't name their children with Chinese names. Swanson was my mother's name; she's Swedish and Norwegian. Kroll is my father's name; we're not sure what he is, but he's Slovenian, English, and maybe German or Polish. I know my parents were trying to be culturally sensitive when they named me Mei Lin, but they didn't realize how difficult it in fact would be for people to say my name properly. I still don't see why some people have such a hard time trying to pronounce it. You say it just like it looks. Mei Lin. It's two words: the first like the month of May, and the second like the American name, Lynn. But people have a tendency to add a "g" at the end of my name, because they think all Asian names have *g*s. They also call me My Lin, Mee Lynn, My Ling, Mia Lim, Mee Ling, Marylyn, Elle, and my own favorite, Melon. So I've found the name to be a bit of trouble.

When I was experiencing an identity crisis in my first year of college, I came across my naturalization papers while I was getting ready to apply for a passport. I saw my orphanage-given name and suddenly had a very strong emotional reaction. That was really all I had when I came to this country: that name. And my parents overlooked it and chose another one. So I began to use Yoon, Chang Hee in writing and in speaking. I've thought about changing my name legally and I still may do it. I want to tell you more about myself, about how I've arrived at these names, and about my sense of identity in a transracial family and in a racist society. It's been quite a journey.

When I was young, I knew that I was adopted and was Korean. I also knew other adopted Koreans and other families with adopted kids, so I thought I was pretty normal. In fact, when I was about three or four I came

Culture Concepts

Race and Culture

Race *commonly refers to certain physical similarities, such as skin color or eye shape, that a group of people share and are used to mark or separate them from others. Contrary to popular notions, however, race is not primarily a biological term; it is a political and societal one that was invented to justify economic and social distinctions. Though racial categories are inexact as a classification system, it is generally agreed that race is a more all-encompassing term than either* culture *or* nation. *Race is often used as the basis for prejudice and discrimination.*

home one day to tell my mother a big secret—something I'd just figured out. I asked her, very confidentially, "Did you know there are some families who don't have any adopted kids?" She said she did know that. I said, "You know, they're just plain white."

In fact, in grade school, my two best friends were adopted Koreans. We thought we were pretty special, like we had a secret language. We often teased other kids and made up things about our relationships. One day we told them we were really sisters. Another day we were cousins. Another day we were friends, just all from different families. It made a difference, obviously, for there to be several of us. I later met Korean adoptees who didn't live near others. They grew up in suburbs with few kids of color, and they always felt alone and outside. I also had the good fortune to have a Korean woman as my day-care provider. I consider her now my godmother. She took care of me during the day and taught me to eat Korean food, sing Korean nursery rhymes, and count in Korean. I loved her and came to love Korean food. I consider her a very important part of the development of my positive cultural identity.

When I was in junior high my parents sent me to a preteen Korean group. I went for several years, enjoying the food and joining in discussions about Korean culture, activities, groups, and (especially) Korean food. But as I got older, I got tired of it. I told my parents I was tired of the same old questions over and over: "How does it feel to be Korean?" "How does it feel to be adopted?" My parents reluctantly let me quit. Looking back, I think that was the beginning of my turning my back on my Korean identity and culture.

Ever since I was little there was always some kind of teasing going on because I was Korean and didn't look like everyone else. My mother tells me that on the first day of public school I came home indignant because some kid had called me Chinese and said I peed in my Coke. My parents were very concerned and asked me how I felt and what I did. I said, "Well, I hit him." They thought that ended that; I'd learned to stand up for myself. They didn't know that the teasing went on all the time and that I was storing up some negative reactions about being different. Once some friends and I were talking about stupid things we had done. I was telling a story about jumping and flipping on my parents' bed. While I was jumping up and down and having the time of my life, I decided to flip over forward. I accidentally overrotated, fell off the bed, hit my mouth on the wall, and started to bleed. My friend then said, "Oh, is that why your face is so flat?" She and another girl just laughed. I just sat there embarrassed and acted as if I didn't hear a thing. I've been told that I look like a Chinese porcelain doll. Some have even asked if I could see out of my eyes. The list goes on and on, but I began in junior high and throughout high school to let people make those comments and pretend I didn't hear or they didn't really say what they said. I think that subconsciously I decided to drop the Korean side of myself and try to fix the other side—the reasons I was teased. I decided to "fix" it by wanting to be white, to be "just like everyone else."

I also felt like an outsider at times within my own family, especially my extended family. It wasn't as direct or as deliberate as the incidents in school, but it happened nevertheless. Once one of my cousins was diddling with her fingers and discovered that when she put her two index fingers together, they parted from each other at the tips. Everyone else decided to put their fingers together to see what it looked like. I knew exactly where this was going. I put my fingers together under the table, where no one could see. When I put my two fingers together, it looked like someone put superglue on them—straight together to the end. There was no separation, not even slightly. I pretended something was in my eye and got up and left—and went to the bathroom where no one could see my tears. I often still feel like an outsider when my extended family gets together, such as when the out-of-town cousins come to visit. Someone always mentions that "the Krolls have a distinct look." Last I checked I was a Kroll too. But they start to point out similarities: who has what eyes, lips, smile, hair thickness, and so on. If someone doesn't fit that mold, it is for some peculiar reason. I never fit. But we don't talk about it—like I'm not there or I don't count. But I feel it—I don't fit, the oddball even in my own family.

When kids get to high school they become concerned with fitting in. I went to a high school that was pretty racially diverse, but I spent my time with a kind of "in" athletic crowd, mostly from my neighborhood, and mostly white. I didn't want to spend time with people who looked like me. I didn't want to spend time with other Asians—I acted like they were foreigners—even other adopted Koreans. An adopted Korean boy asked me to a dance; I said no and avoided him like the plague. I even tried to avoid talking to other Asians. I was so self-conscious and thought that everyone else was looking at us, lumping us together, when I was determined to be like everyone else—not Asian.

In the summer after high school and before college this assimilation plan of mine started to come apart. First it changed because of something positive; then my first year of college demolished it completely. When I finished high school, I was introduced to a group of Koreans by a former high school friend who was Korean. I wouldn't have given him the time of day in high school, but he came often into the Chinese restaurant where I worked so I agreed one night to go with him to somebody's house after work. What I found was so intriguing and amazing—I didn't have to explain or adjust myself to fit in. We all shared this invisible bond. We all had gone through similar experiences in school—and I had thought I was the only one feeling this way because I was adopted. I realized this was a race issue, not just an adoption issue. People pick out differences in how we look. But now I felt like I belonged. I opened up to Koreans, and to Korean culture and to other Asians. I had a whole new ap-

Culture Concepts

Communication and Context

All communication takes place within a setting or situation called a context. *By context we mean the place where people meet, the social purpose for being together, and the nature of the relationship. Thus the context includes the physical, social, and interpersonal settings within which messages are exchanged.*

preciation for being Korean and for Korean culture. I had a new set of friends and they were like me!

In the fall I went away to a college about 70 miles from my home. I went with a group of kids from my high school, but I looked forward to meeting other people. I didn't expect what I found: a new level of stereotyping and racism, beyond teasing. One of my classes was taught by a professor who talked about cultural sensitivity in her classes. On the very first day of class, she asked a Japanese man in the front row if he had a camera. She then looked around the room and at the four Asians in the room—including me—and asked, "I mean, come on, all you Japanese people have nice cameras, right?" All of a sudden she began to laugh, a signal for the rest of the class to laugh too. I just kept looking down at my notebook, while everyone else waited for more jokes. I realized this was just the beginning.

Winter break was coming up and everyone was getting restless. This professor handed out something to several of us; at first I thought it was our grades. Then I saw it was a map. It was an invitation to come to her house for Thanksgiving. I was going up to thank her but decline after class, when I realized only Asian students had received these invitations. She commented to another (white) student who looked curious that she was inviting the Japanese students because they couldn't afford to fly all the way home for Thanksgiving. The ironic thing was that on the first day of class she had us fill out cards telling her where we came from, our name, address, and why we wanted to take the class. My name is Kroll—my address was 70 miles away, I don't have a Korean or a Japanese accent. But she couldn't see me as a person—just a stereotype—and what she automatically assumed about all Asians was applied to us, though only one of the four Asians in that class was Japanese.

It was even harder on a social level. One night my friends from high school talked me into going to a party. I tried to mingle, but people spoke to me v . . . e . . . r . . . ry slo-o-o-w-ly, e-nun-ci-a-ting every word. No one asked me to dance. There wasn't another person of color in the entire room. I had enough; I wanted to go back to the dorm and told my friends so. They asked why I wanted to leave. I told them I didn't feel comfortable and had heard someone whispering to another "and they can't even speak English." One of my friends said to me, "Well, Mei, at least you're not black." I couldn't believe it. I just stood there in total shock while the rest of them kept bouncing to the music and sipping Old Milwaukee beer.

I began to go home every weekend and to spend my free time with my Korean friends. They could understand, so I didn't have to explain. It began to hit me that all the effort I had put into being white wasn't worth it, and of course it didn't really work. Wow! Like a ton of bricks! I had other choices. I knew I had to get off that campus and go to the people who could help me be myself. That would be a better way to get through college. As the year was coming to a close I began hauling my stuff back home, nearly three to four weeks before school actually ended. I just couldn't wait to get off that campus and I looked forward to not ever seeing those people again.

The following year I transferred to a college nearer my home. I got to know more Koreans and spent more of my time, in fact almost all my free time, with other Koreans. I took Korean language classes, as well as classes in Asian history, race and gender relations, and intercultural communication. Things were much better—not because the transfer meant that I would avoid all prejudice, racism, and discrimination. But I was better able to face it because I had the family and friends who are my support network.

I do still encounter incidents and people who don't understand Koreans or Korean culture. At work I was hanging out in the kitchen tossing French fries back and forth with a cook who is African American. He said, "Hey, don't be doing any of that Kung-fu stuff on me! I know you Chinese people!" I said, "Um, I'm not Chinese. I'm Korean." He said, "What's the difference?" like it was unimportant. I said, "It's a big difference. What's the difference between a Jamaican and a Nigerian?" He said, "I don't know." "The difference is culture! Different languages, food, values, beliefs, traditions, music, ways of life!" I've found ways to respond and not just be silent and keep my feelings bottled up inside.

I'm also reminded that people know so little when they expect me to know everything Asian and every aspect of Asian cultures. I was talking to another student who was telling me how amazed he was by the dinner an Asian woman had made for him recently. I asked him what she made. He started to describe it, because he didn't know the name. He was describing it as chicken with red, sweet sauce all over it. I immediately said, "Oh, that's got to be sweet and sour chicken." He said, "Wow! How did you know? Do your parents own a Chinese restaurant?" I said, "Uh, not quite, but I did work in a Chinese restaurant." Then he moved on to the next dish. He described this soup with all kinds of greens and said it was Japanese soup. I said, "Well, you got me there. I don't know what kind of soup that is." He had an unsettled look on his face and insisted that I must know. He said, "This soup is Japanese, though. What do you mean, you don't know?" And I said back, loudly, "I don't know means I don't know. I'm Korean and I worked in a Chinese restaurant. How does that make me a Japanese authority?"

My Korean friends understand and have similar experiences all the time. We recall similar experiences from high school, where practically all our friends were white or of another color. We were all pretty "Americanized." There were times when we hated to be Korean, because we looked so different from our friends. In college most of us changed and began to identify with and spend our time with other Koreans. We can relate to each other better, because we don't have to explain ourselves. I identify more strongly with my Korean heritage and culture, which makes me actually feel in place, comfortable with who I am. All of these experiences that I've written about have made me

Culture Concepts

Interpersonal Communication

Interpersonal communication *involves a small number of individuals who are interacting exclusively with one another and who therefore have the ability both to adapt their messages specifically for those others and to obtain immediate interpretations from them.*

a stronger person and determined to succeed—to prove wrong the people who underestimated me.

My mother and I were talking once and she told me that when she went to Norway to visit her relatives she could feel that bond, not so much because her relatives were Scandinavian, but because this was who she was. She felt at home and understood herself better by seeing them and learning which parts of Scandinavian culture had become part of her. I could relate because that's how I feel about being with Koreans. I think everyone should visit where they originally came from. I don't mean it has to be a physical visit to another land—but merely soul searching—meet people of a similar background and ethnicity, read books about your ethnicity, the country you originate from, whatever it takes to get a better understanding of who you are. If you go, if you find a place, a book, or a person that awakens your inner self or an unrecognized part, you will discover something deep inside that is inexplicable, something priceless. I know my identity and who I am because I know who I am not. I wish others the same.

▶ ▶ ▶ Learning AmongUS

1. Given the definitions of race and culture provided, explain Kroll's search for her identity in terms that are appropriate for these distinctions.
2. Kroll describes herself as a high school student who was not interested in being with students from Asian cultures. Why do you think this happened? Has something similar happened to someone you know personally?
3. Both Kroll and Covarrubias reacted very negatively to the ways their teachers pronounced their names and gave them nicknames. How important is it for teachers to use the "right" names for the students in their classes? Why?

4. Kroll describes different contexts in which her life unfolds, and she explains how those contexts affected her sense of racial and cultural identity. What were those contexts? How did they affect her sense of identity?
5. Is it common or typical to group people from somewhat similar racial and/or cultural groups together? What is this human social categorizing process called?
6. Do you agree with Kroll's conclusion that "everyone should visit where they originally came from"? Why or why not?

Mei Lin Kroll continues her journey to understand her Korean birth culture and to craft an identity that recognizes both her Korean ethnicity and her Minnesota upbringing. Her story contains important and powerful lessons for transracial adoptees and their parents. It is also a remarkable story of a person's quest for personal, racial, and cultural knowledge.

4 Neither Lost nor Found

Mei Lin Kroll

A lot has changed these past years. I've graduated from college, traveled parts of the world, connected with some remarkable people, and also lost cherished souls. I've learned a lot from family, friends, and personal growth. I've come to understand that life is comprised of experiences that test one's character and create one's individuality. Life is lived through such challenges, which can't be predicted or understood beforehand. It's what makes us each unique.

I am now living in Seoul, Korea. While taking intensive language classes to increase my fluency in Korean, I am teaching business communication classes for a local corporation and tutoring children in English. It has taken some time and many experiences to come to this point. Let me explain how I got here.

Growing up, I had to develop a Korean self-awareness and identity; it was a struggle and was by no means automatic. It began when my parents found a day-care giver in the neighborhood who happened to be Korean and who also thought she was finished with the whole day-care thing. But after she discovered that I wasn't just another white kid, she took me under her wing. My mother would pick me up at the end of the day and would find me shedding tears while eating *kimchee,* a spicy cabbage. Alarmed, my mother asked if it was okay for a toddler to be eating such spicy things. Instantly Mama Yun pointed her finger at me replied, "If she doesn't eat it now, she will never eat it!"

My parents put me through Korean culture camp, and I always had a wonderful time there. I enjoyed the experiences because I loved Mama Yun and the things we did together. I remember looking forward to the last day of camp, because that was when all the families would come to watch us perform. The adoptive parents proudly looked at the boys and girls in their traditional *han-boks.* I distinctly remember resting under a tree with Mama Yun and my mother. As I was practicing my *san-ttoki* dance moves, Mama Yun pulled out a beautiful hair pin, sat me down, quickly parted my hair, and whipped it into a bun. I glanced at my mother, and she was beaming with a fulfilled look on her face.

Culture Concepts

Importance of Intercultural Competence

The quality of life in this century will depend on our ability to communicate competently with people from other cultures. Our neighbors may speak different first languages, have different values, and celebrate different customs. Families are also becoming more culturally diverse as marriages and adoptions contribute to the cultural mix. The challenge is to understand and to appreciate cultural differences and to translate that understanding into competent interpersonal communication.

My mother told me that Mama Yun wept contentedly as she watched me dance and sing with the other Korean children. It was a very nostalgic moment for her and it was also a small reflection of her childhood. The feeling of being able to instill a heritage we both shared and loved was more than words could express.

After the performances we would eat the delicious food that the Korean mothers had prepared, and we looked at the items that were available for purchase. I fell in love with the Korean fans. The older girls got to do the fan dance, which looked so graceful and so Korean. I took some fans home and proudly performed the dance by myself.

When I was eleven or twelve, I joined the Korean pre-teen group. Initially I liked the group, but I grew tired of it rather quickly. I thought I was going to go crazy if they asked one more time, "How does it feel to be adopted?" It wasn't like the Korean culture camp, where you could learn about Korea through songs, dance, and Korean writing. Instead, it focused on feelings of identity and adoption. I wasn't ready to talk about myself in front of others whom I didn't know, and I wanted out.

The Asian students in my high school were mainly Southeast Asians. They pretty much "stuck to their own." They spoke various languages and had strong accents, which made them seem "foreign." I tried to avoid these other Asians, because I thought it would attract attention and make me seem foreign as well. Looking back, it made sense that they would "stick to their own." They came from similar backgrounds and were going through their own adjustment processes. It also made sense that they would want to hang out with others who were going through similar experiences and could provide an emotional support system.

In high school I moved away from any sense of Korean identity. I wanted to be like the other kids and not emphasize my differences. I was always teased about how small my eyes were or how flat my face looked, and I internalized what people said about me. Some of my so-called friends would call other Asians "chinks," or "gooks," and they would make racial slurs and jokes in my presence, thinking it was okay. My tongue became paralyzed; I never stood up for myself. Instead, I just laughed with them while hurting inside and wondering what the hell I was doing. After all, though I looked different, I was just as "Americanized" as they were. I wondered why appearances would be so important. My white friends would make racist comments and then say, "But not you, you're different." I didn't want these types of comments to occur, but I also wanted to be "normal" and fit in. So though I chose to hang out with non-Asian kids, I learned to avoid certain topics.

Immediately after high school, I had this self-awakening identity phase. Before that, I never thought I would socialize with other Asians. When I went off to college, however, I found that I was often viewed by others in stereotypical ways. Though I thought I could fit in with white people, during my freshman year of college I discovered that I could not. Everyone automatically judged me without trying to get to know me. I soon realized that no matter how hard I tried to adjust, I would always be seen as "Asian," "other," and therefore as "outsider."

Coincidentally, at about this time I bumped into an old high school classmate who was Korean, and through him I made new friends who were also Korean. They were my first group of friends with whom I felt that I fit. They were my gateway to Korean culture. That was when I began to discover myself and my heritage. That was when I admitted to myself that I felt lost, and I thought I could be found by learning to be Korean. Thus, my first year's college experience sent me on a quest to reclaim my cultural heritage.

The next thing I knew, I was in love with a second-generation Korean. We shared seven years together. What got me was how strikingly Americanized and Koreanized he was. Before meeting him, I had only met people who were either very Americanized or very Asian. I had no clue that one could be both. I was intrigued. In my eyes he was a perfect balance. I also liked that he was able to show and explain Korean culture to me. Everything that for him was just everyday life was fascinating to me. It felt great to experience Korean culture through his personal life, rather than through some TV show or from a travel book. He became part of my life. Everything was exciting and intriguing. For the first time, I felt Korean.

Despite this sense of joy, there were moments when I didn't feel like I fit in with "real" Koreans. Many experiences made me feel foreign. One evening, for example, I was having dinner with some Korean friends when my friend's mother walked in. Immediately, all the chairs screeched. I looked up and saw everyone standing and bowing; I was the only one still sitting down. Quickly, I stood up, too. Moments like those made me realize that I was not culturally Korean. But then there were moments when I was with white people and didn't fit in there either. I was in between two worlds.

I had heard many horrible stories from my Korean friends that some Korean parents would not accept their son's girlfriend because she was an adopted Korean rather than a "real" Korean. Hearing all this made me very anxious to meet my boyfriend's parents. So I went to him and casually asked when I was going to meet his parents. Though I worried that they would not accept me or he would be too ashamed to introduce me, I was hoping that I would hear a positive answer.

My boyfriend explained to me that he could not introduce me to his parents unless he was planning to marry me. I couldn't understand this, because I had introduced him to my parents within a month of our dating. I demanded that he introduce me to his parents if he claimed to care about me. However, after many big arguments and after talking with friends, I realized that this was a huge cultural difference. Later, I also noticed that some of my other Korean friends who were couples had been dating for a few years and their parents also hadn't met their son's or daughter's boy/girlfriend, let alone were aware that their child was even dating. I calmed down, accepted the difference, and looked at it in a new light.

Within a year his parents knew of me and, shortly thereafter, I was about to meet them for the first time. Suddenly the concept of not introducing the girlfriend started to sound pretty good, because the thought of meeting them was nerve-racking! I made sure I looked and dressed properly, and I stood in front of the mirror for hours at a time, practicing my limited Korean. *Annyong-ha-saeyo? Man-na-seo ban-gap-sumnida! Charl moe-gos-sumnida!* I was very nervous about their first impressions of me. Was I going to be Korean enough for their son? What would it be like when we had dinner? How will we communicate? I could try to be funny, but what if I did something horrible and ended up offending them? I was pacing, panicking, couldn't breathe, had to breathe. In the end, the evening went a lot smoother than I expected. His family was very laid-back and was more than welcoming. But throughout the whole ordeal, I was still nervous as hell!

That first dinner was the prelude to many dinners with his family. I was relieved and so happy that they accepted me. I was concerned that, as we got to know each other better, they would tell my boyfriend to tell me that I needed to change, to be more of this and less of that; but they never did. Next thing I knew, his mother is packing Korean food for me to take home, or she is bringing it to my house because she noticed how much I enjoyed it. Believe me, this wonderful woman knew how to cook! Eating at his house was one of the best perks of being with a 1.5 Korean! Before going there, I would make sure that I hadn't eaten much, knowing that her food was mouth-drooling! Eating at his house gave me insights into how Koreans eat together. When I first visited Korea I was taught that the eldest lifts the spoon or chopsticks first, and I made sure that I used those same manners when eating in his home.

Opening their refrigerator was a new world: the *kimchee, pan-ch'ans*, garlic, red pepper paste, soy bean paste, and all the smells of a Korean refrigerator. The whole house smelled Korean. The faint smell of *kimchee* and garlic actually seemed normal to me—almost like a homecoming. It was definitely different from my home, but it wasn't hard to adjust to it. I was learning how everything is prepared and placed on the table, and I was eating authentic Korean food that isn't served in restaurants. And I paid extra attention to how his mother prepared things, because I wanted to be able to cook like her. After all, I couldn't depend on her for Korean food all my life! The things that I found fascinating and intriguing were just commonplace to my boyfriend; this was what he had grown up with every day. Thanks to Mama Yun, I grew up with them too, until the age of nine; then I chose to abandon them. Now, I wanted to recapture them. My boyfriend commented that I ate authentic Korean food very well. It wasn't the style of Korean food that would be given to someone who is new to eating it. It was the hard-core Korean dishes: fish that stunk up the house, soup that had the entire fish in it (bones, head, tail, eyes, everything), raw squid, spicy vegetables soaked in a red-pepper sauce, strong *dwen-jjang chiggae*, and so many others.

It meant the world to me to have my boyfriend's parents, and indeed his entire family, accept me. There was a sense of belonging that can not be described. It's not about being an adoptee; it's wanting to belong. Yes, I know that my adoptive family is my real family; they are my nourishment and without them I wouldn't be who I am today. Yet there was still this gap in my life. My boyfriend's family gave me a taste of what it's like to be a part of a Korean family. This is what my future family could look like, I told myself, if I married this man. My children would grow up with Korean relatives and would experience Korean culture. That sounded so wonderful to me. I had a deeper sense of belonging; my life felt perfect. I had so many great things to look forward to—friends, school, job, marriage, and kids—the unwritten goals of life.

I thought our relationship would last a lifetime. We had built a strong partnership through love, and I believed true love was unbreakable. I was sadly mistaken. Our relationship came to an end. I discovered that my boyfriend had a second life with another woman whom I considered a friend. Life is full of harsh realities. I discovered that the man I knew for years was not the person I thought he was. So much for friendship and loyalty. The relationship that had grown between us and with his family, the relationship we had nurtured for seven years, was instantly gone.

That was and still is my most life-altering experience. I toggled back and forth between anger and sadness. In the midst of the confusion I somehow focused on getting past this adversity. I felt lost and unsure what to do, but I believed a good friend when she told me that everything happens for a reason. I took her words to heart and tried to analyze my whole situation. Was the reason because it wasn't meant to be and that I deserved better? Is this a test to see how weak or strong I am? Without my family and close friends, I don't know if I would have been able to cope. Eventually I was able to look at this experience as character-building, making me a wiser and better person. I don't know how, but I did. I learned that this was a blessing in disguise.

As trite as it sounds, I discovered that life is short. I don't have any time to waste; I need to take charge. There is so much out there for me to experience and I have to take chances in my own life to make things happen. Back home I was stuck doing the same routine day in and day out. I would wake up groggy from the many nights of bartending and making sure I got to my graphic design company on time, while squeezing in volunteer work by teaching ESL at the University of Minnesota a couple of days of the week. Financially I was fine, but emotionally I was at a dead end. No husband, no kids, no house, and I didn't have a job going anywhere fast. Suddenly I realized: what a terrific opportunity this is! I've always wanted to go back to Korea; now I could! I had this liberating feeling that I could do whatever I wanted. And what I wanted was to prove to myself that I could go to Korea on my own and develop a better understanding of Korean culture and life. My goal wasn't to transform myself into a Korean-Korean, because I will never be that. But I wanted to discover myself more, to learn about where I came from, and to enjoy my life.

I call my first trip to Korea, which occurred years earlier, the "Princess Trip," because my friend and his family graciously did everything for me. They knew I was adopted and knew of my passion for discovering my heritage, so they made sure I saw everything, ate everything, and experienced Korean life fully. It was a marvelous and awkward feeling to be in a place where everyone looks like you. I was so used to looking different, that looking like everyone else felt odd. When I was in Korea for the first time, I wanted to squeeze everything in. Part of my itinerary that first trip was to visit the adoption agency I went through. I had such high expectations that I would learn about my birth mother and would meet her. I couldn't stop crying on my way to the agency. Looking at my adoption file was so overwhelming that I was unable to ask questions of the social worker.

My second trip to Korea, during my junior year in college, was a semester abroad at Yonsei University in Seoul. I had taken two years of college-level Korean, and I knew a handful of Korean natives and Minnesota friends who were in Seoul. I thought I was well-prepared and the sojourn would be easy. But I started to doubt the wisdom of my decision to go even before I entered the Minneapolis airport. My stomach was tied up in knots. My heart was beating faster and faster. My body felt heavy. I wondered, in a combination of excitement and terror, "What the hell am I doing?" Through the airplane window I stared at the gate where my family was looking back at me in the tiny airplane window, barely seeing me wave to them.

BOOM! CULTURE SHOCK! OVERLOAD! My second trip wasn't what I had expected it to be. This time I had to find my own way around, I had to use my horrible Korean language skills, I had to do everything for myself! "How do I get to . . . Wait! Say that again? Please speak slower! How do you say that in Korean? I gotta go where?" I felt vulnerable. I felt like a little kid learning how to do things all over again, learning what not to do and what to look out for. Just catching the bus or subway, or directing a taxi driver to where I wanted to go, was so mind-consuming!

After getting situated in Korea on my second trip there, I decided to go back to my adoption agency. This time I was able to find out more information about my mother. And it was also at this time that I met a woman who said she could help me find my mother. She mentioned that there was a support group/organization for women who gave up their children for adoption, and that she could search the names and see if any names matched the one in my adoption file. How did she know of this support group? She, too, had given up her son for adoption and had reunited with him. In fact, he was someone I knew. She gave me hope and the courage to continue.

Toward the end of the semester at Yonsei University, I was anxious to get back home. I wanted to bring many things with me, which perhaps reflected my desire to meld Korean culture into my life at home. A rice cooker! Not just any rice cooker, but a rice cooker that looked like something from the future, or as my dad liked to call it, a miniature vacuum cleaner look-alike. I bought a Korean-style blanket, gifts for family and friends, *keem, oh-jing-o, soju*, and so much more! In an odd sort of way, I'd come full circle. Leaving Minnesota for Korea, I was scared. Now, leaving Korea for home, to my utter amazement I wanted to stay.

Culture Concepts

The Intercultural Family

The increasing number of intercultural families, in which husband and wife have different cultural backgrounds, poses new challenges. Often, the children in these families are raised in an intercultural household characterized by some blending of the original cultures. Differences in the expectations of appropriate social roles—of wife and husband, son and daughter, older and younger child, or husband's parents and wife's parents—require a knowledge of and sensitivity to the varying influences of culture on family communication.

Before I left Korea, I wanted to learn if the woman I had met had found my birth mother. She had. My eyes immediately swelled with tears, thinking we were finally going to meet. "But I not allow this meeting," she added in an unsympathetic tone. I looked at her, dumbfounded. What the hell is this woman trying to pull? She said, "All you want is money, just like my son!" "I don't need money," I replied angrily. "I just want to meet my birth mother." Then I said, "I don't know the relationship you have with your son, but please don't let your selfishness spoil my chances to meet my mother." Being so vulnerable had blinded me to the kind of person she was. She needed comfort and attention, and she was manipulating me to get it. I never did learn what she knew—or even if she knew—about the circumstances of my birth. After that tormenting experience, I was glad to get away. Back to Minnesota!

But now—after seven years with the "love of my life" who turned out to be the love of someone else's life as well—I'm back in Korea for the third time. I've been having many challenging opportunities to learn and to develop my own identity, my own sense of being Korean. I am here in the crowded, busy, vital, urban center of Seoul, trying to navigate my schedule of classes and tutoring, and I'm building relationships with many people who are helping me to make sense of this world and my place in it.

Here in Seoul, there are other Koreans on similar quests—to learn the language, to experience Korean culture at its core, and to discover something about who they are. There is a Korean word for us—*K'yo-bo*—which means a Korean who was raised outside of Korea. Among us *K'yo-bos*, there are second generation Koreans, biracial Koreans, and adoptees from many countries. We have widely differing levels "Koreanness."

I've met some second-generation Koreans who have grown up in Korean families, have a basic level of Korean language skills, and possess a sense of Korean culture. Yet they are here to learn more, because their Korean experiences are limited. Some families emigrated from Korea for education, work, or other reasons. Some of these parents made the swift decision to quit speaking Korean to their children so they could adjust to their new culture. Some parents endured many challenges and difficulties so their children could have more opportunities. While the children usually understand and appreciate these sacrifices, they know that they have lost something, and they regret this loss.

Many Korean children who were raised in other countries feel that they live in two worlds. Home is like a tiny Korea, but once outside they live in a predominantly non-Korean culture. To survive, they've learned to navigate both worlds. It's very interesting to see how their country has shaped their behaviors and values: my Italian-raised Korean friend talks with his hands, wears gold jewelry, and speaks Korean with an Italian cadence and accent; the Scandinavian Koreans speak with that Minnesota-familiar "huta huta" rhythm.

Some biracial Koreans are also in Korea to explore their roots. Though they sometimes have Korean mannerisms and speak Korean like a native, they face challenges because they physically don't look Korean. They, too, live in two worlds, but they also have a different perception of culture. Some of them have experienced discrimination from both sides; not being Korean enough for the Koreans and not being (for example) African American enough for the African Americans. My German-Korean friend, who doesn't look very Korean, says that most people in Germany think he's Turkish because he is tall and has thick, dark hair. Few Koreans would regard him as Korean, either.

The other kind of *K'yo-bo* is the adoptee—someone born in Korea but adopted, usually by a non-Korean/non-Asian family, and raised in another country. There are many such adoptees here. For Korean adoptees, there is typically more need to know where they came from and a desire to absorb as much of the culture as possible. They come to Korea to find answers, to pursue Korean language skills, to start a new life, to pursue goals, to explore roots, to search for family relatives, and for many other reasons. The sad fact is that making the decision to come to Korea too often jeopardizes the adoptees' relationships with their adoptive families. Some come here when their adoptive family relationships are already strained or broken; some face a rift because they chose to come here, especially when the decision involves a search for biological families.

As a transracial adoptee myself, I strongly believe that having exposure to one's heritage, culture, and ethnic resources is important. There is nothing wrong with adoptees who want to explore their roots. It is only natural to wonder how and why they were adopted. Parents should not feel threatened if their adoptive children decide to explore their roots, their beginnings. Adoptive parents may have never felt what it's like to be the only one in the family who looks like no one else. Since most adoptive families are white, they may not have had their children's experiences of discrimination and racism. The choice to do some soul-searching is an individual one, and family members need to view it not as a threat but as an opportunity.

Speaking from my own experiences, I accept that I live in at least two worlds. In one world I am a daughter of two amazing parents—my nourishment. In another I am on a quest to learn and grow as a Korean; Korea is my classroom. One world is my foundation that provides strength and identity; the other constantly challenges me to learn and grow. Having this life has opened my eyes to other people. I understand and appreciate the effects that others have had on my development and maturity. Having two worlds gives me the advantage of melding the best from each of them.

Though I've lived in Minnesota all my life, there are certain feelings, habits, and behaviors that feel very Korean. Reflecting on all my experiences, I realize that I'm not "lost" but I'm also not "found." I'm not traditionally Korean and I'm not solely Minnesotan/American. I'm finding a path that respects and values both cultures, while graciously being who I am—a very special blend of Korean and American. I am able to function well in both cultures and in others. At first, finding that blend among disparate worlds didn't seem possible, and was certainly not easy to accomplish.

Recently, my parents came to visit me in Korea. It was their first time here, and it provided an opportunity for me to show them "my" Korea. During their visit, a close friend got us tickets to Tokebi Storm, a very popular Korean theater performance. The presentation is based on the Tokebi, a traditional character in Korean folklore. But the show was hardly traditional; rather, it was a contemporary production that was adapted from the traditional theater style.

My friend and I laughed at the Korean jokes and behaviors, and we enjoyed the blending of old and new in the use of traditional instruments, rhythms, and patterns. But my parents couldn't understand the performance in the ways we could. They enjoyed it as a wonderful show of drum beats, sight gags, and music, but they couldn't understand the cultural undertones and Korean "insider" knowledge that gave it a depth and complexity that we enjoyed and appreciated.

My Korea is like that performance. I'm learning to understand and appreciate it more, and each new experience is overlaid on the old or traditional ones that create the sense of self that this *K'yo-bo* woman is developing. That's the current metaphor for my life: a work in progress. I'm not "lost" and I don't expect to be "found." I don't even want to be, and am certainly not looking to be, "found." I'm working on my performance, my own Tokebi Storm—a production that is my own style yet is built on a foundation of traditional Korean values and culture. My "Koreanness," my transracial adoptee *K'yo-bo* self, is still under construction. And that's just fine with me.

▶ ▶ ▶ Learning AmongUS

1. Using both of Kroll's essays, describe the development of her cultural, social, and personal identities.
2. When parents adopt a child transracially, what are their responsibilities to assure that the child has contact and knowledge of his or her birth culture?
3. Kroll offers several examples of people who confuse differences in physical features with differences in culture. Have you ever experienced a similar confusion, either as the recipient of the confusion or as the person who was confused?
4. What has Kroll done to improve her ability to be interculturally competent in Korea?

Samuel Edelman describes his personal choices in nurturing and sustaining his Jewish cultural and religious identity in the face of the many pressures to assimilate and thereby blur the lines separating Jews from their non-Jewish neighbors and friends. Through descriptions of his journeys to Central Europe and to his hometown in Pennsylvania, Sam explains the alternative possibilities facing Jews in the United States. This essay also provides a larger framework for understanding the experiences of people who must live among and interact with those from more dominant cultural groups.

5 To Pass or Not to Pass, That Is the Question: Jewish Cultural Identity in the United States

Samuel M. Edelman

Not long ago, with only a few weeks between them, I took two voyages into my past. On the first I toured Poland, the Czech Republic, and Germany with 27 professors of the Holocaust. On the second I returned to my hometown in central Pennsylvania to see my parents and to show my children where their father grew up. I returned from these trips a changed man.

In Poland I discovered memorials to millions of dead Jews. Before World War II Poland had a Jewish population of 3.8 million people; today it is 2,500. Yet with almost no Jews remaining, I also found a schizophrenic Poland—anti-Semitic to the core, yet curious about and searching for a culture that is as Polish as Poland but was eradicated. Poland seems to have a split personality. Much of the wall graffiti is violently anti-Jewish, blaming communism and all of Poland's ills on phantom Jews, on the ghosts of the murdered. Newspapers, politicians' speeches, and Polish parish priests' sermons rail against hidden Jews; during the last presidential election, one of the candidates was "accused" of being Jewish. At the Auschwitz-Birkenau death camp several Polish skinheads even confronted us as we toured. I was stunned by the anger in their words and actions. Yet other Poles forcefully confronted the skinheads, who were ultimately carted off by the police.

The most disturbing image burned into my mind was a sight in the beautiful city of Krakow. Before the war Krakow had one of the oldest and most distinguished Jewish communities in Europe. Now only a hundred or so elderly Jews remain. Krakow boasts of its Jewish section, its fine shops, its restaurants, a cemetery, and an ancient synagogue that is now a museum. It was there that I heard a *klezmer* band playing hauntingly beautiful Jewish melodies. Yet the *klezmer* band had no Jewish members. Jewish culture, burned alive in Auschwitz and Treblinka, was now on display in Krakow at a living museum without Jews.

In Poland I also witnessed a Jewish renaissance without Jews. In Warsaw, Krakow, Lublin, and other places there were Jewish film festivals, Jewish cultural festivals, and Yiddish readings. There were searches for Jewish roots by thousands of young Poles who had discovered that they had Jewish grandparents or that one of their parents was Jewish.

One warm evening we were relaxing at an outdoor café in Warsaw after visiting Jewish cemeteries, monuments, and synagogues. A young man overheard our discussion and asked if any of us were Jewish. Two of us were, and we said so. He asked if he could join us, and we welcomed him. It turned out that he was 36 years old and his father had died a few weeks earlier. Going through his father's papers he had discovered a packet of letters and other family materials; one of the letters was addressed to him. In the letter his father confessed that he was a survivor of one of the worst killing sites in Europe. After his escape, his father was protected and hidden by a young Polish woman, with whom he eventually fell in love and then married after the war. Because of the rampant anti-Semitism in Poland, his father hid his Jewish heritage from his children. Now, as he came closer to death, his father wanted to reveal his roots to his son, hoping that he would search out other Jews, find out more about being Jewish, and decide for himself what to be.

The man's father's death and his discovery of his own Jewish roots were emotionally overwhelming. He asked us if we knew where he could go to learn more about Jews and his heritage. It so happened that we had just returned from the Warsaw Jewish Documentation Center, and we suggested that he go there to discover more. I heard later that he did, indeed, go and began to discover his long-lost Jewish connections.

The man was not alone in his yearning to discover his identity. While anti-Semitism in Poland was growing without Jews, so, too, was interest in all things Jewish. A Jewish journalist told us that to have Jewish roots was "in" among Polish liberals. We learned that the phenomenon of this man's discovery was happening all over the country. The Jewish renewal without Jews was both puzzling and exciting, just as anti-Semitism without Jews was puzzling and disturbing.

My second journey was to my hometown, Altoona, Pennsylvania. When I lived there 40 years ago it was a small community of about 49,000 people in the middle of coal and railroad country. There were roughly five hundred Jewish families, two synagogues, two kosher butchers, and a few kosher bakers. *Yiddishkeit,* or Jewishness, thrived. There was also the standard anti-Semitism of small towns, such as the yearly swastika that was chalked on the sidewalk, soaped on the window, or painted on the front door. And there was the name calling—"Jew-boy," "Kike," "Christ killer"—coupled with periodic cross burnings by would-be Kluxers.

Today the Jewish population of Altoona is substantially reduced. Though there are still two rabbis and two buildings, the synagogues have had to put aside their religious differences to combine into one religious school. There is a struggle to keep going. The Reform and Conservative Jewish cemeteries sit side by side, never to meet formally.[1] There are no butcher shops for kosher meat, and no kosher bakeries. There seems to be a tiredness about the place. What is most frightening is the significant part of the Jewish population that is no longer Jewish. Friends and acquaintances with whom I grew up have married non-Jews and have given up their culture and religion—their children are being raised as Christians. Most of my school friends have either converted to Christianity, have become gastronomic Jews who eat ethnic foods on Saturday night or Sunday morning, or—worse yet—are nothing. They are Jews without Judaism; Jews without culture; Jews without history; Jews at best vaguely aware of their heritage. Only a handful remain practicing Jews. Most are lost forever. A few have spouses who converted to Judaism, and fewer still have spouses who helped their children grow up as Jews even though they did not convert.

These two voyages both point to a common image of Judaism and Jewish culture in the United States at the beginning of the twenty-first century. Jewish culture, religion, and life are at a crossroads in the United States. One path leads to Altoona and Poland, to anti-Semitism without Jews. The other path leads to Jewish renewal and renaissance. One path leads to Jews passing as non-Jews and disappearing; the other leads to community and continuity.

In my parents' time, those who gave up their heritage were in the minority. For my generation, the size of that group grew significantly. Among today's college students, the number of Jews who are lost to Judaism is more than double that of my generation. Many demographers believe that if the trend continues, the Jewish population in the United States will decline until the middle of the twenty-first century, when it will be negligible. Thirty years ago the Jewish population in the United States was 5.8 million people; today, after the arrival of Jewish immigrants from many parts of the world and a sizable increase in the total number of U.S. residents, the Jewish population is essentially unchanged. Where there should have been a substantial net increase, there is none. Zero population growth, coupled with a massive rate of assimilation, is the basis for the fear that within the next 25 years Jewish culture will disappear from America. Ironically, anti-Semitism is probably at its lowest point ever in the annals of the United States. Jewish intellectual, political, and economic power in the United States is strong. Yet the very existence of Jewish culture is facing its greatest threat.

Assimilation has always been a significant part of Jewish life in America, from the first recorded Jewish settlement in 1654 until today. Each wave of immigrants, and the successive generations of their children, has had to choose between passing as non-Jews or publicly embracing and maintaining their Jewish roots as Jewish Americans.[2]

Culture Concepts

Ethnic Group

Ethnicity *or* ethnic groups *are terms that refer to groups who share a language, historical origins, religion, nation-state, or cultural system. The nature of the relationship of a group's ethnicity to its culture depends on a number of important characteristics. For example, many European American people in the United States still maintain an allegiance to the ethnic group of their ancestors who emigrated from other nations and cultures. In other cases, the identification of ethnicity may coincide more completely with culture. It is also possible for members of an ethnic group to be part of many different cultures and/or nations. For instance, Jewish people share a common ethnic identification, even though they belong to widely varying cultures and are citizens of many different nations.*

For the Jewish community in the United States, there are four competing choices in dealing with assimilation and its benefits and threats. One choice, of course, is anchored in the vision of the Protestant majority: the United States ought to be a "melting pot," and any hint of foreignness is a threat to American culture and should be eliminated. Like the view often expressed in Europe following the French revolution and the Napoleonic period, the goal of this choice is the disappearance of Jews—both as a culture and as a religion—into the larger society. The force at play is the attractiveness of Americanization, which is sufficiently seductive that Jews will turn their backs on their "other" culture and eventually disappear. The disappearance of Jewish culture, or ethnocide, is happening all over America. Many American Jews have intermarried and, for a variety of reasons—laziness, a desire to pass, ignorance—watch passively as their children grow up with no Jewish education, intermarry again, and finally lose all touch with their heritage.

The second competing choice about how to deal with assimilation is one emphasized by such Jewish leaders as Rabbi Mordechai Kaplan, the founder of the Reconstructionist Jewish Movement. This choice involves an equilibrium between mainstream America and traditional Jewish values. These two sets of values are not antithetical but flow, one into the other, like a balancing act between particularist and universalist perspectives. Kaplan's view is that Jewish culture, history, and religion—important ingredients in the maintenance of Judaism—can easily live side-by-side with American values and culture. This choice verges on what one might call intercultural communication. Some communication scholars might term this approach "biculturalism."

As an example of this second choice to being Jewish in the United States, consider the experiences of one of my very close Jewish friends. More than 15 years ago he met a Catholic woman. They started to date, fell in love, and eventually were married by a Reform rabbi who wanted to keep intermarried families in the orbit of Judaism. After a few years, they had two girls in quick succession. He was ambivalent about his roots, but she was not about hers and felt a tension between them and her obligations to her children. They struggled with such issues as whether to have a Christmas tree in their house and whether to celebrate Christmas and Easter with her parents. They argued over what messages of ambivalence and inclusiveness would be sent to their children if they permitted both religions in the household. Their decision was to give up all Christian practices, even though she had not converted. This was a wrenching decision for her, which she did for the sake of her children. She also knew that because she had not converted to Judaism, the children would not be considered Jewish under Jewish law unless they chose to convert themselves. She therefore opted to have the girls educated in the synagogue, and when they were older she encouraged them to go through the ceremony of conversion. Recently they completed the conversion ceremony, and both had their Bat Mitzvot in the synagogue. Now she, too, is beginning to study to convert.

The third and fourth choices for dealing with assimilation both involve a separation from American culture, but in very different ways. The third choice involves living in the United States while rejecting secular American values. This alternative is adopted by ultra-Orthodox Jews such as the Hasidim. The Hasidic approach places physical and psychological barriers around the Jewish community to separate it from what its members view as the profane. Television is restricted, pop culture is avoided, and anything not Jewish—according to *halacha,* or strict Jewish law—is not permitted. This ideology, which is similar to that of the Amish and other separationist communities, is at the center of the Hasidic way of dealing with secular American values.

The fourth choice, while not rejecting American culture, involves leaving the United States for a political, cultural, linguistic, and religious existence as a Jewish majority in Israel. This Zionist approach encourages as many Jews as possible to make *aliyah* and emigrate to Israel. The horrors of the *Shoah* (the Holocaust), the unwillingness of the allies and others to save European Jewry, the antagonisms among Jewish political groups that left them splintered and ineffective, and the creation of the State of Israel by the United Nations in 1948 all acted as catalysts for many American Jews to propose Zionism to combat assimilation and extermination. It is mind-numbing to realize that, had a Jewish nation existed, millions of Jews could have survived the *Shoah.* The success of the State of Israel is an important and critical counterbalance to assimilation, conversion, intermarriage, indifference, and anti-Semitism in America and throughout the world. An economically developed, intellectually advanced, and politically stable Israel suggests that Zionism has been successful in achieving its broad goals. The core belief of Zionism is that what happened to Europe's Jews should never happen again. Connection to this idea and to Israel has become a secular religion for many American Jews. While Zionism initially held that one should make *aliyah* to Israel, it now supports the idea that one also serves who stays in America and fights in support of Jewish communities under threat throughout the world.

Culture Concepts

Assimilation and Integration as Forms of Adaptation

Two issues shape the response of individuals and groups to prolonged intercultural contact. The first is whether it is considered important to maintain one's cultural identity and to display its characteristics. The second involves whether people believe it is important to maintain relationships with their outgroups. Assimilation *occurs when people think it is relatively unimportant to maintain their original cultural identity but it is important to establish and maintain relationships with other cultures.* Integration *occurs when people retain their original cultural identity while seeking to maintain harmonious relationships with other cultures. Both integration and assimilation include a desire to maintain positive intercultural relationships.*

Another useful typology for understanding the American Jewish community is provided by Daniel J. Elazar.[3] Elazar describes American Jewry as seven concentric circles that radiate outward from a core of committed Jews toward a vague sense of Jewishness on the fringes. At the core are the "integral" Jews, for whom Jewishness is a central factor in their lives and a full-time concern. Elazar estimates that they represent 5 percent of the Jewish population in the United States. Surrounding the core is a second group of U.S. Jews, the "participants," who regularly engage in Jewish life and who view expressions of their Jewishness as important but not full-time activities. They may be officers in Jewish organizations, participants in pro-Israel activities, contributors to Jewish educational experiences, or professionals employed by Jewish agencies. Elazar estimates that they represent from 10 to 20 percent of U.S. Jews.

The third circle is made up of "associated" Jews, who are affiliated with Jewish institutions or organizations in some concrete way but are not very active in them. This group is made up of synagogue members whose activities are limited to High Holy Day services, participation in Jewish rites of passage, and memberships in Jewish social and political organizations such as Hadassah and B'nai B'rith. Elazar suggests that this group is fairly large, making up about 30 to 35 percent of the Jewish population.

The fourth circle, "contributors and consumers," consists of Jews who make periodic donations to Jewish causes and occasionally use the services of Jewish institutions, but who are at best minimally associated with the Jewish community. He estimates that 25 to 30 percent of Jews are in this circle.

The fifth circle includes what Elazar calls the "peripherals," who are recognizably Jewish in some way but are completely uninvolved in Jewish life. They have no interest in participating in Jewish experiences and rarely make donations to Jewish causes. About 15 percent are in this circle.

The sixth circle, the "repudiators," are Jews who actively deny their Jewishness. Some are extremely hostile to all things Jewish, while others simply react with hostility to their Jewish origins. This group, which once was very large but has experienced an extensive decline, now makes up less than 5 percent of U.S. Jews.

Finally, there is a group Elazar labels "quasi-Jews." They are neither fully inside nor entirely outside the Jewish community. They may have intermarried but have some connection to a personal Jewish label. They make up about 5 to 10 percent of the population.

Growth at both the core and on the periphery of Judaism is increasing. The core grows as young Jews return to Jewish religious life and become *Baal Teshuva,* conforming to Jewish laws and rituals. The proselytizing activities of some of the more aggressive fundamentalist groups, such as the Lebavitcher Hasidim, have been very successful with disaffected Jewish youth. There is also substantial population growth among Orthodox Jews, especially among the ultra-Orthodox. The movement toward religious return and revival, coupled with a phenomenal birth rate, contributes to growth in the core. Simultaneously, however, the intermarriage rate among those in the third and fourth circles of Jewish involvement, who comprise the majority of the U.S. Jewish population, is also on the rise. The intermarriage rate among these Jews—who often label themselves Conservative, Reform, or Reconstructionist Jews—now approaches 57 percent.

Intermarriage has both positive and negative consequences. Although increasing numbers of young Jews are intermarrying, there is also a growing number of their non-Jewish spouses who are converting to Judaism. The rate of conversion has been increasing in the last decade, but the relative numbers are still small. Of greater interest is the number of non-Jewish spouses in intermarried couples who join a Jewish communal group as quasi-Jewish participants. This phenomenon is most evident in rural or small Jewish congregations that exist where the Jewish population is relatively isolated from mainstream Jewish communities. For example, my own community of Chico, California, has one small synagogue and a congregation that dates back to the early days of the gold rush. Over the last 20 years the membership has tripled to about 90 families. Until recently we had an active religious school but only a part-time rabbi, who did not live in the community, to provide our religious services. Now we have a rabbi who lives here. A significant proportion of those who affiliate with the synagogue come from intermarried families in which the non-Jewish spouse is the catalyst for involvement of both the children and the Jewish spouse. Many of these men and women support Jewish communal and religious involvement despite resistance from their Jewish spouses. These Jewish affiliate members, as I call them, are integral to the development and maintenance of Jewish life in our community. This is the reality of what some of us call frontier Judaism.

Colleagues from other small and rural communities report observations similar to mine in Chico. This suggests to me that the most peripheral areas of Jewish involvement may provide the greatest potential for the future of Jewish America. It is because of these non-Jewish yet affiliated members of intermarried couples that Jewish life is transmitted to a new generation of Jews hitherto thought lost to Jewish life. If the Chico phenomenon is typical, then it is clear that a rethinking of the age-old negative vision of intermarriage must be undertaken.

I view myself as among the ranks of what Elazar calls the "integral Jew." I have taken a roundabout path to this place I am now in. Growing up in my hometown, I defined myself in terms of my Jewishness. I never denied it, and sometimes flaunted it. There was even a time when I thought seriously about becoming a rabbi; I still have dreams of doing that. I became, instead, a communication professor. I have experienced various incidents of anti-Semitism. One such incident occurred when I ran for township supervisor in Pennsylvania. Though it was a close race, it was only as election day approached that I discovered a secret my campaign staff and friends had been keeping from me: flyers accusing me of being part of a Zionist conspiracy and a "Christ-killer" had been distributed throughout the district. I doubt that I lost many votes because of these smears, but I did feel pain. I truly felt like an outsider.

I explored the option of making *aliyah* to Israel. I did not move there because, at the time, I couldn't find work and my wife didn't want to go. Nevertheless, I regret that I didn't immigrate, for when I am in Israel I feel truly at ease and not "the other." Instead, I choose to identify as a Jew in the United States, not only in my home but also in my work. Over the last 20 years I have gradually spent more and more time researching and studying Jewish subjects related to communication studies. I now identify more with my Jewish work than with my disciplinary involvement in communication. As I became successful in teaching and researching such subjects as the Holocaust and Israeli public address, I experienced a greater sense of ease. I also feel lucky to have supportive colleagues and friends who have encouraged me to do my own thing. My mentor at Penn State, Gerald Phillips, felt bitter that his peers in the communication discipline never provided him with similar latitude to work on Jewish topics.

Today I coordinate a Jewish studies program and am working toward developing a field of study called Jewish rhetoric. My wife is Jewish and my children are being educated and brought up in the Jewish faith. Even though I live in a small California town, I bring my Jewishness with me. I define myself through it and see the world through Jewish eyes. I am what I am. *Hineni,* here I am. I am content.

Being Jewish to me requires participation in a community, involving oneself in the rituals, ceremonies, and frames of reference that are typically Jewish. There are many types of Jews in the United States, but at the heart of all is the concept of the community—*klal yisrael,* the community of Israel, and *am yisrael*, people of Israel.[4] For many Jews in the United States passing has become a way of life. It is not hard to do. One simply has to choose not to be observant and not be a part of the Jewish community. To be Jewish is to be active, at least to some extent, in the community. Even though the religious law defines Jewishness based on the mother's religion, it is clear that actual affiliation goes far beyond that definition.

The second most defining event for Jews in the twentieth century, that of the *Shoah*, or the Holocaust, eliminated the choice of passing. To pass or not to pass was no longer the choice of the Jew; rather, the Nazis said that you

---

Culture Concepts

Separation, Segregation, Seclusion, and Marginalization as Forms of Adaptation

When people do not want to maintain positive relationships with others, several outcomes are possible. If people do not want positive relationships with another culture and also wish to retain their cultural characteristics, separation *may result. If the separation occurs because the more politically and economically powerful culture does not want the intercultural contact, the result of the forced separation is called* segregation. *If, however, a nondominant group chooses not to participate in the larger society in order to retain its own way of life, the separation is called* seclusion. *When individuals or groups neither retain their cultural heritage nor maintain positive contacts with the other groups,* marginalization *occurs.*

---

were Jewish no matter what. The first most defining event for Jews in the twentieth century was the creation of a Jewish homeland in the State of Israel, which also rejected the idea of passing. Only those who take the action of declaring themselves to be a part of *klal yisrael* can be a citizen of Israel.

As I consider friends and relatives in my old hometown, many of whom have intermarried and have found it easier to reject their connections to their Jewish communal heritage, I see Jews who are as lost to me as my relatives who perished in the *Shoah*. The legacy for their children will be empty synagogues, museums to a culture that disappeared, cemeteries covered with weeds, and *klezmer* music without Jews to play it. Their legacy will be to succeed in doing what the Nazis failed to complete in Europe. Judaism will continue in the United States, but the declining number of those willing to make the choice for communal involvement and against disappearance concerns me.

To be accepted fully by mainstream America has been a benefit that many generations of Jewish immigrants have sought and are finally achieving. Time will tell if Jewish Americans thrive or die because of such kindness.

Notes

1. Reform and Conservative Judaism are separate movements. In the United States they comprise the two largest denominations.

2. There have been four waves of Jewish immigrants to the United States: the initial Sephardi Jews (Spanish origin), who immigrated prior to the birth of the United States; the immigration of German and central European Jews in the first third of the nineteenth century; the largest wave, of almost 3 million immigrants from eastern Europe, between 1882 and 1914; and the most recent wave, after World War II, that has included survivors of the Holocaust and, more recently, Jews from the Soviet-occupied lands, Jews from Arab lands, Iranian Jews, and Israelis.

3. Daniel J. Elazar, *Community and Polity: The Organizational Dynamics of American Jewry* (Philadelphia: Jewish Publication Society, 1976).

4. These terms refer not to the State of Israel but to the biblical children of Israel, or all who call themselves Jewish.

▶ ▶ ▶ **Learning AmongUS**

1. How do the types of choices that Edelman describes overlap with the forms of adaptation described in the reading's Culture Concepts boxes?

2. Edelman describes the personal choices of several families with one parent who is Jewish and another who is from a different religious background. Using those examples, do you believe it is possible within one family to create traditions that honor different ethnicities and religions?

3. In addition to Jews, identify other groups that can be described as an ethnic group. How do these groups differ from cultural groups?

4. Based on your readings and your own experiences, identify one or more cultures that have chosen to follow each of the following five responses to living among other cultures: assimilation, integration, segregation, seclusion, and marginalization.

Our cultural identities come from multiple sources. That is the theme of Alfred Guillaume's story about who he is, what he believes, and what values he tries to instill in his sons. The title of this essay describes the major cultural influences that shaped his identity. In the essay Alfred describes how race, nationality, culture, and religion interact in unique ways to produce beliefs and values that guide his personal and professional choices.

6 To Be American, Black, Catholic, and Creole

Alfred J. Guillaume, Jr.

I am a 50-year-old American. I am black, Roman Catholic, and Creole. This is how I describe myself 50 years in the making. As a young boy growing up in the South I was made to believe that I was different. Images of America did not mirror me. The segregated South wanted me to believe that I was inferior. The Catholic Church taught me that all of God's people were equal. My French Creole heritage gave me a special bond to Native Americans, to Europeans, and to Africans. This is the composite portrait of who I am. I like who I am and can imagine being no other.

What I've accomplished professionally I owe to discipline, a good education, and opportunity. I thank my parents, whose values concerning education shaped my life; they instilled in me the notion that hard work breeds success and opens doors to opportunity. Today I am a senior administrator at Indiana University. I am fortunate that my life has been a wonderful adventure.

I'm an American. I was born in New Orleans, Louisiana, whose sophisticated elegance and alluring exoticism make it America's most European city and also its most Caribbean. Natives call it the Big Easy. From its founding, New Orleans has been a land of dichotomies, of piety and hedonism, a Catholic city that revels in music, food, and good times.

I'm an African American. Just within my lifetime people of African ancestry have been called colored, Negro, black, and sundry derogatory terms that I categorically reject. I am proud to have been born black. My people paid a heavy price through toil and suffering to make America. Their unparalleled creative contributions shaped American culture.

I am Catholic. I thought everyone was Catholic until I went to school and learned that there were Protestants. The nuns taught my schoolmates and me to pray for them and for all other non-Catholics. My values were formed in large part by my religious faith. As a child I dreamed of becoming a priest. I left my parents at age 12 to study for the priesthood with the Josephite Fathers in New York. I made my first long journey on a train with five other seminarians from my parish. I will never forget the memorable sights along the way and my arrival at Grand Central Station and the Port Authority. The bustle of people made it feel like a carnival.

I am Creole. I trace my ancestry to Africa, to Europe, and to Native America. I am proud of my multiethnic ancestry. America is a nation of immigrants. Some came willingly; others came in shackles. The native peoples also call this land home. Race dominates American thought. In an era of increased intolerance; of rapid retreats from affirmative action, civil rights, and human rights; of tightened immigration laws; of fast-paced retrenchment from obligations to the poor and the homeless, America is becoming a society of "us" and "them." But America is not and has never been a land of clearly defined racial groups. Racial groups are not monolithic.

The word *Creole* is used to define Europeans who came to the Americas. But *Creole* also refers to blacks in the Americas, mixed-blood people whose ancestry can be traced to Africa as well as to Europe. Such is my family: gumbo people, a blend of Africa, Europe, and Native America. The first languages of my maternal grandparents were French and Creole, a kind of pidgin French. I regret that my siblings and I never learned to speak the language. We lived in the city and the language was spoken primarily in the rural areas. My mother understood the language but never spoke it to us. Speaking English correctly was important, particularly without the melodic Creole accent so characteristic of natives of southern Louisiana. Yet even without the language, I speak with a regional accent. On my paternal side were the Houma Indians. Pictures of my great-great-grandmother in Indian dress are prized family possessions.

I grew up in the segregated South. My parents shielded us from racism. Our upbringing, our religion, and our schooling protected us. We lived in a middle-class neighborhood, attended a Catholic elementary school run by a black order of nuns called the Holy Family Sisters, and went to Mass at a black Catholic church. We lived in a cocoon in our black, Catholic, Creole world. Because of all the support Creole society provided, it seemed that segregation did not affect us. It was not until the sixties, during my teenage years, that I became fully aware of the dehumanizing effects of segregation.

Creole society could not totally isolate us from racial prejudice. I remember sitting with my maternal grandmother in the colored section of the bus, behind the "Colored Only" sign, when a white patron removed the sign and put it behind us, forcing us to stand and relinquish our seat to him. I remember the separate water fountains, the separate entrances to restaurants, the separate playgrounds, the separate schools and churches. In department stores and other businesses, blacks did menial work; the salespeople and bosses were white. I remember the day my dad took me with him to the post office, where he worked. At the desks and the service counters were only whites; I asked my dad to show me his office. I had no notion then that only whites had offices.

My first recollection that black meant being inferior occurred one morning as I walked to school. In the segregated South, only white children were bused to school. A young white boy, about my own age—eight or so—yelled out the window of the yellow school bus, "Hey, chocolate boy!" When I related this story to my maternal great aunt her response to me was, "Cher (My dear), you

---

Culture Concepts

Defining Intercultural Communication

Intercultural communication *occurs when large and important cultural differences create dissimilar interpretations and expectations about how to communicate competently.*

---

a pretty chocolate boy." Since then I have always taken a particular delight in being "chocolate."

It was not until the sixties, during the civil rights movement, that I began to call myself black. I had always thought of myself as Negro or Creole. As Creoles we grew up believing that we were "different." I remember my maternal grandmother's shock when she saw me sporting an Afro. She wondered why I wanted to make my hair nappy. She firmly believed that we were descendants of France, not Africa—to her I was not black but brown. I didn't understand then, though I understand now, why she could not call herself black. After all, her parents spoke French; she grew up speaking French and Creole; she was Catholic; most of the people in her family were medium brown to fair-skinned. She herself was considered "high yellow" and gave birth to two fair skinned blonde girls.

In the sixties, of course, black was "beautiful," as young blacks shouted it with Stokely Carmichael. James Brown urged us to "Say it loud, 'I'm black and I'm proud.'" We marched with Martin Luther King, Jr., and felt a renewed pride in being black. Throughout the South, in sit-ins and on freedom rides, we sang exuberantly, "We Shall Overcome." In New Orleans I worked tirelessly in voter registration drives to teach blacks the preamble to the Constitution so they would be eligible to vote, only to have them denied that right repeatedly. We marched on city hall and were arrested when we refused to disband. I remember one sweltering day, passing my paternal grandmother's home on my way to jail, waving to her from a police car, singing freedom songs. Right up until her death years later, she recalled that day with horror.

Though the message of segregation was hatred and subjugation, my parents taught my four siblings and me never to feel inferior to whites. We never heard a disparaging word in our home about white people. Rather than thinking that whites were superior, we grew up believing that we were special. We were Americans. And not only were we colored, we were Creole and Catholic. My father took particular delight in repeatedly saying that each of us was a jewel; we were five dazzling jewels, and each was different. My parents taught us to believe in ourselves above all else, and that we were never to forget where we came from. We were never to forget those who helped us along the way. "Never burn bridges once you cross them," my dad would say. "You never know when you might have to cross them again." My parents taught us to have pride always but never to hate or deride another human being. We were taught to respect elders and treat all individuals with dignity. We were never to make fun of those less fortunate and were to be thankful for the graces we did have.

Neighborhoods in New Orleans today are more segregated than I remember as a child. Typical of housing patterns that date back to the eighteenth and nineteenth centuries, and because of the common practices of miscegenation during those historical times, whites and blacks lived close to each other when I was growing up. Our neighborhood was mixed. In a string of modest shotgun houses, white and black families lived adjacent to each other. Our next door neighbor, Miss Gladys, was white. Babette, an old white lady who walked with a limp that scared the children in the neighborhood, lived around the corner. She was always admonishing us to be good and chastised us if she caught us playing in the streets.

Most neighborhoods had two Catholic churches, and ours was no exception. There was St. Francis Cabrini for whites and St. Raymond for blacks. If blacks attended a white church, they sat in special seating in the back and sometimes would be denied communion. It was particularly hard for me, as a little boy, to understand why black and white Catholics should be separated. I believed that God did not segregate the races in Heaven. I prayed for forgiveness for those white Catholics who stood on the church steps citing biblical chapter and verse to prove that God meant the races to be separate. In our own black Catholic church the white priest spoke of God's love for all of humanity during his Sunday homily. As he glanced toward the congregation he said, "Negroes are beautiful in God's eyes. What I see in the church this morning are many hues and colors, as beautiful as the most magnificent flower garden." I was an altar boy at that Mass and those words made a deep impression on me. To this day they remain a source of comfort to me whenever I face the harshness of racism.

My brothers and sisters and I received our religious values from our parents, particularly our mother, who is religious and devoted to the Church. My dad, no matter how exhausted from the day's work—he sometimes worked two jobs—would, without fail, kneel at his bedside, saying his nightly prayers. Often we would find him asleep on his knees. Priests and nuns were frequent visitors to our home. My mom took the nuns for Sunday afternoon rides (at that time nuns did not drive). My brother and I were altar boys; we hated funerals, but we loved weddings because of the tips we received from the grooms. I remember the Monday night parish rosary, which rotated from home to home, and the Tuesday night novenas to Our Lady of Perpetual Help. I would also occasionally accompany my mother to the seasonal novenas to St. Jude, the patron saint of hopeless cases, and to the Shrine of St. Ann, where the devoted climbed stone steps to make the Stations of the Cross on their knees. When the neighborhood where St. Ann's shrine was located grew increasingly black, the Church tried to close the shrine and rebuild it in the white suburbs. Today there are two shrines to St. Ann, one in black New Orleans and the other in white Metairie.

Education was stressed in my family. My siblings and I knew from an early age that we would go to college. My dad would tell us that we could be anything we wanted in life, even bums, but he insisted that we be educated bums. We used to laugh at this idea, but now we understand his wisdom. He finished only high school, but he was an avid reader. He subscribed to the *Readers' Digest of Condensed Books,* and the *Encyclopedia Britannica* was prominently displayed in the living room. He earned a living as a postal clerk. One of eight children, my father shined shoes on Canal Street at age nine when his father died. My mom was a school teacher who taught piano and the

---

Culture Concepts

What Do You Call Someone from the United States of America? I

Many people who live in the United States of America prefer to call themselves American. *However, people from Brazil, Argentina, Guatemala, Mexico, and many other Central and South American countries also consider themselves American because they are all part of the continents known collectively as the Americas.* North American *is commonly used by people from many Central and South American countries to refer to people from the United States. However,* North America *refers to an entire continent, and people from Mexico and Canada are, strictly speaking, also North Americans. We prefer the term* U.S. American *because it retains the word* American *but narrows its scope to refer only to those from the United States. The term retains the advantages of a name that is specific enough to be accurate, yet it does not resort to a form of address that people would be unlikely to use and would regard as odd and insulting.*

---

sixth grade. My parents taught us that everything was within our reach, because success depended on our hard work and persistence. My dad taught us never to give up, that the word "can't" is not in the dictionary. We were Guillaumes, he would say, and a Guillaume never gives up. He exhorted us never to accept mediocrity. He encouraged us in our schoolwork always to aim for an *A*. "It is far better to aim high and miss the mark," he would say, "than aim low and make it." We understood that to mean that if we studied for an *A* and failed, then our reward would be a *B* or no less than a *C*. But if we studied for a *D* and succeeded, the results would be disastrous. He also taught us never to complain about what we didn't have. When we did complain he would say endlessly, "I complained because I had no shoes, until I saw the man who had no feet." I consider myself blessed to have had parents who valued education and who understood the limitless potential education affords.

Most of my formative education was in black schools, from kindergarten through college, and by all measures of assessment I received an excellent education. I spent my first three years of high school studying for the priesthood in Newburgh, New York, with the Josephite Fathers, whose apostolic mission is among African Americans. I finished my senior year in New Orleans with the Josephites at a black Catholic high school for boys. To many, Saint Augustine High was the best high school in the city. The school prided itself on its academics as well as its athletics. It produced many sports championships in the black leagues and graduated the first black presidential scholar. Perennially, it had the highest number of National Achievement Scholars for Negro students among the city's high schools. Its students earned scholarships to prestigious eastern colleges and universities.

Like our mother, all five of us graduated from Xavier University of Louisiana, which is a small, predominantly black Catholic university that was

Culture Concepts

What Do You Call Someone from the United States of America? II

Because their common cultural heritage is predominantly European, we prefer the term European American to refer to white U.S. cultural members. Similarly, we prefer African American *as the cultural term for U.S. Americans of African heritage.* Latino *and* Latina *are cultural terms for U.S. Americans who share the Spanish language and cultural patterns.*

founded in 1913 by the Sisters of the Blessed Sacrament, an order of religious nuns established by Katherine Drexel of Philadelphia. Xavier has a history of excellence in training black teachers and pharmacists, and it is widely recognized for its strong music curriculum. Many of its graduates sang on the opera stages of Europe when discrimination did not permit them to perform in the United States. Xavier is now nationally recognized for its science programs; it consistently sends more blacks to medical and dental schools than does any other institution of higher learning in the United States, and it continues to train a large number of this nation's black pharmacists. Katherine Drexel has been beatified by the Catholic Church, the first step toward sainthood.

Growing up in New Orleans was fascinating. It is affectionately called the Crescent City because of the bend in the Mississippi River that shapes it; jazz and blues singers mournfully lament "Do you know what it means to miss New Orleans?" It has a unique flavor among American cities. It has been memorialized in literature dating from the earliest journeys of travelers to the New World who spoke of its pesky insects, its insufferable heat, and its beautiful women: black, white, and all the muted shades in between. A city nestled in the swamps and bayous of southern Louisiana, it is as enchanting as it is mysterious, blending Native American, African, European, and Caribbean cultures. Music, food, and good times are synonymous with New Orleans.

New Orleanians love to eat. Recipes that blend Native American, African, and European culinary tastes and spices treat the palate to a symphony of pleasure. Gumbo, crawfish etouffee, shrimp creole, jambalaya, stuffed crabs, soft-shell crabs, seafood boil, raw oysters, coushaw (an indigenous squash), mirliton, catfish, stuffed bell peppers, andouille, grits, pain perdu (homemade French bread or French toast), corn soup, red beans, and rice are the foods with which I grew up. You can't leave the home of a New Orleanian without first having something to eat.

Festivals and parties are also very much a part of New Orleans life. The carnival season of debutante balls, masked parties, and parades begins with the feast of the Magi on January 6. The biggest party of the year is Mardi Gras, the hedonistic carnival before Lent, in which New Orleanians feast and dance one last time before the 40 days of fasting and abstinence that precede Easter. My family, like many others, would wear colorful costumes sewn by my mother and watch the parades, yelling, "Hey, mister, throw me something." As young adults we also attended the debutante balls. Other popular festivals included the French Quarter Festival and the Jazz and Heritage Festival, perennial favorites that rival Mardi Gras.

I consider myself a citizen of the world. I have traveled to many countries in Europe, Africa, Asia, and the Americas, and I feel at ease wherever I am. My comfort with other cultures stems, in part, from my ability to speak French and to communicate passably in Spanish. After spending almost my entire high school years studying for the priesthood in the seminary, I had no idea what I wanted to study as a college student. My mother advised me to study what I enjoyed most. Because I liked French in high school, she suggested that I study languages in college. That was perhaps the best advice I've ever been given. Thanks to my parents' sacrifice and support, I was able to study French and Spanish through immersion. As an undergraduate I spent summers in Mexico and in French-speaking Canada. Later, as a graduate student, I studied and traveled in France and French-speaking Africa. In many ways my pursuit of French as an educational goal was, perhaps unconsciously, a way for me to recapture my lost Creole French heritage.

In the United States I am black. In Europe and abroad I am also black, but not in the same way. Race dominates American culture. In my own country I am black and American; abroad I am American and black. There is a distinction. In many places I have traveled, I am not a minority. Skin color is not a major distinctive attribute. In Brazil, where there is a panorama of skin tones and hues, race is not determined by skin color. Some Brazilians consider me white. Cultural identity is more aptly defined by racial groups, such as the blacks in Bahia and the Indians in the Amazon.

As an administrator and a professor at three different universities, I have confronted prejudice. Most of it was subtle. There are some who feel discomfort in accepting a black authority figure. I sometimes wonder whether individuals would respond to me differently as an administrator if I were white. I have noticed that some first-time visitors to my office are surprised to see a black vice chancellor. Our images of power in America show a white male in positions of authority.

Curiously, in northern California, where there is little ethnic and racial diversity, less attention was paid to my racial background. When I was appointed vice president of a midwestern Catholic university, the public and the university press highlighted the fact that I was the university's first black academic vice president. The alumni and the black community took special pride in my appointment. In admissions literature that reached out to African Americans and other minorities, I was prominently featured. When I was appointed provost and vice president at Humboldt, no mention of my race was made in the university's press releases.

Living in Humboldt County was less of a cultural adjustment than I had at first imagined. I suspect that my southern accent, coupled with my expressive and chatty manner, quickly marked me as a nonlocal. I was often asked how I liked it here, since there were so few blacks living in this part of California. When I first arrived, a kind, elderly couple was concerned that I might feel awkward at Mass because there were no black Catholics in the parish.

Culture Concepts

What Do You Call Someone from the United States of America? III

Terms routinely used to describe members of other cultural groups in the United States include Native American, Arab American, Asian American, and Pacific Islander. Each of these labels, as well as those previously described, obscures the rich variety of cultures that the single term represents. The use of these overly broad terms is not meant to deny the importance of cultural distinctions but to allow for an economy of words. There are some inherent difficulties in any choice of cultural terms to refer to U.S. Americans. If precision was the only criterion, it would be necessary to make many further distinctions. But often there is a need for an economy of words and there is also the force of common usage. Remember, however, that the term specific individuals prefer is an important reflection of the way they perceive themselves.

They mentioned their own uneasiness when, during a visit to New Orleans, they were the only whites at Mass in a black Catholic church. I imagine they wanted to let me know that they understood what it is like to be a minority. The couple did not understand that my biggest transition to living in northern California was living in a rural community; it had nothing to do with race. Until then I had always lived in big cities.

I am divorced with two sons, ages 19 and 11. I know that each is trying to find his place in a society that is increasingly multicultural but whose power base remains white. As young black men they struggle with the stereotypical images of what being black connotes in America. This is particularly true for my older son, who learned bitterly what it meant to be black when, as a young boy of 11, he was stopped by campus police at a midwest university and escorted off campus because he did not belong there. He was afraid to tell them that his father was the vice president. My younger son, to my knowledge, has not yet experienced racism at its ugliest. He remains open and accepting of others. He hates talk of black people and white people and proudly boasts that all people are the same. For him the important quality in a person is whether he or she is nice.

I am raising my sons as my parents raised me. I teach them that it is less important that the world sees you as black, and it is more important that the world recognizes you as a person of strength and integrity. As my father taught me, I teach them to be strong and independent, to be individuals. I tell them that they are jewels, that there are no others like them, that they have unique gifts of self, and that they should be willing to share their gifts of self with others. Color is not important; character is. They are special and they honor their father and their heritage.

▶ ▶ ▶ **Learning AmongUS**

1. Alfred Guillaume describes himself as "American, Black, Catholic, and Creole." Based on his essay, which of these aspects of his identity is the most central or important?

2. Which parts of Guillaume's sense of self would you characterize as his personal, social, and cultural identities? What factors influenced the development of each of these aspects of his identity?

3. How does Guillaume's self-description fit with the Culture Concepts boxes that describe various cultural groups in the United States?

Alfred Guillaume's story is about the multiple sources of his identity, strong parental values, and a love of languages. At each step of his personal and professional journey, elements of each shape his choices. His story is also a case example of the intersection of group experiences and those of the individual—his religion, his race, his ethnicity, and his profession all come together to make him who he is. The role of race as a factor in U.S. higher education is also a powerful contribution of this reprise to his earlier essay.

7 Lessons Learned: A University Administrator's Intercultural Journey

Alfred J. Guillaume, Jr.

I am a black, Catholic, Creole American. I see myself not as any one of these traits but as a composite of the whole. Who I am and the values that brought me to my current station in life, I owe to my upbringing as a black, Catholic, Creole who was raised in the South. Well, not exactly the Deep South of Eudora Welty or William Faulkner, but rather the South of Tennessee Williams and Walker Percy, with its exotic European and Caribbean flavor. My four siblings and I grew up in New Orleans, a city lazily nestled among bayous and the Mississippi River. As Southerners we understood segregation and knew "our place." *Colored Only* and *White Only* signs were commonplace and were constant reminders that somehow colored meant inferior.

The South I grew up in included French Creole, the colorful patois spoken by blacks, whites, and the indigenous native peoples. It was the parlance of my grandparents, the secret code among the elders when they wanted to speak privately. My country cousins, who lived along False River in Pointe Coupee Parish north of Baton Rouge, could communicate among themselves in Creole, further isolating my four siblings and me. My parents were of the generation that lived in the city and consciously or unconsciously chose to assimilate more fully into mainstream American culture by abandoning the Creole language. They claimed never to have learned it. In our household, English was the lingua franca. Thus my siblings and I never acquired the melodic cadence typical of Louisianans who speak both French and English. Because I never learned to speak Creole, I've always felt a void in my cultural heritage.

To my parents, who embraced middle-class values and for whom education was important, speaking correctly and growing up properly were essential buffers against segregation. We were taught good manners. "Thank you" was an important grace. We knew when to say "Yes, Ma'am" and "No, Sir."

Culture Concepts

Intercultural Competence

Intercultural competence *is not independent of the relationships and situations within which communication occurs. Competence is not an individual attribute; rather, it is a characteristic of the association between individuals. Because intercultural competence is contextual, someone may be perceived as highly competent in one set of intercultural interactions and only moderately competent in another. Judgments of intercultural competence also depend on cultural expectations about the permitted behaviors that characterize the settings or situations within which people communicate. Consequently, the same set of behaviors may be perceived as very competent in one cultural setting and much less competent in another.*

Adults were addressed as Mister or Miss. Whether single or married, a lady was "Miss." Even today I feel a slight awkwardness when calling an elderly person by her or his first name. Neighborhoods in New Orleans then were not nearly as segregated as they are today. Whites and blacks lived in proximity to one another. Our next-door neighbor was white, as well as several families around the block. We co-existed peacefully, but publicly we respected the boundaries of segregation.

Thanks to the lessons our parents taught us, my siblings and I prevailed in the segregated South. From them we learned self-esteem, pride, and the importance of dignified decorum. We knew we were special; our dad relished repeating that each of us was a jewel, each different, but each precious. Both of my parents preached daily the gospel of respecting self and being respectful of others. We understood that public bad behavior reflected negatively on us and on our race. Being a gentleman or a lady earned respect and admiration. We were taught never to hate and never to allow anger to interfere with clear, rational thought. From an early age, our parents instilled in us that the obstacles of segregation could not prevent us from achieving what we wanted in life.

The Catholic Church was central to our lives. My brother and I served as altar boys. I preferred the high Masses to the low ones. Weddings were fun because the groom gave us tips; funerals were dreaded. Monday evening rosaries to Our Lady of Fatima, Tuesday evening novenas to Our Lady of Perpetual Help, and Thursday evening holy hours were regular devotional rituals in our local parish. These regular devotional ceremonies have all but disappeared within today's Church. Although churches were segregated, I learned a great deal about civility to and respect for others. The priests and nuns who served in colored parishes and schools modeled for us lessons of love, and they taught us to pray for those who advocated and practiced segregation. Through the pulpit and our catechism classes we felt God's special love for the oppressed. Thus, the black Catholic Church served as a buffer against the ugliness of segregation. Despite my parents' counsel against anger, I had a tempestuous temperament that would flare up at the least provocation. I remember that, after a fistfight with my best friend, one of the nuns marched me into the parish church and ordered me to do the Stations of the Cross on my knees and to ask at each station the grace to control my temper. To this day, I have a deep well of tolerance. To a fault, I may allow too much latitude to those who may be causing me personal injury.

Our parents' legacy to my siblings and me was education. It was the pathway for full acceptance into society. All five of us attended all-black Catholic elementary and high schools and historically black Xavier University. My father was resolute in his determination that each of us would be college-educated. He hammered these words repeatedly, "You can choose to be a bum, but you will be an educated bum." He knew that a college education would open doors. Through education we would develop self-confidence. We would not be apologetic about race, nor would we allow it to be a barrier to success. He understood that with self-esteem, opportunity knocks. Both of my parents nurtured in us a sense of pride in being black, Catholic, Creole, and American. My mother, particularly through her pious example, led us to understand the beauty and strength of prayerful devotion, though my own efforts to achieve piety resemble a Sisyphean struggle.

Language has been an integral part of my life. When I graduated from high school, I had no idea what to study in college. My mother gave me the most practical of advice, which I've followed ever since. She told me to study what I enjoyed, and success would follow. I've never regretted studying foreign languages. When I speak French, I become French in thought and demeanor. I am linked emotionally and psychologically to the French people. The same holds true when I am in Africa or the French Caribbean. I am African. I am a man of the Islands. And although I speak Spanish less well, I feel a kinship with Latinos. Language has been and is my entry into many worlds. French has been my re-connection to a lost Creole linguistic heritage.

I continued to pursue my love of language in graduate school at Vanderbilt University. There, in 1968—just several months after the assassinations of Martin Luther King and Robert Kennedy—I encountered the harshest racism of my life. In the center of the campus, on the university quad, I was cruelly taunted and was called "nigger." I felt degraded and lonely. A white classics graduate student befriended me. On Friday evenings, he and I would frequent a local pub. One particular Friday evening, we decided to visit a bar in the black section of town near Fisk University. We were walking home late that evening, shortly after the bars closed at 2 am; just as we crossed the railroad tracks into a white neighborhood, a squad car suddenly appeared. The police officer frisked us and asked my friend what he was doing in a white neighborhood with this "boy." Fortunately for my friend and me, another officer appeared and convinced his fellow officer to let us go, as we were just college kids. When this incident was reported to university administrators, they were outraged and apologized to me. A few days later, a letter from a concerned student appeared in the local newspaper, protesting this police action.

The rest of my time in Nashville was uneventful, as I continued my graduate studies. However, I was able to complete only one semester of graduate school. Shortly after the beginning of my second semester, I was drafted into

---

Culture Concepts

Culture, Subculture, and Co-culture

Subculture and *co-culture* are terms sometimes used to refer to racial and ethnic minority groups that share a common nation-state with other cultures and also share some aspects of the larger culture. Often, for example, African Americans, Arab Americans, Asian Americans, Native Americans, Latinos, and other groups are referred to as subcultures or as co-cultures within the United States. The terms, however, are offensive to some and problematic to others, because they both suggest subordination to the larger European American culture. We refer to these various groups as cultures, rather than as subcultures or co-cultures.

---

the army. I will never forget the morning in downtown Nashville, at the Armed Services draft station, when I stepped forward to pledge to defend my country. I was sent to boot camp at Fort Campbell, Kentucky, where a white draftee from the eastern hills of Tennessee, who slept in the bunk bed above me, confessed that he had never touched a colored person before and asked if he could touch my arm. I was not offended by this odd request, because I truly believed he was sincere. After completion of advanced training in teletype communications at Fort Gordon, Georgia, I was sent to Vietnam. During my entire time there, my mother attended daily Mass for my safety. In Vietnam, French was useful in making friends and getting information. I do not regret having served my country there; the price of freedom sometimes demands personal sacrifices. But I have often wondered what was gained from this conflict. I also felt that my fellow soldiers and I failed to appreciate the traditions of the Vietnamese culture. Through arrogance, ignorance, and perhaps laziness, we imposed Western values while missing a golden opportunity to understand other ways of experiencing the world.

After my service in Vietnam, I returned to graduate school, this time at Brown University in Rhode Island. My undergraduate advisor and mentor, who encouraged me to apply, felt that the racial climate would be more welcoming there. He was absolutely right. Everything there was foreign to what I had known and experienced in the South. Brown University was a multicultural society that was open to all people and to all possibilities.

I am the father of two sons and two stepchildren, all independent adults except for one son in college. My wife and stepchildren are white. We are a loving and supportive family and, like blended families everywhere, there have been adjustments. There are occasional stares, but my wife and I are rarely consciously aware that each is of another race. If there are differences between us, they are that she is from New England and I am from the deep South, and she is Unitarian and I am Catholic. But the similarities between us are more important. Both our parents were hard-working middle-class aspirants who valued education for their children. Her dad was a milkman, mine a postal clerk. Both of our moms were teachers. We both received graduate degrees from Brown University. We both are French professors. We love to travel, cook, do ballroom dancing, and read. We're soul mates because we both value open and honest communication. We make conscious efforts to do the same with our children.

After graduate school in the mid-seventies, it was difficult to find a university position teaching French. Most available positions were one-year temporary replacements, in part because during the Civil Rights and Vietnam era, students clamored for more social relevancy in their college curriculum. Universities often abandoned the traditional core curricula. The result was fewer jobs for French teachers. I spent a year in France on a Fulbright, where I was an American language assistant in a lycée, a French high school. After this year in France, I returned to my undergraduate college, Xavier University of Louisiana, to teach French.

My teaching career began with high hopes. I had dreams of spending the rest of my life in a college classroom, with students as enthusiastically excited about French literature and language as was I. Those hopes quickly vanished. Few students were eager to learn about French Romanticism or seventeenth-century French drama. I enjoyed teaching, and I would have happily remained in the classroom; however, the university president wisely thought my talents could be used more fully elsewhere. In 1978, I began my administrative career by working half-time in the admissions office.

Today, I am a senior academic administrator, with the title of vice chancellor for academic affairs, at a public university in Northern Indiana. As the chief academic officer, I am responsible for oversight of the faculty, academic policies, and campus procedures. Most of my daily work involves interaction with people, which provides an immense feeling of satisfaction. The role of chief academic officer involves organizing resources and facilitating processes that will allow others to achieve desired outcomes. The successful performance of my duties requires active listening, skillful negotiation, and the ability to communicate effectively and interculturally. Faculty, staff, and students bring to each conversation their unique skills, values, and experiences. Moreover, race, gender, religious affiliation, ethnicity, nationality, cultural mores, regional differences, and alternative lifestyles influence approaches to problem-solving and the accomplishment of tasks. Insensitivity to any one of these attributes can undermine goodwill and derail effective communication. By respecting the dignity of each person and acknowledging each person's talents, I am more open to embrace the unique gifts of self that each person brings to the conversation.

Whatever successes I've had in working with people, I owe in large measure to my upbringing. In my childhood home I was taught humility; arrogance and superiority were undesired traits. I was taught to value the humanity in each person, to see everyone as an individual. Race, ethnicity, and gender are secondary factors in communicating with others. It is not essential that I see them as black or white, male or female. And it is equally unimportant that I am seen as black. It is far more important that each recognizes in the other integrity and goodwill. These are the values that define me and by which I strive to live. When asked to describe myself, I begin typically by defining myself as a people person. I have heard others describe me as an affable administrator with a ready smile. Though my work is often tedious, at times frustrating, certainly time-consuming, and usually lacking immediate gratification, I truly enjoy what I do. The daily interchange with others energizes me.

In my work, I have many constituencies—deans, faculty, students, staff, and the public. I am responsible to the chancellor and serve at her discretion. How well I perform depends upon how well I satisfy the interests of each constituency. In many ways I share the same public scrutiny as a politician. Since universities are the most democratic of institutions, effective communication is critical. Important decisions are generally reached through consensus. The prescribed labyrinth of committee structures allows input from across the university, sometimes including community members. Peer reviews and program assessments are mechanisms that assure quality but also promote equity and fairness. Effective university governance includes all stakeholders and a system of checks and balances.

The joys of academic leadership rest not with accomplishments of tasks but with the knowledge that I have been instrumental, at least in some small ways, in helping others to achieve desired outcomes. Along the way, I have been privileged to work with many interesting and fascinating people from varied backgrounds and cultures. Respect for each person is important, but sometimes being astute and sensitive to cultural affinities brings about immeasurable dividends. For example, when I greet an Iranian colleague in the waiting area outside my office, under no circumstance can he be persuaded to enter my office before me. And he will absolutely refuse to sit down unless I sit first. Since I am his immediate supervisor, his deference is a sign of respect. At first it felt awkward, because customarily I would invite someone to my office, follow him or her in, and not sit until he or she is seated. In this instance, I honor my colleague by yielding to his preference.

Occasionally, there are pitfalls for a senior administrator who has an enormous responsibility for the management of human and capital resources. At times, tension and discord arise between well-meaning individuals. Some-

---

Culture Concepts

Language and Thought

Every language has unique features and ways of allowing those who speak it to identify specific objects and experiences. These linguistic features, which distinguish each language from all others, affect how the speakers of the language perceive and experience the world. To understand the effects of language on intercultural communication, questions such as the following must be explored: How do initial experiences with language shape or influence the way in which a person thinks? Do the categories of a language—its words, grammar, and usage—influence how people think and behave?

times those conflicts are between colleagues, and at other times they may be between a subordinate and me. My approach to reaching a resolution is to seek common ground, find areas where both parties can agree, search for outcomes that are in each party's best interests. I begin with the belief that each person is acting from a set of principles that include honesty, civility, and integrity, and that each person sincerely wishes to seek a common understanding. Occasionally I fail, but I do not abandon the effort. There is the rare individual for whom a compromise is regarded as a personal failure, and who will seek every opportunity to undermine colleagues or those in authority. A natural response is to lash back. The more reasonable approach is to remain professional and keep the dialogue open. When all approaches fail, then the hard decision must be made to make the appropriate personnel changes.

As a black man, do I play a particular role in higher education administration? Does race influence decision-making? Do values? These are interesting questions to which I cannot give a firm answer. First, I do not think consciously about race as a factor in the performance of my work. As the cartoon character, Popeye, was fond of saying, "I am who I am." Second, I lead by example. My actions and words must mirror my values. Although I am comfortable with who I am, how do others perceive me? When I speak, are my words received from Alfred the administrator or Alfred the black person? Which comes first? Is it important, or even relevant, that I am black? What influence, if any, does race have on my message? Is race, then, a distraction from the message? I am not sure that I can faithfully respond to these questions. As a professor and administrator at Xavier University, I was simply Alfred, without assignation of race. When I left there for Saint Louis University, the public and university press noted that I was the first black vice president in the university's history. At Humboldt, in Northern California, where I was provost, no mention was ever made in the press about my race. The same was true when I came to Northern Indiana.

Race, however, remains a focal point in higher education. In an age of declining public interest in and support for Affirmative Action, universities resolutely affirm diversity of faculty, staff, and students as necessary to effective learning. Universities compete with each other for the limited pool of black faculty. Prominent research universities enter bidding wars for the most talented among this already small group. Universities make concerted efforts to promote their programs to qualified minority students. Yet challenges remain. If universities wish to hire more minority faculty, the pipeline from kindergarten through college must be broadened. Both increased access to higher education and direct intervention are needed. Students should be encouraged to pursue graduate degrees, and they should be nurtured and encouraged to pursue college teaching and research. Attention to the alarming dropout rate of minority students also needs to be addressed.

I've worked with five different presidents or chancellors, each with his or her strengths and weaknesses. From them, I've learned the importance of being a visionary and how critically important it is to articulate that vision. I've learned the art of passion in expressing a message that resonates with personal conviction. I've learned that trust can only be earned, not expected, and that the way to earn trust is through collaboration and sincere demonstration of respect for others. I've learned the value of taking risks, and that sometimes gut feeling overrides factual information. I've learned that resolute follow-through produces results and earns respect. And from each of them, I've learned that honesty, integrity, and sincere communication are key characteristics of leadership.

I am often asked whether I aspire to be a university president. It certainly is the next logical step in my career, and the answer is yes. I would like to apply to the job of university president the lessons learned while growing up in the South, and the lessons learned from many years of experience as a senior executive in higher education. I am often contacted and have been a candidate. To date, however, I have not been successful. Is race a critical factor in achieving a university presidency? That depends. To some, coupled with my varied experiences, accomplishments, and education credentials, my race may seem to be an asset. To others, it may have no significance at all. For yet others my race may be an attractive asset that creates a diverse pool of candidates, even if I am not likely to be a good fit for the position. I prefer to think that I will be judged on the merits of my accomplishments, on the skills and values I bring to the position, on my potential for success, and, ultimately, on how all of these match the needs of the institution. My race should only be considered an asset after all the above conditions are met.

My success as a person is not contingent upon a university presidency. I have lived a full and complete life as a professor and administrator. I've worked with many wonderful and talented individuals. Like most professionals, I've had successes and failures, and as I look back to the beginning of my administrative career, my achievements far outweigh the shortcomings. There is no work more gratifying than that of a university professor, and by extension, that of a university administrator. I'm appreciative of all my colleagues who have helped along the way.

▶ ▶ ▶ Learning AmongUS

1. When is Guillaume engaging in intercultural communication? When is the difference among interactants so small that he is not communicating interculturally?

2. We have suggested that intercultural communication competence is contextual. Based on this criterion, evaluate Guillaume's intercultural communication competence.

3. Guillaume makes the following statement: "Race dominates American culture." Do you agree or disagree with him? Why?

4. Have you ever experienced the differences in feeling that occur when you speak different languages, as Guillaume describes? If so, what were your experiences like?

5. Guillaume has had a successful professional career in university administration. Does he have a special responsibility in higher education as an African American man? How much of a factor do you believe race will play as Guillaume seeks the presidency of a college or university?

PART TWO

Crossing Cultures

Negotiating Intercultural Competence

8 Cultural Patterns and Intercultural Competence[1]

Myron W. Lustig and Jolene Koester

All cultures differ from one another—some more so, some less—yet there is also something similar, and therefore predictable, about the nature of these differences. For many years, scholars tried to make sense of this puzzle as they described systematic variations both between and within cultures. They found that cultures differ from one another, that there are general tendencies that cultural members "typically" follow, but within every culture are individuals who vary from the cultural patterns most often associated with it. To explain both these cultural-level and individual-level differences, Florence Kluckhohn and Fred Strodtbeck offered four conclusions about the functions of cultural patterns that apply to all cultures:[2]

1. People in all cultures face common human problems for which they must find solutions.
2. The range of alternative solutions to a culture's problems is limited.
3. Within a given culture, there will be preferred solutions, which most people within the culture will select, but there will also be people who will choose other solutions.
4. Over time, the preferred solutions shape the culture's basic assumptions about beliefs, values, norms, and social practices—the cultural patterns.

Kluckhohn and Strodtbeck's first conclusion, that all cultures face similar problems, is not just about everyday concerns such as "Do I have enough money to get through the month?" or "Will my parent overcome a serious illness?" Rather, the problems they focused on are more fundamental because they involve issues about our basic human identities, our relationships with others, and our orientations to the physical and spiritual world. Each culture, in its own unique way, must provide answers to such issues in order to develop a coherent and consistent interpretation of the world.

Their second conclusion is that a culture's possible responses to these universal human problems are limited, and cultures must select their solutions from a range of available alternatives. In short, an unlimited range of possibilities is not available for solving basic problems.

Kluckhohn and Strodtbeck's third conclusion is their response to an apparent contradiction that scholars found when studying cultures. They argued that within any culture, most people will choose a preferred set of solutions.

Not all people from a culture will make exactly the same set of choices, however, and, in fact, some people from each culture will select other alternatives. For example, most people who are part of the European American culture have a "doing" orientation, a veneration for the future, a belief in control over nature, a preference for individualism, and a belief that people are basically good and changeable. But clearly not everyone identified with the European American culture shares all of these beliefs.

Their fourth conclusion explains how cultural patterns develop and are sustained. A problem regularly solved in a similar way creates an underlying premise or expectation about the preferred or appropriate way to accomplish a specific goal. Such preferences, chosen unconsciously, implicitly define the shared meanings of the culture. Over time, certain behaviors to solve particular problems become preferred, others permitted, and still others prohibited.

Kluckhohn and Strodtbeck's ideas have been very influential among intercultural communication scholars, and they form the foundation for understanding cultural patterns. In the following section, we focus on one conceptual taxonomy—probably the most widely referenced taxonomy in the literature on intercultural communication—that can be used to understand cultural differences.

▶ Hofstede's Cultural Taxonomy

Geert Hofstede's impressive studies of cultural differences in value orientations offer a useful approach to understanding the range of cultural differences.[3] Hofstede's approach is based on the assertion that people carry mental programs or "software of the mind" that is developed during childhood and reinforced by their culture. These mental programs contain the ideas of a culture and are expressed through its dominant values.

Hofstede identified five dimensions along which dominant patterns of a culture can be ordered: individualism versus collectivism, uncertainty avoidance, power distance, masculinity versus femininity, and long-term versus short-term orientation to time. Hofstede's work provides a useful summary of the relationships between cultural values and social behaviors.[4]

Individualism versus Collectivism

One of the basic concerns of all cultures involves people's relationships to the larger social groups of which they are a part. People must live and interact together for the culture to survive. In doing so, they must develop a way of relating that strikes a balance between showing concern for themselves and concern for others.

Cultures differ in the extent to which individual autonomy is regarded favorably or unfavorably. Thus cultures vary in their tendency to encourage people to be unique and independent or conforming and interdependent. Hofstede refers to these variations as the individualism-collectivism dimension, the degree to which a culture relies on and has allegiance to the self or the group.

In individualist cultures, the autonomy of the individual is paramount. Key words used to invoke this cultural pattern include *independence, privacy, self,* and the all-important *I.* Decisions are based on what is good for the individual, not for the group, because the person is the primary source of motivation. Similarly, a judgment about what is right or wrong can be made only from the point of view of each individual.

Collectivist cultures often require an absolute loyalty to the group, though the relevant group might be as varied as the nuclear family, the extended family, a caste or *jati* (a subgrouping of a caste), or even the organization for which a person works. In collectivist cultures, decisions that juxtapose the benefits to the individual and the benefits to the group are always based on what is best for the group, and the groups to which a person belongs are the most important social units. In turn, the group is expected to look out for and take care of its individual members. Consequently, collectivist cultures believe in obligations to the group, dependence of the individual on organizations and institutions, a "we" consciousness, and an emphasis on belonging.

Huge cultural differences can be explained by differences on the individualism-collectivism dimension. We have already noted that collectivistic cultures tend to be group oriented. A related characteristic is that they typically impose a very large psychological distance between those who are members of their group (the ingroup) and those who are not (the outgroup). Ingroup members are required to have unquestioning loyalty, whereas outgroup members are regarded as almost inconsequential. Conversely, members of individualistic cultures do not perceive a large chasm between ingroup and outgroup members; ingroup members are not as close, but outgroup members are not as distant. Scholars such as Harry Triandis believe that the individualism-collectivism dimension is by far the most important attribute that distinguishes one culture from another.[5]

Individualist cultures train their members to speak out as a means of resolving difficulties. In classrooms, students from individualistic cultures are likely to ask questions of the teacher; students from collectivistic cultures are not. Similarly, people from individualistic cultures are more likely than those from collectivistic cultures to use confrontational strategies when dealing with interpersonal problems; those with a collectivistic orientation are likely to use avoidance, third-party intermediaries, or other face-saving techniques. Indeed, a common maxim among European Americans, who are highly individualistic, is that "the squeaky wheel gets the grease" (suggesting that one should make noises in order to be rewarded); the corresponding maxim among the Japanese, who are somewhat collectivistic, is "the nail that sticks up gets pounded" (so one should always try to blend in).

Uncertainty Avoidance

A second concern of all cultures is how they will adapt to changes and cope with uncertainties. The future will always be unknown in some respects. This unpredictability and the resultant anxiety that inevitably occurs are basic in human experience.

Cultures differ in the extent to which they prefer and can tolerate ambiguity, and therefore in the means they select for coping with change. Thus all cultures differ in their perceived need to be changeable and adaptable. Hofstede refers to these variations as the uncertainty avoidance dimension, which is the extent to which cultures feel comfortable with or threatened by ambiguous and uncertain situations and therefore try to seek ambiguity by encouraging novelty or avoid uncertainty by establishing more structure.

At one extreme on the uncertainty-avoidance dimension are cultures that have a high tolerance for uncertainty and ambiguity; low on uncertainty avoidance, they believe in minimizing the number of rules and rituals that govern social conduct and human behavior, in accepting and encouraging dissent among cultural members, in tolerating people who behave in ways considered socially deviant, and in taking risks and trying new things. At the other extreme are cultures that are high on uncertainty avoidance and therefore prefer to avoid uncertainty as a cultural value. These cultures desire or even demand consensus about societal goals, and they do not tolerate dissent or allow deviation in the behaviors of cultural members. They try to ensure certainty and security through an extensive set of rules, regulations, and rituals.

Members of cultures that can tolerate uncertainty (i.e., those low on uncertainty avoidance) tend to live day to day, and they are more willing to accept change and take risks. Conflict and competition are natural, dissent is acceptable, deviance is not threatening, and individual achievement is regarded as beneficial. Consequently, such cultures need few rules to control social behaviors, and they are unlikely to adopt religious rituals that require precise patterns of enactment.

Members of uncertainty-avoidance cultures have a powerful need to create a world that is more certain and predictable, and they do so by inventing rules and rituals to constrain human behaviors. They tend to be worried about the future, have high levels of anxiety, and are highly resistant to change. They regard the uncertainties of life as a continuous threat that must be overcome. Consequently, these cultures typically develop many rules to control social behaviors, and they often adopt elaborate rituals and religious practices that have a precise form or sequence.

Differences in level of uncertainty avoidance can result in unexpected problems in intercultural communication. For instance, European Americans tend to have a moderately low level of uncertainty avoidance. When European Americans communicate with someone from a high uncertainty-avoidance culture such as Japan or France, they are likely to be seen as too nonconforming and unconventional, and they may view their Japanese or French counterparts as rigid and overly controlled. Conversely, when European Americans communicate with someone from an extremely low uncertainty-avoidance culture such as that in Ireland or Sweden, they are likely to be viewed as too structured and uncompromising, whereas they may perceive their Irish or Swedish counterparts as too willing to accept dissent.

Power Distance

A third concern of all cultures, and a problem for which they all must find a solution, is the issue of human inequality. Contrary to the claim in the U.S. Declaration of Independence that "all men are created equal," all people in a culture do not have equal levels of status or social power. Depending on the culture, some people might be regarded as superior to others because of their wealth, age, gender, education, physical strength, birth order, personal achievements, family background, occupation, or a wide variety of other characteristics.

Cultures also differ in the extent to which they view such status inequalities as good or bad, right or wrong, just or unjust, and fair or unfair. That is, all cultures have particular value orientations about the appropriateness or importance of status differences and social hierarchies. Hofstede refers to these variations as the power distance dimension, which reflects the degree to which the culture believes that institutional and organizational power should be distributed unequally and the decisions of the power holders should be challenged or accepted.

At one extreme on the power-distance dimension are cultures that prefer small power distances as a cultural value and therefore believe in the importance of minimizing social or class inequalities, questioning or challenging authority figures, reducing hierarchical organizational structures, and using power only for legitimate purposes. At the other extreme are cultures that prefer large power distances. They believe that each person has a rightful and protected place in the social order, that the actions of authorities should not be challenged or questioned, that hierarchy and inequality are appropriate and beneficial, and that those with social status have a right to use their power for whatever purposes and in whatever ways they deem desirable.

The consequences of the degree of power distance that a culture prefers are evident in family customs, the relationships between students and teachers, organizational practices, and in other areas of social life. Even the language systems in some cultures emphasize distinctions based on a social hierarchy. Chinese and Korean languages, for instance, have separate terms for older brother, oldest brother, younger sister, youngest sister, and so on. Many languages—Spanish, French, German, Japanese, and others—have both formal (polite) and informal versions that people use in specific circumstances.

Children raised in high power-distance cultures are expected to obey their parents without challenging or questioning them, whereas children raised in low power-distance cultures put less value on obedience and are taught to seek reasons or justifications for their parents' actions. Similarly, students in high power-distance cultures are expected to comply with the wishes and requests of their teachers, and conformity is regarded very favorably. As a consequence, the curriculum in these cultures is likely to involve a great deal of rote learning, and students are discouraged from asking questions because questions might pose a threat to the teacher's authority. In low power-distance cultures, students regard their independence as very important, and they are less likely to conform to the expectations of teachers or other authorities. The educational system itself reinforces this value by teaching students to ask questions, to solve problems creatively and uniquely, and to challenge the evidence leading to conclusions. In the business world, managers in high power-distance cultures are likely to prefer an autocratic or centralized decision-making style, whereas subordinates in these cultures expect and want to be closely supervised. Alternatively, managers in low power-distance cultures prefer a consultative or participative decision-making style, and their subordinates expect a great deal of autonomy and independence as they do their work.

European Americans tend to have a relatively low power distance, though it is by no means exceptionally low. However, when European Americans communicate with people from cultures that value a relatively large power distance, problems related to differences in expectations are likely. For example, European American exchange students in a South American or Asian culture sometimes have difficulty adapting to a world in which people are expected to do as they are told without questioning the reasons for the requests. Conversely, exchange students visiting the United States from high power-distance cultures sometimes feel uneasy because they expect their teachers to direct and supervise their work closely, but they may also have been taught that it would be rude and impolite to ask for the kinds of information that might allow them to be more successful.

Masculinity versus Femininity

A fourth concern of all cultures, and for which they must all find solutions, pertains to the extent to which they prefer achievement and assertiveness or nurturance and social support. Hofstede refers to these variations as the masculinity-femininity dimension, though an alternative label is achievement-nurturance. This dimension indicates the degree to which a culture values such behaviors as assertiveness and the acquisition of wealth or caring for others and the quality of life.

At one extreme are such cultures that are relatively high in masculinity, which means they believe in achievement and ambition, prefer to judge people on the basis of their performance, and value the display of the material goods that have been acquired. The people in cultures high in masculinity also believe in ostentatious manliness, and very specific behaviors and products are associated with appropriate male behavior. At the other extreme are feminine cultures that believe less in external achievements and shows of manliness and more in the importance of life choices that improve intrinsic aspects of the quality of life, such as service to others and sympathy for the unfortunate. People in feminine cultures are also likely to prefer equality between the sexes, less prescriptive role behaviors associated with each gender, and an acceptance of nurturing roles for both women and men.

Members of highly masculine cultures believe that men should be assertive and women should be nurturing. Sex roles are clearly differentiated, and sexual inequality is regarded as beneficial. The reverse is true for members of highly feminine cultures: men are far less interested in achievement, sex roles are far more fluid, and equality between the sexes is the norm. Teachers in masculine cultures praise their best students because academic performance is rewarded highly. Similarly, male students in these masculine cultures strive to be competitive, visible, successful, and vocationally oriented. In feminine cultures, teachers rarely praise individual achievements and academic performance because social accommodation is more highly regarded. Male students try to cooperate with one another and develop a sense of solidarity; they try to behave modestly and properly; they select subjects because they are intrinsically interesting rather than vocationally rewarding; and friendliness is much more important than brilliance.

Long-Term versus Short-Term Time Orientation

A fifth concern of all cultures relates to its orientation to time. Hofstede has acknowledged that the four previously described dimensions have a Western bias, because they were developed by scholars from Europe or the United States who necessarily brought to their work an implicit set of assumptions and categories about the types of cultural values they would likely find. His time-orientation dimension is based on the work of Michael H. Bond, a Canadian who has lived in Asia for the past thirty years and who assembled a large team of researchers from Hong Kong and Taiwan to develop and administer a Chinese Value Survey to university students around the world.[6]

The time-orientation dimension refers to a person's point of reference about life and work. Cultures that promote a long-term orientation toward life admire persistence, thriftiness, humility, a sense of shame, and status differences within interpersonal relationships. Linguistic and social distinctions between elder and younger siblings are common, deferred gratification of needs is widely accepted, and family life is guided by shared tasks. Conversely, cultures with a short-term orientation toward changing events have a deep appreciation for tradition, personal steadiness and stability, maintaining the "face" of self and others, balance or reciprocity when greeting others, giving and receiving gifts and favors, and an expectation of quick results following one's actions.[7] The Chinese, for example, typically have a long-term time orientation—note the tendency to mark time in year-long increments, as in the Year of the Dragon or the Year of the Dog—whereas Europeans typically have a short-term time orientation and aggregate time in month-long intervals (such as Aries, Gemini, Pisces, or Aquarius).

Comparing Hofstede's Five Dimensions

Each of Hofstede's dimensions provides insights into the influence of culture on the communication process. Cultures with similar configurations on the five dimensions would likely have similar communication patterns, and cultures that are very different from one another would probably behave dissimi-

Table 1   GROUPINGS ON HOFSTEDE'S DIMENSIONS

Type of Culture	Characteristics	Cultures, Countries, or Regions
More Developed Latin	Medium to High PDI High UAI Medium to High IDV Medium MAS	Argentina, Belgium, Brazil, Italy, France, Spain
Less Developed Latin	Medium to High PDI High UAI Low IDV Low to High MAS	Chile, Columbia, Peru, Costa Rica, Ecuador, Guatemala, Mexico, Panama, Portugal, Salvador, Uruguay, Venezuela, Jamaica
Caribbean	Low PDI Low to Medium UAI Medium IDV High MAS	
More Developed Asian	Medium PDI High UAI Medium IDV High MAS	Japan
Less Developed Asian	Medium to High PDI Low to Medium UAI Low IDV Medium MAS	Hong Kong, India, Indonesia, Malaysia, Pakistan, Philippines, Singapore, South Korea, Taiwan, Thailand
African	Medium to High PDI Low UAI Low IDV Medium to Low MAS	East Africa, West Africa
Near Eastern	Medium to High PDI Medium to High UAI Low IDV Medium MAS	Arab Countries, Greece, Iran, Turkey, Yugoslavia
Germanic	Low PDI Medium to High UAI Medium to High IDV Medium to High MAS	Austria, Germany, Israel, Switzerland
Anglo	Low PDI Low UAI High IDV High MAS	Australia, Canada, Great Britain, Ireland, New Zealand, South Africa, U.S.A.
Nordic	Low PDI Low to Medium UAI High IDV Low MAS	Denmark, Finland, Netherlands, Norway, Sweden

Source: Adapted from data reported in Geert Hofstede, *Cultures and Organizations: Software of the Mind* (London: McGraw-Hill, 1991), 26, 53, 84, 113.
Key: PDI=Power Distance Index, UAI=Uncertainty Avoidance Index, IDV=Individualism-Collectivism Index, MAS=Masculinity-Femininity Index

larly. Table 1 uses Hofstede's first four dimensions to group many cultures on the basis of their similarities.

As we suggested at the outset, each of Hofstede's dimensions of cultural patterns represents a universal social choice that must be made by all cultures and that is learned from the family and throughout the social institutions of a culture: in the degree to which children are encouraged to have their own desires and motivations, in the solidarity and unity expected in the family, in the role models presented, and throughout the range of messages conveyed. Hofstede's dimensions describe cultural expectations for a range of social behaviors: individualism-collectivism refers to expected behaviors toward the group, uncertainty avoidance to people's search for truth and certainty, power distance to relationships with people higher or lower in rank, masculinity-femininity to the expectations surrounding achievement and gender differences, and time orientation to people's search for virtue and lasting ideals.[8]

▶ Conclusion

Cultures vary systematically in their choices about solutions to basic human problems. Hofstede's taxonomy offers a lens through which cultural variations can be understood and appreciated, rather than negatively evaluated and disregarded. The categories in the taxonomy can help you describe the fundamental aspects of cultures. As a frame of reference, it provides a mechanism to understand many intercultural communication events. In any intercultural encounter, people may be communicating from very different perceptions of what is "reality," what is "good," and what is "correct" behavior. The competent intercultural communicator must recognize that cultural variations in addressing basic human issues such as social relations, emphasis on self or group, and orientation to time will always be factors in intercultural communication.

Notes

1. Excerpted and adapted from Myron W. Lustig and Jolene Koester, *Intercultural Competence: Interpersonal Communication across Cultures*, 5th ed. (Boston: Allyn & Bacon, 2006).

2. Florence Rockwood Kluckhohn and Fred L. Strodtbeck, *Variations in Value Orientations* (Evanston, IL: Row, Peterson, 1960).

3. Geert Hofstede, *Culture's Consequences: Comparing Values, Behaviors, Institutions, and Organizations Across Nations,* 2nd ed. (Thousand Oaks, CA: Sage, 2001); Geert Hofstede, *Cultures and Organizations: Software of the Mind* (London: McGraw-Hill, 1991).

4. Hofstede, *Culture's Consequences*; Denise Rotondo Fernandez, Dawn S. Carlson, Lee P. Stepina, and Joel D. Nicholson, "Hofstede's Country Classification 25 Years Later," *Journal of Social Psychology* 137 (1997): 43–54.

5. See Harry C. Triandis, *The Analysis of Subjective Culture* (New York: Wiley, 1972); C. Harry Hui and Harry C. Triandis, "Individualism-Collectivism: A Study of Cross-Cultural Researchers,"

Journal of Cross-Cultural Psychology 17 (1986): 225–248.

6. Data from twenty-two countries are reported in Chinese Culture Connection, "Chinese Values and the Search for Culture-Free Dimensions of Culture," *Journal of Cross-Cultural Psychology* 18 (1987): 143–164. Data on the People's Republic of China, added to the survey after the initial publication of results, can be found in Hofstede, *Cultures and Organizations*, 166. Data for the remaining four countries are from subsequent studies conducted by various researchers and reported in Hofstede, *Culture's Consequences*.

7. Hofstede, *Cultures and Organizations*, 164–166; *Culture's Consequences*, 360.

8. Hofstede, *Cultures and Organizations*, 164; *Culture's Consequences*.

Study tours to other cultures allow students to learn firsthand about the relativity of cultural beliefs, values, and norms. Such excursions inevitably provide insights into some of the moral and ethical dilemmas characteristic of those who cross cultures. Thomas Steinfatt's trip to Northern Thailand with a group of U.S. college students provided him with an opportunity to explore issues about cultural differences and the appropriate behaviors of visitors to another culture. Tom guides your understanding of these issues by providing a series of questions that are linked to his narrative. You might want to read this essay twice. The first time, skip the questions that are set apart from the narrative. Then read the story again, along with the questions, and think about your answers to them. Doing so produces an understanding of the original story that is different from the simple description of an excursion by touring U.S. college students.

9   The Shower

Thomas M. Steinfatt

Encountering another culture can occur in locations that vary from the everyday to the exotic. Different value systems and past experiences, as well as different languages and different cultural notions of right and wrong, can create situations in which the intercultural participants are annoyed at each other's reactions and at each other's apparent interpretations of the situation. One such situation occurred a few years ago.

I often teach summer courses in intercultural communication to culturally diverse groups of U.S. college students in Southeast Asia. Part of the course involves the study of hill tribes—indigenous peoples somewhat akin to Native Americans—who live within the countries of Asia yet apart from the dominant culture both geographically and in ways of thinking and behaving. Two of the larger hill tribes in Thailand are the Hmong and the Karen.

Most of the Hmong regard Laos as their original homeland. But the traditional beliefs of the Hmong include the concept that the Lao people and government want to steal their land. These beliefs were exploited by Amer-

---

Culture Concepts

Intercultural Competence Is Appropriate and Effective

Intercultural competence requires behaviors that are appropriate and effective. Appropriate refers to those behaviors regarded as proper and suitable given the expectations of the culture, the constraints of the specific situation, and the nature of the relationship between the interactants. Effective refers to those behaviors that lead to the achievement of desired outcomes.

ica's CIA during the Vietnam War period. The CIA convinced the Hmong to fight against the Pathet Lao communists, who now control Laos. Thus the Hmong believe that they would receive a most hostile reception in Laos were they to attempt to return—likely an accurate perception of reality. The Lao government exerts consistent pressure on the Thais to treat the Hmong as a hostile foreign group. Foreigners often subdivide the Hmong into the White Hmong and the Blue Hmong, according to the predominant color of the women's dress.

Burma is the Karen homeland. The Karen dress less colorfully than other hilltribes, and the Karen are the only group with no identifiable ties to Chinese culture. They are the most willing hilltribe group in adopting lowland agricultural methods. Thai Karen immigrants are usually Sgaw Karen and Pwo Karen, but scattered Padaung Karen live in the area of Mae Hong Son in northwestern Thailand. By tradition, Padaung Karen girls born on a full moon Wednesday have their necks stretched with rings. The rings force the head away from the body during growth. An elongated neck is a much-prized sign of beauty among the Padaung Karen.

> Is beauty an element of nonverbal communication? Which standards of beauty are universal across cultures and across history, and which are variable? Why might a culture adopt a standard that a long-necked woman is beautiful?

A mature Padaung woman may have 24 rings, with a maximum of 32. By the 1980s, demand promoted by tourists wanting to see the "long-necked people" led the Padaung to ring the necks of most of the village girls, regardless of the circumstances of their birth.

> Should tourism to foreign countries be regarded as an ethical issue? Would you apply the answer to that question equally in the opposite direction? That is, Miami depends on tourist income just as the principal source of foreign income for Thailand is tourism. If tourism to Thailand is an ethical issue, can the same be said about tourism to Miami? Why or why not?

The Karen and Hmong both live high in the hills, with the Karen usually choosing the higher elevations. Karen houses are always on stilts and lack a shrine. A common shrine to the local god of the land and water is located on a main path into the village. Both groups are skilled in agriculture, usually of the slash-and-burn variety during the nomadic periods of their histories. As the jungle has gradually disappeared, the nomadic ways and slash-and-burn tactics have given way to more permanent settlements and less transitory methods of agriculture. Poppies are the prized crop for both groups, who both use the opium and trade it for goods. Both Karen and Hmong smoke frequently, often every day, sometimes all day. The women wear a headdress made of a long thin cloth wrapped in layers around the head, from which a pipe may almost always be seen protruding.

> Drugs that are commonly used in one culture may be illegal in another. What do you think about the use of "illegal" drugs? Why did the British fight two "opium" wars with the Chinese? Were the British trying to stop Chinese drug use? Are you familiar with the history of attempts to suppress the drug trade in Asia? What were the results of several hundred years of attempted suppression? Do the lessons of Asian history apply to the West? Some people believe that drug use is immoral. If you encountered drug use in a hilltribe culture, how would you react to it? How should one react to it?

Early one morning, during one of our student trips, a group of four men and three women from U.S. universities left Chiang Mai in Northern Thailand with me. Two male Karen guides, Chi and Nong, rode with our group in the back of a pickup truck. Nong was bilingual in Karen and Hmong, and Chi spoke Karen, Thai, and limited English. The truck took us about 35 kilometers on twisting earthen roads, stopped at the edge of the jungle, let us out, and left. While I had cautioned everyone to bring enough water, several had listened to Chi's promise from the night before to provide enough water for everyone, a feat that would have been most difficult to accomplish. The water would be too heavy for one person, Chi tended to be on the forgetful side with respect to supplies, and Chi's water consumption estimates, though he was familiar with foreigners, were based on Karen norms. The Karen are used to arduous mountain treks. Westerners tend to be larger and softer, regardless of the physical shape they are in—or believe themselves to be in. It is particularly common for Western males on such trips to overestimate their physical abilities, and then to be too macho to admit it and ask for help. Females generally simply stop and say they have to rest.

> Chi is represented as forgetful. Is this a characteristic of an individual or of a culture? While the text states clearly that it is Chi who is forgetful, some readers may make the inference that this is a characteristic of less developed peoples in general, or of the Karen. Though such an inference is unwarranted, some students have suggested that the characteristic of forgetfulness should not be ascribed to Chi since such an ascription may lead to the attribution by some readers that all less developed peoples are forgetful. What do you think? Should individual characteristics be described accurately, or should "political correctness" be invoked? If you argue for "political correctness," on what basis would you propose distinguishing between when accuracy versus political correctness is most important? Are the characteristics of "large, soft, and macho" politically incorrect? Does it matter? What if the ascribed characteristics were positive rather than negative, such as the Thai smile referred to later in the story? Should the positive or negative direction of the comments make a difference?

Culture Concepts

Knowledge, Motivation, and Skilled Actions

Intercultural competence requires sufficient knowledge, suitable motivations, and skilled actions. Each of these components alone is insufficient to achieve intercultural competence.

A 30-minute wait ended with unmistakable sounds and movement of the ground, and eventually of the trees, vines, and ferns, that only a herd of elephants can produce. Actually there were only five, and one was a nursing infant, but it sounded like a herd from ground level. Each adult elephant had been fitted with a rectangular basket mounted across the forward part of its back. The mountainside where the truck had let us off was steep enough at points that the students could get on the elephant from the uphill slope. Each elephant had a mahout, a boy or young man who lives in a symbiotic relationship with his mount. Our mahouts were Karen, who also tame and train elephants, practices not found in other hilltribes. Elephant and mahout need each other for protection and for survival in a human-dominated environment. In the city the mahout sells bananas to tourists and city dwellers, who then feed the elephant by hand. The mahout uses the proceeds to eke out a living and to buy more bananas and other food for the elephant. Most Thai elephants with a mahout find survival easier in the city than in the countryside. Elephants without a mahout are driven away from villages and are often hunted down and killed in response to the damage they do in trying to find food.

> What does it say about the moral superiority of humanity over other animal species that humans have created a society in which many species can no longer live in their traditional environments and without the support of humans?

At first we followed a narrow path weaving up the side of the mountain, elephants and baskets lurching from side to side along with their occupants. As the path became treacherous and slippery in spots, the elephants veered off it and through virgin jungle. This slowed our progress, since it was now more difficult for the mahouts to keep their charges from devouring the foliage they were uprooting and pushing aside as we moved slowly through the jungle. It was at this point I recalled that I had once again failed to apply "Steinfatt's First Law of the Jungle," learned on many previous journeys but temporarily forgotten: *Always ride on the front elephant.* Food appears to go through an elephant rather rapidly.

To control their mounts, the mahouts use a long bamboo stick as a whip around the animal's feet. If that and threatening yells don't work—and they usually don't—the mahouts use a pick, which is a piece of wood about half a meter in length that has a sharp, curved metal spike tied at a 90° angle to the wood. As I watched, blood seeped from half a dozen spots on our elephant's head where the mahout had applied the pick. The students appeared clearly upset, both at the flailing picks and at me for not "doing something." One student had tears in her eyes. We had a brief discussion of this point while lurching through the brush, and a more extended one later in the day.

After several hours, the mahouts stopped their beasts and urged us off. From here on up, the trail was too steep and rocky for elephants. I alighted from my elephant and placed my camcorder on the ground while gallantly attempting to help one of the women down from her basket. She assured me that she did not need any such help. Unfortunately, the camcorder's designer had not anticipated that its user might place it on the ground next to an elephant.

> Was I wrong, insulting, or "genderist" for offering to help a woman down? Was the woman wrong or insulting for refusing the offer?

Elephants are normally quite cautious and gentle about where they step, but when they step, they step. While my university was quite gracious after we returned and responded to my request for a new camcorder, I got some rather strange looks as people read the section of the report explaining how the damage had occurred: "An elephant stepped on it."

> Do you see any problems with using a camcorder or a camera in intercultural settings? How does one decide between respecting the rights of people not to be photographed, and the rights and desires of an individual who wishes to record the experience? Does the fact that the persons on the trip are university related give them more rights, fewer rights, or equal rights to anyone else to take such photographs? Are you familiar with your university's institutional review board (sometimes called a human subjects committee) and its position on this point? Should students and professors have fewer rights to photograph, record, and videotape than other U.S. citizens and citizens of the world?

An hour's climb and walk led to a Hmong village where Nong was able to negotiate a refill of our water bottles for some of our food. Potable water, which might be "free" elsewhere, is a precious commodity when it is scarce. We parted with very little in exchange for the water, and a student suggested that we should pay for the water with Thai baht, another ethical decision to be discussed the following day.

> How does one decide the worth of a trade in intercultural settings? Is it acceptable to simply let the individuals involved come to a mutually acceptable agreement? Would you be willing to apply that standard to Native Americans selling Manhattan to Europeans for trinkets?

It was afternoon by now. Beautiful as the jungle was, and as interesting as the birds, monkeys, and other assorted wildlife we encountered were, fatigue began to set in, along with the inevitable "Are we there yet?" comments. Our water was gone by now, and the small springs and streams of the jungle were tempting. But Chi steered us away from them as unwise, saying good fresh water was just ahead. Diseases associated with snail larvae are commonly associated with some jungle water supplies. Chi continued for more than two hours to say that fresh water was just ahead, which was perhaps a good persuasive tactic on his part. Eventually we topped a ridge and all of Northern Thailand seemed to spread out below us. Only a kilometer down the other side, a spring gushed forth with icy water that formed a small and rapidly flowing stream. All drank deeply but for Chi and Nong, who just looked on in puzzled amusement.

Several hundred meters further down, someone had apparently discarded a plastic milk jug right in the middle of the stream. A student went to pick it up and put it in our ever-expanding trash bag, but Chi stopped him with a gentle hand on his arm. Chi pointed to the plastic pipe taped on to the mouth of the bottle. The bottom of the jug had been cut away and was facing upstream. It was the source of the fresh running water supply for the Karen village, which soon appeared out of the growing evening mist, a half-kilometer below.

> Since things may not be what they seem in another culture, how does one decide how long to wait and whom to ask and to believe when encountering events such as the apparent "trash" of the milk bottle?

Wearily—except for Chi and Nong, who were as fresh and talkative as they had been that morning—we entered the village and followed a diminutive pipe-smoking Karen woman, who greeted us with a killer smile worthy of a Thai, to an empty bamboo hut set off the ground on bamboo stilts. The double-sloped thatched roof formed most of the walls as well, and the hard, uncovered bamboo floor felt as soft and welcome to us as might your favorite overstuffed couch. Half the group was all for skipping dinner and going to sleep immediately, and they were making significant progress in that direction. The rest wanted to look around by firelight and see what were the sources of some of those delicious smells wafting through the air from other huts.

This debate was halted by the reappearance of the tiny woman, still puffing away, who gave us a five-minute speech of welcome, translated by Chi. The essence of the speech was the honor our visit had bestowed on the village, woven together with how cold it gets in the village at night. Indeed, a chill had already settled in, as I pointed out in whispered tones to the three sleeping beauties, gently nudging them from their prone positions to upright but exhausted stances as I did so. I was not sure of the Karen norms on sleeping through a speech of welcome, but I felt reasonably sure that upright had to be more acceptable than "prone and drone."

The speech reached its climax by pointing out the obvious: none of us had sleeping bags or blankets, since Chi had said they would be provided by the various villages where we would stay. The village would provide two blankets for each person, said the little woman, one for under and one for over. At this

> Suppose a foreigner who walked into your home went straight to sleep in the guest room. What would you think? Would you be likely to attribute rudeness to the individual, or rudeness to the culture that the stranger represents? Or would you be more generous and assume the individual was just tired? How would your attributions change if the person was quiet and uncommunicative in the morning? Is the existence of a language barrier sufficient reason to avoid communication with people from another culture?

point I had the feeling that Chi was translating into more polite form the woman's words that, from her nonverbal behaviors, seemed likely to indicate "smelly foreigners who do not bathe before going to sleep." But Chi simply said that anyone who wanted blankets had to bathe, and now.

> How universal is the assumption that foreigners "smell funny"? Would knowing that other cultures sometimes regard Americans as unclean and smelly make Americans less likely to regard other cultures as "bad" because of their different smells?

Though quite a reasonable request, after the woman left it was met with limited enthusiasm within our group. It was already cold, several people pointed out, and taking a shower would only make us colder. And besides, where was the shower?

That proved to be the key question. Mustering my most authoritative manner, I strongly suggested the displeasure I would feel toward anyone who declined to accept the Karen's kind offer of a shower. Glumly, the troop followed Chi through the smoke of the cooking fires to the single water outlet in the village. It was the other end of the milk bottle pipe we had seen earlier, a series of right angles of PVC pipe ending in a spigot about a half-meter off the ground. "Of course it's going to be cold," I said, "but just get it done so we can all eat and get some sleep." The males met this comment, which seemed reasonable to me, with acquiescence, but it was met from the females, who stared at me with a unified and purposeful glare, with a silence colder than even the piped water was likely to be.

Not totally certain of the cause of this apparent displeasure, I looked around. The spigot was the central feature of the village, with the majority of the huts facing it, perhaps 10 to 20 meters away. As we stood there, a young woman from the village approached, smiled at us, and washed her body,

Culture Concepts

Knowledge

Knowledge *refers to the cognitive information needed about the people, the context, and the norms of appropriateness that operate in a specific culture. Without such knowledge, correct interpretations of the meanings of other people's messages, are unlikely; nor is it likely that a person will be able to select behaviors that are appropriate and effective. The kinds of knowledge that are important include culture-general and culture-specific information.*

while deftly and easily keeping the bits of cloth she had with her between herself, the foreigners, and the other villagers. The latter were going about their business as she was going about hers, with no one except the foreigners paying much attention to the events. She finished, dried herself, and walked off, with only limited compromise to her modesty.

I wanted to say, "See, that's how it's done," but thought better of it. The males in our group began to strip and shower, shivering from the cold water and holding up towels as the young woman had done with her cloth. The females in our group made a point of turning their backs and looking away. The presence of a group of foreigners in the middle of the village, all strangely dressed and acting in an unusual group manner, must have attracted attention, and it was after dinner by this time so the villagers were beginning to gather on their porches.

The men in our group were finished showering, but the added attentions of the villagers now upped the ante for the women students. All village eyes were fixed upon the spigot and the obvious discomfort of the foreigners. I thought of trying to explain that many cultures find no shame in the exposure of the human body in nonsexual circumstances. It seemed a reasonable comment from my perspective, knowing that students dutifully take in stride such cultural points in on-campus classroom settings. Professors always want to give lectures. But I held my tongue, guessing that such pedantic comments would not be particularly helpful while we were immersed in the actual situation.

> How should nudity be viewed in this and other intercultural settings? Whose norms apply? The individuals involved are Western, yet the circumstances, culture, country, and village are not. Is nudity simply wrong? Is the fact of embarrassment of some individuals an important consideration? How important? Why would women be more embarrassed then men? Would this be true in other cultures? What of the Karen woman who bathed?

The resolution was for the male students to hold up towels in front of the female showerers while averting their eyes. This behavior in itself brought peals of laughter from the villagers, who likely would not have left this show to watch TV, had that option been available to them.

> Do you regard the laughter of the villagers as impolite or as normal? Would you regard Americans laughing at foreigners, in a situation that the foreigners perceived as embarrassing, as impolite? Are your answers the same for both cases? What do your answers say about your perception of "political correctness" norms?

The laughter only increased when it became apparent that it is difficult to coordinate the behavior of one's hands holding towels when one's eyes cannot see where the towels are and where the towels are moving versus where they are supposed to be. No slapstick comedy could have been better, I was later told by several villagers through Chi as they watched the towel holders respond to the squeals of the shower-takers that the towels were moving out of place. The response, quite naturally, was to look to see where the towels were. These efforts were met with even greater squeals by the showerers, along with a resounding slap or two, which did little to steady their hands and the towels they held. Eventually the showers were finished, the blankets distributed, and the cold night passed with our group huddled together for warmth on the hard bamboo floor, open to the wind both through the walls and up through the floor itself.

We awoke to the sounds of the pigs and chickens living beneath our hut as they rooted in the dirt searching for food, and the barking of the dogs whose job it was to keep the other animals from straying. Students were talking about the stream we would follow to the next village, and the promised pools and waterfalls. At a breakfast of fresh eggs and vegetables, which Chi cooked, the little Karen lady was able on request to come up with a few cans of warm Coke. Many villagers came by, bowed, nodded, and smiled, taking the opportunity to thank the comedy troop of foreigners for their wonderful performance the night before and assuring us that the village would welcome a repeat performance any time we chose to return.

▶ ▶ ▶ Learning AmongUS

1. Assess the intercultural competence of the students in the group Steinfatt was escorting around Northern Thailand. Provide some examples of appropriateness and effectiveness, or lack thereof.
2. Consider the description of the guide's comments and promises to the students about the availability of water. Using the framework of intercultural competence that includes knowledge, motivation, and skilled actions, analyze the students' intercultural competence.
3. Where might the students on the trip have gotten the knowledge that would have improved their intercultural competence?
4. Answer the questions that Steinfatt poses throughout his essay.

A very common—indeed very ordinary—conversational sequence in which we all engage is the introduction. This conversational pattern is so ordinary and taken for granted that most of us tend to be unaware of how scripted and culturally grounded it actually is. Donal Carbaugh and Saila Poutiainen describe conversational introductions as cultural communication events. Their essay focuses on those events in which people are being introduced to each other by a third party. They present differences in Finnish and American cultural premises, sequences, and forms associated with introducing people. Note that they write about the cultural dimensions and features of communication practices, not about the personalities of specific people. Though anyone from a particular cultural group may use, resist, deny, or exaggerate that culture's way of communicating, doing so relies partly on an understanding of those ways. Thus Donal and Saila call our attention to the subtle requirements that must be performed to interact in an interculturally competent manner.

10 By Way of Introduction: An American and Finnish Dialogue[1]

Donal Carbaugh and Saila Poutiainen

I (DC) had been anticipating my trip to the University of Suomi, in Finland, for a couple of weeks.[2] My family and I were living as foreigners in a city south of the University of Suomi, where I had begun my research and teaching at another university. I had been fortunate to receive a Fulbright professorship to Finland, with the Fulbright arrangement involving me in activities at universities there. So after settling in at our home, I was excited about traveling to Suomi, where I would meet the Finnish colleagues with whom I would be working over the next few months.

Upon arriving at the university, I marveled at the modern facilities and the advanced technologies available in classrooms and computer rooms. I also felt energized by the natural landscape—the main part of the university was located on a hill with views through pines onto a large lake. It was a beautiful winter day, with a deep blue sky above a snow-covered ground. I felt energized and was ready to go.

But I was not ready for what happened next. Upon meeting my Finnish host, Professor Silvo, we began walking through the building where my office would be located. As we moved down a hallway of office suites, I noticed that some people—upon seeing us—seemed to be avoiding us by moving into their offices. After this happened a couple of times, I asked my host if I'd be able to meet my future colleagues, especially Professor Virtanen. I knew we shared

---

> **Culture** Concepts
>
> ### Nonverbal Communication
>
> Nonverbal communication *can occur when someone intentionally tries to convey a message nonlinguistically or when someone attributes meaning to the nonverbal behaviors of another, whether or not the person intended to communicate a particular meaning. Nonverbal communication messages function as a silent language and impart their meanings in subtle and covert ways. Contributing to the silent character of nonverbal messages is the fact that most of them are continuous and natural, and they tend to blur into one another.*

some interests in our studies and thought that perhaps I'd seen him out of the corner of my eye, going into an office. Professor Silvo replied that perhaps we could meet him at my next visit, in a couple of weeks.

Given my customary ways, these introductory events were, for me, puzzling and cumbersome. I wondered to myself, "Why can't Professor Virtanen at least say 'hi'? And why aren't the others here more forthcoming with their greetings?" I was accustomed to meeting people quickly, with perhaps a "hello" and a quick exchange of smiles, names, and pleasantries. But nothing of the sort was happening here on my first trip to Suomi. I was puzzled. Moreover, upon meeting someone, the exchanges seemed, at least to me at times, quite cumbersome. I had heard and read about "the silent Finn" and wasn't sure when I should step into a conversation. Moreover, when I did so, I wasn't sure what to say, how long I should speak, or what obligations I had to open or close the conversation.

What follows is a record of one such meeting that occurred upon this, my first trip to Suomi. The meeting involved me with a group of colleagues that I had only met that day, but who eventually, over the years, have become my good friends. The introductory event, on this occasion, involved a Finnish university administrator, two Finnish faculty members, and me. In particular, the event involved me in my role as an American Fulbright professor who was to meet this Finnish university administrator (Professor Jussi Virtanen, male). More specifically, in this exchange, I, the American professor (Donal Carbaugh, male), was being introduced to the administrator by a Finnish professor (Anna Silvo, female). We were accompanied by another Finnish professor (Jussi Levo, male). The event begins as the two Finnish professors escort me down a university corridor to meet the administrator, Jussi Virtanen. He is visible through a slightly opened door.

1. (Anna Silvo knocks on the door.)
2. Jussi Virtanen: Jaa. [Yes.]
3. Silvo: Hei, anteeks, voinko mä esitellä sulle meidän uuden Fulbright professorin? [Hi, excuse me, could I introduce to you our new Fulbright professor?]

4. Virtanen: Joo. [Okay.] (Virtanen rises from his desk, walks around in front of it so he is facing Silvo on his right, Carbaugh in front of him, and Levo on his left.)
5. Silvo: Jussi, I would like you to meet Dr. Carbaugh.
   And (Silvo looks at Carbaugh while gesturing to Virtanen) Professor Virtanen.
6. Virtanen: Hello. (Shaking hands with Carbaugh)
7. Carbaugh: Good to meet you.
8. (10- to 16-second pause)
9. Virtanen: So, uhm, when did you arrive?
10. Carbaugh: Well, we arrived in early January and we've been here for about a month now.
11. And it's been very good to be here. We've been able to see just a little bit of Finland but
12. what we've seen we like very much. We feel like we're at home. With the good help of
13. people like Anna and Jussi, they've made us feel even more at home.
14. (12- to 20-second pause)
15. Virtanen: Have you been meeting people here?
16. Carbaugh: Well, yes, uh, we met several people this morning and uh I've heard a little bit
17. about their research projects and that's been very interesting. It sounds like there are
18. many interesting things going on here. And uh I'm just so impressed with your physical
19. facilities. The buildings are so nice and your lab seems very well equipped.
20. (10- to 16.9-second pause)
21. Virtanen: So what are you going to do while you are here?
22. Carbaugh: Well uh mainly I have teaching obligations at another university. I have a
23. couple of lecture series. And then here at Suomi I'll be teaching and doing some
24. seminar work. And so most of my time will be spent teaching here and there.
25. (10- to 13.5-second pause)
26. Carbaugh: Well, it's been very good to meet you and I look forward to spending time at your university.
27. Virtanen shakes hands with Carbaugh, nods, smiles, and bows slightly. Silvo, Levo, and Carbaugh turn and leave.

As this event began, I felt rather comfortable, up through line 7 at least. However, at that point, as the event unfolded, I met what was for me a pause in the conversation that went well beyond any I had encountered before. As the seconds ticked by, and as is typical for me when sensing something may have gone awry, alarms began to sound in my mind. Perhaps I had done something wrong, or perhaps I was supposed to be doing something different, or saying something else. Why was this pause lasting so long? Finally, and thankfully from my view, Professor Virtanen filled the silence and asked me when I had arrived. I told him when we arrived and how things were going, and tried to indicate that Anna and Jussi had been fine hosts to me. I tried to offer some information that he could take up, ask me about, or build on. After doing this, however, there was no uptake on the matters I had mentioned, but instead an even longer pause—perhaps up to 20 seconds long! What was going on? Had I done something wrong? My collar began to moisten as I looked to Jussi and Anna for nonverbal cues about what to do next. Both were delightfully calm, small smiles at the corners of their mouths. Were they smiling at me? All nonverbal indications from them seemed positive. Evidently, from their view, things were proceeding quite well, thank you. At the time, I found this hard to believe, especially when the next question from Professor Virtanen did not seem to relate to anything I had said earlier, but initiated another topic altogether, about the people I had been meeting.

And so the event went. As we cycled through the question-answer-silence sequence another time, it occurred to me that perhaps it was my responsibility to conclude our meeting. After all, I thought—perhaps unwittingly initiating an escape from the conversation—I may be taking too much of the administrator's valuable time. So eventually, after the fourth and shortest of the pauses I broke in with a closing, thanking Professor Virtanen for meeting me and indicating an interest in seeing him again.

Two weeks after this exchange, I was having lunch with Professor Silvo. We were discussing a student project about uses of silence when the exchange above came to mind. I asked her about it and she said, yes, the use of long pauses in conversation—at least longer "when compared to the ones you Americans tend to do"—is common in Finnish conversation. But also, she said, these pauses are especially long when conversing with Professor Virtanen, even by Finnish standards! After discussing this for a while, I asked her a question to which I thought I already knew the answer. "Should I have waited for Professor Virtanen to close the conversation?" She smiled kindly, said again how long his pauses tended to be. "You know," she said, "he's very Finnish." Then she answered my question: "Yes, it is up to him to close the conversation. He wanted to give the proper amount of time to meeting you." I had not known enough to give Professor Virtanen, and this event, the "proper amount of time."[3]

We have provided some initial reactions to this event as they were formed, early on, by the American (DC). Now let us add additional reflections about this same event from a Finnish view. How might the conduct of this event, and initial reactions to it, be formulated by a Finnish participant?

When I (SP) look at this exchange, I cannot help but hear some common and important features of Finnish communication. According to my experience, these features are present and active in many intercultural communication situations, like this one between Finns and others. For example, consider Professor Silvo's response to DC about pauses in Finland being longer "when

---

Culture Concepts

Structure of Conversations

Conversations within a culture have a similar structure or pattern. A standard set of scenes or topics is used to initiate and maintain conversations, and the conversations flow from beginning to end in a more-or-less predictable pattern, which is typically understood and followed by the interactants. However, there are important cultural differences in the ways that conversations are organized and sequenced. Thus, from one culture to another, conversations can vary on a number of important dimensions: how long each person talks; the nature of the relationship between the conversants; the kinds of topics discussed; the way information is presented; and how signals are given to indicate interest and involvement.

---

compared to the ones you Americans tend to do." Professor Silvo's comment reflects her own considerable intercultural experiences and expertise, including living in the United States for several years. Clearly she knew firsthand how Finnish and American pauses differ in length. Perhaps more generally, comments like these may reflect the strong sense Finns have about their way of communicating and how it compares to the ways of others, such as Americans, Germans, and Japanese. For various reasons, Finns are interested in knowing what others think about Finns and Finnish communication. The images Finnish people have about themselves, relative to others, are partly based on images of others they have contacted personally or, especially for the younger generation, perhaps seen in Finnish popular culture and television. Many popular American television programs are shown on Finnish television, thus providing a daily contrast between this mediated "American" world and the Finnish one. Based largely on these contacts and images, some Finns—especially those who have not traveled to the United States—may believe they "know" how Americans communicate, how they talk, and what they sound like. Thus, Finns may know that their pauses are at times much longer than those that are typical in "America." When considering this kind of intercultural encounter from the Finnish perspective, it is important to remember this: One's prior personal contacts, experiences, and exposure to mediated images may establish expectations about others' communication, for example of Finns as being relatively silent or of Americans as being talkative, with those expectations perhaps shaping parts of this kind of encounter.

A second important point to stress is the perceived language skills of the Finnish speakers. While often in situations of speaking a foreign language with cultural others, and in spite of an obvious fluency with a foreign language, Finnish speakers may lack confidence or assurance in using that foreign language.[4] In the scenario above, English is required of the Finnish speakers; this may be the second, third, or even fourth language of a Finnish speaker.[5] Recall, in this scene, that Virtanen has to speak English not only with a respected native English speaker (DC), but also in the presence of two of his coworkers, who are important to him.

To focus on the kind of interaction described above, one event that may have been taking place when DC first visited the Finnish universities might be called, from the Finnish perspective, "getting to know, or getting acquainted with the workplace or house" (in Finnish this is *tutustua taloon*). When "getting acquainted with the workplace," a main initial activity involves walking around and seeing the facilities, the important offices, and hearing from the host about the workplace, its history, the people, the relationships, and the preferred practical daily procedures. Perhaps Silvo and Levo, and other faculty, were engaging in activities that are deemed appropriate to that kind of Finnish activity—that is, to helping DC "get acquainted with the department, workplace, or house." In Finland such an activity doesn't necessarily involve verbal introductions with the people working in that department. The main activities in the Finnish activity of "getting acquainted with the house" would involve seeing the facilities and hearing about the workplace from a host or hostess. Naturally, of course, one might see people during such a visit, but here's an important point: in Finland, during this *tutustua taloon* activity among Finns, there would be no felt need to talk with visitors or to be verbally introduced to them. A nod, a slight smile, and/or a "hello" if passing them in the hallway would be quite enough. "Getting acquainted with the workplace"—that is, in this Finnish way—may require very little by way of verbal interaction with those besides the host that one sees. Minimizing verbal interaction can also be a way of not wasting DC's, and other participants' time in relatively "superficial" matters.

At this first visit, the host, Silvo, mentioned to DC that it may be best to meet some of her colleagues, including Professor Virtanen, after the first visit, at a later date. Indeed, Finnish readers of the introduction episode have called the event a "handshaking delegation" that can seem very distant and formal. Perhaps this is because of several reasons. Formal introductions are not part of the normal, daily professional communication in this Finnish scene, nor typically a part of initial visits. Formal introductions can require special preparation. As contrasted with a Finnish greeting such as an exchange of nods, a formal first meeting may—perhaps even should—involve exchanging information and ideas that are special and worthy of the occasion. To get to know someone, or to meet someone formally, takes more time and is usually done directly and concisely by discussing one's official affairs, business, and duties. Professor Virtanen may have wanted the time to prepare for his first meeting with Professor Carbaugh, a highly respected guest, and perhaps Professor Virtanen wanted to make sure that the first meeting would be rewarding and productive for both Professor Carbaugh and himself. That kind of Finnish interaction might involve the Finnish style of talking *asiaa,* or "matter-of-fact" speaking. This style, prevalent in scenes of education, consists not so much of small talk, pleasantries, and getting acquainted but of significant and substantial exchanges of important information on a variety of matters or

---

Culture Concepts

Talk and Silence

There are large cultural differences in the extent to which talk is regarded as a useful and necessary means of communicating. African Americans and European Americans, for example, regard words as very important. In informal conversations, the spoken word is seen as a reflection of a person's inner thoughts. In this characteristically Western approach to communication, people need words to communicate accurately and completely with one another. Conversely, silence is often taken by many Western Europeans and European Americans to convey a range of negative experiences—awkwardness, embarrassment, hostility, disinterest, disapproval, shyness, an unwillingness to communicate, a lack of verbal skills, or an expression of interpersonal incompatibility. Some cultures are far more hesitant about the value of words. Asian cultures, such as those of Japan, Korea, and China, and southern African cultures, such as those of Swaziland, Zambia, and Lesotho, share this alternative evaluation of words and talking.

---

topics. As such, talking *asiaa* involves direct, concise, and substantial discussion about one's official affairs, business, and duties.[6]

Notice then, from the Finnish perspective on these matters, several features: Finnish interactions of this kind can presume something about American speaking based on the ways Americans have acted in the past. As a result, in scenes like the one above, Americans may be relied on—by Finns—to talk a lot. Finns, on the other hand, may prefer to speak very little in such situations, especially when speaking a foreign language, including English. Accentuating these differences are Finnish folk events, such as "getting acquainted with the workplace." Only the assigned host is required to entertain the guest. Moreover, Finnish events like this one do not necessarily incur the obligation from others of verbal communication with the guest. As a result, workers may move into offices quite appropriately without speaking to a visitor. Further, when being introduced to a visitor in Finland, very little information needs to be exchanged verbally. If one is involved in a more formal meeting, this may take place one on one, in a small group, and at a specified date and time. Both third-party introductions and formal one-on-one meetings may be conducted through talking *asiaa,* which is rather straightforward, direct, and matter-of-fact, about official affairs and duties. Note that this is quite unlike American "small talk," which may involve lengthy exchanges of "pleasantries."

Being mindful of these few Finnish cultural features, then, a participant might monitor the above encounter somewhat differently than DC did initially. Perhaps Finnish communication, here, moves between actions one does when "getting acquainted with the workplace" and a more formal and meaningful meeting through the matter-of-fact, *asiaalinen* style. With it, participants may anticipate a direct style of speaking, exchange information matter-of-factly, and interpret ideas accordingly. Understanding the exchange in this way suggests the following additional insights about it.

After Silvo introduces DC and Virtanen to each other (lines 5–7), Virtanen asks DC about his time of arrival (line 9). DC's response to that question is on line 10, "we arrived in early January," but is followed by several more utterances about Finland, his feelings, and friends. Note how that same pattern is repeated as Virtanen asks his second question (line 15): "Have you been meeting people here?" DC's answer is on line 16, "we met several people this morning," but again is followed by additional descriptive commentary about research projects, physical facilities, and laboratories. From a Finnish perspective, especially one accustomed to a kind of talking *asiaa* that is concise and direct, DC has given a sufficient answer on line 9, and again on line 16. Such answers, like these, are what might be preferred as *asiaa,* something short, matter-of-fact, and directly responsive to the queries. No more speaking is required. As a result, the rest of DC's responses, while descriptive—and perhaps produced in a spirit of American "small talk" or exchanging pleasantries—are not so significant, at least to Finns. A Finnish listener might even wonder: why are these details forthcoming? In fact, a Finn might, indeed, ask silently: What is he talking about? Isn't DC saying something else than what Virtanen asked of him? For example, when DC says on line 12, "We feel like we're at home," or on line 13, "Anna and Jussi, they've made us feel even more at home," a Finnish listener might wonder if DC is indeed telling the truth and being honest. Having said so much in this way, DC may easily be heard, like those Americans seen on TV, as so very American, talkative, even exaggerating, and maybe even being stereotypically superficial ("Can he really feel at home, as he says?"). Is he speaking the truth or "just being nice"? From a Finnish point of view, especially one mindful of talking *asiaa,* he may easily be heard as saying more than was required in this situation and therefore be deemed guilty of stretching the truth a bit.[7]

Focusing for a moment on the Finnish pauses that are active in this exchange, we might ask why they are so long—at least when compared to those Americans might expect in their place. As mentioned above, one reason is this: Professor Virtanen is known for using long pauses, even longer than is typical by Finnish standards. More generally, pauses tend to be much longer in Finnish than in American communication. There are several reasons for this. First, it is customary for Finnish conversations to be punctuated by lengthy pauses, even if they are rarely as long as the ones in use here. Second, the long pauses might result from the Finnish speaker's speaking a foreign language, thus taking considerable time both to interpret the English being spoken and to formulate the proper responses in English. Third, introducing a foreigner (DC in this scene) is to create a scene that is perhaps a bit unusual to some Finnish participants. The foreigner may do something unusual, like the expressive "small talk" behavior, whereas a Finn might prefer or expect a more short, matter-of-fact talking *asiaa.* As a result, Finnish expectations must be adjusted, which takes time. Together, then, these features of the conversation lay some possible cultural ground for such long pauses in this situation.

What we have tried to do in our analysis is to notice features in one communication encounter that are deeply cultural. An American may notice people who are, in his words, not talking very much, not trying to avoid long pauses, and, when speaking, saying little. Perhaps unwittingly, the American produces an American folk version of communication, "small talk," and in so doing, does not quite meet the expectations the Finnish participants may have. A Finn may notice an American who, as expected, likes to talk a lot. Ready for verbal action, he says more than the occasion seems to warrant; he also says things other than expected, bringing informal affairs to a more formal occasion. Perhaps unwittingly, Finns may produce folk versions of communication including a Finnish form of "getting acquainted with a workplace" and "talking about matters of fact." To summarize with a metaphor, the encounter involves two scripts for the same play, two sets of lines for the same scene, and thus the stage is set for an intercultural drama.

We have come to understand the above encounter, and others that are similar, through American and Finnish cultural features that are active when a foreigner in Finland is being introduced by a third party. Introductory encounters, as this, can provide a kind of intercultural play. As such, we note the preparation and propriety that may be preferred for a Finnish version, as Professor Silvo said of Professor Virtanen: "He wanted to give the proper amount of time to meeting you." As a Finnish reader of this essay commented: "When meeting someone we want to make sure there is enough time to really talk about something." A proper, formal meeting, from the vantage point of this script, requires time and adequate preparation. When we discussed this kind of scene with other Finns, they made such comments as, "The whole scene certainly sounds very familiar! Slow pace, pauses, direct questions"; it sounds "delightfully familiar"; it "reminds me of formal parts of weddings and birthday parties"; and it is like "thousands of similar events when introducing foreign visitors to university officials. Very typical, delightfully typical." The intercultural dynamics seem to strike a chord. Yet understanding them is a tall order indeed.

Our understanding has come partly through ideas of propriety and preparation, in a Finnish version of the play. Propriety means that one should conduct a formal introduction in the proper way, with the appropriate degree of decorum and respect. If possible, one should give the event forethought, learning what one can about the visitor, and preparing questions that are fitting for the occasion. In fact, the questions used in this encounter—"When did you arrive," followed by "When will you leave," "Have you been meeting people," "What are you going to do while you are here"—are typically used in such exchanges between Finns and foreigners. Moreover, silence and patience in such exchanges are an acknowledged way of giving the occasion its proper due. Exchanges such as this should not be too short, and thus one expects silence as a sign that the occasion is being conducted properly, politely, and respectfully.

Culture Concepts

Rules for Interactions

Cultures provide an implicit set of rules for interaction. Verbal and nonverbal codes come with a set of cultural prescriptions that determine how they should be used. Some of the ways in which conversational rules can vary are illustrated in the following questions: How do you know when it is your turn to talk in a conversation? When you talk to a person you have never met before, how do you know what topics are acceptable for you to discuss? In a conversation, must your comments be directly related to those that came before? If you want someone to do something for you, do you ask for it directly or do you mention it to others and hope they will tell the first person what it is you want? If you decide to ask for something directly, do you go straight to the point and say, "This is what I need from you," or do you hint at what you want and expect the other person to understand? When you speak, do you use grand language filled with images, metaphors, and stories, or do you simply and succinctly present the relevant information? Cultural preferences for what constitutes competent communication will produce many different answers to these questions.

As many Finns are quick to point out, good human relations, like Finnish coffee, take time to brew. Giving the event the proper amount of time makes it that much better, and one cannot hurry the process. So Finnish standards of propriety and preparation are active in silence, signifying that the visitor and the occasion are being treated respectfully and properly.

As a result of these cultural ideas, a Finnish interactional script can be produced during an introduction: pacing tends to be slower "than Americans tend to do"; verbalizations might be prepared ahead of time; and silence is quite comfortable and acceptable to prolong the situation and thus make it more meaningful and more respectful of social relations. Further, there are important nonverbal messages that may be difficult to notice in the conversation above but are nonetheless worthy of comment. Notice that Virtanen rises from his desk and walks in front of it to stand directly in front of DC. This is a gesture of respect from Virtanen for the occasion and the visitor. Further, Silvo and Levo are situated on either side of DC. This is a gesture of support by them. More nonverbal subtleties are also active here, including differing uses of the eyes and face. Noticing these nonverbal actions helps us understand how this event, and scene, was structured in a Finnish way to convey respect and support of DC, the other participants, and the occasion.

A popular American version of this play is different, for there are, of course, other features operating. Ideas perhaps active in American professional and business scripts may come to the fore, particularly with regard to introductory lines, quantity, and efficiency. Upon arriving, one may walk through a hallway and meet a large number of people, the feeling being that one has been greeted by, and introduced to, the whole group. Unlike the Finnish ideas of propriety and respect, an American idea may be "to get to know"—in this way—as many people as quickly as possible. Cultural notions of efficiency and quantity may be active. The American interactional script accompanying these ideas may be conducted at a quicker pace, with short pauses; spontaneous verbalizations play into the scene rather than prescripted comments; and the words, more than the nonverbal actions, tend to be the crucial site of communicative messages. Against this backdrop, within this American version of the play, silences of even a short duration, "compared to those Finns produce," can be sources of discomfort for some Americans. As one Finnish observer noted about the above exchange, DC "suffers from the pauses!"

We have offered a series of observations on some initial interactions and an intercultural encounter as they occurred in actual situations involving Americans and Finns. We have interpreted some of the features involved in this one encounter from Finnish and American perspectives. Based on several other similar events, we believe that these features suggest ways of structuring acts and sequences of this kind. We have thus noticed how these communication practices are shaped by cultural terms for those practices, such as "getting acquainted with the workplace" and talking *asiaa* in Finnish, or "small talk" in American English. Each draws attention to a cultural form of communication, through cultural terms, that perhaps identifies the kinds of communicative practices each produces. Further, we discussed various cultural premises about verbal and nonverbal action, about what is proper and preferred communication in such scenes in Finland and the United States. By focusing our attention on specific and actual intercultural interactions, by interpreting them through cultural terms, and by exploring some of the premises active in these interactions and terms, we have provided an admittedly partial and suggestive account of Finnish and American communication, by way of introduction. We hope also to have introduced, by discussing interactions and cultural terms, a way of understanding and enhancing intercultural communication.

Notes

1. The authors acknowledge the helpful suggestions for improving the essay from several students of Finnish culture and communication, including Marjatta Nurmikari and Michael Berry among others. To them, we extend our heartfelt thanks but no blame.

2. The names of people and places that we use in this paper have been changed to honor the confidence of our colleagues.

3. We note here that uses and interpretations of silence vary not only by speaker but also by region within Finland. As a Finnish reader of this essay commented, "A Karelian Finn may have filled some of these pauses," unlike Virtanen, a Häme Finn.

4. This is especially difficult when native Finnish speakers are expected to do things in a second language, such as an American version of "small

talk," that are not done quite that way in Finnish. On a related point, Finns themselves may be quite reticent in using their own language. This is a source of the oft-repeated joke, from Finns to others: "Why, Finnish people can be silent in several languages!"

5. It is not unusual for Finnish students to have studied and be fluent in English, Swedish, and German in addition to Finnish.

6. There is a special Finnish attitude associated with this style; it suggests that the discussion should be done "istua rauhassa," without any hurry. For these observations we are drawing partly on Richard Wilkins's dissertation work at the University of Massachusetts on "talking *asiaa*" in Finland.

7. In Finland and many European countries, "Americans" are often regarded as "superficial" because of such behaviors.

▶ ▶ ▶ Learning AmongUS

1. Using the description of nonverbal communication provided, describe the meanings Carbaugh attributed to the nonverbal communication of the Finns.

2. When Carbaugh first arrived at the Finnish university and was being shown around, what did he notice about some people?

3. Using the idea that cultural conversations can be structured differently, analyze the dialogue presented near the beginning of the essay.

4. For the Finns, what is the main activity associated with "getting acquainted with the workplace"?

5. During "getting acquainted with the workplace," what is the role of talk for Finns?

6. What is the Finnish style of "talking *asiaa*"?

7. During introductions between Finns and foreigners, what is the role of silence and patience?

Zhong Wang and Rui Shen knew each other from their hometown of Beijing. They both came to the United States to study: Zhong on the East Coast, and Rui on the West. Their essay is derived from personal exchanges between them, and it shows the emotional, cultural, and linguistic difficulties that are often experienced in adjusting to a foreign culture. They describe the painful, joyous, busy, confusing, complex, and rewarding processes of acculturation to the United States.

11 Acculturation in a Foreign Land

Zhong Wang and Rui Shen

▷ Rui: The First Attempt at Involvement

Dear Zhong,

It is really great that we have re-connected with each other in America.

I arrived in the United States two months ago. When I landed in Eugene, Oregon, it was one o'clock in the morning. The time difference from China to America's West Coast confused me about how long it took me to fly across the Pacific Ocean. Once I landed, a middle-aged couple warmly greeted me. Entrusted by the International Student Office of the University of Oregon, the couple would host me for my first two weeks in this new country. The hostess, Sheila, drove us "home" while we talked and laughed. After arriving at their house, she treated me with homemade pies and juice, and then we chatted some more for a while. When I went to the bedroom upstairs, I couldn't believe it was already daybreak.

Probably one or two hours after I fell into sleep, Sheila woke me up. She said: "Rui, a new Bible class will start today. You might be interested in going there with us." Thus, within six hours after I arrived in the United States, I seated myself in an American church. It was the first time I had gone to church throughout my life.

The woman preaching had a beautiful voice. She read a certain chapter of the Bible and explained it sentence by sentence. Then she read a letter from her friends who were American missionaries in Africa. We learned that her friends had built a church in a remote African village, and a lot of people there had accepted Christianity. The audience fervently applauded and was greatly moved. After the meeting, everybody filled in an application form to join Bible study class. I did too, because I thought, being "fresh off plane," the Bible class would help me get to know American society faster. A week later, I was in-

---

Culture Concepts

Motivations

Motivations *include the overall set of people's emotional associations as they antic-ipate and actually communicate interculturally.* Feelings *refer to the emotional or affective states experienced when communicating with someone from a different culture. Feelings of happiness, sadness, eagerness, anger, tension, surprise, confu-sion, relaxation, and joy are among the many emotions that can accompany the in-tercultural communication experience.* Intentions *are what guide choices in a par-ticular intercultural interaction. People's intentions are the goals, plans, objectives, and desires that focus and direct their behavior.*

---

formed that I had been accepted into the class. Some new friends, whom I only met once in church, called to congratulate me on my acceptance. I was touched by their warm and nice words. When I looked up at the bright-blue autumn sky above this new land, I felt blessed.

I went to the Bible class several times, but then I became too busy with my schoolwork to continue going. Whenever the class was over, some women I did not know very well would come over and hug me before they left: "Thank you for coming, I'm glad to see you again," they'd say.

Their kindness and piousness amazed me. Most of them were well-educated career women. After daytime work, they voluntarily came to the class. What motivated and called them to do so? A woman walked close to me and asked: "Ma'am, are you Christian?" I recognized that she was the other foreigner in our study group. She was from Iran. I wondered if we were the only two foreigners in the whole class.

"No," I shook my head quietly, "and how about you?"

"I was born into a Muslim family. Are you Buddhist?"

"No, I am not," I hesitated for a second, "I don't have specific religious be-liefs. But I believe in Confucius and Lao-tze. They were great philosophers of my country. Their philosophies have been in existence for two thousand years. They told us to develop perfect morality and live with nature harmoniously."

I did not know how I could explain my religious perplexity and the rapid cultural changes that have happened in the recent decades of China. I couldn't tell her that when I hold the hymns with the red cover, I am suddenly re-minded of my early childhood experiences in the "Great Proletarian Cultural Revolution" of the late 1960s in China. During that time, every Chinese, young or old, held Chairman Mao's red book and sang for him. I terrified myself with this analogy. In substance, Christianity did not share any similarities with the idolatry of Mao Zedong during the period of 1966–1976 in China. However, I found a similarity in power—the power of religion and quasi-religion. Good or bad, they both have profound social impacts. Eugene, a city with only 100,000 people, has over a hundred churches. All of these reminded me that in the new culture, there are too many layers to be fully understood immediately.

As you see, I have been busy since my very first day in the United States. I felt overwhelmed. In China I "learned" a lot about America from either academic channels or government propaganda. No matter what I learned, positive or negative, I never felt alien to the "America" that I constructed from those secondhand materials. But after I came here, I found I was totally a stranger.

I have suspended my church activities because I am getting really busy with my schoolwork. I noticed that American professors rarely lecture the whole class. Usually, they use fifty percent of class time to lecture and fifty percent to pose questions for discussion. At the beginning, I was very nervous and highly focused. Sometimes, I could only understand one third. I was especially lost when students conducted discussions. I was worried. I went to my professor after class. She consoled me: "Don't worry, Rui. One step at a time. You'll get better." But how long will it take me to "get better"? I don't know, but I can't wait to get there.

How are your studies? Are you OK? You've been here for a year. I guess you don't have language problems, do you?

—Love, Rui

▶ Zhong: A Language Issue

Dear Rui,

You mentioned several times in recent letters about your difficulty with the language. In fact, I have also had painful experiences adapting to a new language environment. To the foreign students who study humanities or social sciences, the biggest challenge is language, linguistically, culturally, and academically. Once admitted, you are assumed to share the same language level with your American classmates.

It is said that most Asian students are quiet. I, unfortunately, fall into this category. I would not be very silent if I had strong confidence in my articulation. During the first two months, I felt bad whenever I failed to greet people well in a hallway, in a classroom, or in front of my office. For example, one day I encountered a woman from another department in the school elevator. She said: "Hi, how are you doing today?" Then I was stuck and I did not know how to go on. After an embarrassing three-second silence, she nicely offered a conversation topic. I wanted to respond to her in the same comfortable way, but before I could finish my process of translation, the elevator reached the first floor. She said "take care" and "bye" sweetly and I had to answer in a hurry without being fully detached from the translation process. I watched her walk away. I wondered how I became so slow? So dumb? So awkward? Yes, "awkward." This is the best word I can think of to describe myself during my first three months.

In China, language was an instinct. I never needed to organize my thoughts before speaking. In Chinese, I can talk properly, persuasively, and humorously. My humor was an intelligent one. It could make groups of people laugh. My talk showed my insights about life. My talk made me a pleasant, gracious, and delightful person.

Culture Concepts
_____

Cultural Variations in Organizational Preferences

Cultures have distinct preferences for organizing ideas and presenting them in writing and in public speeches. These preferences influence the ways people communicate and the choices they make to arrange ideas in a specific pattern. The organizational pattern preferred in the formal use of U.S. English can best be described as linear. This pattern is a series of steps or progressions that move in a straight line toward a particular goal or idea. In contrast, the preferred pattern in Japanese is a series of stepping-stones that depend on indirection and implication, rather than on explicit links, to connect ideas and provide a main point. The rules for language use in Japan demand that speakers not tell the listener the specific point being conveyed; to do so is considered rude and inappropriate. Rather, the Japanese delicately circle a topic in order to imply its domain. The U.S. English concepts of thesis statements and paragraph topic sentences have no real equivalent in many languages. Studies of Korean, Thai, Chinese, and Japanese language use indicate that in these languages the thesis statement is often buried in the passage, if it exists at all. In sum, the "right way" to organize ideas within one culture may be regarded as illogical, disorganized, unclear, and perhaps even rude, discourteous, and ineffective in another.

Language, a thing that I've taken for granted for 26 years in China, became a luxury in America. Without the power of language, I felt I was disabled or abnormal. I identified myself with deaf-mute people. I dreamed about speaking English fluently. Words came out of my mouth, like a spring meandering along a mountain and merging into a long river.

Language is a resource that can externalize my inner self. I have a strong desire to articulate my ideas eloquently, logically, beautifully, and to be an accomplished scholar in English, my new language.

I have no doubt that I learned a great deal after I dove into a new culture. However, the more I learn, the more I notice how much more I need to learn.

I often ponder what it means to be "successful"? It means you figure out what you want to do, what you can do, and finally you do it. I guess to reach what we consider "success," we need to go through a painful process.

Tell me more about your life after you finish your final exam.

—Love, Zhong

▶ Rui: School Life

Dear Zhong,

I finished my finals last week. The most important reward of my first term was acquiring a learning method, an active learning style. I was required to read almost 100 pages per day and write a book report every week. However, the purpose of reading is not merely for understanding but also for learning to think and critique. I am glad that now, whenever I read academic materials, I read them actively instead of passively.

The first term was very tiring. One professor required twelve textbooks for his class. The learning pace of the first ten weeks was like speeding. I worked very hard to keep up. Toward the end of the final exam, all my old illnesses that were healed years ago came back: stomachaches, serious headache, and insomnia. The rain is endless during winters in Eugene. Holding my books and notes, looking at the misty drizzles outside my window, I can't help asking myself: "Why am I here? Why did I bother to fly thousands of miles from China to Eugene? Yes, I am here to study. But why did I choose such hardship and misery?" I miss my husband, I miss my son, and I miss my home city.

Last Friday was my birthday. I finished my last exam of the term. I spent the whole day in the computer room typing. I was stressed and did not eat anything. I never touched a computer before I came to Eugene, so I had to learn everything from scratch and struggle every minute with frustration. I went out of the school building. It was rainy, windy, and chilly. Yellow leaves were scattered on the ground. I asked myself again: "Why am I here? Studying, reading, reading, and studying? Is this the life I am supposed to have? Having arrived in the United States for ninety days, I have not had a chance to go to any malls yet. I have no idea what American shopping malls look like. I do not have time to watch TV or videos. I do not have time to chat with old friends and make new ones. I do not even have enough time to sleep. This was my life for my first three months in America. This was the life I worked very hard to maintain and endure. This was the life I tried to treasure, because this was the life I chose.

I walked across the campus. In my mind, I whispered to my family in China. I talked to my husband, my son, and my parents. Life was hard and I was alone. I wanted to quit and go home.

I stopped before the Smith Family Book Store. The word "family" was dear to me. I walked in and climbed the old, narrow, steep stairs to the second floor. I walked between the bookshelves aimlessly. Suddenly, a familiar pocket picture jumped in front of my eyes: it was the picture of my favorite American woman poet, Anne Sexton. I squatted down and opened the book. A letter caught my attention. It was a letter written by Anne Sexton to her sixteen-year-old daughter Linda Sexton. And this letter was found after she committed suicide many years later.

Dear Linda,

I am in the middle of a flight to St. Louis to give a reading. I was reading a New Yorker *story that made me think of my mother and all alone in the seat I whispered to her, "I know, Mother, I know." (Found a pen!) And I thought of you—someday flying somewhere all alone and me dead perhaps and you wishing to speak to me.*

And I want to speak back. Linda, maybe it won't be flying, maybe it will be at your own kitchen table drinking tea some afternoon when you are 40—Any-time—I want to say to you.

    1st I love you.

    2. you never let me down.

    3. I know. I was there once. I, too, was 40 and with a dead mother whom I needed

    still.

    . . .

I want to thank you for loving me!

    . . .

This is my message to the 40-year-old Linda. No matter what happens you were always my bobolink, my special Linda Gray. Life is not easy. It is awfully lonely. I know that. Now you too know it—whenever you are, Linda, talking to me. But I've had a good life—I wrote unhappy—but I lived to the hilt. You too, Linda—Live to the HILT! To the top. I love you, 40-year-old Linda, and I love what you do, what you feel, what you are! Be your own woman. Belong to those u love. Talk to my poems, or talk to your heart—I'm in both if u need me—I lied, Linda. I did love my mother and she loved me. So there!

                               —xoxoxo Mom

While reading the letter, tears filled my eyes. At the moment when I felt terribly lonely, my favorite woman poet "came" and talked to me softly about loneliness, love, life, and hopes. Zhong, have you had a moment like this before?

                               —Love, Rui

▶ Zhong: Homesickness

Dear Rui,

    You are not alone. I have been there many times—I have been very home-sick, too. It almost destroyed my faith in my capability of "hanging in there." That happened during my first two months here. . . .

    One day, having finished a night class, I went back home. I still did not feel that I fully understood the content the professor lectured that day. I ate something tasteless. It was not appetizing food. I didn't have time to cook. After I washed my dishes, I lay on the bed, feeling very tired. I had very little furniture. The only things in my bedroom were a twin bed, a desk, a floor lamp, and two big suitcases that I brought from Beijing. The international airlines only allowed two suitcases. I crammed them with several books, dictionaries, as well as some clothes. Fortunately, I came to Florida, and I didn't have to bring winter clothes. I looked around the empty room and felt my mind was just as empty, unbearably empty. I felt myself shrinking, and at that moment, I needed someone's hand on my shoulder to keep me physically visible. I leaned forward, picked up my pillow, and held it tightly, as if the pillow was a life-saver and I was drowning

Culture Concepts

Actions

Actions *refer to what we say and do. Thus actions refer to the behavioral skills necessary to be competent.*

in water. It was dark outside. I did not cry. The strong fear and homesickness held my throat. I picked up the phone and dialed. I heard Mother's voice, so clear and dear: "Weih—who is it?"

"Mom—" I answered with a trembling voice.

"Oh! IT'S ZHONG!" Mother raised her voice, stimulated and concerned: "How are you? Are you OK?"

"Yes, I am fine. Really, I am fine. How about you?"

"I AM FINE. Don't worry about me, Zhong. It is nice to receive your call. But you don't have to call me so often. I am really fine. I take care of myself very well. Forget about me and concentrate on yourself and your studies. How are your studies going this week? It must be very difficult for you in your first semester. It has been 35 days since you left. I count every day."

Tears fell from my eyes. I couldn't say a word. Being silent myself, I heard my Mom continue in a very soothing voice: "Don't be afraid. You will be all right. Nothing is too difficult if you put your heart into it. Try to make some friends. Try to talk to your professors if you have problems."

"Yeah, Mom, you are right. People here are very nice, actually. I probably spend too much time studying. I will try to socialize and relax a little bit." I tried very hard to keep my voice normal. I tried to calm down but the tears just trickled down my cheeks.

"Take care of yourself. Keep yourself in good shape. You wouldn't want to ruin your health for your degree, right? Don't worry too much about your studies. Even if you do not perform ideally, you are still my daughter!"

"Thank you Mom." This time, the tears flooded.

I hung up the phone and buried my face into a towel. "Mom, Mom," I called in my mind. My dear, loving, supportive, aging, widowed mother. What a sin it is that I left her alone in China. How weak I felt without seeing her. In that moment, I thought about returning to China at once. I thought I would call the airlines that night and book a ticket. I must see her in two days. I couldn't wait. I felt my face burning. Was I crazy?

The next day, I recovered after an eight-hour sleep. I didn't go back to China. I went to school. I greeted people. And people responded with a high spirit. I was influenced. I greeted the next person in a very pleasant way. And I was responded to even more pleasantly. My mood changed. I went to my office. How lovely my office is. My office mate, Christine, looked very beautiful that day. She brought me a book, *Handbook of Human Communication,* and said it might be helpful to me as a newcomer to the field. I chatted with her for a few minutes before she had to teach her class. I sat down. Recalling the previous night, I realized that calling back home and crying did not help me except to let me unload some emotional burdens.

The homesickness became cyclical. But the next time I experienced it at home, I sat and calmed myself down, recalled something pleasant that occurred during the day, and thought about the tasks I had to do before the weekend. After a while, I got up, turned on the lamp, and spread out my books and notes. I reviewed and previewed readings until midnight. It seems the loneliness was peacefully overcome.

Dear Rui, believe me, you will be fine.

—Love, Zhong

▶ Rui: Am I Too Critical?

Dear Zhong,

How have you been? Time went fast. It has been nearly a year since I came here. This term, I am a teaching assistant for two sessions of an undergraduate Chinese class. One day after teaching, Cathy ran into me. She is a graduate student majoring in Chinese fine arts history.

"Hi, Rui, imagine you drive your car into a gas station. While you have your gas filled, you run fast into McDonald's, buy a hamburger and a drink, come back in a hurry, pull out, and drive directly to your workplace. How is that?" Cathy asked.

"Doesn't sound bad," I replied pleasantly, without knowing her purpose.

"But if that happened in China, I mean if you ate fast food while driving cars in China, how does that sound?" she said.

"That sounds even better." I affirmed.

"Rui, I am not kidding!" Cathy looked serious: "I just read a report. It says China will step into the 'fast food culture.' Isn't that bad!"

"So, what do you expect of China's future?" I asked her.

"I don't know," She hesitated, "But definitely not 'fast food culture.'"

Cathy is getting her master's degree this spring. She has been to China several times and fell in love with Dun Huang caves—the Chinese ancient art gallery in the desert, which is located at the west end of the ancient Silk Road. She just received an acceptance letter and a fellowship from a prestigious university and will start her Ph.D. in Chinese history next fall. The other day, several graduate students in our department, including me, got together in a Korean restaurant and celebrated with her.

I think Cathy is in love with Dun Huang caves—the great Chinese art of one thousand years ago. I hope her rejection of the Chinese "fast food culture" does not mean she expects China is still "primitive": Women wear traditional gowns, men marry many wives, people socialize in Peking Opera theater.

The other day, an undergraduate student selecting Buddhism Studies came to me and asked a very strange question.

"Ms. Shen, would you please tell me more about this? I heard there is a god or goddess in Chinese religious legend. He or she is both male and female. It sounds fantastic!" the student said.

I was puzzled; what is he talking about? For a few seconds, I suddenly realized that he is talking about Avalokitesvara, a Bodhisattva in a famous Temple in Zhejiang province, China. I replied: "Sorry, I know very little about

Buddhism." I ended the conversation politely, but I felt sad that Chinese culture is often regarded as something novel or exotic. Am I too sensitive and too critical?

—Love, Rui

▶ Zhong: Looking at Other and Self

Dear Rui,

Your story reminds me of Said's ideas about Orientalism, the knowledge of the "othered" culture constructed by European and American experiences, which is said to show relationships of power, domination, and hegemony. But I *don't* want to use this concept to name your stories. Rather, I would link this to ethnocentricity.

It is said that all human beings grow up and tend to rank themselves at the center of the universe and rank themselves over other ethnic groups accordingly. Both you and I were born in Beijing. I guess you still remember the sense of pride deeply rooted in the Beijingnese's minds. During my undergraduate years, I had a lot of students coming from remote provinces and cities. They were brilliant and diligent. However, a group of Beijingnese students in the class often made fun of their accents and expressions of their dialects. I never made fun of my provincial classmates, but I never tried to empathize with them. Now it's my turn to sound funny.

I study communication in America. One principle of communication is to respect the differences of diverse people and appreciate the rational and emotional commonalities among human beings. This philosophy makes me feel at home. For two years, I think I have benefitted a lot from this philosophy.

As time goes by, my homesickness, as well as language and cultural barriers, become less and less tormenting to me. I notice a lot of similarities between my American professors and my Chinese professors, as well as similarities between my American schoolmates and my Chinese schoolmates. These familiarities provide me with a sense of security, making my surroundings and future predictable.

Being a foreign student seems to be a mixture of both loss and gain, pain and joy. The homesickness and loneliness in a new place always intertwine with the joy of having new friends and a new cultural learning experience. The delight of surviving and thriving in a new educational institution also accompanies the fear of being a failure. The enrichment of learning another culture also brings the risk of transgressing my old cultural integrity and raises questions about who I am, what I can do, and who I will be.

I want to question why and how I became emotionally and intellectually vulnerable after I dove into a new culture. I want to inquire why my sense of self, which was based on where I came from, is challenged and re-constructed in a changing environment.

Let us continue our exchange on this topic. Take care.

—Love, Zhong

▶ ▶ ▶ **Learning AmongUS**

1. Describe the impact of Wang's and Shen's motivations (feelings) on their adaptation to the United States.

2. How did each of these Chinese women attempt to adjust her actions (behaviors) in order to be more interculturally competent?

3. As each woman was learning to function in another language and culture, what comments did she make that illustrated the impact of cultural differences on her preferences for organizing ideas, using logic, and making persuasive messages?

What are the cultural expectations for men and women? Are gender roles completely determined by cultural patterns and expectations, or can they be negotiated and changed? Are there intergenerational differences in gender-role expectations? Based on her experiences as an Asian American/Pacific Islander who was raised in male-dominated cultures, Rona Tamiko Halualani describes her struggles to navigate the difficult terrain of culture/gender expectations.

12 *"This Is the Way Things Are!"*: Making Sense of Gender Roles in Cultures

Rona Tamiko Halualani

As a child, I always looked forward to the summer. That's when I would see my Japanese grandparents, who would travel from Honolulu to California to visit my two older brothers and me. (I am of mixed background: half Japanese, part Hawaiian, and part English). My grandfather was six feet tall, a strong man with an infectious laugh and a big heart, usually buying us anything we wanted. My grandmother was quite different. She was just under five feet tall, with a petite frame and a soft voice. I loved them both with every fiber of my being. But each time I saw them, I started to notice peculiar things specifically in terms of their gender roles. For example, when I was eight years old, I sat down at the dinner table. I immediately noticed that my grandmother was scurrying around, grabbing dishes to set the table, making sure that the tea was hot enough and the fish was fully cooked. Grandpa was always the last to enter the kitchen; when he finally did, all the food was on the table. I understood from moments like these that my grandfather *expected* specific things of my grandmother: the preparation of food to his liking and on time, and the completion of all housework maintenance duties (such as laundry, cleaning, and grocery shopping). With such implicit rules, I never witnessed my grandmother complaining and Grandpa never outwardly demanded such behavior. It was as my grandmother once told me, when at age sixteen I asked about the clear differences in their gender roles: "This is the way things are!" The gender role differences I observed therefore took on this "natural" quality; the rules and expec-

Culture Concepts

Culture and Gender Roles

Cultural patterns often prescribe appropriate behaviors for men and women. In some cultures, very specific gender-related behaviors are expected; other cultures allow more ambiguity in the expected roles of women and men.

tations for how women and men behaved were the "normal" outcomes of culture and tradition (and these outcomes would reproduce themselves over time).

What was odd was that, when my grandparents were around, my brothers and I implicitly accepted the roles of my grandparents. We never lifted a finger to help my grandmother, even as she moved around the house frantically to address all of our needs. Simply put, we had unconsciously and consciously acquiesced to the gender scenarios that are embedded in Asian cultures. Our tacit acceptance of such gender roles was especially odd given our immediate family context at home in California. My parents were nothing close to "traditional." Both my parents were highly educated, worked full time, and held progressive views about gender roles. Specifically, my parents created an egalitarian household for their children. Mom and Dad shared all household duties and childrearing responsibilities. In fact, some of the first memories I have as a child were those of my father taking care of my brothers and me. In addition, once my brothers and I grew tall enough to load a dishwasher or stand on a stool to wash rice (a daily chore in our house), my parents initiated us into a world of equal sharing of chores and responsibilities. I remember my mother telling me, "Girls and boys alike need to partake in housework and taking care of the family." We were expected to treat other girls and boys with equal respect and value. There were also no boundaries imposed on how we envisioned our futures; Mom and Dad encouraged the three of us to "be" whatever we wanted, and to enter professions that were not expected of our genders. (By contrast, as a child, my mother was always encouraged to be either a schoolteacher or a nurse, which were two professions deemed "suitable" for women.)

As the youngest and the only daughter in the family, I considered my parents' modern philosophy about gender roles as incredibly important. Throughout adolescence and into my college years, I continued to notice how different the gender roles were between my parents, compared to those between my grandparents. I realized that there were no "clear" or "natural" rules and expectations about gender roles and behaviors. My parents, who were raised in traditional households, did not reproduce the gender portraits to which they were exposed. Instead, we were always working to make sense of seemingly automatic gender roles and negotiate for ourselves our own gender identities.

Like culture, gender is socially learned and fashioned in relation to all of the people in your life (your parents, grandparents, family members, neighbors, friends). Thus, while we assume that we will immediately invoke the gender roles of our parents, there may be much more to it than this. Our gender identities are informed by all of our accumulated experiences and memories. In addition to observing the gender roles within my family, I remember going to my friends' homes and observing mostly traditional roles for wives and husbands (with the mother completely tending to the home while the father served as the breadwinner and family decision maker). I was initially shocked that other families were not like mine. That impression has stayed with me. Asian cultures are presumed to adhere to strict gender role divisions: males fulfill the breadwinner roles and females the domestic roles. While I saw it firsthand with my grandparents, this image grated against the divergent view offered by my parents. I internalized these contrasting experiences, which influenced the development of my own gender identity as a mixed Asian American/Pacific Islander woman.

I remember one of my Asian classmates in middle school, Susan, who asked why my mother was so "different" from all the other Asian mothers. "How is she different?" I asked. My friend responded, "She works and she seems to call the shots at your house. Is she really Japanese?" The question shocked me. Why was it so odd to my friend that my mother worked outside of the home? And because my mother did not stay at home or act in accordance with certain cultural (Asian) norms, her cultural background was being questioned? For years, I did not really understand this interaction. I could not quite grasp how gender and cultural norms are intertwined so tightly. To many of my family members and friends, to be traditionally "Japanese" was to model and perform all of the expected gender roles and behaviors. To go against such expectations (especially as a woman raised in a patriarchal culture) threatened one's cultural authenticity and membership. I had been told family stories about how my grandmother "went along" with the gender expectations of her as a Nisei Japanese woman, and that my mother—a strong-willed Sansei—fought every gender rule placed upon her. How did this happen to two women who were linked to the same traditions but were taking different paths toward gender role expectations? Perhaps it was easier for my mother to diverge away from the gender expectations of the time, given that she was of a later generation, but I also noticed that other female relatives who were my mother's age acted like my grandmother: soft-spoken and subservient.

From about age ten through high school, I grew increasingly curious about how my grandmother and mother were so different from each other in that one adhered to tradition and the other (though raised in a traditional household) broke away from gender and cultural norms. I became curious because I was trying to sort out my own gender identity and behaviors. Fearful that I would become more deferential like my grandmother, I began to act out—especially against males. I would constantly rebel against my male classmates in every subject in school. One instructor in my middle school complained to my mother that I was overly "aggressive" and "competitive" with the boys in class. Hearing this, my mother smirked and told me later that she was "very proud" of me.

Even at a young age, I was very aware of the gender stereotypes and expectations of Asian women, and I did not want to be trapped as a woman in such cultural norms. In fact, I did everything I could to go against the grain of the gender rules that framed my grandmother's life: academically competing with other males throughout college and graduate school, and sounding off at any hint of chauvinism from my female and male friends and family members. This eventually spilled over to how I act today. I am a tenured university professor on a large campus and often "overcompensate" to shatter the notion that I am a weak, passive Asian woman who can easily be taken advantage of. For example, I have a wonderful department chair and I have found myself snapping at him or coming across in a verbally aggressive manner so that I will not be misrecognized as a docile Asian American woman. I want to be taken seriously but find that I act in response to my accumulated memories of the gender roles I have seen in my life. I have had to reflect upon these "habits" of mine and work toward openly discussing my feelings and perceptions with my colleagues and friends. The tight-knit relationship between gender and culture always shifts in relation to the interpersonal contexts. Three years ago, I married a wonderful man, which raised yet another gender role consideration. My husband is the eldest Chinese (1st generation) son in his family, and he was raised to be a "strong" male figure. This means that he was not expected to engage in any household or familial duties, since it was deemed "inappropriate" for the eldest Chinese son to do such chores. The differences in our gendered upbringing became difficult in our first year of marriage. We had to openly discuss the ways in which we were raised (as the eldest Chinese son and the youngest daughter in a mixed family), and we had to negotiate "new" gender roles and expectations for ourselves. I exposed my husband to the egalitarian philosophy of my parents, while also being sensitive to the Asian way of gender socialization. In turn, my husband and I would have long discussions about our memories of our parents, and he always emphasized how difficult it is for individuals to change and rethink traditions and rules—especially gender rules—that center their culture. From these discussions I realized that gender norms and roles are always up for negotiation and reconfiguration, though often this is done subtly and indirectly. I started to think back to the anecdotes and stories my mother would tell me (and that I had forgotten) about how my grandparents negotiated the strict gender norms in their lives. My grandmother—a stubborn and silently strong-willed woman—wanted to work outside the home, so she went against my grandfather's wishes, got her driver's license, and took her first job. Realizing he couldn't change the situation, my grandfather relented and later expressed appreciation for the money my grandmother earned for the household. My grandfather even began to shift his previously held views on gender roles; in his elder years he took on some of the household responsibilities, encouraged my grandmother to try new things, and persuaded her to travel more. I know now that the notion that gender and cultural norms can't change because "This is the way things are!" is not entirely true. Rather, we can share our gendered/cultured experiences with others, and we can negotiate what "gender/culture" means in our specific relationships and at specific times in our lives.

Culture Concepts

Knowledge of Our Own Culture

Knowledge of our own cultural system may be very closely linked to intercultural competence. Though often overlooked, knowledge of our own culture provides important insights that facilitate understanding of other cultures.

▶ ▶ ▶ **Learning AmongUS**

1. What is the relationship between Halu-alani's cultural background and her be-liefs, values, norms, and cultural prac-tices? How does this background affect her sense of the appropriate roles for females and males?

2. Think about Halualani's story from the standpoint of cultural patterns. Using Hofstede's framework (see pages 64–71), explain the views of Halualani's grand-parents, parents, and husband.

3. How important was it that Halualani had knowledge of her own cultural background as she and her husband addressed differ-ing expectations that each had for the other?

4. What expectations do you have for appro-priate gender-related behaviors? Do these expectations occur as a result of your cul-tural background? Have you ever had to negotiate contested gender roles, as Halu-alani has done? If so, describe the experi-ence(s) and the outcome(s).

Charles Braithwaite gives us the opportunity to understand his experiences in crossing from his European American culture to that of the Navajo. This essay moves between descriptions of the communicative interactions he witnesses among the Navajo people and his interpretations of what might be happening. It provides a model for understanding a culture that is different from your own. In your own intercultural experiences, do as Chuck does: begin by describing what you observe, in specific and nonjudgmental language. Then attempt to interpret and understand the rich dynamics of that other culture, always maintaining a sense of tentativeness and openness because your interpretations may not be accurate.

13 Roast Mutton, Fry Bread, and Tilt-a-Whirls: Cultural and Intercultural Contact at the Navajo Nation Fair

Charles A. Braithwaite

The Navajo Nation is the largest sovereign Indian nation in the United States. More than 200,000 Navajo live in an area the size of New England: seventeen million acres, which includes lands in Arizona, New Mexico, Colorado, and Utah. For 51 years the Navajo people have been attending the largest tribal gathering in the continental United States: the Navajo Nation Fair in Window Rock, Navajo Nation (Arizona). Around the first week of September, easily 150,000 people, more than 90 percent of whom are Navajo, gather for five days of powwows, rodeos, music, arts and crafts, food, midway rides, and other activities associated with "state" fairs. The Navajo Nation Fair Parade, which covers a two-mile stretch of road outside the fairgrounds, alone draws more than 80,000 people. For six years I have attended the Navajo Nation Fair, spending more than 150 hours participating in and observing the activities. Below I provide accounts of four important aspects of the Navajo Nation Fair to help you understand

Culture Concepts

Ethical Dilemmas in Intercultural Interaction

All intercultural interactants must confront three key ethical dilemmas. The first asks how much a person ought to be willing to change in order to adapt to others' cultural patterns. The second asks if cultural values are relative or if it is possible to judge another's beliefs, values, norms, and social practices as morally reprehensible. The third relates to the consequences of intercultural interaction and asks whether intercultural contacts should be encouraged or discouraged.

some dimensions of Navajo culture and intercultural communication. Each account has two sections: (1) a narrative description of events, and (2) a cultural perspective that includes contextual information and interpretative analyses that will help you understand the significance of what you are reading. You may choose to read the accounts in this essay in one of at least two ways. One way is to read the narrative section first, without being influenced by my analysis. The second is to read the cultural perspectives section first, thereby giving you a "lens" through which to view what you are reading.

▶ 1: Air Jordan and Walking Buffalo

As I head toward the Navajo Nation Fair from Gallup, New Mexico, about 25 miles from Window Rock, I tune in to KTNN ("The Voice of the Navajo Nation") on the radio. During the half-hour drive I hear songs by Garth Brooks, Van Morrison singing "Gloria," bluegrass music, traditional powwow music, and advertisements for local businesses in both English and Navajo. Just as I arrive in sight of the fair an old version of "Down in the Boondocks" comes on the air.

Entering the fair, the midway is straight ahead, with carnival rides to the right, and the Navajo Nation Warrior's Powwow Arena on the left. Next to the arena, which is about one-third full of people listening to the drumming and singing, a booth is set up selling cassettes and CDs of a variety of Native Indian music: traditional powwow, peyote songs, song and dance, and contemporary Native American. Three young Navajo boys are lined up to make purchases. One is wearing a shirt with "Metallica" on the back, another wears a "Megadeth" sweatshirt, and the third has a Nike hat and an "Air Jordan" T-shirt. Each boy is buying two or three tapes of traditional powwow music from groups such as Walking Buffalo, Fly-In-Eagle, and Pipestone Creek. Later I see these same boys holding up microcassette recorders over the powwow drummers and singers to make their own recordings of the music.

As I look down the midway, I see a group of about 12 Navajo standing around an "old time" photo booth, the kind you see at almost all U.S. state fairs. Several families are patiently waiting for their turn to go into the trailer and change into costumes and have their pictures taken: the Navajo women and girls dressing up as "dance hall" girls, and the Navajo men and boys dressing up as "cowboys." Two of the Anglo workers from the booth are dressed as western gunfighters. They point their six-guns at little Navajo children while the parents smile and take pictures.

Cultural Perspective #1

The juxtaposition of different cultures is a common feature on the Navajo Nation. Although many Navajo still live far from the influence of Anglo culture, the vast majority of people readily embrace aspects of cultures that initially appear incongruent with Navajo life. There is a willingness, for example, to associate with "cowboys" (as evidenced by the 700-plus participants in the all-Indian rodeo that runs throughout the length of the fair), even though it was the Spanish, Mexican, New Mexican, and United States "cowboys" who have helped to steal land from the Navajo for the past 400 years. Navajo history is filled with examples in which the people borrowed and adapted aspects of those cultures with which they came into contact while simultaneously maintaining the important aspects of their traditional ways: corn was adopted from the Pueblo people; horses, sheep, and goats were adopted from the Spanish; and mining and forest development, which (at an estimated $50 million per year) provide the greatest source of tribal income in the United States, were learned from the U.S. Americans. Young Navajo apparently experience no cognitive dissonance when they listen to Snoop Doggy Dogg on headphones while waiting for elderly Navajo women to finish up the fry bread competition so they can sample the tasty bread and honey.

▶ 2: Shorts and Sandals on Sacred Ground

The Navajo Nation Warrior's Powwow Arena includes a small stage, used mainly for public address equipment, and grandstands that hold more than one thousand spectators. Around the arena is a camping area where people from throughout North American and Canadian Indian Nations can stay when they come to participate in the intertribal dances. There are contests for adults, juniors, teens, and "tiny tots," which includes babies and toddlers who need assistance even with just walking. After the competitions judges tally scores but no awards are given out at the time, although partway through the fair a "powwow princess" is chosen and crowned. Groups of drummers and singers come from all over the United States and Canada and take turns playing for the dances and the "grand entries" that occur twice a day.

Of the few Anglos that attend the fair, most come to buy jewelry at the arts and crafts exhibit hall and to attend the rodeos. However, some do wander over to the powwow arena. One reason the Anglos usually stand out is the way they are dressed. During one four-hour period, I saw ten Anglo women come to the powwow wearing shorts and halter tops. In all fairness, I should point out that the temperature was in the mid–80s at the time. Most of the Anglo men also wore shorts and carried cameras or camcorders, with which they walked into the arena to shoot pictures of the dancers. Sometimes the photographers would actually step out into the arena so they could take a picture. Few Anglos would sit more than about a half hour to an hour before moving on, even though the dances would go on from about 10:00 A.M. until sometimes 2:30 A.M. The day at the powwow arena would begin with a gourd dance, followed by the presentation of the colors (U.S., Navajo, and P.O.W. flags), followed by an invocation. One invocation was delivered by an elderly Navajo man in a wheelchair. Though using a microphone, he could barely be heard because he spoke so softly and occasionally let the microphone drop to the side. All the dancers and drummers in the arena stood for the speaker, and most of the people in the grandstand also stood, with the majority of men removing their hats. Even the Navajo teenagers showed respect, although with a slight

---

Culture Concepts

When in Rome . . .

When people are in the midst of another culture, to what extent should they be willing to alter their behaviors to fit the beliefs, values, norms, and social practices of others? Whose responsibility is it to attempt to take into account cultural differences in communication? Is it the responsibility of the visitors, newcomers, or sojourners to adjust their behaviors to the cultural framework of the host culture, or should members of the host culture adjust their communication and make allowances for the newcomers and strangers? To what extent must individuals adapt their cultural beliefs, values, norms, and social practices to the dominant cultural patterns?

---

air of indifference, too. However, most of the Anglos continued to film and talk and eat and often walked away when a speaker went on "too long."

Cultural Perspective #2

A powwow arena is a place for celebration by Native Indian people. It is an opportunity for Native Indian people from all parts of North America and Canada to share their music and their communal beliefs in the nature of life. As one powwow host stated before an initiation ceremony for a young girl, "This circle (the powwow arena) is the Creator's circle. It's a sacred place." For many Native Indian people, attending a powwow has the same characteristics as attending church. However, most Anglos usually cannot see the analogy. A "religious" service has different qualities for Anglos, and the celebratory atmosphere of powwows, as well as the presence of contests and vendors and grandstands, makes it difficult for many Anglos to recognize the sacred nature of what is occurring in front of them. Further, when Anglos behave inappropriately at powwows by being scantily clad or by walking into the arena to take pictures, few Native people will overtly criticize their actions. This is especially true when visitors are perceived as "guests." Numerous times I was encouraged to move ahead of Navajos when waiting in line for activities, told as they moved aside, "You're our guest." There may often be disapproving glances toward the Anglos, especially from the elderly Indians, but no direct confrontations. Except for children and some teenagers, most Native peoples at the powwows wear long pants or long skirts and do not expose their bodies unnecessarily.

▶ 3: "Be Diné and Proud"

I remember attending state fairs with my parents, and the moment we entered the fairgrounds we split up: kids going in one direction and parents in another (after trying in vain to get the children to agree to a meeting place and time for later in the day). What catches my attention at the Navajo Nation Fair is the many groups of intact family units that walk around together: very elderly Navajo women wearing velvet dresses of turquoise or purple with many beautiful pieces of jewelry, holding the hands of very young children, followed by older children and parents or other adult relatives. The fair has numerous locations devoted to caring for the elderly and children: special tables reserved for elderly, special booths set up to give water and food to the elderly, and an extensive effort to make sure children are "tagged" (a name tag attached to each child's clothing) in case children stray too far from their families. What strikes me about the family interaction is how easy it appears to be for adults to cope with the few disruptions caused by children. I notice how remarkably quiet it is at the fair, given the thousands of people there. Few children or teenagers are running and yelling across the grounds, and few people are voicing the kind of complaints that are typical at events such as this (e.g., waiting in a long line, waiting for food, waiting for the bathroom). When a child does start to fuss, particularly a young child, it appears that an adult has simply to give the child "the look," often accompanied by a movement of the index finger in a short sweeping motion, to silence the complaint quickly.

The prevalence of multigeneration groups is especially evident at the Navajo Nation Fair parade. Beginning as early as sunrise, Navajo people begin gathering along the fair route. Vendors of roasted corn, "kneel-down" bread, sno-cones, watermelon, and sodas stake out areas to feed the more than 80,000 people who will sit or stand in the sun until as late as 2:00 P.M. to watch the 250-plus entries: floats, bands, politicians, tribal agencies, and local businesses. Room is always made up front for the elderly to sit down, and the parade itself has many floats and groups that *feature* the respected elders of the tribe. Singled out for particular honor are groups of military veterans/warriors from World War II to Bosnia. The Navajo "code-talkers," U.S. Marines who spoke coded Navajo during the war in the Pacific and whose code was never broken by the Japanese, receive tremendous applause while leading a group of warriors. The crowd also shows great respect to veterans carrying a P.O.W. flag, which represents the men believed to have been left behind after the Vietnam War. The themes illustrated by the floats, most constructed on the back of trucks or small wagons, emphasize ideas such as "pride," "young people," "future," and "prosperity." As the various entries go by, it is common for the riders to toss hard candy into the crowd that is then chased down by the little children.

Cultural Perspective #3

The centrality of the family to Navajo life cannot be overstated. One's identity as a person is interwoven with one's place in a large family affiliation or clan. There are approximately 30 Navajo clans that emerged from the four original clans created by Changing Woman (one of the original holy people of the Navajo): Near the Water Clan (To'ahani), Tower House Clan (Kinyaa'aanii), Bitter Water Clan (Todich'iinii), and Mud Clan (Hastlishnii). The traditional

Culture Concepts

Do the Ends Justify the Means?

*Which intercultural contacts should be encour-
aged or discouraged? Are the outcomes of all intercultural contacts positive? Are all circumstances appropriate for intercultural contact? In
short, do the ends justify the means?*

Navajo way of relating is based on
identifying oneself with the mother's
clan, the father's clan, the maternal
grandfather's clan, and the paternal
grandfather's clan. When introducing
themselves, even in writing, Navajo
begin by stating their kinship—for example, "I am of the Honaghlaanii clan,
born of Bitter Water, and my paternal
grandparents are Naalani, my maternal grandparents are T'achiinii." A
high value is placed on clan affiliation and on the teachings of one's elders.
When asked to write an essay for a Navajo Nation Fair magazine, one Navajo
author said he chose to get his information by talking to women who

> speak the Dineh (Navajo) language and speak limited English, and with none
> or limited Western/European education, those who possess livestock, a corn-
> field, participate in traditional Dineh ceremonies, who wear the traditional
> Dineh *tssii'* (hair bun), have a *hogan* (traditional Dineh home), and those who
> did not have all of the modern conveniences of indoor plumbing, electricity, ca-
> ble TV, telephone, etc.[1]

Of the 40 lessons the above author learned from these women, at least 22 concerned the sense of family. The abandonment of Anglo elderly and the free
rein given young Anglo children are sources of wonder and often disgust for
many Navajo. The respect for the elderly holds true for the value placed on
those who contribute to the tribe, such as warriors. Those who served and
those who gave their lives in battle are highly regarded throughout the
Navajo Nation. A large park near tribal headquarters is devoted to honoring
all veterans. The Navajo believe a warrior takes into battle only two things
that belong to him: his spirit and his shadow. For this reason, the veterans'
memorial at the park will have large sheets of glass suspended horizontally
over the ground, with the names of the fallen warriors inscribed in the glass.
This is so you can look up through the glass toward the sky and the spirits;
each man's name will appear as a shadow on the ground.

▶ 4: Juniper Berries

It is a 350-mile drive back to Phoenix, so I take off about halfway through the
Navajo Nation Fair parade. I turn on the radio to listen to the announcers describe the floats and marching bands, which they do in both English and
Navajo. Although I have a six-hour drive ahead of me, I want to make one
more stop before leaving the Navajo Nation, so I head north toward Canyon de
Chelly. At the base of the Chuska Mountains, along the Arizona–New Mexico
border, are two canyons: Canyon de Chelly, which extends about 27 miles, and

an 18-mile branch called Canyon de Muerto. The canyon walls range from 200 feet to more than 1,200 feet high. Rains and runoff water create washes throughout the canyon, which are sometimes completely dry while at other times surging with water that will submerge a truck. Throughout the canyons are farms that grow beans, corn, and squash and raise flocks of sheep or goats. Although designated a national park by the U.S. government, the canyons are home to many Navajo, who live on the rim during the winter and down in the canyons during the summers. I am always awed by the stunning beauty of the canyons: lush cottonwoods lining the wash; rocks in all shades of red, beige, black, and white; scattered patterns of crops and livestock; and a big blue sky ascending over the flat plateaus of the rim. The Grand Canyon is certainly better known, but I consider Canyon de Chelly to be the most spectacular site in the Southwest.

I drive to the extreme northeastern rim of Canyon de Muerto, to a place overlooking Massacre Cave. It was along this part of the canyon that Spanish troops cornered Navajo warriors, women, and children at a ledge high on the sheer canyon walls and killed more than 120 people. Almost 200 years later, bullet holes can still be seen where the Spanish soldiers fired into the cave. As I came down the path toward the canyon, I saw a woman and a very little girl sitting on sheepskins under a piñon tree with a red Ganado blanket out in front of them. There were only three necklaces and one "dream catcher" displayed on the blanket, with a dirty piece of tape that said "$2." As I slowed down to look, I didn't expect to stop because I had seen and purchased jewelry from Navajo at the fair. However, as I was passing I saw a bandage on the child. Covering her right foot was gauze with the yellow stains of medicine or maybe infection. I then looked at the woman, who seemed to be somewhere between 20 and 40 years old, dressed in a faded blue velvet blouse and skirt with a small squash blossom necklace. As I looked, the woman and child stared at my face, which

---

Culture Concepts

Questions for the Ethical Intercultural Communicator

As an ethical intercultural communicator, some of the following questions must be confronted: Is it ethical to go to another country or culture, for whatever reason, if you are naive and unprepared for cultural contact? Should intercultural contacts be encouraged for those who speak no language but their own? Should those who are prejudiced seek out intercultural contacts? Is it ethical to send missionaries to other countries? Is it acceptable to provide medical assistance to help a culture resist a disease, when in providing the assistance you may destroy the very infrastructure and nature of the indigenous culture? Is it justifiable for a person from one culture to encourage a person from another culture to disregard his or her own cultural values? While there are no simple answers to any of these questions, the competent intercultural communicator must consider them.

was an unusual sensation on the Navajo Reservation. What was more unusual was that I stared back in silence. After a minute she said, "Juniper berries." Looking down at the necklaces on the blanket I saw they were made of the dried brown seeds and a few bits of colored plastic or glass. As I squatted down to take a closer look, the woman said, "They keep away evil spirits"; the entire time, the woman never took her eyes off my face. Then she pointed to the necklace in the middle. I got out three dollar bills and stepped over to pay her. When I looked at the little girl's foot, the woman told me that the child had stumbled into the fire that was heating up water for the child's bath, which is something they had to do because there was no running water in their hogan. But the mother said the child would be well soon, or so she was told by the nurse at the public health service in Chinle, 20 miles away.

Cultural Perspective #4

A sense of "place" is central to the life of most Navajo people. The people talk about how important it is to live among the "four Sacred Mountains": Blanca Peak to the east, San Francisco Peak to the west, Mt. Hesperus to the north, and Mt. Taylor to the south. Few places within the Navajo Nation carry as much significance as Canyon de Chelly. The canyon is central to many stories concerning the holy people, the deities in traditional Navajo beliefs, and the home of any Anasazi ruins, some more than 1,000 years old. In addition, this place played a vital role in the Navajo struggles against Spanish and U.S. American invaders. Because of the sheer rock cliffs and winding tributaries, the canyon has been an important stronghold for Navajo who fought or needed to hide from those who came to take their land. It was into the canyon, in the 1860s, that Kit Carson and the U.S. Army drove many Navajo before forcing them to surrender and take the "Long Walk" to a reservation 500 miles away from the sacred mountains. To deprive their enemy of food and shelter, the U.S. Army destroyed all the crops and livestock they found in Canyon de Chelly, including 4,000 fruit trees, in less than a month. Today the land is being farmed again. Land is not held in private ownership among the Navajo of the canyon, but it is passed down through the mother's line based on family and clan relationships. Although there are rich places such as the Canyon de Chelly, poverty afflicts many on the Navajo Nation. Unemployment can be as high as 40 percent, and it is common to find homes without running water or electricity. The vast size of the Navajo Nation, as well as the continuing cutbacks of funds from the U.S. government and the Bureau of Indian Affairs, means that basic health services are hard to come by for many Navajo. However, there is much pride and hope for the future among the Navajo. The theme of the 1997 Navajo Nation Fair was *"Yódi dó nitl'iz nihidahaazljágo bee nei'ni'ji'yiikahdoo"* (Natural resources, spiritual wealth, and economic development create prosperity). The special relationship the Navajo Nation and the Navajo people have with Mother Earth and their Creator has sustained them through many years of hardship, and it appears to be a driving force in the continued success of the largest Indian nation in the United States.

Notes

1. Navajo Nation Fair Office (1997). *Fiftieth Anniversary Program, Navajo Nation Fair.* Window Rock, AZ: Navajo Nation.

▶ ▶ ▶ Learning AmongUS

1. Braithwaite describes what he regards as contradictions in the behaviors of some Navajo (for example, listening to traditional powwow music while wearing a Metallica T-shirt). Do you agree that these behaviors are contradictions? If so, are these "contradictions" negative? Why do you think they occur?

2. Braithwaite describes as culturally insensitive the behavior of some Anglos who visit the powwows. Using the ethical dilemma titled "When in Rome" in the Culture Concepts box, how would you characterize the behavior of those Anglos? What do you believe their behavior should have been?

3. Does the Navajo way of treating their elders differ from the behaviors of your own culture? Do you think that the Navajo way is better? Why or why not?

4. Apply the three ethical dilemmas described in the Culture Concepts box to Braithwaite's observations of the Navajo people and their interaction with others from outside their culture.

5. Answer the questions in the Culture Concepts box related to issues for the ethical intercultural communicator.

Peter O. Nwosu provides an account of an African immigrant's experiences in the United States. The narrative describes and explains some of the problems he encountered and the intercultural growth that occurred on his American journey. The narrative style of the essay reflects the nonlinear approach to storytelling that is common among Africans. African narratives include interconnecting ideas; the story typically begins somewhere, breaks off into another but related subject, and eventually returns to the main body of the narrative. This essay provides both an example of the African narrative style and an analysis of the ingrained cultural patterns that we bring to intercultural interactions.

14 Cultural Problems and Intercultural Growth: My American Journey

Peter O. Nwosu

The entire family gathered to wish me farewell. Little did they realize that I would probably be spending quite some years in the United States. In keeping with family tradition my mother, the matriarch of our large and extended family, had organized a reception in my honor and had invited many people to see me off.

I had been offered a graduate fellowship by Nigeria's Federal Agricultural Coordinating Unit, a World Bank program to manage all of the bank's integrated rural development projects in the country. The fellowship enabled me to pursue a master's degree in liberal studies, with a specialization in communication and instructional media technology, at Towson State University. Towson State, in Baltimore, is a predominantly European American institution. Later I went to the mainly African American Howard University in Washington, D.C., to pursue doctoral work in human communication studies, with an emphasis in communication processes across cultures.

My arrival at Dulles International Airport near Washington, D.C., on September 19, 1985, was accompanied by mixed feelings and perceptions. The flight had lasted nearly 13 hours. I had a great curiosity about a land I had been told flowed with "milk and honey." The things I saw upon my arrival seemed to confirm my expectations: a magnificent airport infrastructure; huge paved roads that I observed as I trucked along the freeway with an in-law who had come to the airport to greet me; numerous high-rise buildings; and lighted streets. It was as if the roads had been swept. Truly, it appeared to be a land flowing with milk and honey. Yet in the midst of this grandeur, I had flashbacks of stories I had been told of race relations in the United States. I recalled the negative images of blacks that were portrayed on Nigerian television, images of the buffoonery behavior of J.J. in the old-time sitcom *Good Times,* images of blacks in subservient or supporting roles. Those images heightened my initial fears about living in the United States, and I wondered about the opportunities that would be available to a person with my background. I also wondered about the nature of relationships that would emerge between my African American relatives and me.

I had left Nigeria with the impression that African Americans were confined to a life of silliness and crime in America, and that the experience of slavery had wrought considerable havoc on the psyches of blacks. My experiences in Nigeria with some African Americans living and working there (my boss was African American, as was one of my good high school friends) did little to alter the very negative perceptions reflected in media images that had become the prism through which I saw life in America. My initial interactions with African Americans upon my arrival in the United States were therefore filled with curiosity, because I wanted to get to know them, and caution—one could even say fear—because of the negative media portrayals. Such fear was manifested in my polite refusal of an offer from a young African American male staffer to assist me with my luggage at Dulles; yet I felt safe when a similar offer came, moments later, from a white male attendant! For most newcomers into a foreign land, their knowledge of a place is typically informed by media images. Clearly the distorted depictions of blacks helped to condition my perceptions of and relationships with that group upon my arrival in the United States. Fortunately, those perceptions had changed by the time I went to Howard University for my doctorate.

At Towson State University I continued my American journey. A predominantly white institution located on a pristine campus, Towson had more than 16,000 students; when I was there I was the only black face, or one of the very few black faces, in several of my classes and on the campus. I had never been exposed to such a sea of white faces in my life! It was there that I encountered some initial cultural problems. They came in many shapes and sizes. The first was in the use of the English language.

In my initial interactions with U.S. Americans, I had difficulties related to use of verbal and nonverbal codes, including the meanings assigned to various actions or behaviors. One such difficulty arose during my first encounter with snow. I had never seen snow until I came to the United States. There is no word in Igbo (my language) for it.

My knowledge of snow came from watching television and from classroom discussions at St. Mary's Elementary School (later renamed Niger Close Primary School) in Enugu, Nigeria. The teacher would liken snow to ice formations in one's refrigerator. For someone who has not experienced snow, that description does not capture the phenomenon. My sister had warned me of the need to be careful during winter,[1] since large tracks of snow tend to turn into ice. On one particular morning in Baltimore I woke to the sight of snow and was clearly enthused by it. My college friend, Sam, who is African American, had joined me at my apartment as I prepared for class that morning. A few

> ## **Culture** Concepts
> ### Intercultural Interactants in Social Episodes
> *In social episodes that include intercultural interactions, those involved may—and in all likelihood will—have very different expectations and interpretations about people's behaviors and intentions. As the interaction becomes more and more ambiguous, the expected behaviors that provide a sense of pattern to the social episode also become more unpredictable and problematic. Though a culture teaches a particular interpretation of the meanings and behaviors in social episodes, other cultures may provide their members with very different interpretations of these same experiences.*

minutes later, we both left the apartment and walked down the stairs, which had been partially covered by the snow. Not remembering my sister's warning, I tripped and rolled down to the bottom of the stairs. I was in pain, and of course I expected my friend to say that he was sorry about the incident while assisting me up from the ground. Instead, he kept asking "Are you all right, Peter? Are you all right?" The more he asked the question, the angrier I became. When I finally managed to get up, I wasted no time in telling him how inconsiderate he was. Sam could not understand why I would expect him to say "sorry" when he was not responsible for my fall.

Years later, at Howard University, when I was able to reprocess that interaction, it became clear that our remarks regarding appropriate behaviors and linguistic norms were a function of our cultural backgrounds. I began to feel a sense of both awareness and understanding of these differences—a sense of intercultural growth. Among Africans, when a person is hurt, regardless of the circumstances, it is appropriate for the others who are present to indicate their sympathy by saying "I am sorry." The phrase is not an indication of responsibility; rather, it is one's way of showing concern. Duty also requires one to assist physically in extricating the injured person from the source of the pain. Among U.S. Americans, however, the predominant cultural norm is that a person should display concern through questions like those Sam asked. How a question is posed—its tone, pitch, and rate—indicates the degree of concern. In fact, if one is badly injured, the cultural rule in the United States is that the person would call for medical help, since any attempt to assist physically might exacerbate the pain or injury. There are a few exceptions to this rule, as in the case of administering cardiac pulmonary resuscitation (CPR) when needed.

In spite of my proficiency in British English, American English, for the most part, was incomprehensible to me because of differences in pronunciation and the use of words. There were numerous instances of miscommunication when I felt embarrassed because my accented speech was misunderstood or the way I pronounced or used words was wrong. For example, what the

---

Culture Concepts

Role of Language in Intercultural Communication

Intercultural communication often involves interactions among people who speak different languages. Even when the individuals seem to be speaking the same language—a person from Spain interacting with someone from Venezuela, a French Canadian conversing with a French-speaking citizen of Belgium, or an Australian visiting the United States—the differences in the specific dialects of the language and the different cultural practices that govern language use can mystify those involved.

British pronounce *schedule (shedyool)* is pronounced *skedyool* by most American students. Once I used the word *stroke* to explain intrapersonal/interpersonal communication in one of my classes. The students were clearly confused by the term because the U.S. American way of saying intrapersonal/ *(stroke)* interpersonal communication would have substituted the word *stroke* with the word *slash*. It was another lesson for me in communication, whose goal is shared meaning. In addition, my accent was different from the U.S. norm, and in the company of many U.S. Americans, it was a constant reminder that I was an outgroup member who did not belong. It was a struggle to understand both my instructors and my classmates. In numerous instances I laughed at jokes when I did not understand their meanings or their cultural contexts, simply to cover my "deficiency."

Another equally perplexing issue centered on the use of first names to refer to people in authority or who were higher in status or age. I could not understand the general informality of my new environment, and I wondered why people would be so "disrespectful." Why, I asked rhetorically, would fellow classmates address the instructor by his or her first name? My relationship with authority figures and with people older than me was guided by an expectation that they should be treated with deference, which is displayed, in part, through one's greeting styles (handshakes, bowing, or kissing the hand or forehead). To observe students address the instructor, an authority figure, without such deference was perplexing. In contrast to these experiences of white students' relationships with their instructors at Towson State, I saw a profound difference in the way African American students related to their instructors—referring to them by their formal titles—at Howard University. At California State University, Sacramento, where I first taught, it took me a while to refer to my colleagues by their first names, since doing so (given my cultural background) was a sign of disrespect. In fact, during the initial period of my teaching, the chair of my department insisted (although jokingly) that he would stop speaking to me if I continued to address him using the honorific title Doctor! In spite of my growth and adjustment in this area, I am still somewhat uncomfortable when students refer to me or to other instructors by first name.

The initial period of my American journey included other instances of communication failures. At the college cafeteria and at public restaurants, I always ordered the same meals. On public transportation, I paid my fare with large bills to mask my ignorance of the currency. I felt too embarrassed to ask questions, since my accent would give me away and expose me to vulnerabilities. On a few occasions I had to withdraw from the sources of pain because, as for so many immigrants who come to the United States, the transition involved not just a tremendous adventure but, at times, near overwhelming stress, feelings of alienation, and low self-esteem. At no time did it occur to me that the frustrations I experienced on a daily basis were a symptom of the stress associated with adjustment to a new environment, or the phenomenon commonly known as "culture shock."

When I first left Nigeria I believed, like most African-born immigrants, that my life and experiences in my country had prepared me fully for life in another country. After all, when I graduated from college my parents had encouraged me to accept employment in the western part of Nigeria, in an area inhabited by Yorubas, who are one of the major ethnic groups in the country. My parents, who are Igbos,[2] had lived in western Nigeria, and they speak the Yoruba language fluently. The Igbos represent one of the three major ethnic groups in the country. My parents also lived for more than a quarter of a century in northern Nigeria, where I was born. The North is inhabited largely by Hausas and Fulanis, and my parents also speak the Hausa language fluently. However, the rise of ethnic antagonisms against the Igbos in the region a few years after Nigeria's independence in 1960 compelled my parents to return to eastern Nigeria, their place of origin. In 1967 eastern Nigeria seceded from the rest of the country to form the Republic of Biafra. Following the collapse of talks to resolve the crisis between the East and the Nigerian government, a bloody civil war ensued. The war, which lasted nearly 30 months, claimed more than one million lives. The period of the Biafra-Nigeria conflict (1967–1970) was a very dark chapter in the country's history, and many accounts of that ugly experience have been written. Just as the history of slavery shaped black-white relations in the United States, the history of the Biafra-Nigeria war shaped interethnic relations in Nigeria. Communication in such areas as politics, education, the military, the economy, and infrastructure development has been tainted by these historical circumstances, yet it was difficult for me to recognize the profound impact of my country's history on my perceptions of race relations in the United States. I will return to this point later.

Although I was born in the northern region of Nigeria, I cannot claim that as my place of origin. According to Igbo custom, one's father's place of birth (not one's mother's) is the person's place of origin. In other words, my father's place of birth, in the eastern region of Nigeria, is my place of origin. In the same manner, my father's place of origin is his father's place of birth. Consider, for example, the following: according to my culture, if my father was born in California and I was born in Arkansas, California would constitute my place of origin. However, if my grandfather was born in California, my father was born in New York, and I was born in Arkansas, both my father and I would hail from California, which is my grandfather's birthplace. This is how Africans generally maintain their family lines and group identities from one generation to the next. In the United States a person's own place of birth is his or her place of origin. Thus, if someone is born in California, that state would constitute the person's place of origin, regardless of where his or her father was born. Initially I had difficulty and a sense of disconnection in my conversations with U.S. Americans because I could not comprehend their sense of casualness about something as important as origins and group identities.

In any case, my period of residence in the North, East, and West of Nigeria exposed me to three vastly different cultures in the country. My work with the World Bank project, in the western part of the country, provided further exposure to other cultural and ethnic groups, as I had the opportunity to travel to 18 of Nigeria's 19 states.[3]

At the World Bank project, I worked with many expatriate workers from several countries, including Ghana, the United States, the United Kingdom, Canada, India, Pakistan, Bangladesh, and China. My daily interactions with these workers, in addition to my exposure to the various cultural and ethnic groups in Nigeria, convinced me that I was fully prepared to deal with the challenges of life in another society. But this was not the case.

My world view collided with fundamental teachings about what is viewed as logical and illogical in Western society. For example, old age in African society is valued positively and held with a high degree of respect, whereas most U.S. Americans place a high value on youth rather than old age. The value placed on communal or group responsibility for rearing a child ("it takes a village to raise a child") contrasts with the Western notion of individualism ("only parents can raise their child"). The Igbo value placed on the extended family system contrasts greatly with the value placed on the nuclear family in the United States. The most fundamental principle in Igbo society is "I am because we are; since we are, therefore I am." One does not exist in isolation from the group. The unbridled individualism in the United States is therefore hard to comprehend, especially for a new immigrant from a communally based culture.

An equally perplexing experience for me was the reaction of most U.S. Americans to my family background. I come from a fairly large extended family with some history of polygyny. Polygyny is the union between a man and two or more wives. (Polygamy, a more general term, refers to marriage among several spouses, including a man who marries more than one wife or a woman who marries more than one husband.) Polygyny is an accepted and respected marriage form in traditional Igbo society. My father, Chief Clement Muoghalu Nwosu, had two wives. My paternal grandfather, Chief Ezekwesili Nwosu, was married to four. My great grandfather, Chief Odoji, who also married four wives, was the chief priest and custodian of traditional religion in my town, Umudioka town, a small rural community in Anambra State of the Federal Republic of Nigeria.

My maternal grandfather, Chief Nwokoye Akaigwe, was from the royal line of the Akaigwe clan and was the traditional ruler of Enugwu-Ukwu, which is a medium-sized community in Anambra State. Chief Akaigwe was

---

Culture Concepts

Cultural Variations in Persuasion

The effective use of persuasion varies greatly among cultures. There are differences in what cultures consider to be acceptable evidence, who is regarded as an authority, how evidence is used to create persuasive arguments, and what ideas are reasonable. These preferred ways to convince others are called the culture's persuasive style. When people from diverse cultures communicate, the differences in their persuasive styles are often very evident. The underlying cultural patterns function as assumptions in the persuasion process. Because these vary among cultures, there will be differences in the ways people prefer to arrange their evidence, assumptions, and claims.

---

known for several firsts (the first warrant chief[4] in Enugwu-Ukwu, the first to own and ride a bicycle, the first to own a car in eastern Nigeria, and the first to build a "zinc" house—metal roofing as opposed to a thatched roof—in Enugu-Ukwu). He was married to 24 women! I found myself explaining to my curious, and sometimes amazed, U.S. friends that the traditional economic structure in Igbo society dictated this familial arrangement whereby a man would have more than one spouse and produce several children, who would then assist him with farm work, which is regarded as the fiber and glue of economic life in traditional Igbo society. Each wife and her own children live in a separate home built by the husband. Each wife is responsible for the upkeep of her immediate family, with support from her husband.

One of the traditions of my extended family is the family reunion, held every two years. Families who are unable to attend for any reason are required to send pictures so that other members of the extended family, who are present at the reunion, may know them. The goal of the family reunion is to encourage unity, promote awareness of one another, and prevent the potential for incest or marital union between and among family relatives, considered an abomination in Igboland.

In traditional Igbo society it is acceptable for a man to marry many women to support the economic well-being of the family. In an agrarian lifestyle, where people's livelihoods depend on subsistence farming, it makes sense that the institution of polygyny would be a fundamental pillar of traditional Igbo economy and society. Indeed, marriage to more than one wife was often regarded as a measure of a man's wealth and status. Today, however, a man marries more than one wife mostly only if his first wife fails to conceive a male child, which is a requirement for perpetuating the family and ancestral lineage.

Although the extended family system exists in the United States, it is typically much less important than in Africa. During the initial period of my journey, it was clear that in the United States the nuclear family was the norm, although other kinds of families (e.g., single-parent families) did exist. I was surprised to learn that most U.S. couples were not concerned whether their unborn child was male or female. This is certainly not the case in Africa.

A related and perplexing issue centered on my perception of differences in matrimonial life between my culture and that in the United States. Among the Igbos, marriage doesn't just bring husband and wife together into matrimonial life; it also unites two families into a stronger relationship. Couples do not establish independent families; instead, they enter into already existing ones. The U.S. ideal of exclusivity, of mutual love just between spouses, was an aberration to me. In the Igbo culture, family love is multidimensional. One enters into love not only with one's spouse but also with all members of both families. Marriage for the Igbo people is a community affair, a joyful reality, a covenant between two *umunnas* (extended families), not merely an arrangement between a man and woman.

In the United States a core value of social life is a sense of personal freedom and a commitment to oneself. As an African, it was difficult for me to contrast this personal freedom and commitment to self with the commitment to interdependence and community affiliation that are at the core of social life in Africa. The nonindividuality of the African, which is such a vital part of the African cultural ethos, often is responsible for the numerous misperceptions and misinterpretations of U.S. cultural values.

Let me now return to the profound impact of historical forces on my initial interactions in the United States. These forces include slavery, conflict, war, colonialism, famine, and prosperity. To deny or ignore that history is to deny the experience of the group to which that particular history occurred. To deny the Holocaust, for example, is to deny the experience of the Jewish people and a major historical force that shaped how Jews have come to view the world around them. To deny the internment experience for the Japanese is to deny their suffering in the United States during World War II. To deny the discrimination experiences of the Irish in the 1840s in Boston is to deny a major historical force that shaped their lives in this country. In the same manner, to deny or ignore the experience of slavery for blacks is to deny or ignore a major historical force that shaped and continues to shape the collective wisdom of African Americans in the United States. There is considerable evidence to show that people bring their histories to their communication events. When African Americans react negatively to Ross Perot's choice of the words "you people" in an address to them in Texas during the 1992 presidential campaign, their reaction stems from the experience of slavery, in which a "master-servant" relationship existed between blacks and whites. The term "you people" is a reminder that they (blacks) are different, and are often regarded by whites as lower in status.

Some of my initial cultural problems in the United States emerged from a lack of a deep sense of understanding of some of the forces of history that have shaped U.S. domestic relations, and their implications for competent communication in a variety of contexts. I recall my encounter with an African American classmate at Howard University. I had used the term "old boy" in referring to him during a conversation. While in Nigeria this is regarded as a positive term in referring to friends, my African American friend took offense at what appeared to suggest a master-servant relationship. During and after the slavery period in the U.S., Africans were referred to as "boy" by the white master. However, through discussions we were able to recognize that no offense was intended, and we both grew from the experience. One of the major indicators of intercultural growth when one confronts a cultural problem must be a willingness on the part of those involved to engage in genuine dialogue, which helps to sort out the cultural differences that created the miscommunication. Through such dialogue, intercultural understanding is enhanced.

As a newly arrived African-born immigrant from a society in which race was not necessarily an issue, initially I had difficulty understanding why both intellectual and lay discussions about domestic relations were so much anchored by race. For most Africans, ethnicity and national origins, rather than colors, were the critical factors. My experience living in the United States has made me look for deeper meanings. The perceptual differences between black Americans and native Africans stem, perhaps, from the fact that in Africa, black people under the control of Europeans were subjected to the institution of colonialism, an institution that while very limiting allowed certain basic freedoms and protections under the law. In the United States, blacks under the control of Europeans were subjected to the institution of slavery, an institution that denied them every right under the law. To understand why black Americans may view reality from the perspective of race, one must put the experience of slavery in its proper historical context.

Overall, growth for me throughout my American journey has produced a greater degree of adaptability, such that I am now able to experience cultural differences with better understanding while at the same time functioning well in my host culture. Although my expectations are still grounded in Igbo cultural values, nevertheless they have become shaped through frequent travels and interactions with host culture nationals in both small communities and large cities across the United States. I have visited more than 30 states since my arrival in the United States, from large urban cities such as Washington, New Orleans, New York, Chicago, Los Angeles, San Francisco, Miami, and Atlanta, to mid-sized towns such as Sacramento, Portland, Nashville, East Lansing, and Albuquerque, to small communities such as Oakdale, Myrtle Beach, and Plains (hometown of former President Jimmy Carter). I have participated and immersed myself in the various historical, institutional (government and religious), and community events that cut across racial, ethnic, and cultural boundaries—events such as church services of other faiths, Latino Cinco de Mayo celebrations, African American Juneteenth, Native American Pow Wows, German Oktoberfests, Chinese New Year's festivities, East Indian weddings, and Thanksgiving dinners.

Culture Concepts

Culture Shock

Culture shock *is said to occur when people must deal with a barrage of new perceptual stimuli that are difficult to interpret because the cultural context has changed. To assure some degree of understanding, things taken for granted at home may require virtually constant monitoring in the new culture. The loss of predictability, coupled with the fatigue that results from the need to stay consciously focused on what would normally be taken for granted, produces the negative responses associated with culture shock.*

In fact, it is safe to say that I have become so functionally adapted in the United States that when I return home to Nigeria I experience the stress of reverse culture shock as I readjust to my own culture. The stress results because the new ideas that I have acquired living in the United States often are in conflict with my native customs and traditions. For example, during my father's funeral in 1995 a number of the native beliefs and values regarding funeral rites seemed very strange to me, but I quickly adapted, after a few days, with help from family members still living within the culture.

When I first entered the United States, I was a stranger in this land. I was unsure how to behave properly, and I was anxious and insecure about what I would experience. Through prolonged and varied experiences, I have gradually acquired the communication skills necessary to cope with the challenges and to realize the promises of my new environment. This, for me, has been and continues to be a wonderful American journey.

Notes

1. There are four seasons in the United States—winter, spring, summer, and fall—but there are only two seasons in Nigeria: the dry season, which lasts from November through February, and the rainy season, which runs from March through October.

2. The Igbo people of Nigeria rank as one of the largest ethnic groups in Africa. Their population ranges from 15 to 25 million, according to various estimates. They occupy a land area that encompasses 7 of Nigeria's 36 states and stretches from the southeastern corner to the midwestern part of the country. The Igbos are a tenacious, adaptable people who also maintain a considerable presence beyond this geographical region.

3. Nigeria's four regions—North, West, East, and Midwest—were initially divided in 1967 into 12 states as a way to end interethnic tensions and bring the government closer to the people. Successive military governments in Nigeria have created more states since then, bringing the total to 36, including the Federal Capital Territory in Abuja, which is considered a state.

4. The institution of warrant chief was introduced in eastern Nigeria by the first British governor-general of Nigeria, Lord Frederick Lugard, as a system of indirect rule (governance through proxy) of subject territories.

▶ ▶ ▶ Learning AmongUS

1. Using the concepts provided, explain at least two of the social episodes that Nwosu describes.
2. Why did Nwosu expect his roommate to say "I'm sorry" after Nwosu fell down icy steps? Identify two or three examples from your own language use that could be similarly confusing to others.
3. What kinds of problems did Nwosu encounter because of his use of British English?
4. What does Nwosu mean when he says, in Igbo culture, "family love is multidimensional"?
5. What is the Igbo custom concerning one's place of origin? How does this differ from your culture's definition of place of origin?
6. Nwosu's reaction to the use of first names in the United States reflects cultural differences in formality and informality. How does your culture treat formality and informality?
7. What are the potential negative consequences of forgetting the history of slavery and other injustices committed by whites in the United States?
8. Did Nwosu experience culture shock?

In Vicki Marie's essay, we witness the process by which an outsider attempts to understand and adjust to living within another culture. With enthusiasm and respect, Marie moved to Micronesia, only to discover that her preferences about a variety of common social experiences (greeting others, resolving conflicts, desiring privacy, displaying courtesy and respect) had different meanings among her Micronesian colleagues and neighbors. Marie's essay also introduces some of the inevitable ethical issues that occur when crossing cultures: how and when should we conform to behaviors that are inconsistent with our own beliefs, values, and experiences?

15 Living in Paradise: An Inside Look at the Micronesian Culture

Vicki Marie

In 1988 I was an adjunct instructor at several nearby colleges and universities. One day, while commuting between campuses, it occurred to me that while I was waiting for a full-time position, I could be teaching abroad. I researched overseas teaching opportunities and sent out a dozen resumes. I received three job offers. The assistant professorship of language arts at the College of Micronesia was the most appealing. I accepted an eighteen-month contract, left California a few months later, and arrived on Pohnpei in January 1989.

Except for holiday travel, I had lived in California my entire life and knew little about Micronesia. I read eagerly about Micronesian history, geography, and culture, and talked with people who had lived in Micronesia and taught at the college. Yet I arrived in Pohnpei believing that my Micronesian students would be motivated by the same values and would aspire to the same goals that I considered worthwhile. I was surprised to discover that my worldview was uniquely European American and my attitude ethnocentric. Pohnpei became the classroom and textbook that taught me about cultural relativity and intercultural communication. I discovered I had much to learn about Micronesia and even more about myself.

▶ Background

The U.S. and Micronesian governments have been intertwined since the end of World War II, yet many Americans are unaware of the vast northern ocean area of Micronesia. Micronesia, meaning "tiny islands," comprises a string of more than 2,100 islands and atolls lying in four major archipelagos: the Mariana, the Caroline, the Marshall, and the Kiribati islands. These islands are scattered across an area as large as the continental United States, yet they are so small that their combined land mass amounts to approximately 1,000 square miles, about the size of Rhode Island. The inhabited islands are home to more than 375,000 people, who make up five constitutional governments. While these political divisions also represent linguistic, ethnic, and cultural differences, the people native to the islands are all classified as Micronesians.

Despite 175 years of contact with foreigners, Micronesians have maintained their traditional politics, languages, and family organizations. Changes, though, are inevitable. As a result, I found island life to be an amalgam of traditional and Western influences. Micronesians wear Western-style clothing, drive imported cars, eat in Japanese restaurants, and socialize in American-style bars. Yet these same people are equally comfortable wearing traditional island *lava lavas,* reciting ancient folklore in native languages, and masterfully pounding *sakau,* the local kava drink.

▶ Cultural Patterns

Although Micronesians can move easily between ancient traditions and modern ideas, they have distinct value systems unlike those in the West. I found that it wasn't always easy to consider—much less appreciate—our contrasting worldviews. And what huge differences in worldviews we had! The following list summarizes some of the significant differences in cultural assumptions that I encountered while living among Micronesians:

Micronesian	*European American*
Nature will provide for us in time.	We must change our world, control nature, and make it work for humankind.
What will be, will be. Human life is controlled by destiny.	We create our own future by what we do.
There's no use rushing away from what I'm doing now. There's always plenty of time	I have to hurry and meet somebody now. See you later.
Worry about tomorrow when tomorrow comes.	Save for the future.
Work a little, rest a little. Whatever you do, try to keep other people happy.	If I work hard enough, someday I'll make it to the top.
What I have is yours. What you have is mine.	What's mine belongs to me.

The wise person is one who knows his place in the world, respects authority, and does what he is supposed to do.

Sensible people strike out on their own, learn to do things for themselves, and make their own decisions.

The feelings of others are more important than an honest answer.

Always tell the truth, no matter how much it hurts.

My life belongs to the family and God.

I am a god.

As you can tell from this list, the potential for intercultural misunderstandings is great. I found these cultural differences to be interesting, irritating, amusing, or stressful, depending on the situation.

As time passed, I moved through predictable and trying phases of adjustment and assimilation. The first few months I was euphoric just to be in Micronesia, and everything seemed perfect and beautiful. I walked around with a big smile on my face and wrote letters to my family that recounted every blissful event. My euphoria plummeted the morning I discovered two flat tires on my Jeep. As a prank, the boys in the village had let the air out of the tires. I took it very personally and cried. A few days later, someone stole my sandals off the porch. I wasn't sure what to expect next in my new surroundings. I coped with the uncertainty by writing letters to everyone I knew "back home," socializing primarily with American and European expatriates and occasionally retreating to the solitude of my bungalow. Eventually I settled into a routine in which uncertainty became entertaining more than threatening. I reached out to people with varied cultural backgrounds and broadened my social circle.

I enjoyed new cultural experiences. I drank *sakau* and ate eel at feasts, visited with neighbors, hiked in the rainforest, learned to scuba dive, and enjoyed the challenge of teaching English to Micronesian students. With each experience I gained valuable insights into the culture and into myself. As I learned about Micronesian ways, I came to better understand my own cultural conditioning.

My American assumptions were often laughable in the Micronesian context. I felt anxious about wasting time and reprimanded students who were late to class. I was impatient when meeting times were disregarded. I took pride in accomplishing a list of goals each day. Then one day a Micronesian dean questioned why another American professor always walked so fast. "What's his hurry all the time?" the dean wondered aloud. Knowing that I easily outpaced my American colleague, I realized the question was indirectly aimed at my own task-oriented style. I felt embarrassed about looking foolish to the dean, but it seemed right to use my time wisely.

My notions of being direct and straightforward also were challenged. One day my friend Maggie stood me up at the hospital. I had agreed to assist her by talking with a physician on her behalf. She had health problems that she didn't fully understand and agreed to meet me at the hospital for an 11 A.M.

Culture Concepts

Monochronic and Polychronic Cultures

An important aspect of a culture's time system is the degree to which it is monochronic or polychronic. A monochronic time system means that things should be done one at a time, and time is segmented into precise, small units. In a monochronic time system, time is viewed as a commodity; it is scheduled, managed, and arranged. A polychronic time system means that several things are being done at the same time. Those who use polychronic time systems often schedule multiple appointments simultaneously, so keeping on schedule is an impossibility that was never really a goal. Those with a monochronic time system, of course, are upset when they are kept waiting for a scheduled appointment, particularly if they discover that they are the third of three appointments that have been scheduled at exactly the same hour.

---

appointment. I took a taxi and arrived at the hospital 10 minutes early. After reading a book for 20 minutes I roamed around the hospital, looking for Maggie. I was concerned and wondered if a problem was keeping her from being on time. After I'd been there 45 minutes, Maggie's brother found me, staring at the main door, and told me that Maggie was sorry but she couldn't make it that day. I was disappointed and frustrated. Unlike the earlier interaction with the dean, the cultural implications were not obvious. Months later, after observing similar incidents between others, I realized that Maggie never intended to meet me that day. Apparently she felt that saying "no" would have insulted me.

▶ Political Structure

Shortly after moving to Pohnpei, I discovered that an important key to understanding Micronesian culture lies in the pervasive traditional political structure, which is a hierarchical social system with strongly embedded political and relational values and social norms. Even when Micronesian communities are affected by the maneuvering of government politicians, the traditional system factors strongly into negotiations and outcomes of most political transactions. For example, the negotiations required for paving the road that encircled Pohnpei were lengthy and complicated. Government officials proposed a plan that had to be approved by each of the five districts' leaders. The negotiations for land rights took months of meetings, discussions, gifts, and other traditional courtesies. Eventually, after each traditional chief felt satisfied that his community had been sufficiently compensated, the road construction began.

Typically, each district on an island operates within a status hierarchy: hereditary nobility, landed gentry, and commoners. On Pohnpei, each island district is ruled by a *nanmwarki,* or "high chief." Below the *nanmwarki* is a group of high-titled nobles. A second set of nobles is headed by the *nahnken,* or "talking chief." Each male title has a female equivalent. The male leaders, however, are the decision makers and the most highly revered in traditional culture. They are bestowed with much respect; others must address them in a "high language," which is an honorific language with special vocabulary reserved for nobility and authority.

Commoners and outsiders like me are expected to stand when talking to nobility, to respond to rather than initiate communication, and to cast our eyes downward to convey humility and respect. One evening I was introduced to a *nahnken* who had entered the restaurant where I was dining with a colleague. As the *nahnken* approached us, my friend quickly coached me: "Stand up, shake his hand, and cast your eyes down." I reluctantly followed his direction, feeling very awkward. In that instance I was abiding by the local custom but violating behaviors that I considered to be courteous and comfortable. I prefer to use direct eye contact and a sincere smile and believe such gestures conveyed confidence, honesty, and mutual respect. At that moment, I struggled to avoid eye contact and felt resentment and a tightness in my stomach as I tried to abide by social norms that collided with my own standards of equality and status.

▶ Gender Roles

Unlike in U.S. society, where equality is the desired value, the roles of men and women in traditional Micronesian cultures are quite well defined. Many gender roles were apparent. In the morning, women hung their laundry, prepared meals, and swept their living areas. Men returned from early-morning fishing outings to repair homes or head for their jobs in town. During the day, men built houses, repaired canoes, sailed, fished, and gathered breadfruit and coconuts. Women prepared meals, cared for the children, cleaned, and tended the taro patches. In the early evenings, men met at the "men's house" for socializing or all-male community decision making. After their homemaking chores, women played cards or walked through the village, visiting with friends along the way.

In business and government centers on the more developed islands such as Pohnpei and Palau, many women have moved into the workplace, operating businesses or working in government offices. As women's roles have changed, so have gender communication norms. Traditional hierarchies still dictate the intrinsic status of women, but the subtleties are not obvious to an outsider. I learned about social status by talking to Micronesian men and women.

Traditionally, social expectations in Micronesia dictate where and to whom women may speak, but norms have shifted as women have taken responsible positions in community affairs. In more traditional settings, however, predictable gender communication norms remain intact. Women, for instance, are not supposed to speak during village or community meetings.

Above all, women should not challenge or confront men. As a European American woman, I found that notion foreign. I learned the hard way about hierarchical gender communication in Micronesia.

My bungalow was situated between a *sakau* bar and a beer bar in Porakiet village. Over the winter holiday season, both bars had ongoing parties. Because *sakau* is a soporific, the more the patrons drank, the quieter they became. The beer had the opposite effect on the patrons in the second bar. As the evening progressed, people and music became louder, and the noise continued until dawn. After two sleepless nights, I approached the bar owner with a direct but courteous plea to end the party at a reasonable hour. He reluctantly agreed to turn the music off by 10 P.M. and close the bar at midnight. I felt relieved, but that evening the music continued past midnight. I walked over to the bar, asked to speak to the owner, and pleaded with him to turn off the music. I made, I thought, a reasonable and polite request, but the music continued into the early morning.

On my way to campus that morning I was confronted by the owner's daughter, who accused me of casting shame on her father. Although the owner and I had had a private conversation, my directness was perceived as aggressive and disrespectful. I tried to explain my position to the daughter, but she wouldn't listen. As an outsider and a woman, I had overstepped my boundaries and never had a chance of persuading the owner to comply with my request. Interestingly, my landlord, a well-respected businessman, eventually intervened. From that night on, the owner conformed to a 10 P.M. curfew, and I finally got some sleep.

Even in family settings, women must temper their comments. A Pohnpeian colleague once explained that if she was bitterly angry with her brother's wife, she would not dare say anything to her brother about her feelings. To do so would be disrespectful to her brother and would cast shame on herself. She said she limits her conversations with her brother to "asking for his help or advice."

I learned that women who initiate conversations with men are considered forward or flirtatious. The college maintenance man went out of his way to help me set up my office and bungalow. I thought he was very nice—until he made a pass at me. I was informed that my outgoing personality and friendly small talk had been interpreted as romantic interest. I thought it was silly, so I just ignored the misunderstanding. To avoid an unnecessary conflict, however, I was courteously warned by my Micronesian friends about the man's jealous Chuukese wife and told to avoid him.

A similar situation occurred after I stopped one day to look at a hotel construction site near the lagoon. One of the owners, who was married to the college secretary, was on the premises. I was pleased to meet him and chatted about his new hotel. A few days later, his wife told me that he thought I was flirting with him. Thankfully, she didn't take him seriously. My Micronesian friends trusted me and guided me when necessary to avoid misperceptions. I was grateful for the support as I maneuvered my way through a new culture.

I learned, for instance, that despite the cultural constraint of gender, Micronesian women hold a position of power and community esteem in island life. When a dispute occurs, the first-born woman, who is the female head of her clan, is sent to settle the conflict and reconcile the two sides. Her judgments are almost always obeyed, because if they are not there is the risk that the conflict could reemerge to plague the community.

True to their collectivist nature, the Micronesian people consider social harmony an important cultural value that is critical to community welfare. Women are called on to ensure that such harmony prevails.

▶ Family and Children

Like most European Americans, I tend to belong to several unrelated groups. Micronesians, however, belong to one relatively unchanging group: their family. Having grown up in a small family I found it intriguing that Micronesian families include all relatives in their clan. The extended family is composed of generations of matrilineal relationships. Several members of the extended family commonly share a single household. The larger clan is composed of descendants of a common female ancestor. As a Westerner, I was confused by the matrilineal nature of Micronesian families. Descendants always come through the woman and are considered members of the mother's clan. Children refer to their mothers, aunts, grandmothers, and other significant women as "mom." Their siblings and cousins are considered "brothers and sisters." When the girl next door told me that she had 19 brothers and sisters, I laughed because I thought she was joking. When I asked Millie, the daughter of my friend Maggie, how many brothers and sisters she has, she began counting on her fingers but finally threw up her hands and exclaimed, "I don't know. A lot!"

Rank in the clan comes from birth order, not age. The children of the oldest daughter will have higher rank than the children of a younger daughter, regardless of their ages. For example, if the older daughter's son is 25 years old, and the youngest daughter's son is 35 years old, the older daughter's son would have the higher rank. He would be regarded as a big brother by the older but lower-ranking man. Rank for females follows the same pattern. Grandparents, by virtue of their position in the family, are highly honored and treated with great respect, love, and care by their children and grandchildren.

Respect is the most important value to Micronesians. It is expressed in the guiding rule to "be humble; don't put yourself up." This social rule, which extends to all relationships, discouraged our college freshmen from initiating conversation with sophomores. In some circumstances, though, such as in a classroom, students switched to an egalitarian style for practical reasons. But they did so with discomfort.

I asked my college students to explain status norms. One responded, "The rule about talking to higher-rank people is to be polite. We honor the higher-title person." Another said, "We use high language for leaders and important people like the elders. If you don't use appropriate language you are considered impolite and disrespectful. Following the rules in our culture is very important, which is why I don't like to communicate at feasts with traditional leaders."

Culture Concepts

Culture and Nonverbal Communication

Cultures vary in their nonverbal behaviors in three ways. First, cultures differ in the specific repertoire *of behaviors that are enacted; movements, body positions, postures, vocal intonations, gestures, spatial requirements, and even dances and ritualized actions are specific to a particular culture. Second, all cultures have* display rules *that govern when and under what circumstances various nonverbal expressions are required, preferred, permitted, or prohibited. Third, cultures vary in the* interpretations *or meanings attributed to particular nonverbal behaviors. Three possible interpretations could be imposed on a given instance of nonverbal behavior: it is random, it is idiosyncratic, or it is shared. An interpretation that the behavior is* random *means it has no particular meaning to anyone. An* idiosyncratic *interpretation suggests that the behaviors are unique to special individuals or relationships, and they therefore have particular meanings only to these people. A* shared *interpretation occurs when people jointly attribute the same meaning to a particular nonverbal act. However, cultures differ in what they regard as random, idiosyncratic, and shared. Thus behaviors regarded as random in one culture may have shared significance in another.*

In general, only a few expectations constrain children's behavior. Parents allow their children to do whatever they please as long as they display respect for others. One afternoon I sat visiting with my friend while her three young children played nearby. During our four-hour conversation, her children would stop to listen to us talk but did not once interrupt. Occasionally my friend or I would speak to her kids. They responded immediately to their mother but were more hesitant toward me.

Respect is the value embedded in the strict rules that prohibit children from initiating conversations with elders. An elder is loosely defined as anyone older than the child. When responding to an elder, children are expected to use "high language." They use honorific language to answer their parents, grandparents, or older siblings, especially the first-born son. Micronesian children will rarely vie for attention or interrupt adults. So, although children are included in all community events, they are typically "seen but not heard."

If a child does something displeasing, the parent will usually attempt to modify the behavior by making the child feel ashamed. For instance, if a girl uses her mother's money to buy something without permission, the parent may talk about the child within her hearing range to make the child feel ashamed for spending the family's money. Disputes among family members are strongly discouraged. Children are taught this value at a very early age and are made to feel great shame if a dispute occurs. Courtesy, respect, and politeness are constant themes found in each household and in the community. Intentional rudeness or malevolent behaviors are looked down on. A person exhibiting such behaviors is considered *amalgam tekia,* a Chuukese phrase meaning "haughty."

Micronesian parents do not praise their children for good deeds. Children might hear indirectly from a third party how pleased their parents are with their behavior, but Micronesians find it awkward to express and receive compliments directly. I would tell children how beautiful or talented they were and would be surprised to hear in reply "I'm not." My Micronesian friends were more likely to express their appreciation through caring, gifts, or favors. In fact, providing enough food is the primary way in which a parent shows affection for a child. Being hungry would imply to others that the child is not taken care of properly and is, therefore, unloved.

Family members who are hungry are expected to help themselves to food. But a hungry person may be too embarrassed to ask for food, for fear of implying that the family is neglectful. To avoid embarrassing family members, Micronesian people assume that any person coming into the house, including a visitor, is hungry and is thus greeted with an offer of food. Family members generally serve themselves from the communal bowl. Eating together goes beyond the mere intake of food to satisfy hunger. The spirit of sharing is a way of showing oneness and, more significantly, mutual trust and love.

Displays of affection among family members, as practiced by many groups in the United States, do not exist in Micronesian families. Children display affection for their parents through loyalty and by performing certain duties or responsibilities for the family, such as sweeping the floor without being asked. Although Micronesians seldom hug or kiss children, a mother will lovingly nuzzle her child's nose.

I attended a church wedding in Pohnpei and was surprised that the Western tradition of the husband kissing the bride was eliminated from the ceremony. I was told later that public displays of affection are considered inappropriate. Holding hands with others outside the family circle is more common, especially among those of the same gender. The only time one is likely to observe hugging and kissing in a family is when an adult is playing with a baby. In fact, children are not allowed to observe kissing. Millie told me that it made her *shake* (nervous) when she saw Americans kissing, because it was bad. I had seen her cover her eyes during a kissing scene in a film. She told me that her mother said she should never see kissing. In Pohnpei, I heard stories of teenage girls being punished for inadvertently witnessing Westerners kissing at the airport. The taboo is apparently a strategy for discouraging promiscuity.

▶ Language

Many language differences exist in Micronesia, although each language derives from a common Malayo-Polynesian source. Several major languages, with dialect variations, are spoken in Micronesia. The islanders I encountered knew their native language and at least one other Micronesian language. On the islands that were heavily influenced by Japan, inhabitants know some conversational Japanese. Because of the diversity of native languages, English has emerged as the lingua franca used in government, education, and other intercultural contexts. For most Micronesians, English is a second language; for others, it is their fourth or fifth and, thus, the language with which they feel the least secure.

At the College of Micronesia students appeared confident when switching between Micronesian languages but seemed reticent when communicating in English to me. I spoke with students who had varying degrees of English proficiency. Some disclosed that they were afraid of appearing "stupid" to native English speakers.

I taught an evening class for two weeks before I realized that the majority of students didn't understand me. They pretended to understand by simply nodding and smiling. When I spoke to them individually after class, I realized that in fact they understood very little English. Micronesians who live and work in city centers and who have frequent contact with native English speakers are able to express themselves as clearly in English as they do in their native languages. When they speak fluent English, it is easy to forget that our cultural perceptions may actually block clear communication.

I sometimes wondered about the illusion of shared meaning that existed during my intercultural conversations. There were times I'd expect a particular outcome but it wouldn't occur. I learned, over time, not to take the language for granted. I tried to be empathetic toward students who spoke in a foreign language, especially when I heard them struggling to express themselves clearly. Actually, I admired their ability to speak multiple languages.

▶ Communication Norms

Micronesians seem to be simultaneously extroverted and introverted. As a group Micronesians find it easy to talk with others, and they perceive themselves to be friendly, dramatic, and animated. They also appear interested in others, demonstrating goodwill when they communicate.

Because it is difficult to accept compliments, Micronesians generally do not openly give compliments. They admire people silently or indirectly. Generally, if a person wants to compliment another, he or she will pass the compliment through a relative rather than acknowledge the person directly.

When I praised our student clerk for a job well done she giggled, blushed, and turned away from me. I observed the same reaction when I openly praised students for well-written essays or other course work. One day in front of my office, I encouraged a young man to present his exceptionally good speech at our upcoming speech festival. He turned his body away from me as he flipped his hand chest-high in a gesture that meant to communicate "stop" or "go away," because it was difficult for him to accept the compliment. Each time I encountered these common nonverbal responses, they were coupled with self-effacing statements that were said with a smile, but it was quite clear that the student was extremely uncomfortable. One student explained: "People are uncomfortable with praise because they do not want to be perceived as thinking they are 'big' or better than anybody else." Modesty is an important characteristic of the Micronesian personality. Micronesians believe that it is generally virtuous to be quiet. Even in childbirth, a woman is expected to keep silent and show as little pain as possible.

Pohnpeians find very few situations in which they can show pride in their accomplishments or possessions without fear of criticism. This attitude was evident at the conclusion of our college speech festival, when all the student speakers disappeared immediately after the awards ceremony. The young man who won first place for his persuasive speech left to avoid criticism for pretentiousness or "acting big." Runners-up left because they felt ashamed. In a collectivist community where such public competition is rare, the fear of ridicule or gossip seems sufficiently strong to enforce an apparent pattern of exaggerated modesty, humility, and shame.

Micronesian communication style uses less verbal exchange and looks for implicit meaning in the situation. In contrast, my European American communication style is one in which talkativeness is valued and the message is conveyed explicitly. In everyday encounters I commonly misinterpreted silence as introversion, shyness, or disinterest. Over time, I better understood notions of context as I heard conversations similar to one between our department secretary and a European American professor. As the professor walked away from the exchange, the secretary grimaced. When I asked, "What's wrong?" she answered, "He talks too much." She explained that talkative people are less respected in Pohnpeian society. People who are reserved or quiet are admired. This greatly influences the way in which Pohnpeians conduct themselves in public. "Generally," she explained, "people rarely initiate conversations, particularly if they are meeting someone new. During childhood we are told not to speak to adults, and if we did speak we were to be careful of the language to be used." Talkativeness casts shame on oneself and one's family. Such perceived threats contribute greatly to Micronesians' willingness to communicate with others.

▶ Nonverbal Communication

Differences in nonverbal communication, or body language, are often subtle and can be the source of intercultural misunderstanding. During my first few days at the College of Micronesia, the division secretary was on sick leave. When she returned I introduced myself and asked, "Are you feeling better?" She answered "Yes" nonverbally by raising and lowering her eyebrows. I interpreted her response to mean "What did you say?" So I repeated the question a little more slowly, and again she raised her brows. I asked the question a third time, receiving the same nonverbal response. Out of frustration, I finally said, "I hope you are feeling better soon." About a week later, when I learned that raised eyebrows mean "yes," I realized that the secretary must have thought me dense for repeatedly asking the same question.

Micronesians use the same shake of the head as Americans as a way to say "no." A frown accompanied by a wave of the hand at chest level is an emphatic "no!" or "stop it!" Micronesians throw their heads slightly back and to the side to indicate "over there." Depending on the context of the question, the

Culture Concepts

Touching as a Nonverbal Code

Cultures differ in the overall amount of touching they prefer. People from high-contact cultures, such as those in the Middle East, Latin America, and southern Europe, touch each other in social conversations much more than do people from noncontact cultures, such as those in Asia and northern Europe. These cultural differences can lead to difficulties in intercultural communication. Germans, Scandinavians, and Japanese, for example, may be perceived as cold and aloof by Brazilians and Italians, who in turn may be regarded as aggressive, pushy, and overly familiar by northern Europeans. Cultures also differ in where people can be touched and in their expectations about who touches whom. Finally, cultures differ in the settings or occasions in which touch is acceptable.

response could mean a few blocks away or the next island over. The apparent ambiguity of that particular response was sometimes confusing. Similarly, if I, as an outsider, were to summon a Micronesian by repeatedly curling my index finger upward, the gesture would imply that the receiver had the status of an animal. More than a few times, I had to control my impulse to use that common American gesture.

Much more difficult was remembering that the proper nonverbal gesture for summoning someone in Micronesia is to make a downward movement of the hand from the level of the head to the shoulder. The first time a Micronesian beckoned me in this manner, I thought he was telling me to "go away." I stood in utter confusion until he finally asked me to "come here."

Height

I often learned through my mistakes. I once reached out to ruffle a little boy's hair only to have my hand quickly pulled away by a colleague who saved me from cultural transgression. From my American perspective, I was expressing affection toward the child. I was surprised to learn that I was conveying the exact opposite meaning by violating a Micronesian perception of height, an important concept in Micronesian cultures. Generally speaking, the higher something or someone is, the more sacred it is. The head is the highest part of the human body; to touch another person's head is considered disrespectful, and such behavior is strictly prohibited.

Height also acts as a type of checks-and-balances system. When passing others who are sitting, Chuukese people say "Tirow" (excuse me) or "Tirow wom" (high language used to excuse oneself) to elders and others higher in rank. "Tirow wom" is usually accompanied by a bow from the waist, which demonstrates respect by lowering one's height in relation to the people who are sitting.

In the Chuukese culture, a woman is forbidden to be physically higher than a man at any time. I heard Westerners mistakenly categorize this behavior as sexist. From the Chuukese perspective, however, the behavior is practical: A woman should never stand when a man is sitting because she runs the risk of drawing attention to her thighs. A woman's thighs are considered sexually stimulating by Micronesian men. Therefore, her behavior would appear sexually suggestive.

If a woman's brother is sitting, she would either walk past him at a distance while bowing at the waist, walk past him on her knees, crawl, or simply sit down and wait for him to stand up. She would not, under any circumstances, directly ask him to stand up, because that would imply that he didn't respect her. She could, however, ask another person to point out her presence to him or wait until he noticed her. As an outsider, I was generally exempt from these strict cultural rules and was excused when I inadvertently violated social expectations. Still, I tried my best to be sensitive to cultural norms.

Before I left California, I read about the Micronesian perception of female thighs. I was prepared to teach while wearing long skirts and to play while wearing modest, knee length walking shorts. I found most outsiders to be equally sensitive toward this cultural norm. Peace Corps volunteers and other expatriate women adopted the Pohnpeian style of swimming in skirts. It was easier to swim or dive out on the reef, away from the island, because we could swim in bathing suits and cover up with *lava-lavas* (wrapped skirts) as soon as we got within sight of the island. One afternoon, while returning to the lagoon in our boat, some friends and I were engrossed in conversation and didn't remember to cover our legs. We snapped back to reality as we passed the docks and were jeered with whistles and wolf-calls. Interestingly, my friends and I felt very exposed and embarrassed and quickly learned to abide by cultural tradition.

Time

As members of a "doing" culture, European Americans are very concerned with time, compartmentalizing it carefully to avoid wasting it. Micronesia is a "being" culture. Micronesians are more likely to listen to their natural impulses—to eat when they are hungry and sleep when they are tired—than to the hands of a clock. Cooking, fishing, and other tasks are determined by mood, weather, or ocean tides. In the remote villages and outer islands, much time is spent relaxing and socializing. The men meet to discuss community affairs or play games. The women weave or socialize over a card game. I had difficulty relating to people in the village who appeared to spend a great part of the day just sitting around doing nothing. I would have been bored but, interestingly, the word "bored" does not exist in Micronesian languages.

In city centers, where people are expected to abide by work hours and class times, Micronesians find the transition to schedules unnatural and confining. It is not considered unusual or rude for Micronesians to come later than their appointed time. It would, however, be unusual to meet a Micronesian who was in a hurry or anxious over a deadline. Because European Americans typically view time as a commodity, the time issue causes many misunderstandings. It took most of the first semester for me to understand that student tardiness was not a sign of disrespect or apathy.

During the fall semester I was asked to present a communication workshop to local radio announcers. I had very little time to design the workshop, so I gave the support staff the course materials to duplicate and assemble. Two days before the workshop was scheduled I discovered the duplicating hadn't been completed. I expressed my concern about having the materials on time but was assured that they would be ready. I heard indirectly that if I was in such a great hurry I should do the job myself. Surprisingly, the materials were delivered one hour before I left for the radio station.

I arrived at the station ten minutes early and found only one person there. The general manager and three announcers trickled in over the next 20 minutes. As I was about to begin, the electricity shut down, leaving us without air conditioning or lights. The general manager suggested we move the workshop to the college campus. By the time we drove to the campus and settled into a classroom, 15 minutes were left of the scheduled time. I had time only for a brief introduction and an ice-breaker activity. I was disappointed that we lost virtually an entire session and that my preparation had been in vain, yet none of the participants seemed inconvenienced.

Space/Privacy

The Micronesian lifestyle is communal. Traditionally, many Micronesians live in shared areas where everything is used collectively. This idea is emphasized in the Chuukese proverb: "Meta aai epwe oomw, mea oomw epwe aai," or "What is mine is yours, and what is yours is mine." This notion remains an ideal cultural value but is mostly theoretical. In reality, Micronesians have personal property and regard it as such. Personal property may be loaned to others, but it is considered proper to ask the rightful owner for permission. Most of the time the owner will grant permission. In fact, about the only time the owner would withhold permission is when he or somebody else was using the object in question.

While the concept of private property does exist, Micronesians tend to be less attached to their belongings than are European Americans. Acquaintances who were Peace Corps volunteers on Pohnpei said this was a frustrating cultural difference that they found difficult to accept. They explained that if they wanted to keep personal possessions such as hair clips, books, or cassette players for themselves, they would have to put them away in a private place. Their Pohnpeian family's attitude toward such items was one of detachment, which is generally true for most Micronesians. For instance, if something is borrowed and subsequently lost or damaged, the owner will not express anger, because people are much more important than possessions. In contrast, European Americans tend to react to losing a possession with varying degrees of anger and, depending on the object, may perceive a loss almost as a loss of part of oneself. In the collectivist Micronesian societies, in contrast, the personality of each person is well known, but people express their individuality by their behaviors rather than their possessions.

The issue of privacy was a challenge for me in Pohnpei. As a typical European American, I highly value my privacy, but the concept of privacy is strange in Micronesian cultures because togetherness is the norm. Although most Micronesians have been exposed to American cultural patterns and accept them, they still do not fully comprehend the need for "quiet time" or privacy. Being alone is generally associated with strong emotions—for instance, avoiding an individual or group to keep from expressing strong anger toward others or hiding because of feelings of sadness or great shame. Micronesians may also think that someone desiring solitude is *mas* or "physically sick and wants to be alone."

The day I moved into my two-bedroom bungalow, the landlord sent his son over to make some repairs on the house. His three sisters followed him over, walked into my living room, tied up the curtains to let the breeze in, and sat down for a chat among themselves. They were as relaxed and natural as if they were in their own home. I, on the other hand, didn't quite know what to do. Should I offer them something to drink? Make small talk? Try to entertain them in some way? The young women were fully engaged in their conversation in Pohnpeian language, so I retreated uncomfortably to my back room to work until everyone was ready to leave. On other occasions, the children in the neighborhood would pile onto my back porch to watch the video playing on my TV. They seemed as interested in what I was doing as in the plot of the film. After some time, I noticed my boundaries relaxing, but I was never fully comfortable with the territorial differences. The most disturbing violations of my privacy were when the young men in the neighborhood looked into my windows at night. The nocturnal habits of a single *menwai* (outsider) woman were apparently entertaining.

Night-Crawling

The Chuukese term for night-crawling is *teefan*. This is the behavior in which a young man sneaks to a young woman's house at night to meet her. Strictly speaking, the man could go night-crawling only when the couple had made an arrangement. It is expected that the woman will help the man in their attempts to get together. In days gone by, the process was much easier. Houses were thatched, and all the man had to do was poke his carved wooden "love-stick" through the thatched wall and await an answer. The woman could either invite him in or ask him to wait outside by a simple push or pull of the stick. It was obviously necessary that the woman know the love-stick design of her intended lover.

Today the ritual is complicated by cinder-block or wooden walls that make the love-stick ineffective. Night-crawling continues but with an arrangement made between the lovers. Frequently I discovered evidence of such trysts near my bungalow. Large banana leaves had been used to pad the ground where young couples met. Crawling around without such prearrangement constitutes *inkikich* or peeping. The boys in my village occasionally whistled into my windows and on one occasion actually invited my visiting mother to join them in the night air. She just laughed. But night-crawling can be risky, and a man who night-crawls should expect to meet challenges. It is perfectly acceptable for the man to be beaten up by the woman's relatives if he is caught.

▶ Conclusion

I moved back to California in 1990, when I accepted a teaching position at San Joaquin Delta College in Stockton. The first day on campus I met a visiting professor who had been a Peace Corps volunteer in Micronesia. He encouraged me to teach intercultural communication because, he said, "It's an important course, great fun, and a forum for Micronesian tales."

I am glad I took his advice, because each time I share a story with students I am transported to Pohnpei. I remember the riches I gained by living among Micronesians: I was able to move beyond my ethnocentrism and better understand and value variations of human behavior. I became aware of the culturally programmed beliefs, values, and norms that determine my behaviors. Most importantly, I developed lasting intercultural relationships.

Recently, my husband and I invited Millie, now eleven years old, to live with us. She arrived from Micronesia eighteen months ago and is attending the elementary school near our home. These months together have been joyous for us all but particularly meaningful to me. Millie is Maggie's daughter—Maggie, my dear friend and former student in Pohnpei. I consider Pohnpei my second home and Maggie and her children my Micronesian family.

Now that Millie is with us, I have a renewed sense of connection with my Micronesian home and family. Each day with her brings discoveries about our life experiences and cultural assumptions. As I help her learn about American culture, I develop a deeper dimension of love for Micronesia and a greater appreciation for cultural diversity and relativity.

▶ ▶ ▶ Learning AmongUS

1. Apply the concept of monochronic and polychronic time to Marie's experiences in Micronesia.

2. What are your own expectations about touching? Whom is it appropriate for you to touch, and when, and where? How would those expectations fit with the cultural norms for touching in Micronesia?

3. Using the Micronesian and European American cultural patterns that Marie describes at the beginning of her essay, articulate your own culture's views of these dimensions.

4. Did Marie experience culture shock?

5. Which of the several exchanges that Marie recounts can best illustrate the important differences that a culture places on communicating a thought or point of view directly and indirectly to someone else?

6. In Part IV, we provide a Culture Concepts box on the distinction between high- and low-context messages. Use this distinction to interpret Marie's description of Micronesian society.

In this continuation of her earlier essay, Vicki Marie is living in the United States and raising three Micronesian children. This reading offers descriptions of intercultural competence in action as Marie and her children work to understand each other's cultural beliefs, values, norms, and social practices. The essay presents poignant moments of the joys and perils of creating and re-creating an intercultural family. Marie challenges some of the taken-for-granted assumptions about family, parenting, and cultural patterns. She also provides a case study of the ethical choices we must often confront when engaging in intercultural communication, and how her family is addressing those choices.

16 Living Interculturally: Confessions of a Menwai Nonoh

Vicki Marie

I have discovered that when I travel to a foreign land, the first person I meet when I step on its shores is myself.

That came as a surprise the first time it happened, about seventeen years ago. I had accepted a two-year contract to teach Communication in Pohnpei, Micronesia, and I arrived expecting to look around, meet new people, eat some exotic foods, and, after a couple of years, return home with a pack full of good stories. It turned out that living in a foreign culture was an enormous exercise in self-awareness. When I stepped out of the U.S. American culture, I saw it in a new light and discovered its unique dimensions—invisible dimensions that had shaped my worldview.

I discovered that values and behaviors that I took for granted—like rugged individualism, a fast-paced lifestyle, direct communication, and, for that matter, do-it-yourself home repairs—were part of a unique cultural repertoire. My new Micronesian friends did not necessarily share my perceptions of what defined the good life. In fact, from their community-oriented, gentle-paced, be-in-the-moment perspective, my approach to life seemed odd. Living on Pohnpei Island taught me about the U.S. American and Micronesian cultures and about intercultural communication. It also profoundly changed the course of my life in ways I could not have imagined.

Culture Concepts

Beliefs

Beliefs *are ideas that people assume to be true about the world. Culturally shared beliefs are so fundamental to assumptions about what the world is like and how the world operates that they are typically unnoticed.*

Culture Concepts

Values

Values *involve what a culture regards as good or bad, right or wrong, fair or unfair, just or unjust, beautiful or ugly, clean or dirty, valuable or worthless, appropriate or inappropriate, and kind or cruel. Because values are the* desired *characteristics or goals of a culture, a culture's values do not necessarily describe its* actual *behaviors and characteristics.*

Immersed in island culture and in intercultural communication research, I discovered the deeper meanings of Micronesian values. I grew emotionally attached to Pohnpei and now consider it my second home. I also became fascinated with other cultures, which launched me into world travel and led me to teach intercultural communication in California.

The most surprising twist, however, is that my husband, Forrest, and I are now raising three Micronesian children. We laugh because we are still surprised at the course our lives have taken to create our intercultural family. But we are having the best time of our lives and revel in the joy of watching Millie, Joma, and Yasuwo as they meet themselves on foreign shores.

The children's ethnicity is Micronesian and Filipino. Until they began arriving in California about eight years ago, their mother, Maggie, raised them on Pohnpei Island. Forrest is third-generation northern European American raised in Indiana, and I am second-generation Italian American raised in California. Our contrasting cultural landscapes have shaped our individual cultural perceptions and orientations. So although Millie, Joma, Yasuwo, Forrest, and I live together as a family in California for 10 months each year, our cultural lenses each project somewhat different versions of our shared reality.

The children's Micronesian beliefs, values, norms, and cultural practices are in sharp contrast to Forrest's and my European American ones. They have been socialized in a collectivistic culture; Forrest and I are individualists. They fear being harmed by evil spirits; we believe we are in control of our destinies. They prefer "being," and we enjoy "doing."

Our concepts of time are vastly different. The children expect to rest before and after they accomplish a task. They don't share our notion of wasting time, and because they view tasks as burdensome, they often procrastinate. Eventually, after many diversions and a little nudging, they will usually finish their jobs. Forrest, a product of his midwestern upbringing, has a strong work ethic but strikes a balance between work and play. I have a "rest is for sissies" approach to life and always put task before play.

I make a concerted effort to modify my "doing" temperament in relation to the children, but I admit that such cultural style-flexing isn't especially easy. To me, life is a to-do list, so when the children are "being," I perceive it as not accomplishing anything. When I ask them, "What are you doing?" and they reply, "Nothing," I may respond with "Oh, that's nice," but I actually feel mildly annoyed. Most of the time, if their homework or chores are completed, I am able to remember that "being" is a legitimate state, and I walk away. But to be honest, I do so with some discomfort. Thankfully, intercultural awareness and a sense of humor save us when my compulsive monochronic work style encounters their

Culture Concepts

Norms

Norms *are the socially shared expectations of appropriate behaviors. When a person's behaviors violate the culture's norms, social sanctions are usually imposed.*

easygoing polychronic approach to life. Understanding that our cultures have shaped us helps our family appreciate and value our differences.

Long before Millie, Joma, and Yasuwo came to live with us in California, I was introduced to Milton Bennett, the director of the Intercultural Institute in Oregon. Dr. Bennett, who had served on Chuuk Island, Micronesia, as a Peace Corps volunteer in his youth, was the keynote speaker at a convocation at Delta College in Stockton, California, where I have taught for fifteen years. That morning he advised me to consider teaching intercultural communication, humorously adding that it would provide a venue for all of my Micronesian stories. Little did I know how prophetic his advice would be. I eventually did develop and still teach an intercultural communication course at Delta College.

All the while, I had continued to correspond with my friends at the College of Micronesia, especially one Pohnpeian student, Magdalena Johnson. When Maggie bestowed on me the honor of becoming *Menwai Nonoh*—white godmother—for her daughter, Joma Marie, the loving gesture deepened our friendship. A few years later, I spent a summer on Pohnpei teaching at the College of Micronesia and reuniting with old friends, including Maggie and her family. Maggie told me then that she considered me her "promise sister," a status bestowed on very close friends.

By the end of the summer, when I returned to California, the family ties with Maggie and her children had grown even closer. It is difficult to convey the heart connection I felt with the children, despite our long-distance relationship. When Maggie would write and share her family stories, it was easy to imagine the environment, family dynamics, and sounds of their voices, because my memories of them and of living among Micronesians were so vivid. Forrest hadn't yet been to Micronesia, but through anecdotes, photos, video recordings, and telephone conversations, he came to share my kinship with Maggie and her children.

Culture Concepts

Social Practices

Social practices a*re the predictable behavior patterns that members of a culture typically follow. Social practices are the outward manifestations of beliefs, values, and norms. They can be informal, including everyday tasks such as eating, sleeping, dressing, working, playing, and talking to others, or formal, such as saluting the flag, praying in church, honoring the dead at funerals, getting married, and many other social practices.*

Eventually, we extended an invitation to Millie, Maggie's eldest daughter, to study in California. Millie was only 10 years old, but she traveled halfway around the world to live in a foreign country with people she barely knew. Soon after she arrived, it became apparent to everyone that Millie would live with us for as long as she wanted. Millie is a wonderful girl and is very persuasive, so within five years her siblings—nine-year-old Yasuwo and eleven-year-old Joma Marie—joined us to complete our intercultural family.

Considering the various configurations of U.S. American families and the multicultural nature of the United States, we think of ourselves as a typical family. We go to school and work every day. The children play sports and take dance and music lessons, and we all share the household chores. We help the kids with their homework, watch *Survivor* together on Thursday nights, and play on the weekends. We have a typical family routine.

Still, many people have been curious about our arrangement. During the school year, Millie, Joma, and Yasuwo live in California with Forrest and me, their *Menwai* parents. During summer vacations they travel home to Pohnpei to reunite with their family, friends, and culture. Some American acquaintances have told us they can't imagine how Maggie could "let her children go." But on Pohnpei, a collectivistic island culture, children are part of a large extended family that cooperates in their care. As Maggie's promise sister, I am a member of her extended family. And from a practical perspective, Maggie is a concerned mother who recognizes the limitations of the Micronesian educational system—compared with the opportunities of an American education—and who wants the best for her children. We believe our arrangement to co-parent with Maggie provides a solid education for the children so they can eventually return to Pohnpei as educated Micronesian citizens.

Some American acquaintances have predicted that the children won't want to return to Pohnpei after they complete their education. We understand that people who live in a developed Western country can't imagine living without conveniences and material wealth. In fact, the children appreciate the opportunities and amenities in the United States, but they are Pacific Islanders through and through. They adapt to and enjoy their day-to-day Californian lifestyle, but they prefer, and often yearn for, their Pohnpeian culture. They miss their family and friends, the easygoing island lifestyle, their favorite foods, and living in the rainforest. They ultimately want to return to Pohnpei to live, work, and contribute to their Micronesian community.

In the meantime, our arrangement has enriched their lives and ours. What began as a simple invitation has bloomed into a joyful family experience and an ongoing experiment in intercultural living.

Before they moved to California, Millie, Joma, and Yasuwo hadn't been exposed to a world outside their immediate village community except through American movies. They watched videos but couldn't understand the English dialogue, so they would fantasize their version of the story. By the time Millie arrived in California, Hollywood images had defined her expectations of American culture—rich, attractive, white people with perfect lives living in beautiful homes. Surprisingly, she also expected that her brown skin would turn white when she lived in the United States.

By the time Yasuwo and Joma left Pohnpei, satellite television had been pumping sitcoms, world news, and advertising into Pohnpeian homes for four years, so the younger children were more prepared for U.S. culture than Millie had been. They arrived with limited English proficiency but had picked up phrases from American programming such as "Think outside the bun" and "There goes the neighborhood."

During Millie's first few weeks in California, everything evoked a big "Wow!" Neighborhoods with manicured yards, grocery stores gorged with food, and Barbie dolls—ubiquitous Barbie dolls—were all exciting and new experiences for Millie.

When she first spotted the freeway elevated over the city streets, she gasped, "Oh, wow, look at that!" We did, and she was right, the freeway looked alien-like as it hung above the street seeming to defy gravity. She oohed and aahed at high-rise buildings, stared at the bright neon signage, cranked her neck to watch every airplane and helicopter and covered her eyes whenever she observed public affection. We couldn't have anticipated more than a fraction of the new experiences she would encounter, because we took our surroundings for granted until Millie's enthusiastic curiosity brought them to our awareness. Simultaneously, we were learning about Millie and she about us.

The first day she arrived, Millie was enchanted by the idea of an American peanut butter and jelly sandwich for lunch. Half a sandwich later, the spell had been broken by my unfortunate choice of whole-wheat-berry bread. So she began asking for soup—*malek* soup.

Our first obvious language barrier followed as I asked, "What is *malek* soup?"

"You know, *malek, malek,*" Millie said with the confidence of knowing that *malek* is *malek*.

Wanting more than anything to understand and please her, I said, "Honey, I don't know what *malek* is. Can you describe it to me?"

She puckered her lips. "Coo, coo, coo, coo," she demonstrated.

"Ah, chicken!" I said triumphantly, and both of us felt the thrill of having surmounted the language barrier.

Unfortunately, Campbell's doesn't offer *malek* soup. Although I tried, I could never replicate Maggie's *malek* soup.

The coveted Barbie doll quickly became a popular family narrative after the day I delivered an impromptu dissertation on Barbie and her perilous effect on young, innocent girls' self-concepts. That day, as Millie and I sat on the floor in the aisle of our neighborhood supermarket holding Shopping Barbie, I painstakingly explained how Barbie's unreal, Anglo-featured, big-bosomed, high-heeled, credit-card-holding image projected messages to girls about unattainable, superficial values. I ended my heartfelt speech with ". . . and that is why we don't like Barbie."

Millie pondered my boorish babble for the few seconds it took to stand up, look at me, look at Shopping Barbie and announce, matter-of-factly, "I like Barbie." She pushed the cart and sang several verses of her improvised "I like Barbie" song as we shopped for groceries. As my comeuppance, Millie happily received plenty of Barbie gear from friends and family for her birthday.

Then there was the spring day I was walking Millie home from school and she suddenly stopped in her tracks, pointed to a neighbor's lawn and, in a panicked tone, asked, "What's that?" I looked for something alarming—a dead squirrel, rotting garbage—but saw nothing. She insisted, "That, Mom!" Finally, she gathered her courage to walk closer and pointed to an automatic sprinkler head. On Pohnpei Island, which is mostly rainforest, the rainfall is 200 to 400 inches annually. For obvious reasons, there are no sprinklers. Through Millie's eyes, the automatic sprinklers looked like aliens popping up through the earth.

Other differences we saw through her eyes weren't so funny. Once a culturally insensitive teacher assumed Millie would not have an American fable to share in a class performance, so Millie was excluded from the event. In fact, she had practiced a fun Pohnpeian fable about children who stole fish from the pond of a giant. But Millie could not assert herself because of a cultural taboo that forbids children to question a teacher. When I arrived at the performance and discovered her sitting on the sidelines, I was livid. Millie had practiced her fable and was being benched, but I could see that she was even more concerned that her assertive *Menwai* mom might say something to cause the teacher to lose face. Millie asked me not to speak to the teacher. I respected her request, but after I left the school, I cried.

On Pohnpei, grandmothers, aunts, and godmothers are called Mom and are significant family caretakers. Older children bathe and often feed their younger siblings and are expected to entertain them while parents work or rest. In our California home, we are two parents who attempt to provide for all our children's needs.

Initially, Forrest and I engaged in predictable first-time parenting behaviors as we tried to make everything perfect for Millie. She loves teasing us about the organic whole-grain cereal she gagged down until she finally complained that we were trying to poison her with sawdust. But we gag when the children mix their favorite islander snack of dry Kool-Aid combined with ramen noodles. On Pohnpei, they also love to make *koko,* a favorite treat: green papayas mixed with Kool-Aid, soy sauce, salt, and pepper. Spam and canned corned beef are also considered delicious foods. Forrest and I find it impossible to fill the children's requests to buy the canned meats, because we believe they are unhealthy. On the flip side, the kids think Forrest and I are weird because we think certain foods are appropriate only for breakfast.

On the surface, the children appear to behave similarly to and show all the same likes and dislikes of typical American kids. And it is true that many elements of U.S. and Micronesian cultures overlap.

A look at Micronesian history reveals why Pohnpei has such cultural diffusion. Pohnpeian wardrobes are an amalgam of traditional and Western fashion. On Pohnpei, girls might wear traditional Pohnpeian skirts or blue jeans. Choices of cuisine also are broad. A hungry person can eat traditional foods—coconuts, bananas, breadfruit, fish, and rice—or dine on Japanese sushi or American-style hamburgers. Some Micronesian children play with toys fashioned from native materials—spears out of tree limbs or hula-hoops out of old garden hoses—but since Western hardware stores opened on Pohnpei, families that can afford to do so buy mass-produced, imported toys, bicycles, and compact-disc players.

So it might appear that Micronesian children have much in common with U.S. American children, but the significant cultural differences that shape their worldview are invisible to most outsiders. Forrest and I learn about the kids' worldview mostly through their questions (and sometimes complaints) about the curious behaviors of Americans. Some examples: "Why do people change into different clothes at night rather than sleeping in the clothes they wore that day? Why are males expected to do housework? Why are females expected to share the outdoor chores? Why isn't it OK to laugh when someone gets hurt? Why is it rude to stare? Why is it rude to burp out loud? Why is it rude to smack your lips while eating? Why don't you use your hands to eat rice? Why do Americans plan everything in advance?"

As we attempt to answer their questions, Forrest and I recognize the cultural transaction that, in effect, creates a third culture within our family.

To help them succeed in the U.S., we encourage the children to acknowledge the presence of adults, to look at people when they talk, to speak loud enough to be heard, to use direct communication, and to negotiate conflicts. They have learned that it is acceptable to tease but that they are also expected to apologize if they hurt someone's feelings. They understand our value of honesty and of making amends when a promise is broken. They are given an allowance but are expected to earn and save extra money. They are reminded to plan ahead. They own their clothes, toys, and books but are expected to share some things and be generous with others. They are told to ask before they borrow something and to return it to its owner in good order. They are taught that their opinions count in family decisions. But even though some of these values and behaviors overlap with Micronesian values, most of our expectations are distinctly U.S. American.

The most challenging task for Forrest and me—in particular for me, because I pride myself on promoting cultural relativity—is knowing where to draw the line. We often question ourselves: Are we violating the children's cultural values by not abiding by privileges bestowed on siblings according to age and gender? How can we avoid ridiculing a cultural norm, like fighting, when we strongly believe that it is unacceptable? How can we effectively teach critical-thinking skills when they collide with the Micronesian belief that one's fate can be attributed to spirits and magic? The answers are not simple. We know that our behaviors help to shape the children's worldview and that as a result of living biculturally, Millie, Joma, and Yasuwo have already adopted many U.S. American behaviors. They have learned to choose behaviors that are appropriate for their surroundings. Yasuwo, for example, has learned that although it is completely normal for Pohnpeian boys to hold hands, American boys may find it odd and pull away. Joma has learned that Americans are insulted if she laughs at their misfortunes. Fortunately, all three children understand cultural differences and have strongly maintained many of their Pohnpeian attitudes and beliefs, especially about respect, family, and other important values. This is especially evident each summer when they are ecstatic about going home where everything and everyone is comfortably familiar.

I've asked the children if it is difficult to switch their thinking and behaviors when they move between cultures. "A little," they say, explaining that it is easier to move from California to Pohnpei because Micronesian culture is slower-paced and less demanding. Millie says that when she goes home to Pohnpei, cultural expectations are easy to remember because they are common sense. Every once in a while, she says, she behaves in an assertive American manner and receives a pinch or warning glance from her mom, Maggie, with the admonishment *kilmesul*, which translates as "thick-headed." The Micronesian idiom *kilmesul* is loosely equivalent to the American English idiom "to be dense" and means that a person should just know how to behave without being told directly—a clear example of Pohnpei's high-context culture.

I asked Millie if Micronesians' willingness to initiate conversation had changed over the years. She asked, "You mean like in the States when you ask someone for the time? Well, first of all, Mom, nobody cares about the time. If you just go up and start a conversation, they will think you are putting yourself up and that you are *kilmesul*. We aren't like Americans who think they can do anything they want."

She illustrated: "If a Pohnpeian is walking with a friend or cousin and meets up with an acquaintance, there are no formal introductions. If they continue walking together the conversation between the three will eventually blend without any obvious effort, but if you make a big deal about introducing everyone, they'll think you're weird—unless you are a *Menwai*, and in that case, Pohnpeians just know that's how you are."

Most of the differences in our perceptions and experiences are funny and relatively inconsequential. But having Millie, Joma, and Yasuwo in our lives has heightened our awareness of everyday racism in the United States. As European Americans, we've always known racism is culturally harmful to all people but until we lived with the kids, our Eurocentric culture with its invisible privileges had sheltered us from the gut-wrenching, heartbreaking effects of prejudice that children of color often encounter. We've experienced stress when our child, who had limited English proficiency, was assigned a desk in the back of the classroom, neglected by the teacher, and forced to depend on the kindness of new friends to help her understand the homework assignments. We've felt irritated when a teacher constantly mispronounced our child's name, which, in turn, caused her classmates to mispronounce it, too. We felt horrible when our child was hurt and frightened by bigoted remarks from classmates. We were infuriated when a teacher who hadn't checked her cultural bias at the classroom door excluded our child from a class performance. We were saddened when our child expressed self-rejection because of his skin color and ethnicity. Racism became very personal and utterly unacceptable when we found ourselves dealing with its effects firsthand.

As parents of Micronesian children, we can barely tolerate the occasional acquaintance who attributes others' prejudiced behavior to coincidence, misperception, or oversensitivity on our part. We've heard the well-meaning platitudes—"Oh, I doubt if she meant anything by it," "Maybe you are being too sensitive," "Well, just ignore it"—but as parents who have seen the effects of prejudice on our children's self-concepts, dismissing it as an imaginary problem is insulting. We try to counterbalance the negative messages with positive messages about our children and about all cultures. The indirect experience of prejudice has made me, as a college instructor, more empathetic and has strengthened my resolve and commitment to include unlearning racism concepts in my communication studies courses. And as a mom, I would do anything to protect my children from the negative effects of racism.

It has been interesting to watch how the kids have adapted to the U.S. American culture without losing themselves. Socially, it was easier when they were in elementary school, where diverse groups of children blend naturally in the classroom and on the playground. It seemed more difficult when, as a preteen, Millie entered middle school where culturally diverse students positioned themselves by class, ethnicity, and race. Since middle school, Millie is most comfortable socializing with people of color. Wherever we are, all three kids notice who is present and who is missing in social situations. They look for people they can relate to and can spot Pacific Islanders a mile away. During two family vacations—one on the California central coast and one in the foothills east of Sacramento—Millie remarked that the areas are beautiful but that she would never be comfortable living in the communities there because they have too few people of color. To be honest, I hadn't noticed the lack of diversity in those areas until Millie brought it to my attention. When we took her to tour the universities in Hawaii, she was just as interested in the cultural diversity of the student population as she was in the academic programs and class offerings. As Millie matures, she expresses a deep yearning to socialize with culturally similar others—especially other Pacific Islanders.

In our California home it is impossible to simulate living in the rainforest, or to replicate Maggie's home cooking, or to step fully into the cultural mindset of our children. But in addition to serving considerably more chicken, rice, and mangoes at mealtime than we would otherwise, each day we invite Pohnpei and Maggie into our lives through photographs, Micronesian handicrafts displayed throughout our home, and daily conversations about our Pohnpeian family. We often read about Pohnpei, and the children frequently talk with Maggie on the telephone and over the Internet. Every day they listen to island music, sing Pohnpeian songs while they wash the dinner dishes, and use their native language exclusively with each other. They attempt to teach their *Menwai* parents a few Pohnpeian words—more for their entertainment than our enrichment. Their unbridled laughter makes it obvious when they are enjoying inside jokes and Pohnpeian humor. The girls wear their traditional Pohnpeian skirts and have joined a Polynesian dance troupe. We have an occasional visitor from Micronesia, but Millie communicates frequently with other Micronesians through Internet chat rooms. And, of course, they spend every summer soaking up their Pohnpeian culture and the cultural fuel that propels them through the next school year.

In our wildest imaginations, Forrest and I could have never guessed we would be parenting three Pohnpeian children. We shifted from happy, self-indulgent yuppies to happier, homework-weary parents who are grateful for each day we share as an intercultural family. We have watched Millie, Joma, and Yasuwo become impressively bicultural as they maneuver their way

> ## **Culture** Concepts
>
> ### Description, Interpretation, and Evaluation
>
> *The interaction tool called description, interpretation, and evaluation allows people to understand how they think about, and then verbally speak about, the people with whom they interact and the events in which they participate. This skill trains people to distinguish among statements of description, interpretation, and evaluation. These statements can be made about all characteristics, events, persons, or objects. A statement of* description *details the specific perceptual cues and information a person has received, without judgments or interpretations—in other words, without being distorted by opinion. A statement of* interpretation *provides a conjecture or hypothesis about what the perceptual information might mean. A* statement *of evaluation indicates an emotional or affective judgment about the information. By separating description, interpretation, and evaluation, you can control the meanings you attribute to the verbal and nonverbal symbols used by others.*

through the U.S. culture with grace and ease. We love reminding the kids how courageous and capable they are and how much we adore them. In concert with Maggie, we want more than anything to help these children grow into intelligent, responsible people who have a strong sense of themselves, their culture, and the world in which they live.

▶ ▶ ▶ Learning AmongUS

1. What should Marie's role be in affirming or sustaining the cultural beliefs, values, norms, and cultural practices of Micronesia while the three children are living with her in the United States?

2. Marie describes Millie's reactions to many of the taken-for-granted assumptions Marie has about her physical and social world. Look at your physical and social world and identify as many assumptions as you can.

3. Using the three ethical dilemmas previously presented in Culture Concepts boxes, evaluate the choices that Marie is making by raising Micronesian children in the United States. How would you solve these dilemmas if you were her?

4. Take one of the stories that Marie relates, and apply the tool of description, interpretation, and evaluation to it.

PART THREE

Othering

*Racism and Prejudice
AmongUS*

17 Cultural Biases and Intercultural Communication[1]

Myron W. Lustig and Jolene Koester

Interaction only within our own culture produces a number of obvious benefits. Because the culture provides predictability, the threat of the unknown is reduced. When something or someone that is unknown or unpredictable enters a culture, the culture's beliefs, values, norms, and social practices tell people how to interpret and respond appropriately, thus reducing the perceived threat of the intrusion. These cultural patterns also allow for automatic responses to stimuli; in essence, cultural patterns save people time and energy.

Intercultural communication, by definition, means that people are interacting with at least one culturally different person. Consequently, the sense of security, comfort, and predictability that characterizes communication with culturally similar people is lost. The greater the degree of interculturalness, the greater the loss of predictability and certainty. Assurances about the accuracy of interpretations of verbal and nonverbal messages are lost.

Terms that are often used when communicating with culturally different people include *unknown, unpredictable, ambiguous, weird, mysterious, unexplained, exotic, unusual, unfamiliar, curious, novel, odd, outlandish,* and *strange.* As you read this list, consider how the choice of a particular word might also reflect a particular value. What characteristics, values, and knowledge allow individuals to respond more competently to the threat of dealing with cultural differences? What situations heighten the perception of threat among members of different cultural groups? To answer questions such as these, we need to explore how people make sense of information about others as they categorize or classify others in their social world.

▶ Social Categorizing

Three features in the way all humans process information about others are important to your understanding of intercultural communication. First, as cognitive psychologists have repeatedly demonstrated, people impose a pattern on their world by organizing the stimuli that bombard their senses into conceptual categories. Every waking moment, people are presented with literally hundreds of different perceptual stimuli. Therefore, it becomes necessary to simplify the information by selecting, organizing, and reducing it to less complex forms. That is, to comprehend stimuli, people organize them into categories, groupings, and patterns. As a child, you might have completed drawings by connecting numbered dots. Emerging from the lines was the figure of an animal or a familiar toy. Even though the form was not completely drawn, it was relatively easy to identify. This kind of recognition occurs simply because human beings have a tendency to organize perceptual cues to impose meaning, usually by using familiar experiences.

Second, most people tend to think that others perceive, evaluate, and reason about the world in the same ways they do. In other words, humans assume that other people with whom they interact are like themselves. Indeed, it is quite common for people to draw on their personal experiences to understand and evaluate the motivations of others. This common human tendency is sometimes called "ethnocentrism."

Third, humans simplify the processing and organizing of information from the environment by identifying certain characteristics as belonging to certain categories of persons and events. For example, a child's experiences with several dogs that growled and snapped are likely to result in a future reaction to other dogs as if they will also growl and snap. The characteristics of particular events, persons, or objects, once experienced, are often assumed to be typical of similar events, persons, or objects. Though these assumptions are sometimes accurate, often they are not. Not all dogs necessarily growl and snap at young children. Nevertheless, information processing results in a simplification of the world, so that prior experiences are used as the basis for determining both the categories and the attributes of the events. This process is called "stereotyping."

Please note that we are simply describing these human tendencies, not evaluating them as good or bad. Their obvious advantage is that they allow people to respond efficiently to a variety of perceptual stimuli. Nevertheless, such organization and simplification can create genuine obstacles to intercultural competence because they may lead to prejudice, discrimination, and racism.

▶ Ethnocentrism

All cultures teach their members the "preferred" ways to respond to the world, often labeled "natural" or "appropriate." Thus people generally perceive their own experiences, which are shaped by their own cultural forces, as natural, human, and universal. This belief that the customs and practices of one's own culture are superior to those of other cultures is called *ethnocentrism*.

Cultures also train their members to use the categories of their own cultural experiences when judging the experiences of people from other cultures. Our culture tells us that the way we were taught to behave is "right" or "correct," and that those who do things differently are wrong. William G. Sumner, who first introduced the concept of ethnocentrism, defined it as "the view of things in which one's own group is the center of everything, and all others are scaled and rated with reference to it."[2] Sumner illustrates how ethnocentrism works in the following example:

> When Caribs were asked whence they came, they replied, "We alone are people." "Kiowa" means real or principal people. A Laplander is a "man" or "human being." The highest praise a Greenlander has for a European visiting the island is that the European by studying virtue and good manners from the Greenlanders soon will be as good as a Greenlander. Nature peoples call themselves "men" as a rule. All others are something else, but not men. The Jews divide all mankind into themselves and Gentiles—they being the "chosen people." The Greeks and Romans called outsiders "barbarians." Arabs considered themselves as the noblest nation and all others as barbarians. Russian books and newspapers talk about its civilizing mission, and so do the books and journals of France, Germany, and the United States. Each nation now regards itself as the leader of civilization, the best, the freest, and the wisest. All others are inferior.[3]

Ethnocentrism is a learned belief in cultural superiority. Because cultures teach people what the world is "really like" and what is "good," people consequently believe that the values of their culture are natural and correct. Thus people from other cultures who do things differently are wrong. When combined with the natural human tendency to prefer what is typically experienced, ethnocentrism produces emotional reactions to cultural differences that reduce people's willingness to understand disparate cultural messages.

Ethnocentrism tends to highlight and exaggerate cultural differences. As an interesting instance of ethnocentrism, consider beliefs about body odor. Most U.S. Americans spend large sums of money each year to rid themselves of natural body odor. They then replace their natural odors with artificial ones, by using deodorants, bath powders, shaving lotions, perfumes, hair sprays, shampoos, mousse, gels, toothpaste, mouthwash, and breath mints. Many U.S. Americans probably believe that they do not have an odor—even after they have routinely applied most, if not all, of the artificial ones in the preceding list. Yet the same individuals will react negatively to culturally different others who do not remove natural body odors and who refuse to apply artificial ones.

Another example of ethnocentrism concerns the way in which cultures teach people to discharge mucus from the nose. Most U.S. Americans purchase boxes of tissues and strategically place them at various locations in their homes, offices, and cars so they will be available for use as needed. In countries where paper products had historically been scarce and very expensive, people blow their noses onto the ground or the street. Pay attention to your reaction as you read this last statement. Most U.S. Americans, when learning about this behavior, react with a certain amount of disgust. But think about the U.S. practice of blowing one's nose into a tissue or handkerchief, which is then placed on the desk or into a pocket or purse. Now ask yourself which is really more disgusting—carrying around tissues with dried mucus in them or blowing the mucus onto the street? Described in this way, both practices have a certain element of repugnance, but because one's culture teaches that there is one preferred way, that custom is familiar and comfortable and the practices of other cultures are seen as wrong or distasteful. Ethnocentrism can occur along all of the dimensions of cultural patterns. People from individualistic cultures, for instance, find the idea that a person's self-concept is tied to a group to be unfathomable. To most U.S. Americans, the idea of an arranged marriage seems strange at best and a confining and reprehensible limitation on personal freedom at worst.

One area of behavior that quickly reveals ethnocentrism is personal hygiene. For example, U.S. Americans like to see themselves as the cleanest people on earth. In the United States, bathrooms contain sinks, showers or bathtubs, and toilets, thus allowing the efficient use of water pipes. Given this arrangement, people bathe themselves close to the toilet, where they urinate and defecate. Described in this way, the cultural practices of the United States may seem unclean, peculiar, and even absurd. Why would people in a so-called modern society complete two such contradictory functions next to each other? People from many other cultures, who consider the U.S. arrangement to be unclean and unhealthy, share that sentiment. Our point here is that what is familiar and comfortable inevitably seems the best, right, and natural way of doing things. Judgments about what is "right" or "natural" create emotional responses to cultural differences that may interfere with our ability to understand the symbols used by other cultures. For example, European Americans think it is "human nature" to orient oneself to the future and to want to improve one's material status in life. Individuals whose cultures have been influenced by alternative forces, resulting in contrary views, are often judged negatively and treated with derision.

To be a competent intercultural communicator, you must realize that you typically use the categories of your own culture to judge and interpret the behaviors of those who are culturally different from you. You must also be aware of your own emotional reactions to the sights, sounds, smells, and variations in message systems that you encounter when communicating with people from other cultures. The competent intercultural communicator does not necessarily suppress negative feelings, but acknowledges their existence and seeks to minimize their effect on his or her communication. If you are reacting strongly to some aspect of another culture, seek out an explanation in the ethnocentric preferences that your culture has taught you.

▶ Stereotyping

Journalist Walter Lippmann introduced the term *stereotyping* in 1922 to refer to a selection process that is used to organize and simplify perceptions of others.[4] Stereotypes are a form of generalization about some group of people. When people stereotype others, they make assertions about the characteristics of all people who belong to a given category. The consequence of stereotyping is that the vast degree of differences that exist among the members of any one group may not be taken into account in the interpretation of messages.

To illustrate how stereotyping works, read the following list: college professors, surfers, Marxists, Democrats, bankers, New Yorkers, Californians. As you read each of these categories, was it relatively easy for you to associate particular characteristics and traits with each group? Now imagine that a person from one of these groups walked into the room and began a conversation with you. In all likelihood you would associate the group's characteristics with that specific individual.

Your responses to this simple example illustrate what typically occurs when people are stereotyped.[5] First, someone identifies an outgroup category—"they"—whose characteristics differ from those in one's own social ingroup. Next, the perceived dissimilarities between the groups are enlarged and accentuated, thereby creating differences that are clearer and more distinct. Sharper and more pronounced boundaries between the groups make it more difficult for individuals to move from one group to another.[6] Concurrently, an evaluative component is introduced, whereby the characteristics of the outgroup are negatively judged; that is, the outgroup is regarded as wrong, inferior, or stigmatized as a result of given characteristics. Finally, the group's characteristics are attributed to all people who belong to the group, so a specific person is not treated as a unique individual but as a typical member of a category.

Categories that are used to form stereotypes about groups of people can vary widely, and might include the following:

- Regions of the world (Asians, Arabs, South Americans, Africans)
- Countries (Kenya, Japan, China, France, Great Britain)
- Regions within countries (northern Indians, southern Indians, U.S. midwesterners, U.S. southerners)
- Cities (New Yorkers, Parisians, Londoners)
- Cultures (English, French, Latino, Russian, Serbian, Yoruba, Mestizo, Thai, Navajo)
- Race (African, Caucasian)
- Religion (Muslim, Hindu, Buddhist, Jewish, Christian)
- Age (young, old, middle-aged, children, adults)
- Occupations (teacher, farmer, doctor, housekeeper, mechanic, architect, musician)
- Relational roles (mother, friend, father, sister, brother)
- Physical characteristics (short, tall, fat, skinny)
- Social class (wealthy, poor, middle class)

This list is by no means exhaustive. What it should illustrate is the enormous range of possibilities for classification and simplification. Consider your own stereotypes of people in these groups. Many may have been created by direct experience with only one or two people from a particular group. Others are probably based on secondhand information and opinions, output from the mass media, and general habits of thinking; they may even have been formed without any direct experience with individuals from the group. Yet many people are prepared to assume that the stereotype is an accurate representation of all members of a specific group.[7] Interestingly, stereotypes that are based on secondhand opinions—that is, stereotypes derived from the opinions of others or from the media—tend to be more extreme, less variable from one person to another, more uniformly applied to others, and more resistant to change than stereotypes based on direct personal experiences and interactions.[8]

Stereotypes can be inaccurate in three ways.[9] First, as we have suggested, stereotypes often are assumed to apply to all or most of the members of a particular group or category, resulting in a tendency to ignore differences among the individual members of the group. This type of stereotyping error is called the *outgroup homogeneity effect* and results in a tendency to regard all members of a particular group as much more similar to one another than they actually are.[10] Arab Americans, for instance, complain that other U.S. Americans often hold undifferentiated stereotypes about members of their culture. Albert Mokhiber laments,

> If there's problem in Libya we're all Libyans. If the problem is in Lebanon we're all Lebanese. If it happens to be Iran, which is not an Arab country, we're all Iranians. Conversely, Iranians were picked on during the Gulf War as being Arabs. Including one fellow who called in who was a Polynesian Jew. But he looked like what an Arab should look like, and he felt the wrath of anti-Arab discrimination. Nobody's really free from this. The old civil rights adage says that as long as the rights of one are in danger, we're all in danger. I think we need to break out of our ethnic ghetto mentality, all of us, from various backgrounds, and realize that we're in this stew together.[11]

A second form of stereotype inaccuracy occurs when the group average, as suggested by the stereotype, is simply wrong or inappropriately exaggerated. This type of inaccuracy occurs, for instance, when Germans are stereotypically regarded as being very efficient, or perhaps very rigid, when they may actually be less efficient or less rigid than the exaggerated perception of them would warrant.

A third form of stereotype inaccuracy occurs when the degree of error and exaggeration differs for positive and negative attributes. For instance, imagine that you have stereotyped members of a culture as being very efficient (a positive attribute) but also very rigid and inflexible in their business relationships (a negative attribute). If you tend to overestimate the prevalence and importance of the culture's positive characteristics, such as its degree of efficiency, while simultaneously ignoring or underestimating its rigidity and other negative characteristics, you would have a "positive valence inaccuracy." Conversely, a "negative valence inaccuracy" occurs if you exaggerated the negative attributes while ignoring or devaluing its positive ones. This latter condition, often called *prejudice,* is discussed in greater detail later.

The problems associated with using stereotyping as a means of understanding individuals is best illustrated by identifying the groups to which you belong. Think about the characteristics that might be stereotypically assigned to those groups. Determine whether the characteristics apply to you or to others in your group. Some of them may be accurate descriptions; many, however, will be totally inaccurate, and you would resent being thought of in that way. Stereotypes distort or hide the individual. Ultimately, people may become blind to the actual characteristics of the group because not all stereotypes are accurate. Most are based on relatively minimal experiences with particular individuals.

Stereotype inaccuracy can lead to errors in interpretations and expectations about the behaviors of others. Interpretation errors occur because stereotypes are used not only to categorize specific individuals and events but also to judge them. That is, one potentially harmful consequence of stereotypes is that they provide inaccurate labels for a group of people that are then used to interpret subsequent ambiguous events and experiences involving members of those groups. Ziva Kunda and Bonnie Sherman-Williams note:

> Consider, for example, the unambiguous act of failing a test. Ethnic stereotypes may lead perceivers to attribute such failure to laziness if the actor is Asian but to low ability if the actor is Black. Thus stereotypes will affect judgments of the targets' ability even if subjects base these judgments only on the act, because the stereotypes will determine the meaning of the act.[12]

Because stereotypes are sometimes applied indiscriminately to members of a particular culture or social group, they can also lead to errors in our expectations about the future behaviors of others. Stereotypes provide the basis for estimating, often inaccurately, what members of the stereotyped group are likely to do. Most disturbingly, stereotypes will likely persist even when members of the stereotyped group repeatedly behave in ways that disconfirm them. Once a stereotype has taken hold, members of the stereotyped group who behave in nonstereotypical ways will be expected to compensate in future actions to "make up for" their atypical behavior. Even when some individuals from a stereotyped group repeatedly deviate from expectations, they may be regarded as exceptions or as atypical members of their group. Indeed, stereotypes may remain intact, or may even be strengthened, in the face of disconfirming experiences; those who hold the stereotypes often expect that the other members of the stereotyped social group will be even *more* likely to behave as the stereotype predicts to "balance out" or compensate for the "unusual" instances they experienced. That is, stereotypes encourage people to expect future behaviors that compensate for perceived inconsistencies, and thus allow people to anticipate future events in a way that makes it unnecessary to revise their deeply held beliefs and values.[13]

The process underlying stereotyping is absolutely essential for human beings to function. Some categorization is necessary and normal. Indeed, there is survival value in the ability to make accurate generalizations about others, and stereotypes function as mental "energy-saving devices" to help make those generalizations efficiently.[14] However, stereotypes may also promote prejudice and discrimination directed toward members of cultures other than one's own. Intercultural competence requires an ability to move beyond stereotypes and to respond to the individual. Previous experiences should be used only as guidelines or suggested interpretations rather than as hard-and-fast categories. Judee Burgoon, Charles Berger, and Vincent Waldron suggest that mindfulness—that is, paying conscious attention to the nature and basis of our stereotypes—can help reduce stereotype inaccuracies and thereby decrease intercultural misunderstandings.[15]

▶ Prejudice

Prejudice refers to negative attitudes toward other people that are based on faulty and inflexible stereotypes. Prejudiced attitudes include irrational feelings of dislike and even hatred for certain groups, biased perceptions and beliefs about the group members that are not based on direct experiences and firsthand knowledge, and a readiness to behave in negative and unjust ways toward members of the group. Gordon Allport, who first focused scholarly attention on prejudice, argued that prejudiced people ignore evidence that is inconsistent with their biased viewpoint, or they distort the evidence to fit their prejudices.[16]

The strong link between prejudice and stereotypes should be obvious. Prejudiced thinking depends on stereotypes and is a fairly normal phenomenon.[17] To be prejudiced toward a group of people sometimes makes it easier to respond to them. We are not condoning prejudice or the hostile and violent actions that may occur as a result. We are suggesting that prejudice is a universal psychological process; all people have a propensity for prejudice toward others who are unlike themselves. For individuals to move beyond prejudicial attitudes and for societies to avoid basing social structures on their prejudices about groups of people, it is critical to recognize the prevalence of prejudicial thinking.

What functions does prejudice serve? We have already suggested that the thought process underlying prejudice includes the need to organize and simplify the world. Richard Brislin describes four additional benefits, or what he calls functions, of prejudice.[18] First, he suggests that prejudice satisfies a *utilitarian* or adjustment function. Displaying certain kinds of prejudice means that people receive rewards and avoid punishments. For example, if you express prejudicial statements about certain people, other people may like you more. It is also easier to simply dislike and be prejudiced toward members of other groups because they can then be dismissed without going through the effort necessary to adjust to them. Another function that prejudice serves is an *ego-defensive* one; it protects self-esteem.[19] If others say or do things that are inconsistent with the images we hold of ourselves, our sense of self may be deeply threatened, and we may try to maintain our self-esteem by scorning the sources of the message. So, for example, people who are unsuccessful in business may feel threatened by groups whose members are successful. Prejudice may function to protect our self-image by denigrating or devaluing those who might make us feel less worthy.[20]

Still another advantage of prejudicial attitudes is the *value-expressive* function. If people believe that their group has certain qualities that are unique, valuable, good, or in some way special, their prejudicial attitudes toward others is a way of expressing those values. Finally, Brislin describes the *knowledge function* as prejudicial attitudes that people hold because of their need to have the world neatly organized and boxed into categories. This function takes the normal human proclivity to organize the world to an extreme. The rigid application of categories and the prejudicial attitudes assigned to certain behaviors and beliefs provide security and increase predictability. Obviously, these functions cannot be neatly applied to all instances of prejudice. Nor are people usually aware of the specific reasons for their prejudices. For each person, prejudicial attitudes may serve several functions.

▶ Discrimination

Whereas *prejudice* refers to people's attitudes or mental representations, the term *discrimination* refers to the behavioral manifestations of that prejudice. Thus discrimination can be thought of as prejudice "in action."

Discrimination can occur in many forms. From the extremes of segregation and apartheid to biases in the availability of housing, employment, education, economic resources, personal safety, and legal protections, discrimination represents unequal treatment of certain individuals solely because of their membership in a particular group. Teun van Dijk conducted a series of studies of people's everyday conversations as they discuss different racial and cultural groups. Van Dijk concluded that when individuals make prejudicial comments, tell jokes that belittle and dehumanize others, and share negative stereotypes about others, they are establishing and legitimizing the existence of their prejudices and laying the "communication groundwork" that will make it acceptable for people to perform discriminatory acts.[21]

Often, biases and displays of discrimination are motivated not by direct hostility toward some other group but merely by a strong preference for, and loyalty to, our own culture.[22] Thus the formation of our cultural identity can sometimes lead to hostility, hate, and discrimination directed against nonmembers of that culture.

▶ Racism

One obstacle to intercultural competence to which we want to give special attention is racism. Because racism often plays such a major role in the communication that occurs between people of different races or ethnic groups, it is particularly important to understand how and why it occurs.

The word *racism* itself can evoke very powerful emotional reactions, especially for those who have felt the oppression and exploitation that stems from racist attitudes and behaviors. For members of the African American, Asian American, Native American, and Latino cultures, racism has created a social history shaped by prejudice and discrimination.[23] For individual members of these groups, racism has resulted in the pain of oppression. To those who are members of cultural groups that have had the power to oppress and exploit others, the term *racism* often evokes equally powerful thoughts and emotional reactions that deny responsibility for and participation in racist acts and thinking. In this section we introduce some ideas about racism that illuminate the reactions of both those who have received racist communication and those who are seen as exhibiting it.

Robert Blauner has described racism as a tendency to categorize people who are culturally different in terms of their physical traits such as skin color, hair color and texture, facial structure, and eye shape.[24] Dalmas Taylor offers a related approach that focuses on the behavioral components of racism. Taylor defines racism as the cumulative effects of individuals, institutions, and cultures that result in the oppression of ethnic minorities.[25] Taylor's approach is useful because it recognizes that racism can occur at three distinct levels: individual, institutional, and cultural.

At the individual level, racism is conceptually similar to prejudice. Individual racism involves beliefs, attitudes, and behaviors of a given person toward people of a different racial group.[26] Specific European Americans, for example, who believe that African Americans are somehow inferior exemplify individual racism. Positive contact and interaction between members of the two groups can sometimes change these attitudes. Yet as the preceding discussion of prejudice suggests, people with prejudicial beliefs about others often distort new information to fit their original prejudices.

At the institutional level, racism is the exclusion of certain people from equal participation in a society's institutions solely because of their race.[27] Institutional racism is built into such social structures as the government, schools, and industry practices. It leads to certain patterns of behaviors and responses to specific racial or cultural groups that allow those groups to be systematically exploited and oppressed. For example, institutional racism has precluded both Jews and African Americans from attending certain public schools and universities, and at times it has restricted their participation in particular professions.[28] Repeated instances of institutional racism, which commonly appear in the popular media, can be especially difficult to overcome. By focusing on some topics or characteristics and not on others, the media often prime people's attention and thereby influence the interpretations and evaluations we make of others. Such biased portrayals can be particularly salient when the media provide people's primary or only knowledge of particular cultures and their members. Consider, for example, Elizabeth Bird's insightful analysis of the ways in which Native Americans are marginalized by the popular media's portrayal of their sexuality:

> The representations we see are structured in predictable, gendered ways. Women are faceless, rather sexless squaws in minor roles, or sexy exotic princesses or maidens who desire White men. Men are either handsome

young warriors, who desire White women, or safe sexless wise elders, who dispense ancient wisdom. Nowhere, in this iconography, do the male and female images meet. The world where American Indian men and women love, laugh, and couple *together* lurks far away in the shadows. These days, representations of American Indians are more accurate, in terms of costume, cultural detail, and the like than in the 1950s, when White actors darkened their skins to play American Indians. As far as suggesting an authentic, subjective American Indian experience, though, there has been little progress.[29]

As Bird concludes of such portrayals, "the lovely princess and American Indian lover of the 1990s may be more benign images than the squaw or the crazed savage, but they are equally unreal, and ultimately, equally dehumanizing."[30]

At the cultural level, racism denies the existence of the culture of a particular group;[31] for example, the denial that African Americans represent a unique and distinct culture separate from both European American culture and all African cultures. Cultural racism also involves the rejection by one group of the beliefs and values of another, such as the "negative evaluations by whites of black cultural values."[32]

Though racism is often used synonymously with *prejudice* and *discrimination,* the social attributes that distinguish it from these other terms are oppression and power. *Oppression* refers to "the systematic, institutionalized mistreatment of one group of people by another."[33] Thus racism is the tendency by groups in control of institutional and cultural power to use it to keep members of groups who do not have access to the same kinds of power at a disadvantage. Racism oppresses entire groups of people, making it very difficult, and sometimes virtually impossible, for their members to have access to political, economic, and social power.[34]

Forms of racism vary in intensity and degree of expression, with some far more dangerous and detrimental to society than others. The most extreme form of racism is *old-fashioned racism,* in which members of one group openly display obviously bigoted views about members of another group. Judgments of superiority and inferiority are commonplace in this kind of racism, and there is a dehumanizing quality to it. African Americans and other cultural groups in the United States have often experienced this form of racism from other U.S. Americans.

In *symbolic racism,* the form currently prevalent in the United States, members of one group believe that people from some other group threaten their traditional values, such as individualism and self-reliance. Fears that the outgroup will achieve economic or social success, with a simultaneous loss of economic or social status by the ingroup, typify this form of racism. In many parts of the United States, for instance, this type of racism has been directed toward Asians and Asian Americans who have achieved economic success. Similarly, symbolic racism includes the expression of feelings that members of cultures such as African Americans and Mexican Americans are moving too fast in seeking social change, are too demanding of equality and social justice, are not playing by the rules established in previous generations, and simply do not deserve all they have recently gained. Paradoxically, while symbolic racists typically do not feel personally threatened by the successes of other cultures, they fear for their core values and the continued maintenance of their political and economic power.[35]

Tokenism as a form of racism occurs when individuals do not perceive themselves as prejudiced because they make small concessions to, while holding basically negative attitudes toward, members of the other group. Tokenism is the practice of reverse discrimination, in which people go out of their way to favor a few members of another group to maintain their own self-concepts as individuals who believe in equality for all. While such behaviors may increase a person's esteem, they may also decrease the possibilities for more meaningful contributions to intercultural unity and progress.

Aversive racism, like tokenism, occurs when individuals who value fairness and equality among all racial and cultural groups nevertheless have negative beliefs and feelings about members of a particular race, often as a result of childhood socialization experiences. Individuals with such conflicting feelings may restrain their overt racist behaviors, but they may also avoid close contact with members of the other group and may express their underlying negative attitudes subtly, in ways that appear rational and can be justified on the basis of some factor other than race or culture. Thus the negativity of aversive racists "is more likely to be manifested in discomfort, uneasiness, fear, or avoidance of minorities rather than overt hostility."[36] An individual at work, for instance, may be polite but distant to a coworker from another culture but may avoid that person at a party they both happen to attend.

Genuine likes and dislikes may also operate as a form of racism. The cultural practices of some groups of people can form the basis for a prejudicial attitude simply because the group displays behaviors that another group does not like. For example, individuals from cultures that are predominantly vegetarian may develop negative attitudes toward those who belong to cultures that eat meat.

Finally, the least alarming form of racism, and certainly one that everyone has experienced, is based on the *degree of unfamiliarity* with members of other groups. Simply responding to unfamiliar people may create negative attitudes because of a lack of experience with the characteristics of their group. The others may look, smell, talk, or act differently, all of which can be a source of discomfort and can form the basis for racist or prejudicial attitudes.

▶ Overcoming Cultural Biases

Ethnocentrism, stereotyping, prejudice, discrimination, and racism are so familiar and comfortable that overcoming them requires a commitment both to learning about other cultures and to understanding one's own. A willingness to explore various cultural experiences without prejudgment is necessary. An ability to behave appropriately and effectively with culturally different others, without invoking prejudiced and stereotyped assumptions, is required. Although no one can completely overcome the cultural biases that naturally exist, the requisite knowledge, motivation, and skill can certainly help minimize the negative effects of prejudice and discrimination.

As inhabitants of the twenty-first century, you will no longer have a choice about whether to live in a world of many cultures. The forces that bring people from other cultures into your life are dynamic, potent, and ever present.

The tensions inherent in creating successful intercultural relationships, communities, and nations are obvious. Examples abound that underscore how difficult it is for groups of culturally different individuals to live, work, and play together harmoniously. The consequences of failing to create a harmonious intercultural society are also obvious—human suffering, hatred passed on from one generation to another, disruptions in people's lives, and unnecessary conflicts that sap people's creative talents and energies and siphon off scarce resources from other important societal needs.

To improve your intercultural communication by building positive motivations, or emotional reactions, to intercultural interactions, take an honest inventory of the various ways in which you categorize other people. Can you identify your obvious ethnocentric attitudes about appearances, foods, and social practices? Make a list of the stereotypes, both positive and negative, that you hold about the various cultural groups with which you regularly interact. Now identify those stereotypes that others might hold about your culture. By engaging in this kind of self-reflective process, you are becoming more aware of the ways in which your social categorizations detract from an ability to understand communication from culturally different others.

There are no simple prescriptions or pat answers that can guarantee competent intercultural communication in all settings. Nor has anyone discovered how to eliminate the destructive consequences of prejudice, discrimination, and racism. Nevertheless, the joys and benefits of embracing an intercultural world are many. As the world is transformed into a place where cultural boundaries cease to be impenetrable barriers, differences among people become reasons to celebrate and share rather than to fear and harm. The opportunities to understand, experience, and benefit from unfamiliar ways are unprecedented.

The intercultural challenge for all of us now living in a world in which interactions with people from different cultures are common features of daily life is to be willing to grapple with the consequences of prejudice, discrimination, and racism at the individual, social, and institutional levels. Because "prejudice" and "racism" are such emotionally charged concepts, it is sometimes difficult to comment on their occurrence in our interactions with others. Individuals who believe that they have perceived discriminatory remarks and actions often feel that they cannot risk the resentment of their coworkers, fellow students, teachers, or service providers that would likely occur should they demand interactions that do not display prejudice against them. Conversely, those who do not regard themselves as having prejudiced or racist attitudes and who believe they never behave in discriminatory ways are horrified to learn that others might interpret their attitudes as prejudiced and their actions as discriminatory. While discussions about prejudice, discrimination, and racism can lead to a better understanding of the interpersonal dynamics that arise as individuals seek to establish mutually respectful relationships, they can just as easily lead to greater divisions and hostilities between people.

The need for an intercultural mentality to match our multicultural world, the cultural biases that must be overcome in the quest of such a goal, the excitement of the challenges, and the rewards of the successes are summarized in the words of Troy Duster:

> There is no longer a single racial or ethnic group with an overwhelming numerical and political majority. Pluralism is the reality, with no one group a dominant force. This is completely new; we are grappling with a phenomenon that is both puzzling and alarming, fraught with tensions and hostilities, and yet simultaneously brimming with potential and crackling with new energy. Consequently, we swing between hope and concern, optimism and pessimism about the prospects for social life among people from differing racial and cultural groups.[37]

We urge you to view your intercultural experiences as steps in a lifelong commitment to make the world a place where people from all cultures can live and thrive.

Notes

1. Excerpted and adapted from Myron W. Lustig and Jolene Koester, *Intercultural Competence: Interpersonal Communication Across Cultures,* 5th ed. (Boston: Allyn & Bacon, 2006).

2. William G. Sumner, *Folkways* (Boston: Ginn, 1940), 27.

3. Ibid.

4. Walter Lippmann, *Public Opinion* (New York: Harcourt, Brace, 1922), 25.

5. See Carl Friedrich Graumann and Margret Wintermantel, "Discriminatory Speech Acts: A Functional Approach," in *Stereotyping and Prejudice: Changing Conceptions,* ed. Daniel Bar-Tal, Carl F. Graumann, Arie W. Kruglanski, and Wolfgang Stroebe (New York: Springer-Verlag, 1989), 183–204.

6. Henri Tajfel, *Differentiation Between Social Groups: Studies in the Social Psychology of Intergroup Relations* (New York: Academic Press, 1978).

7. Marilynn B. Brewer, "Social Identity, Distinctiveness, and In-Group Homogeneity," *Social Cognition* 11 (1993): 150–164; Klaus Fiedler and Eva Walther, *Stereotyping as Inductive Hypothesis* (New York: Psychology Press, 2004); Bonnie L. Haines, *Bigger Than the Box: The Effects of Labeling* (Oacoma, SD: Unlimited Achievement Books, 2004); E. E. Jones, G. C. Wood, and G. A. Quattrone, "Perceived Variability of Personal Characteristics in In-Groups and Out-Groups: The Role of Knowledge and Evaluation," *Personality and Social Psychology Bulletin* 7 (1981): 523–528; John T. Jost and Brenda Major (eds.), *The Psychology of Legitimacy: Emerging Perspectives on Ideology, Justice, and Intergroup Relations* (New York: Cambridge University Press, 2001); Charles M. Judd and Bernadette Park, "Out-Group Homogeneity: Judgments of Variability at the Individual and Group Levels," *Journal of Personality and Social Psychology* 54 (1988): 778–788; Paul Martin Lester and Susan Dente Ross (eds.), *Images That Injure: Pictorial Stereotypes in the Media,* 2nd ed. (Westport, CT: Praeger, 2003); Toni Lester (ed.), *Gender Nonconformity, Race, and Sexuality: Charting the Connections* (Madison: University of Wisconsin Press, 2002); P. W. Linville and E. E. Jones, "Polarized Appraisals of Out-Group

Members," *Journal of Personality and Social Psychology* 38 (1980): 689–703; Craig McGarty, Vincent Y. Yzerbyt, and Russell Spears (eds.), *Stereotypes as Explanations: The Formation of Meaningful Beliefs About Social Groups* (New York: Cambridge University Press, 2002); Brian Mullen and L. Hu, "Perceptions of Ingroup and Outgroup Variability: A Meta-Analytic Integration," *Basic and Applied Social Psychology* 10 (1989): 233–252; Thomas M. Ostrom, Sandra L. Carpenter, Constantine Sedikides, and Fan Li, "Differential Processing of In-Group and Out-Group Information," *Journal of Personality and Social Psychology* 64 (1993): 21–34; Michael Pickering, *Stereotyping: The Politics of Representation* (New York: Palgrave, 2001); David J. Schneider, *The Psychology of Stereotyping* (New York: Guilford, 2004).

8. Micah S. Thompson, Charles M. Judd, and Bernadette Park, "The Consequences of Communicating Social Stereotypes," *Journal of Experimental Social Psychology* 36 (2000): 567-599; Vincent Y. Yzerbyt, Alastair Coull, and Steve J. Rocher, "Fencing Off the Deviant: The Role of Cognitive Resources in the Maintenance of Stereotypes," *Journal of Personality and Social Psychology* 77(3) (1999): 449–462.

9. See Charles M. Judd and Bernadette Park, "Definition and Assessment of Accuracy in Social Stereotypes," *Psychological Review* 100 (1993): 109–128; Carey S. Ryan, Bernadette Park, and Charles M. Judd, "Assessing Stereotype Accuracy: Implications for Understanding the Stereotyping Process," in *Stereotypes and Stereotyping*, ed. C. Neil Macrae, Charles Stangor, and Miles Hewstone (New York: Guilford, 1996), 121–157.

10. Marilynn B. Brewer, "Social Identity, Distinctiveness, and In-Group Homogeneity," *Social Cognition* 11 (1993): 150–164; E. E. Jones, G. C. Wood, and G. A. Quattrone, "Perceived Variability of Personal Characteristics in In-Groups and Out-Groups: The Role of Knowledge and Evaluation," *Personality and Social Psychology Bulletin* 7 (1981): 523–528; Charles M. Judd and Bernadette Park, "Out-Group Homogeneity: Judgments of Variability at the Individual and Group Levels," *Journal of Personality and Social Psychology* 54 (1988): 778–788; P. W. Linville and E. E. Jones, "Polarized Appraisals of Out-Group Members," *Journal of Personality and Social Psychology* 38 (1980): 689–703; Brian Mullen and L. Hu, "Perceptions of Ingroup and Outgroup Variability: A Meta-Analytic Integration," *Basic and Applied Social Psychology* 10 (1989): 233–252; Thomas M. Ostrom, Sandra L. Carpenter,

Constantine Sedikides, and Fan Li, "Differential Processing of In-Group and Out-Group Information," *Journal of Personality and Social Psychology* 64 (1993): 21–34.

11. David Barsamian, "Albert Mokhiber: Cultural Images, Politics, and Arab Americans," *Z Magazine* (May 1993): 46–50. Reprinted in *Ethnic Groups,* vol. 4, ed. Eleanor Goldstein (Boca Raton, FL: Social Issues Resources Ser., 1994), art. no. 73.

12. Ziva Kunda and Bonnie Sherman-Williams, "Stereotypes and the Construal of Individuating Information," *Personality and Social Psychology Bulletin* 19 (1993): 97.

13. John J. Seta and Catherine E. Seta, "Stereotypes and the Generation of Compensatory and Noncompensatory Expectancies of Group Members," *Personality and Social Psychology Bulletin* 19 (1993): 722–731.

14. C. Neil Macrae, Alan B. Milne, and Galen V. Bodenhausen, "Stereotypes as Energy-Saving Devices: A Peek Inside the Cognitive Toolbox," *Journal of Personality and Social Psychology* 66 (1994): 37–47.

15. Judee K. Burgoon, Charles R. Berger, and Vincent Waldron, "Mindfulness and Interpersonal Communication," *Journal of Social Issues* 56 (2000): 105–127.

16. Gordon W. Allport, *The Nature of Prejudice* (New York: Macmillan, 1954).

17. John F. Dovidio, John C. Brigham, Blair T. Johnson, and Samuel L. Gaertner, "Stereotyping, Prejudice, and Discrimination: A Closer Look," in *Stereotypes and Stereotyping*, ed. C. Neil Macrae, Charles Stangor, and Miles Hewstone (New York: Guilford Press, 1996), 276–319.

18. Richard W. Brislin, *Cross-Cultural Encounters: Face-to-Face Interaction* (New York: Pergamon Press, 1981), 42–49.

19. For a test of the ego-defensive functions of attitudes, see Maria Knight Lapinski and Franklin Boster, "Modeling the Ego-Defensive Function of Attitudes," *Communication Monographs* 68 (2001): 314–324.

20. Steven Fein and Steven J. Spencer, "Prejudice as Self-Image Maintenance: Affirming the Self Through Derogating Others," *Journal of Personality and Social Psychology* 73 (1997): 31–44.

21. Teun A. van Dijk, *Communicating Racism: Ethnic Prejudice in Thought and Talk* (Newbury Park, CA: Sage, 1987).

22. Marilynn B. Brewer, "The Psychology of Prejudice: Ingroup Love or Outgroup Hate?" *Journal of Social Issues* 55 (1999): 429–444. See also Marilynn B. Brewer and Wendi L. Gardner, "Who Is This "We"? Levels of Collective Identity and Self Representations," *Journal of Personality and Social Psychology* 71 (1996): 83–93.

23. For a discussion of the causes and consequences of some forms of racism, see Joe R. Feagin and Hernán Vera, *White Racism: The Basics* (New York: Routledge, 1995).

24. Robert Blauner, *Racial Oppression in America* (New York: Harper & Row, 1972), 112.

25. Dalmas A. Taylor, "Race Prejudice, Discrimination, and Racism," in *Social Psychology,* ed. A. Kahn, E. Donnerstein, and M. Donnerstein (Dubuque, IA: Wm. C. Brown, 1984); cited in Phyllis A. Katz and Dalmas A. Taylor, "Introduction," *Eliminating Racism: Profiles in Controversy,* ed. Phyllis A. Katz and Dalmas A. Taylor (New York: Plenum, 1988), 6.

26. Katz and Taylor, *Eliminating Racism,* 7.

27. Blauner, *Racial Oppression.*

28. James M. Jones, "Racism in Black and White: A Bicultural Model of Reaction and Evolution," in *Eliminating Racism: Profiles in Controversy,* ed. Phyllis A. Katz and Dalmas A. Taylor (New York: Plenum, 1988), 130–131.

29. S. Elizabeth Bird, "Gendered Construction of the American Indian in Popular Media," *Journal of Communication* 49 (1999): 78.

30. Ibid., 80. See also Richard Morris, "Educating Savages," *Quarterly Journal of Speech* 83 (1997): 152–171.

31. Jones, "Racism in Black and White," 118–126.

32. Katz and Taylor, *Eliminating Racism,* 7.

33. Jenny Yamoto, "Something about the Subject Makes It Hard to Name," in *Race, Class, and Gender in the United States: An Integrated Study,* 2nd ed., ed. Paula S. Rothenberg (New York: St. Martin's Press, 1992), 58.

34. For discussions of racism and prejudice, see Linda Jacobs Altman, *Racism and Ethnic Bias: Everybody's Problem* (Berkeley Heights, NJ: Enslow, 2001); Joseph F. Aponte and Laura R. Johnson, "The Impact of Culture on the Intervention and Treatment of Ethnic Populations," *Psychological Intervention and Cultural Diversity,* 2nd ed., ed. Joseph F. Aponte and Julian Wohl (Needham Heights, MA: Allyn & Bacon, 2000), 18–39; Martha Augoustinos and Katherine J. Reynolds (eds.), *Understanding Prejudice, Racism, and Social Conflict* (Thousand Oaks, CA: Sage, 2001); Michael D. Barber, *Equality and Diversity: Phenomenological Investigations of Prejudice and Discrimination* (Amherst, NY: Humanity Books, 2001); Benjamin P. Bowser, Gale S. Auletta, and Terry Jones, *Confronting Diversity Issues on Campus* (Newbury Park, CA: Sage, 1994); Bernard Boxill (ed.), *Race and Racism* (New York: Oxford University Press, 2001); John C. Brigham, "College Students' Racial Attitudes," *Journal of Applied Social Psychology* 23 (1993): 1933–1967; Richard W. Brislin, "Prejudice and Intergroup Communication," *Intergroup Communication,* ed. William B. Gudykunst (London: Arnold, 1986), 74–85; Brislin, *Cross-Cultural Encounters,* 42–49; Charles E. Case, Andrew M. Greeley, and Stephan Fuchs, "Social Determinants of Racial Prejudice," *Sociological Perspectives* 32 (1989): 469–483; Farhad Dalal, "Insides and Outsides: A Review of Psychoanalytic Renderings of Difference, Racism, and Prejudice," *Psychoanalytic Studies* 3 (2001): 43–66; Samuel L. Gaertner and John F. Dovidio, "The Aversive Form of Racism," *Prejudice, Discrimination and Racism: Theory and Research,* ed. John F. Dovidio and Samuel L. Gaertner (New York: Academic Press, 1986), 61–89; Ellen J. Goldner and Safiya Henderson-Holmes (eds.), *Racing and (E)Racing Language: Living with the Color of Our Words* (Syracuse, NY: Syracuse University Press, 2001); Harry Goulbourne (ed.), *Race and Ethnicity: Critical Concepts in Sociology* (New York: Routledge, 2001); Edgar Jones, "Prejudicial Beliefs: Their Nature and Expression," in *Racism and Mental Health: Prejudice and Suffering,* ed. Kamaldeep Bhui (Philadelphia: Jessica Kingsley, 2002), 26–34; David Milner, "Racial Prejudice," in *Intergroup Behavior,* ed. John C. Turner and Howard Giles (Chicago: University of Chicago Press, 1981), 102–143; Scott Plous (ed.), *Understanding Prejudice and Discrimination* (Boston: McGraw-Hill, 2003); Peter Ratcliffe, *The Politics of Social Science Research: Race, Ethnicity, and Social Change* (New York: Palgrave, 2001); Albert Ramirez, "Racism toward Hispanics: The Culturally Monolithic Society," in *Eliminating Racism: Profiles in Controversy*, ed. Phyllis A. Katz and Dalmas A. Taylor (New York: Plenum, 1988), 137–157; Paula S. Rothenberg (ed.), *Race, Class, and Gender in the United States: An Integrated Study,* 5th ed. (New York: W. H. Freeman, 2001); James R Samuel, *The Roots of Racism* (New York: Vantage, 2001); David O. Sears, "Symbolic Racism," in *Eliminating Racism: Profiles in Controversy,* ed. Phyllis A. Katz and Dalmas A. Taylor (New York: Plenum, 1988), 53–84; Key Sun, "Two Types of Prejudice and Their Causes," *American Psychologist* 48 (1993):

1152–1153; Nicholas J. Ucci, *The Structure of Racism: Insights into Developing a New Language for Socio-Historical Inquiry* (Centereach, NY: Cybergraphic Fine Art, 2001); Ian Vine, "Inclusive Fitness and the Self-System: The Roles of Human Nature and Sociocultural Processes in Intergroup Discrimination," in *The Sociobiology of Ethnocentrism: Evolutionary Dimensions of Xenophobia, Discrimination, Racism, and Nationalism,* ed. Vernon Reynolds, Vincent Falger, and Ian Vine (London: Croom Helm, 1987), 60–80; Bernd Wittenbrink, Charles M. Judd, and Bernadette Park, "Evidence for Racial Prejudice at the Implicit Level and Its Relationship with Questionnaire Measures," *Journal of Personality and Social Psychology* 72 (1997): 262–274.

35. Jacqueline N. Sawires and M. Jean Peacock, "Symbolic Racism and Voting Behavior on Proposition 209," *Journal of Applied Social Psychology* 30 (2000): 2092–2099.

36. Brigham, "College Students' Racial Attitudes," 1934.

37. Troy Duster, "Understanding Self-Segregation on the Campus," *The Chronicle of Higher Education,* (September 25, 1991): B2.

A move from the racially segregated but predictable world of Mississippi to northern California thrust Chevelle Newsome into a different cultural realm. It also set in motion a series of events that would allow her to understand the causes and consequences of prejudice, discrimination, and marginality. Chevelle recognizes that, in all likelihood, she will always operate from a position of marginality; but she has learned to draw strength and purpose from that place. Her story is that of a successful African American woman who has encountered, and continues to experience and combat, many forms of racism.

18 Finding One's Self in the Margins

Chevelle Newsome

When I was in high school in California, I discovered that I had the same birthplace—a small town on the Gulf Coast of Mississippi named Moss Point—as Michele, who was my high school academic counselor. Like most towns in the south, Moss Point was segregated in the early 1960s when Michele and my mother graduated from high school. Michele and my mother had been high school homecoming royalty the same year in Moss Point, but in different high schools. While they had only lived five miles from one another, because of racial segregation they attended different schools. Their lives would intersect again, some 20 years later and some 3,000 miles away from our common birthplace, through their relationships with me.

During my senior year in high school I was crowned homecoming queen, an event that, at least on the surface, symbolized for Michele, my mother, and me a bridge between the racially segregated world in which we were all born and the ostensibly desegregated world we lived in some 20 years later. My coronation seemed to blur the lines that had separated them when they were young women. Michele's words to my mother when I was crowned homecoming queen indicate their sense of progress and change: "This is the way it should have been back then. That's our girl up there." Her words suggested progress and change for African Americans away from segregation, discrimination, and racism. Though I understand the hope and optimism in Michele's statement, what she did not realize was that I still experience, on a daily basis, marginalization born from racism and discrimination as I move between the segregated world of my birthplace and the seemingly integrated world of modern-day California, where I now live.

Writing this essay has triggered for me an awareness of the struggles I have experienced as I made the journey between two worlds, both pivotal to my identity and both demanding that I explain myself, because success and comfort in one world inevitably render me marginal in the other. In this essay I share my experiences and offer others who are similarly torn between different cultural worlds an understanding of the quest for cultural identity grown and nurtured on the margins of dual cultural worlds.

My story is about finding myself as I made the transition between a rural town in Mississippi, where segregation was the norm, and a city in northern California, where physical integration is tolerated. In the search for my own cultural identity I struggled to understand the complexities of race, ethnicity, discrimination, and communication between people from different cultural groups. As I sought to understand my own experience, I read the works of many African American scholars and discovered the words of Franklin Frazier, which helped me to understand the similarities between my situation and those of other African Americans. Frazier (1957) wrote:

> What may appear as distortions of American patterns of behavior and thought are due to the fact that the Negro lives on the margins of American society. The very existence of a separate Negro community with its own institutions within the heart of the American society is indicative of its quasi-pathological character, especially since the persistence of this separate community has been due to racial discrimination and oppression. (p. 234)

I have had to reconcile the discrepancies between living in segregated and integrated communities, and the words of Frazier have helped me to do this.

Neighborhoods in Moss Point remain segregated to this day. During the 1960s civil rights movement, Michele, my mother, and I resided in a small town where the lines between the black minority and dominant whites were clearly marked. As a child I watched members of my family's older generation, my second cousins and grandparents, quietly cross the boundaries between the racially segregated worlds to work in factories and to clean the homes and offices of European Americans. Some of those who crossed the boundaries during that time supported the idea that the boundaries were beneficial. As a child I heard comments such as "You can't trust them white folks; they ain't got nothin' for us. It's better we stay on over here and they stay over there." The arguments of the separatists, in both the black and the white communities, have been that the separation of the races helps to maintain each group's traditions and cultures. Such ideas resonated with some members of each culture, including some of the older members of my family. However, it was the oppression and devaluation of blacks as human

Culture Concepts

Dialects

Dialects *are versions of a language with distinctive vocabulary, grammar, and pronunciation that are spoken by particular groups of people or within particular regions. Dialects can play an important role in intercultural communication because they often trigger a judgment and evaluation of the speaker. Dialects are measured against a standard spoken version of the language. The term* standard *describes historical circumstances, rather than inherent or naturally occurring characteristics.*

beings that sharply marked the divergence of the ideas of the black and white separatists. As members of our community moved between the two worlds the physical segregation was tolerable, and in some instances welcomed, but it was the economic oppression and abusive language—products of racism—that were and still are intolerable.

Many of the children who were born in Moss Point have, like me, moved on to other places. Moss Point is a town where the residents still live in the shadows of the segregated South. About a decade ago, when my grandmother died and the funeral home personnel were being very difficult, my father, who was born and raised in California, suggested that we have my grandmother's body moved to the "white" funeral home that had opened on the highway. His suggestion would seem reasonable to most people, but to the other members of my family and to me, it was inconceivable. In our town, "black folks" would never allow a "white mortician" to handle the bodies of their loved ones. It was an unwritten rule that even the cemeteries were supposed to be segregated. We lived "outside" the boundaries of the dominant European American culture in that town, and we would never consider crossing that boundary. In death as in life, we operated under a set of rules that placed us outside the mainstream social structure.

I have a vivid image of a European American man who gave me one of my first lessons in racism and the marginalization of my people. My parents and grandparents were moderately educated. Both of my parents had graduated from high school, and in our town that was an accomplishment. Although my parents were employed, there was not an excess of money for medical and dental treatment. Thus, when a group of dentists came to our area to do community service and to provide free dental check-ups, my parents took me to see them. Despite my fears of this strange place, my parents were not allowed in the dental examination room. The dental assistant was friendly and attempted to make me feel comfortable in this unfamiliar environment. Her efforts worked until the dentist entered the room, and then the atmosphere changed. He entered the room, slammed the door, and stated, "I'm tired of these poor nigger children. They're like li'l rats." Needless to say, the words and tone assured disaster. During the examination he was rough and cut the inside of my mouth with his cleaning instrument. I retaliated by biting his finger. He responded by pinching my nose to force me to take a breath and open my mouth, thus releasing his finger from the clutches of my teeth. He rattled off several obscenities and racial slurs and refused to finish the cleaning. The comfort and carefree attitude that I had developed in my segregated community had not prepared me for the reality of an interaction with an individual who openly expressed racist views against a group to which I belonged. From this encounter, I learned quickly and forcefully that racism creates boundaries and margins between my cultural group and that of the dominant European American culture.

Recognizing the lack of economic opportunities in Mississippi, in the early 1970s my parents moved to California, which represented economic opportunity. California also presented an opportunity for me to live in an integrated neighborhood and to attend an integrated school. In that environment I met people from different cultures and explored my own cultural identity in new ways. I vividly remember the song "California Girl," and as I sang along with the record my pride in being viewed as a Californian was palpable. For me the song represented a shift in my cultural identification. I was a girl with new-found allegiances to her adopted home state.

Despite my enthusiasm to meet new people and learn more about them and their cultures, I also longed to return to the comforts of my original home and people in Mississippi. When I visited Mississippi during the holidays and summer vacations, I experienced divided loyalties. I felt conflicted because California had taught me to fulfill many of the behavioral expectations of my European American friends, but in order to fit in with members of my culture from Mississippi I had to relearn many of my old behaviors and language choices.

The marginalization I experienced in moving between my worlds in Mississippi and California is linked to the language used by members of the dominant European American culture. The language we learn and use helps us to develop our social reality. For example, in the United States we learn to associate white with good things and black with bad things. The image that "black" is dirty is pervasive. One day I entered a store and the sales clerk refused to allow me to try on a dress after my European American friend had just done so. She stated, "Your skin might soil the dress." The implication was that my "black" skin might rub off on the fabric. This example illustrates how conceptions of color marginalize African Americans. The clerk's conception of color turned a day of shopping with friends into an event marked by blatant racism.

While the experience with the sales clerk illustrates the detrimental effects of color labels, my own use of language shows me the cultural margins in which I operate. While in California, I had become formally socialized into using standard American English, and I had dropped my southern accent. Members from my southern culture began to tell me that I spoke like a "white girl." They viewed me as an outsider to the culture we once shared, and I began to adjust to the idea that there was one "best" form of English to use. Thus, language that had once bonded me to my culture was becoming divisive. The conflicting messages I was receiving caused me to question my identity as a person and as an African American.

In my search for cultural identification as an African American, I had fallen victim to one of the pitfalls that Frazier had written about years ago. Frazier argued that African Americans are socialized to forget their heritage and to embrace the ideology of the dominant group. In California I had been socialized to believe that I could attain success only by discarding the language and behaviors of my African American cultural group in Mississippi. In the process of being socialized, I was being separated from the poor and disenfranchised in my culture—my family members who crossed the racial barriers in my hometown.

Through my experiences and education in California, I had learned to adapt my behaviors, values, and attitudes to accommodate to the views of the dominant culture. Though my parents tried to maintain my connection with Mississippi by sending me there during summers and other holidays to visit with relatives and friends, I was immersed in a new environment for the majority of the year. In this new environment I had to learn to tolerate—and in some respects to accept—a world that excluded the people I knew back home.

When I began studying rhetoric, learning about political communication, and reading the works of Frazier, Asante, hooks, and other African American scholars, I began to understand fully that although I had been living the middle-class life provided by my parents, I was still operating on the margins of the European American culture and world. It was not only the lower-income African Americans who were marginalized by the language and behaviors of the dominant class, but also people like me who were socialized to accept the language of the dominant class and in so doing to give up part of our racial and cultural identities. I thought about my European American friends and realized that many of them did not see me as an African American. In their eyes, I was not like the African American elevator operator who took us to our offices in the state capitol each morning, or the African American janitor who cleaned our offices and worked double shifts to earn the money to meet his mortgage payment each month. Those hard-working African American individuals, with whom I so closely identified because they reminded me of the people in my family and my neighborhood in Mississippi, were not viewed as being from the same community as me. They were somehow different because the color of their skin was darker, they were not college educated, and their speech did not always conform to standard European American English. I understood then that not only were they marginalized, so was I.

This idea troubled me, because I had worked so hard to represent my culture and attain an education and status in the dominant culture. By not being recognized as a member of a culture that I so passionately thought defined me as an individual, I was once again forced to realize that the margins created by racism do exist. At that moment, I was back in that dentist's chair and again felt the dynamics of racism. I was reminded of Angela Davis's observation that social marginalization often creates political activism. African Americans fought for the right to be politically active within the formal political structure, and they were given the right to vote by legislation, but the dominant group subverted their rights by using verbal and physical violence. In my case, members of the dominant group attempted to strip me of my cultural identity by denying that I was an African American. Some of my European American friends, who considered me to be "one of them," thought their attitude was proof that they were not racist. From my perspective, however, it was a sign of cultural insensitivity at best, and racism at worst. As an African American, I was clearly *not* one of them. To ignore or deny my reality forced me to the margins of the European American culture, from which I had to operate every day.

In an effort to assert my cultural identity as an African American, I was called to political activism. I had an intense need to explain the value of my cultural identity to myself, to my African American friends, and to my friends

---

Culture Concepts

Verbal Codes

A verbal code *is a set of rules about the use of words in the creation of messages. Verbal codes include both oral (spoken) language and nonoral (written) language. Five different but interrelated sets of rules combine to create a verbal code, or language. The basic sound units of a language are called* phonemes; *the phonological rules of a language tell speakers which sounds to use and how to order them. Phonemes combine to form* morphemes, *which are the smallest units of meaning in a language. The study of the meaning of words is called* semantics. *The fourth component of language is* syntactics, *which is the relationship of words to one another. Finally,* pragmatics *focuses on the effects of language on human perceptions and behaviors, or how language is actually used.*

---

from the European American culture. I began to read and examine the practices of dominant groups in dealing with members of minority groups. I also began a reflective process in which I examined my actions in dealing with my friends from my culture in Mississippi.

Many of my friends and relatives have left our small town in Mississippi, and my visits there are far less frequent than when I was a child. However, in that town I discovered my community of origin and a recognition of the differences between two cultures. While I may represent progress in overcoming discrimination, which Michelle expressed when I was crowned homecoming queen so many years ago, I am also an individual who, because of racism, constantly speaks from the margins. As a person of African descent, I cannot afford to lose touch with my heritage. Because of a renewed interest and quest for knowledge about the plights and successes of members of other cultural groups, I frequently share information and debate social issues with friends and colleagues from other cultures. It is a healthy dialogue that allows me to reaffirm my own ethnic identity.

In a discussion with a European American woman about the status of affirmative action, long before the issue became publicly controversial, I was urged to withdraw my support of affirmative action programs because "there would soon be too many others like you and then you would not be special." Her comments devalued my racial identity by supporting tokenism, and it marked me as marginal to her world. It was once again clear to me that racism draws boundaries and creates margins, so that I must validate my cultural identity and speak in support of those who, as I do, operate and live along the margins.

The study of language use among African Americans illustrates the need for self-validation. Scholars have reported on the African use of pidgin language by slaves on the plantations. When white scholars studied pidgin, they reported that it was obvious that African Americans used pidgin because they were inferior and incapable of learning the English language. Labeling African Americans as inferior allowed and justified their mistreatment. In my life I have watched and experienced how language is used to degrade and demean people. I have only to think back to that dentist in Mississippi to learn this lesson again. The language he used allowed him to categorize me as insignificant. I was no longer a small child who needed dental care, but a nigger, a rat, a pest, and, in his view, insignificant. When people are marginalized through racism, as I was, then it is acceptable to deny them the right to live in the neighborhood of their choice or to feel comfortable in a particular store.

Language is often used to create and shape a hierarchical structure that maintains power and control. However, I have learned that, just as the dominant group can use language to maintain control, the dominated group can use language to gain control. For example, in the late 1960s and early 1970s, there was an offshoot of the Civil Rights movement called the Black Power movement. Leaders of the movement, in conjunction with popular music artists and many ministers, used language to empower African American people. Songs such as "I'm Black and I'm Proud," and chants such as "Black Power," were heard across the United States and in my home. I vividly remember the Afros and dashikis worn by members of my family, including me. The clothes, music, and chants served as elements of empowerment. As I reflect back, I now understand it as a self-affirmation by the members of a marginalized culture.

By immersing myself in the history and rhetoric of the leaders of my culture, I recognized the important role that higher education has and can play in helping people to develop their cultural identities. I was exposed to ideas and interests that I had not fully considered. I recognized how I was being and had been oppressed by language. For I believe that understanding the power of language was a key component in the development of my cultural identity and my understanding of my role as a person on the margins.

bell hooks calls for minorities to use the margins as a catalyst for rebellion. According to her, the margins—and not the center of the dominant culture—are where the dialogue for equality should originate. For minority groups, their social marginalization is also based on their status in relation to the dominant group, which in the United States is typically comprised of European American males. For African Americans, in particular, marginalization creates an ongoing battle that began when the first slave arrived. It continues to this day. As Angela Davis, Franklin Frazier, and bell hooks proclaim, African Americans have made many advances, but the fight against oppression and racism must continue. As my life demonstrates, the margins can be used to rebel and to become an activist for this cause.

My search for cultural identity is both challenging and fulfilling. In that search, I am becoming a strong African American woman who speaks from the margins as a representative for herself and for others who are similarly marginalized.

▶ ▶ ▶ **Learning AmongUS**

1. In Newsome's view, how was language used to separate and marginalize her?
2. Describe experiences you have had in which language was used to separate you from others and/or was used to make you feel powerless.
3. Is the amount of racism and discrimination in a society related to the negative treatment of individuals who speak a dialect? Explain.

4. Newsome describes some of the difficulties she encountered in living in California but visiting and maintaining strong ties to her family and culture of origin. Do you agree with her parents' decision to send her back to Mississippi to maintain those connections and that identity? Why or why not?

References

Asante, M. K., & Asante, K. W. (Eds.). (1985). *African culture: The rhythms of unity*. Westport, CT: Greenwood Press.

Davis, A. Y. (1981). *Women, race & class*. New York: Random House.

Davis, A. Y. (1990). *Women, culture, and politics*. New York: Vintage Books.

Frazier, E. F. (1957). *Black bourgeoisie: The rise of a new middle class in the United States*. New York: Free Press.

hooks, b. (1990). *Yearning: Race, gender, and cultural politics*. Boston: South End Press.

The perils of silence and inaction in the face of racism, prejudice, and discrimination form the basis of Elane Geller's essay. Because of anti-Semitism and the genocide directed against Jews, Elane spent five years in concentration camps in Europe. While the descriptions of her experiences chill and horrify, her message is a call to vigilance and action whenever differences in culture, race, religion, or language become the basis for oppression. Geller reminds us that the Jewish Holocaust occurred and could occur again unless every individual assumes some responsibility to speak out about the moral character of our world.

19 The Holocaust and Its Lessons: A Survivor's Story

Elane Norych Geller

The Jewish sages say that, as human beings, we are obligated to leave this world better than we found it, and that we should dedicate our lives to this end. This directive may sound very lofty and intimidating, which would give us an excuse to ignore it. Actually, it is too simple to avoid. We are not expected to solve the world's problems with one grand deed. Quite the opposite, the sages instruct that we improve the world through the practice of decency in our daily behavior. Many people performing many small kind and decent acts on an everyday basis adds up to improvement on a global scale. Changing the world is within the reach of every one of us. Once we understand our capabilities, we cannot avoid our responsibilities.

I travel around the country sharing my story as a survivor of the *Shoah*, the Holocaust. I do not tell my story to win the personal sympathies of my listeners. Nor do I tell it in order to show that the Jews have suffered more than others. I tell it to teach the necessity of accepting personal responsibility for the world. While my "credentials" as a speaker come from my experiences as a Holocaust survivor, I speak not as a Jew, a woman, or a mother. I speak as a human being to other human beings of all creeds, colors, and religions. I am a witness to what can happen when humanity remains indifferent and silent in the face of intolerance. My goal is prevention.

For the most part I speak to students. Almost always I am approached by students after my talk who ask, "What can I do to prevent prejudice or intolerance?" Although we have this sense that the problem is too big for one person to do anything about, it is entirely curable—and it takes no special skills. Even young children have the skills. What it takes is the ability to judge between right and wrong, to care about the difference, and to speak up. I tell the students that it is in their power to combat intolerance of all kinds—they just need to say something, write a letter, make a phone call. It is actually that simple. It is only in an atmosphere of silent acceptance that these ills can flourish. To prevent something like the tragedy of the Holocaust from ever happening again, I hope to teach people, especially young people, that they do have the skills to eliminate racism, bigotry, anti-Semitism, and hatred of various kinds, and that it is simple to use their skills. Most of all, I believe it is our duty as human beings, as the beneficiaries of the gift of free will, to make the choices that will keep this planet ethically and morally safe for all of us.

I have to admit that I was not always an activist. Because I was a child survivor, I had the luxury of deferring the examination of my history. I was too busy becoming an American, going to school, running a household, and raising a family. About 20 years ago, when the revisionists surfaced, I knew I could no longer be silent. The revisionists are folks who say that the Holocaust never happened. What is especially scary about them is that they are "regular" people. They are not kooks. They are teachers, professors, mailmen, secretaries, and trash collectors. They are mainstream people who have decided for whatever reason that the Holocaust never happened and want to "set the record straight." When you think about it, it is a bit crazy to deny the Holocaust because much of what we know about the period comes from German archives. The Nazis were meticulous about keeping records. To a survivor, the kind of media exposure given the revisionists is very painful. In our media-worshipping society, the fact that such people appear on television or in the papers legitimizes their point of view. Picture, if you will, that tomorrow morning all the papers of the world say on the front page, "Eminent Harvard historian, after ten years of research, has concluded that there was no slavery in the United States." I would, of course, expect my fellow Americans who are black to be outraged. But if they were the only people who were outraged, I would be frightened beyond belief. This was the situation with the Holocaust revisionists. These people were going on talk shows and speaking at conferences, and their views were treated by the mainstream as though they were sufficiently grounded in reality to be worthy of consideration. I was outraged at the revisionists, but I was more terrified by the silent acceptance with which their views were treated by the general public. The silence is really the problem, because it allows the hatred to go unchecked.

Hitler's views were also met largely with silent acceptance. While information was available for the world press—the camps were not exactly hidden—the reports of the genocide appeared in the back pages of our newspapers. But it is important to acknowledge that there were some exceptions. Not absolutely everyone was silent. There were some good Poles, and there were some good Germans. There were also some good whites who helped black Americans during slavery. These people should be celebrated

Culture Concepts

Genocide

Genocide *is the systematic destruction of an ethnic group or a nation.*

as heroes. But the existence of some people who behaved ethically and morally does not provide us with license to ignore the overall lesson of history. Mostly, people were silent and accepted the genocide of the Jews; otherwise it could not have happened.

It is essential to remember the political and economic contexts of the Holocaust. After World War I, Germany was suffering economically, and the people were desperate. It was a perfect climate for an extremist. Hitler came in through the ballot box with the answer to Germany's suffering. Then, all of a sudden, like magic a place called Auschwitz pops up. The people in the surrounding area could see the smoke of Auschwitz, smoke that smelled of human flesh burning, and suddenly they had jobs. They were making pillows out of human hair, and jewelry out of gold inlay, and fertilizer out of bones, and nobody said, "Where are these jobs coming from?" German businessmen went into government offices, bid on government contracts for extraordinary amounts of Zyclon B gas and striped cloth and barbed wire, and without question business was picking up for them. It played well because it played into already-existing anti-Semitism: get rid of the Jews and everything will be better. Because of the economic advantages, people wanted to accept Hitler's program despite the knowledge of the atrocities involved. They wanted economic stability so much that they accepted the idea of a master race of tall, blond, blue-eyed people that was given to them by a short, brunette man with brown eyes. This occurred in a country considered to be one of the most educated and most cultured in the world.

Of the six million Jews murdered, there were a million and a half children under the age of seventeen. An additional five and a half million non-Jews were also murdered in the camps: gypsies, gays, political dissidents, and Jehovah's witnesses, for example. Those souls are every bit as precious, every bit as missed as the Jewish souls. But again, we have to be aware of the politics. Only the Jews were targeted for genocide. I was four years old when the war began. From that time until I was almost nine, I was in one prison, one concentration camp or another.

I was born in a small town in Poland called Voygislav. The town had a healthy proportion of Jews; about 2,500 out of 4,000 people were Jewish. My family consisted of mother and father, two older brothers, an older sister, aunts, uncles, cousins, and grandparents. Of course, we all knew that this madman Hitler was loose, and that he was in fact conducting two wars: the war of conquest and the war against the Jews. We knew that the war was bad for everyone but that it would be worse for us. The Jews were persecuted in Poland long before Hitler. He did not invent anti-Semitism; he just perfected it. We were a dispersed people, without land or riches. Jews lived in Poland for hundreds of years; we paid taxes, we served in the army, we did everything required of good citizens, and yet we were never considered first-class Polish citizens. So we knew it would be worse for us, and of course it was.

What my father did in preparation, as did some other people in our community, was to hire a young seminarian to tutor me in the kinds of things that I would need to know to pass as a Christian child of age four in that setting;

some bible stories, hymns, and prayers. I got a false birth certificate and a false baptismal certificate. An arrangement was made with a Christian family: should the Nazis come to our town, I would be taken to their home and left there until the war was over. At that time, whoever survived would come and claim me. These types of arrangements were not unusual. It is fair to say that many of these arrangements were carried out exactly as agreed on, and many were not.

The day arrived when the Nazis came into our town and began to gather all of the Jews on their knees in the town square. The earliest memory I have is my father dressing me in what seemed to me to be an enormous amount of clothing, so much that I could barely put my hands to my sides. We were to walk over quietly and unnoticed to the Christian home where he was going to leave me. On the way he noticed that here and there a door would open up with what looked to be the head of the household, a small child at his side. He would walk the child up to the SS and say, "I don't know who this is, this is not my child. It must be a Jewish child who wandered in here by mistake." The child was killed immediately. The family of the child was located and they were killed in front of everybody, as an example. My father decided at that point to keep me with him. He felt that, at least that way, he would know what my end was. As we survivors are getting older and there are fewer and fewer of us left, there is no doubt that some of us have gone to our graves not certain that the child we left behind wasn't either turned over to the Nazis at some point or hidden from the Jewish family when they came to reclaim the child after the war. Some families became very close to these children, baptized them and raised them, as their own. So my father decided to gamble and we joined my family in the town square.

By the time we got there—it took about 20 minutes—two of my uncles were already dead. My father's youngest brother had a loaf of bread under his arm and in that bread was some jewelry to be used as bribes for favors. The bread fell and broke open, and the SS saw the jewelry and killed him and my aunt's husband with him. Around the large group of Jews were smaller clusters of Jews who were pulled out of the community for various reasons. Maybe they were very strong men and they could dig ditches; maybe they were barbers or other artisans the Nazis needed. I could see that the Nazis were shooting at one of the small clusters near us. People were bleeding and screaming and dying and falling down. In that group were my grandparents and my mother. In the case of my grandparents, they were quite elderly and the Nazis did not consider it worthwhile to send them to a camp. My mother, I was told, was recovering from minor surgery. Again, the Nazis were not going to go through the effort to put her on a gurney and wait for her to heal. Hitler's motto was *Juden rein,* clean of Jews. Zero Jews. No soldier had to explain one less.

After the shooting and the chaos and the screams, we were moved out of town to a camp not far away. The camp was surrounded by electrified barbed wire. We were given armbands marked with yellow stars of David. This was the end of our freedom. Different family members were sent to different work camps or death camps. One had no idea where they were, or if they would ever be seen again. From that first camp, my 16-year-old sister was sent to Auschwitz, where she died in the ovens.

My father's sister—the one who was married to the uncle who was killed—and I were sent to another camp called Stekachine, not far away. My aunt was very courageous; she told the Nazis that she was my mother. This was courageous because the Nazis often sent mothers and children to the gas chambers together.

In the beginning, my father tried to keep us all together. From an incoming prisoner who knew the family, he found out where my aunt and I were. He bribed someone to have us sent to the camp where he was. He made an arrangement for my aunt and me to be sneaked out in the middle of the night. I was thrown over electrified barbed wire onto a large truck filled with coal. My aunt and I were buried under the coal and told not to sneeze or make any noises, because the vehicles were inspected with enormous searchlights. For a very brief time we were reunited with my father and brothers. We were all sent to an enormous work camp in Poland called Skarzysko. The camp had different sections, and it was so large that I never saw my father and brothers again until after the war was over. Indeed, they were not a fact of my life. I did not know whether they were in another camp or another country, or even if they were dead or alive. It was not an issue for me.

My aunt was put to work in a munitions factory, where they made guns and bullets. There were a few other children in the camp. We speculate that children were kept there as pets, since it was not a problem to kill us at any time. Possibly the higher officers missed their own children; they were far away from home and decided a few little children running around were okay. They probably enjoyed it. Still, my aunt would say to me, "When I'm not with you, stay in the barracks, don't be in anybody's way. Hide. Do not call attention to yourself." And I obeyed her or I would not be here today. Many times when children wandered out, we were forced to watch hangings. We were told to hold hands, and look up while they hanged rows and rows of people. For some reason this was very amusing to the young Nazi soldiers. One time when I wandered out, two bored SS soldiers looked at me and said, "Look at this hair, it's too pretty for a Jewish child." They shaved me bald. When my aunt came back and cried because she could hardly recognize me, they beat her with a rubber hose. Another time, for fun, the soldiers addressed a huge pack of German shepherds, talked to the dogs as if they were human and I was the dog. *"Menschen, bitss dem Hundt"* (People, bite that dog.) The dogs attacked me. I begged and pleaded for help and eventually, for reasons unknown to me, the dogs were called off. The physical scars are well healed, but the emotional scars are not. To this day I go nowhere until I make absolutely certain that the pet you love and cherish is behind a locked door. When I am confronted with a loose animal, I have a flashback, much like a soldier. I become that child of the Holocaust again, begging and screaming and pleading for mercy. As you can imagine, with it comes a loss of dignity. Sometimes I'm fine, but other times it takes me much longer before I am comfortable wandering out of my home.

Culture Concepts

Consequences of Genocide

Genocide *is accomplished by mass killings and also by actions in the political, social, cultural, economic, physical, religious, and moral aspects of living that destroy the essential foundations of the life of an ethnic group.*

From Skarzysko we were packed into railroad cars, the conditions of which I cannot even begin to describe. Suffice it to say that all one's bodily functions were performed right where one stood. What I remember most of all is my aunt's screams as she begged the other prisoners not to eat me alive. That train took us to a camp called Bergen-Belsen. Sometimes people ask if I knew Anne Frank, who died there.

I did not know her. She was about nine years older than me and died very quickly after she got to Belsen. It was a very infested and diseased camp, probably one of the most infested. The trains stopped a great distance outside the barracks, and we marched to the barracks on ground that was solid ice. It was winter, and our feet froze so badly that when my feet began to thaw out, my aunt stuck her fist in my mouth so I would not scream and call attention to myself. Any excuse to silence a Jew was worth it, because the war was coming to an end.

When we arrived in Belsen there were women coming in from all parts of Europe: from Hungary, Romania, Czechoslovakia, Bulgaria, and France. Many of these women, if not all, had already lost their children, and the sight of a small child literally broke their hearts. By then I was a little past eight. I had been infected with typhoid, typhus, and tuberculosis; none of it was ever treated. I had lice and rats in my hair. I stole, I ate toothpaste, and I drank urine. I did whatever was necessary to fill my belly and stay alive. I would approach a broken-hearted mother and ask her to teach me a song in her native language. Then I would go off into a corner and practice it. When I thought I knew the song, I would go back to the woman and, with my palms open, I would sing to her so she would give me her food. She would cry and give me her food, although she needed it more than I did. The intake of a Holocaust prisoner was only 400 calories a day, consisting of a triangular piece of black bread and some dirty water in a squat aluminum container that passed as soup. I did not care one little bit that I was forcing them to give me their precious food. I was like a little animal trying to stay alive.

The British liberated my aunt and me from Bergen-Belsen. One of my brothers was liberated from Buchenwald. My other brothers and my father were liberated in Czechoslovakia in a place called Theresienstadt. We were then put into refugee camps. We needed medical attention and documentation. We needed to find a way to get off German soil. All the aid organizations of the world came there to help. My older brother put ads everywhere saying "I am Jacob Norych, I am looking for family in the U.S." My father had a brother who recognized the name and we came to the United States on the first boatload of refugees. I was almost nine.

This is not ancient history. It happened a mere 50 years ago. Also, for me this is not a horror story. My purpose is not to terrify, but to inform those who

were privileged enough not to be living in Europe during that time what occurs when hatred and bigotry go unchecked by those who should know better.
How can anyone remain silent when we know what can happen? They can and
they will, but my goal is that more will speak up.

I believe that there are no mistakes in this world. The higher power created people of all colors and shapes and with all types of belief systems. I
think there may always be racism and anti-Semitism and bigotry of various
kinds. The degree to which they exist in our world is our daily challenge, all
our lives. What this higher power gave us is free will. It is how we use our free
will that is the challenge. One can become so angry that one is immobilized, or
one can become empowered and an activist and do something to stop intolerance. As the Jewish sages say, it is very simple to speak up. When someone
says "All blacks are this" or "All Asians are so and so," that is the start of the
cancer of racism and bigotry. The horrible spread of the cancer is caused when
people are silent in the face of these racist comments. A response is required.
We need to say, "That is wrong. You do not know all Jews, blacks, Hispanics,
or Asians." The spread of the cancer can be stopped in those small ways. As
simplistic as that seems, it is a powerful start to leaving this world better than
we found it.

When I came to this country everyone said America is like a large melting
pot. I do not believe that that metaphor is accurate. I think the Reverend Cecil
Murray of the First A.M.E. church in Los Angeles says it much better: America should be like a large tossed salad—all the ingredients retain their flavor.
The peppers have different colors, the radishes, the tomatoes—everyone lives
in harmony in one salad bowl with a common dressing. This is not to say that
I expect an ideal world where everyone is in love. I do not expect everyone to
like me. On one level it makes no difference. Even if the Nazis thought I was
nice, they still would have killed me for being a Jew. More important than
everyone liking each other and being friends is the goal of tolerance and decency toward every human being.

We can all see from the lessons of history what can happen when we abandon our efforts to maintain civility. We know the depths to which humans can
sink. I know it personally, having been subjected to inhumanity in the camps,
which in turn caused me to forage for food and steal and become less than human myself. We must accept that we are capable of such behavior, but we also
must accept that we are capable of rising above it. We have no excuses, for we
make the choices. We must choose to be vigilant in maintaining our civility
every day. It is not enough that we have laws on the books that require that
all people be treated equally. The fact that we have laws to protect our decency does not absolve us individually from the responsibility to make a continuous effort. After all, it is we who put those laws into practice. All must
make their own individual commitments to be decent. It is a daily and lifelong
pursuit. The power and the responsibility of our free will should be an honor,
not a burden.

It is extraordinary to me that after all that I have witnessed and endured,
I am nevertheless filled with hope for the planet. There was a time that as a

Jewess from eastern Europe I would have feared living in a multicultural society. I am no longer in fear. In fact, I welcome it. I have heard from and met many, many people who take seriously their duty to improve the world by speaking out to their friends and in their schools and communities against hatred and intolerance in its many forms. I am therefore optimistic that if we continue to emphasize the dangers of silence and our responsibilities as human beings, we can greatly decrease the incidence of intolerance. I am pleased to have witnessed the many improvements that have been made in our society. But that is not a reason to rest. Protecting the quality of our humanity is a lifelong pursuit.

▶ ▶ ▶ **Learning AmongUS**

1. Geller argues that each of us has a personal responsibility to make the world a better place. Do you agree or disagree with her? Explain.

2. Use your local newspaper to identify stories in which individuals or organizations are acting on Geller's admonition to make the world a better place by correcting injustices. What types of injustices are being addressed? Do you think that the individuals involved are making a positive difference in the world?

3. Geller talks about the insidious consequences of silence in the face of racism, prejudice, and discrimination against others. Have you ever remained silent in the presence of a person who made racist or prejudicial statements about another person based on her or his race, religion, ethnicity, or gender? Do you see yourself as complicit in supporting racism and discrimination because of such silence?

4. Geller's descriptions of the despicable treatment of Jews in the concentration camps of Germany during World War II are graphic, unsettling, and just plain frightening. Yet she remains optimistic about the possibility of managing the forces of evil that created the Holocaust. Do you think another holocaust could happen? Why or why not?

5. What other instances of genocide have occurred throughout the world? Conduct an Internet search to learn about several of these horrific events.

Juan Gonzalez's essay tells the story of a family's world as immigrants in the United States. Growing up with the American dream as his vision, Juan describes a universal story that is similar to those of millions of other immigrants. Like his family, they do so to improve their standard of living and to make a better world for their children. His is a story of hard work, family love, experiences of discrimination, and the fragility of economic gains. Juan's story also exemplifies the importance of the U.S. educational system in providing a pathway to success for many of those immigrants.

20 Living the American Dream

Juan C. Gonzalez

As a young child I dreamed the American dream. Being a cowboy like the Lone Ranger was a distinct possibility. Becoming a famous hero like Superman was almost within reach; I, too, wanted to stop bullets, to fly faster than an airplane, and to be more powerful than a speeding locomotive. Yes, a poor, second-generation Mexican-American boy raised in the 1950s could dream the same dreams of many other young boys in the United States.

My story is not very different from those of children whose parents recently immigrated to the United States. In fact, as I have seen in my studies of the colorful history of other immigrants to the USA, there are many similarities. Many of our forefathers arrived in America almost penniless, filled with ambitions and dreams. It was believed that if one worked very hard, the future would be filled with the bounties of the typical American dream. I have studied the history of immigration in our country, and it is an absolute truth. The British, Germans, Irish, Chinese, Japanese, Costa Ricans, Africans, Iranians, Jewish, Polish, and Mexicans have all arrived in the United States with their own stories, sacrifices, pains, sorrows, and dreams. I do not intend to write about all of these individual histories. My intent is to bring to light that all of our histories—those of our great-grandparents, our grandparents, our parents, and even our own journeys—have been heavily influenced by how accepted, embraced, rejected, avoided, discriminated against, or favored we were because of our race, culture, or appearance.

Culture Concepts

Reasons for Immigration

Immigration can occur voluntarily or involuntarily. Voluntary migrants willingly leave their home country, typically with the goal of improving their standard of living. Involuntary immigration occurs because of war, fear, or persecution.

My parents were each brought to the United States as children. They arrived without money, friends, or family connections. They left Mexico during the Mexican Revolution, which occurred from 1910 to 1924. As children, my parents witnessed firsthand the horror of war; they were uprooted from their homes in the state of Jalisco, which is in Central Mexico. They met in Texas as young adults, married in 1931, and settled in Amarillo. Though neither completed elementary school, they both recognized their lost opportunities and constantly spoke about the importance of education. My father learned to speak English without an accent. He then taught himself how to read in English, achieving this by reading our local newspaper from the first page to the last. As he chauffeured my mother for her shopping, he would typically wait in the car and read his newspaper. I do not recall seeing him read books, but he certainly was an avid reader of periodicals.

My father supported his family by working as a brakeman for the Rock Island Railroad. He also had side jobs as a gardener, a plumber, and a general handyman. To support his family, he took just about any job he could get.

My father's normal workday was extremely long and arduous. His railroad work began at 11:00 P.M. and ended at 7:00 A.M. He would return home while we were getting dressed, eating breakfast, and preparing for school. My sisters and brothers now fondly recall how our father would help with breakfast. He would make oatmeal, or fresh tortillas, or scrambled eggs and toast. Breakfast was not optional; we were expected to arrive at school with a full breakfast in us, and to behave in a respectable manner while there. After my father's breakfast duties, he would take a two- or three-hour nap. By 11:00 A.M. he would leave to mow lawns and do handy work until 5:00 P.M. At times, he would pick me up after school so I could help him with this work. It was common for me to join him in mowing lawns, raking leaves, cutting trees and shrubs, hauling and collecting trash, and many other tasks. It was common for men in the barrio in the '50s and '60s to have "la otra entrada," another job and another source of income. My father's sense of duty, integrity, and responsibility for family and community was simply incredible.

My father was my role model. He was brave, hardworking, and willing to tackle all jobs, tasks, and roles. I recall how proud I was when he would take me to the railroad yard. His coworkers would greet him and ask if I was being prepared to take his job. As an eight-year-old, I thought working with these huge trains was exciting. I recall being fascinated with my father's tools. My biased perception was that he could fix anything or do anything.

My mother would have an early dinner ready. My family would eat together, and my father would take another nap for two to three hours. He would leave for the railroad about 10:30 P.M.

My mother had an equally demanding work schedule; she would leave home about 4:30 P.M., to clean offices in one of the city's largest banks. She would return home about midnight, after my father had left. In essence, both my parents worked constantly. Because of this schedule, and as was common in the 1950s, our meals were very important; they were rigorous, loud, fun, and delicious. Though we had plenty to eat, my mother was adamant that we eat everything on our plates. Wasting food, choosing not to finish our vegetables, simply was NOT an option. My mother always reminded us of the starving children in her homeland of Mexico, and we were to count our blessings. My mother was the front-line parent in raising ten children (the first child of the ten passed away in her early infancy). The challenge for my parents was raising nine children in a predominantly white, hostile, Protestant, English-speaking environment.

My parents raised us children based on several fundamental values: love and believe in our Catholic faith; love and cherish our family; accept and demonstrate that hard work was good and was required at all times (at home, school, church, and work); and obtain an education and graduate from high school. Both parents expected us to be young adults who worked hard in service to others. We were expected to help our priest, the nuns at church and school, our neighbors, friends, and the community.

As the youngest of the ten children, I was the "spoiled" one. My brothers and sisters had "proof" of this from the first day of my life; I was the only one born in a fancy, clean hospital. I would counter that I was sent out into the cold, sterile, white world and did not enjoy the warm comfort of being born at home. Nevertheless, being the youngest in a large family placed me in a cherished, and perhaps envied, position.

We were all raised in the barrio of Amarillo, Texas, with an awareness that we lived in "our" side of town, the Chicano side of town. Literally on the other side of the railroad tracks, we had our own church, school, grocery stores, barber shops, and cemetery. We were always very cognizant when we crossed those tracks and went shopping "downtown." My mother made certain we were dressed "correctly," and she knew where we were walking and when to expect our return. It was understood that our corner of the world was the barrio; our safety, security, and well-being were determined by us knowing our place. Life on our east side of the tracks was like living within an extended family. We all knew each other, and the adults understood and accepted the responsibility to monitor the behavior of all of the children. Neighbors felt perfectly comfortable to intervene when they observed bad behavior and to report such incidents to my parents. Though it was not clear to my friends and me, the adults of our barrio understood how the behavior of a few affected everyone. The phrase "police profiling" had not yet been invented, but it was very much practiced. The first time I was stopped, questioned, and searched by the police, I was eleven. This practice was common and an ever-present reminder that we were considered suspects at all times.

In the barrio, we were all very similar to each other. We spoke Spanish, went to the same schools, prayed at the same churches, and played on the same playgrounds. When we crossed the railroad tracks, the concept of "otherness" was made very apparent by the manner in which we were monitored as we shopped, or went to the public library, or entered the post office. We were treated as outsiders.

I also experienced "otherness" when I watched television. Mexicans and Chicanos were rarely seen on television. From the very beginning of televi-

---

Culture Concepts

Importance of Language

Language is used to identify people in a group, either by the group members themselves or by outsiders from other groups. Some important questions include the following: How important is language to the members of a culture? What is the role of language in the maintenance of a culture? Why do some languages survive over time and others do not? What role does language play in the relationship of one culture to another? The importance that cultures attribute to language has been well established. In fact, some would argue that the very heart of a culture is its language and that a culture dies if its language dies.

---

sion, Latinos were rarely portrayed; if they were, it was through a negative stereotype. They certainly were not part of the sports culture. During the 1961 baseball season, the great home run race between Mickey Mantle and Roger Maris took place. Tremendous attention was paid to Babe Ruth's record of 60 home runs in a single season. My particular favorite was Roger Maris, who broke the record that had stood for 34 years. I loved baseball, and my childhood dreams and fantasies held very few boundaries. As a typical nine-year-old, I dreamed of being like my idols: cartoon superheroes, television stars, and King Arthur knights. Yet as a child I could not help but dream of being a New York Yankees baseball player. When Mickey Mantle and Roger Maris had their fantastic home run race in 1961, I was totally taken by their heroics. Though I knew my place, I dared to dream of becoming like them.

One of the saddest days of my life was on October 27, 1967; I was fifteen and a sophomore in high school. At about 5:00 A.M., my father was at work checking the brake line between two box cars. As the train engineer moved the train forward, the movement knocked my father down; unconscious, he was run over by the train and lost both of his legs above his knees. That morning I was awakened by my mother and was asked to take on the role of a man. Very simply, my mother and father needed me to step up and serve. I did. For the next several years I became my father's caretaker. I became familiar with hospitals, doctors, physical therapy, prosthetics, insurance, health coverage, settlement terms with the railroad, and access ramps for my father's wheelchair. Because of the accident, I learned to provide support for my mother's stresses and burdens. Very quickly I came to grips with my new role. As the youngest of ten and the only one still living at home, I had a new set of responsibilities. These new roles and responsibilities took a toll at school. I almost failed my sophomore year, based solely on the number of absences from school. My mother was asked to visit with the principal about my attendance, since attending school was not a priority for me; my desire was to be at my father's side.

I received my entire K-12 education in Catholic schools. In my family, Catholic faith, education, and hard work were the cornerstones of our existence. My brothers, sisters, and I finished high school, but rarely were we told about or encouraged to attend college. Because of my academic preparation, my high school counselor clearly advised me NOT to apply to a college or university. His best advice at the time was to go into the military—in essence, to skip college and go straight to Vietnam.

There was a reason my high school counselor advised me against higher education. His direction was based on my potential academic performance. He understood that my academic preparation was mediocre at best. Due to my sixth-grade reading level, I failed my first semester of college. This performance was a direct result of how and what we were taught, particularly in high school. My high school divided my class into two sections: the A group and the B group. The A group was clearly college-bound, white, and our class leaders. Group B members were being trained for the "world of work": technical and vocational training and the military. This latter group consisted of Mexican Americans, African Americans, low-income kids, and student athletes. This orientation and socialization made very clear our options after high school. In Texas, we celebrated high school athletes but not academic performers. As a group B student, I focused my energy and attention on football, fun, cars, and girls. I was being true to my parents' aspirations: I would graduate from high school. However, I did not excel sufficiently to go to college. Eventual success in my undergraduate studies was primarily due to a set of very special programs. These federally funded programs were specifically designed to assist and encourage students like me to attend and succeed at a university. One such program literally advocated for and secured my admission into the university, and it subsequently taught me how to read.

This short account is presented only to depict my early experiences and my own set of circumstances upon entering higher education. The fact that I was one of very few poor, Mexican-American high school graduates to attend college, and that I started out with an extremely inadequate academic preparation, is not unique. Many other poor students, regardless of race, culture, or academic preparation, have succeeded in college, most often because of assistance via initiatives like the program I was in.

My entry into higher education was due to the 1960s civil rights movement and the federally funded programs designed to increase the number of minority students entering college. The reality of current educational efforts is that, all too often, "special programs" are still the principal means by which institutions of higher learning admit diverse student populations. Although my particular experience some 35 years ago is perhaps explainable, an almost identical situation exists today for many minority students.

As a young Chicano freshman, I stepped into the "ivory tower" environment and immediately felt marginalized. There was a distinct feeling that I was a liability to the institution. Though I may not have possessed a college-level reading ability as an entering freshman, it was rather simple to detect both the explicit and implicit messages transmitted to me: my language, culture, and experiences were not valued. In my History 101 course, for example, I can recall classmates asking aloud, for all to hear, what I was doing in college. They were loud, explicit, and direct as they questioned my presence on campus. Even today, in the work that I do as a university administrator, students express feelings of isolation, marginality, and a general lack of belonging that is similar to what I experienced in my undergraduate days. As I speak to minority staff, faculty, and students, there is consistent agreement that many things have not changed.

I believe my successes, and those of my sisters and brothers, are firmly based on our parents providing us with a set of values and experiences that helped us interpret our world, our worth, our self-confidence, and our role within the American society. My older brothers and sisters provided excellent role models for me; they were all trailblazers and demonstrated an ability to be resilient against all odds. Society in general—schools, universities, and work environments—may not have been ready for the Gonzalez family. But our parents made certain that we were prepared to succeed, by instilling in us a sense of integrity, hard work, and willingness to serve others.

So what relevance do my experiences in the 1950s, '60s, and '70s have on today's high school and university students? I believe that Latino, African American, and other ethnic minority students continue to be treated and served differently. There is no parity, no equality, and no commensurate education readily available for all students. The United States has traveled a long road to improve the life of all its citizens, yet we continue to have a long and difficult road ahead of us. The U.S. is not fully inclusive, and discrimination based on race, ethnicity, and gender continues.

The future of the United States requires an understanding and appreciation that diversity is NOT the problem; inequity is the problem. Diversity should be seen as an enrichment and an added value to our society. The solution for this expanded view reminds me of a famous quote by Albert Einstein: "We cannot solve the problems we have created with the same thinking that created them." That is, we must step out of our traditional mental boxes and use our creativity, courage, and imagination to embrace and accept all members of the U.S. American society.

Culture Concepts

Power

Not all groups within a nation or region have equal access to sources of institutional and economic power. When cultures share the same political, geographic, and economic landscapes, some form of a status hierarchy often develops. Groups of people distinguished by their religious, political, cultural, or ethnic identity often struggle among themselves for dominance and control of the available economic and political resources.

My mother used to say that *no hay mal que por bien no venga,* which means "some good comes from every bad thing." There is much wisdom in this saying, as we enjoy the benefits of the considerable pain we have experienced. My hope is that I—and we!—will continue to live a full life, aware and proud of our roots and our history, and that we transform our individual experiences into collective actions that will help others to discover and become the best of who they are.

▶ ▶ ▶ Learning AmongUS

1. Are the goals and dreams of Gonzalez's parents, when they first immigrated to the United States, shared with other immigrants? What other reasons might people have for leaving their home country/culture and moving to another?

2. How does it affect people to know that they have to behave differently when they go to the "other" side of town?

3. What is lost and what is gained when immigrants "give up their language" in order to be successful in their new country?

4. How important is it to a person's sense of self-worth to "see" people like himself or herself in the newspapers, on television, in magazines, and in other media outlets?

5. Do you think that the presence of new technologies, such as the Internet, DVDs, and chat rooms, makes it more likely that future immigrants to the United States can and will maintain their connections to their home culture? Is technology, then, a positive or negative force?

6. Do you agree with Gonzalez that students from many different groups still experience isolation and marginality? If so, what could you or others do to change that?

What does it mean to be black in the United States? How black is black enough? Mark McPhail and Karen Dace describe the pressures to conform to the prevailing interpretations of political and social events that reflect on a cultural group. Though they write from their experiences as African American scholars, Mark and Karen explore issues that pertain to all cultures. Who can speak for the members of a particular culture? Who can be critical of members of a culture? What social expectations govern what can and cannot be said?

21   Black as We Wanna Be: From Identity Politics to Intercultural Competence

Mark Lawrence McPhail and Karen Lynette Dace

In his book *Bad as I Wanna Be,* Dennis Rodman asserts his right to define his own identity by challenging many of our most basic assumptions about race, gender, and difference. Admired by many, and criticized by just as many others, Rodman discusses his life before and after becoming a celebrity and provides interesting insights into what we will call in this essay "identity politics": that is, the tendency of marginalized or oppressed groups to establish notions of "authentic" identity that are used to determine who is and is not included in the group. For African Americans, identity politics is expressed in the idea that some of us are "not black enough" to be considered a part of "the community," and therefore the insights and observations that we have to offer are neither representative nor relevant. This exclusion creates an identity dilemma that Rodman addresses in these words: "Before I got the fame and the money, I wasn't accepted by black people, and I wasn't accepted by most white people. I wasn't the right color for any situation I found myself in. I'm sure a lot of kids and young people go through that. They think like I did: I want to be the right color."[1]

One of the most important lessons that the study of intercultural communication teaches is that the belief that there is a "right" color is at best wrong and at worst dangerous. Consequently, we wish to explore the issues raised by Rodman and consider how they have affected us both personally and professionally. As intercultural communication scholars (and fans of the Chicago Bulls), we would like to expand on Rodman's insights by examining how students and scholars, when engaging in identity politics, run the risk of rejecting ideas that can increase their understanding of intercultural and interracial communication.

The issues we address are certainly not limited to specific cultures, communities, or shared identities. Rather, our extended story should be viewed

---

Culture Concepts

Uncertainty and Anxiety Management

While some degree of unpredictability exists in all interpersonal relationships, it is typically much higher in intercultural interactions. Two broad components are involved in the management of uncertainty behaviors: uncertainty and anxiety. Uncertainty refers to the extent to which a person lacks the knowledge, information, and ability to understand and predict the intentions and behaviors of another. Anxiety refers to an individual's degree of emotional tension and her or his inability to cope with change, to live with stress, and to contend with vague and imprecise information.

---

more generically, as an exemplar that provides insights into the predominant assumptions about the nature of race, culture, gender, and the prevailing orthodoxy that can be used to silence ideas requiring critical self-reflection within a community. We speak from our own experiences as African American communication scholars who have advanced positions that critically analyze ideas about gender and race in contemporary African American culture. We also speak as scholars whose work has been dismissed and resisted because it explores issues that some do not want us to address.

Our story begins with an essay on interracial communication that we wrote together and was rejected by an intercultural communication anthology because it incorporated "white" scholarship. We then explain how the rejection of that essay evolved into a larger conflict with an editor of the anthology; this experience, we believe, illustrates the danger of identity politics. Finally, we offer some conclusions and suggestions for students and scholars of intercultural communication that we believe will help facilitate a richer and more inclusive agenda for understanding and appreciating identity, difference, and diversity.

▶ The Politics of Inclusivity: Blackness, Whiteness, and Intercultural Exclusivity

The conflict we recount here began several years ago, when we were invited to submit an article to an intercultural communication anthology that solicited essays dealing specifically with biracial relationships. Before submitting the essay we spoke with one of the editors about an idea we had that looked at how communication can function positively in interracial communication. Mark McPhail's portion of the essay focused on how performance could be used to bridge racial divisions, and Karen Dace's portion of the essay examined her friendship with a European American man she had known for several years. Initially we were told that the essay would work well in the anthology; after submitting it, we received an email from the editor who had invited us to submit it that said that it had been received, and that offered a tentative evaluation of our work: "I love it," was the response from this editor, and so we looked forward to the publication of our work.

Several months later, however, we received a letter indicating that the editors could not include our essay in their anthology. We were informed that, after careful consideration and discussion, they had decided the essay would not be appropriate because it incorporated and validated those types of scholarship they felt were at odds with the basic assumptions of their project. Specifically, they criticized Mark's portion of the essay because it affirmed and incorporated the insights of white men and focused on the notion of "empathy," which the editors believed was an inadequate concept for the development of "authentic" intercultural understanding. "Doesn't Mark's personal narrative reinforce the claim that white men espouse 'universal' ideas that 'speak' to everyone, but that persons 'limited' by 'nonwhite' ethnicity can only absorb, not contribute, such universals?" asked one editor. A second added, "Not only is the conceptualization of empathy problematic for us, but also the 'essay ends where it begins, as it hints at how to perform empathy interculturally.'" Although the essay evidently could be read this way, Mark suggested in conversations with both editors that what they had done was basically the same thing they accused white men of doing: rejecting positions because they did not fit into a predetermined agenda. One editor candidly acknowledged that this might well be the case, but the other responded by saying, "I never thought of myself as someone with an agenda."

One thing intercultural communication teaches us, we believe, is that we all have agendas. Fortunately, the essay fit into the agenda of another group of intercultural scholars,[2] who agreed to publish the same essay after minor revisions, none of which involved the critiques we had received from the editors of the first anthology. These latter scholars, whose anthology aimed at integrating the diverse voices of intercultural scholarship (including those of white men), believed that the essay made an important contribution to our understanding of intercultural communication and interaction. Still, we felt that the issues raised by the rejection of the essay by the first group of editors needed to be examined more fully, so we attempted to address them in a second essay, which was presented on a panel at a communication conference. One of the editors of the first anthology was a respondent to that panel. The panel addressed the concerns of African American men as communication scholars, and the invitation to appear on the panel included a quotation from an African American feminist scholar, bell hooks, who suggested that the voices of black women as well as black men need to be heard if we are to "redefine in nonsexist ways the terms of our liberation."

We saw this invitation as an excellent opportunity to incorporate both of our voices in an essay that addressed our concerns about racial exclusivity in intercultural communication. Although we did not mention our earlier essay, we explored how assumptions about the nature of race and gender in African American communication scholarship can be used to silence research that calls for critical self-reflection. We have included both narratives, as they were presented on that panel, below. Our story continues with Karen Dace's narrative, which focuses on issues of gender in contemporary African American culture, and Mark McPhail's, which deals with resistance to the theoretical perspectives he has developed in response to an important concept in African American communication scholarship known as Afrocentricity.

▶ Karen Lynette Dace: Disciplining Black Feminism

In their essay "Disciplining the Feminine," Carole Blair, Julie Brown, and Leslie Baxter examine how scholarly norms in the field of communication can, when accepted uncritically, affirm the notion that "institutional or professional power are deemed superfluous to the substance and character of our scholarly efforts."[3] My own experience, like theirs, suggests otherwise, and I believe that issues of power and control are as much at work in academic institutions and practices as they are in the society as a whole. While their analysis focuses on issues of gender, my concerns relate to those situations in which gender and race intersect, and issues of domination become somewhat more complex. One example of this intersection was revealed in the confirmation hearings for Supreme Court Justice Clarence Thomas, where issues of race, class, and gender were so deeply entwined with each other that issues of power and control became somewhat obscured: for some, the hearings were about male domination; for others, they were about racial discrimination; and for others, the hearings were a site of intraracial conflict. It is this last consideration, I believe, that provides important insights into the problems and possibilities of complicity in intercultural communication inquiry.

My entrance into feminist scholarship as it intersects race began not with the Clarence Thomas Supreme Court confirmation hearings, however, but with the Mike Tyson rape case. Both Clarence Thomas and Anita Hill were vital, vocal, and active members of a conservative power structure that excluded most folks like me—African American and female. Although the hearings were an alarming and sad event in American and African American history, the discourse surrounding Mike Tyson and Desiree Washington (the then 18-year-old woman who charged the boxer with rape) was even more disturbing. Conversations with friends and family revealed sympathy for Tyson and contempt for Washington. An examination of cultural artifacts, including African American publications, music, and television programs, pointed to a deep sense of commitment to Tyson at the expense of Washington. The result of that research was a conference paper titled "Let's Set the Bitch on Fire: The African American Community's Response to Desiree Washington." The title of the paper came from a scene from Spike Lee's film *She's Gotta Have It,* in which several African American women are discussing the film's lead character, a woman named Nola. Nola is depicted as a "threat" to these women, and as they discuss how she should be dealt with, one of the women states "Let's set the bitch on fire." The sentiment seemed similar to the responses that I heard from some of those who criticized Washington, who felt that she somehow constituted a threat to African American unity by accusing Mike Tyson of rape. It was this notion of African American unity that troubled me, since it seemed to suggest that women should be silenced, even dominated, for "the good of the race."

I found that the silencing of women within the race was not simply a matter of patriarchal domination; it also revealed how notions of "black authenticity" obscured issues of gender domination within some segments of various African American communities. In an attempt to understand and challenge this rigid notion of "blackness," I looked to "revolutionary feminist thinking," which according to bell hooks is "more concerned with how sexism and sexist oppression are perpetuated and maintained by all of us, not just men."[4] The paper that emerged provided an analysis of African American discourse concerning the Tyson case. Great and powerful institutions and people, including the National Baptist Convention, Louis Farrakhan, and an assortment of popular cultural institutions, joined together to communicate "community" support for Mike Tyson. As for Washington, the possibility that her accusations were true were discussed within the community. The prevailing messages about her behavior were (1) she should have known what to expect from this "strong, active black man" (the racism inherent in that reasoning was ignored by the speakers) or (2) Washington should remain silent in order to show African American solidarity and support Tyson. Many within the culture seemed "convinced that the struggle to 'save' the black race is really first and foremost about saving the lives of black males."[5]

Writing the paper on Mike Tyson was both therapeutic and enlightening. Ever concerned with uplifting the race, I found that many African Americans, both male and female, made the leap in reasoning that Tyson, too, must be saved and lifted out of the hands of his jailers. He needed the community to rescue him from an unjust judicial system and a certain conviction that would rob him of what could be his most viable boxing years. Tyson was an African American hero, and the discourse suggested that there are far too few African American males who wear that label. I felt that the essay provided some important insights into the complex character of African American responses to situations in which race and gender become intertwined, and that the essay at least provided some useful directions for scholarly inquiry. As the essay evolved from a convention paper to an article submitted for publication, however, I began to see the complexity of the very issue I had attempted to study in the responses of reviewers from two journals, the first of which focused on intercultural communication and the second on issues of gender.

The essay was first presented during a national communication convention in 1994, and it has been submitted to two scholarly journals, one of which rejected the essay outright and the second of which invited revision and resubmission. Perhaps the comments I received after its initial presentation shed some light on my failure to find a publishing outlet. Immediately after the convention presentation and throughout the remainder of the conference,

African American women approached me to offer their congratulations on the paper. Many were impressed with my "courage," saying: "I'm so glad you said what you said," or "A lot of us feel that way," or, my personal favorite, "I can't believe you actually wrote what so many of us have been feeling." Reflecting on these remarks, it becomes apparent that these women recognized that the essay made a connection between theory and practice, between revolutionary feminist thought and how it applies to our everyday lives. As scholars we seek to explore, analyze, critique, explain, and sometimes predict. When our explorations, analyses, critiques, explanations, and predictions go against or call into question the status quo or deeply held convictions, they become problematic.

After making revisions and readying the paper for publication (with the assistance of my colleagues), the essay was sent to an intercultural communication journal that emphasizes African American issues, culture, and sensibilities. The first review that arrived (normally all reviews arrive together) charged me with racism, a bias against African American men, and a lack of understanding of the culture. My sense is that the author of that review believed I had to be one of those European American feminists who has no right to explore issues African American. The implication was that no self-respecting or "authentic" black woman would write such an analysis. The reviewer recommended against publishing the analysis because it was "highly generalized," without a "detailed method," and because it "contradicted its own conclusions." The failure of the reviewer to accept feminist analysis, introduced on page one, as an appropriate method was something I had expected. But the tenor of the critique was not: the essay was likened to "a gossip column," and at one point the reviewer asked, "Is this a letter to the editor?" The reviewer rejected the essay as "more a broadside than a piece of scholarly research." The second review arrived several weeks after the first. It contained no remarks or commentary on the manuscript, simply circles on a form identifying the work as "weak" and unworthy of publication.

When sent to a feminist journal, the essay was not rejected; instead, the editor enthusiastically encouraged me to revise the essay, to include more background information about feminist scholarship, and to resubmit it for possible publication. I am in the process of working with these reviews in hopes of finally seeing this piece published. It is apparent that its "acceptance" by the feminist journal is the result of reviewers acknowledging and embracing black feminist scholarship. The analysis of the Mike Tyson rape case was approached from a black feminist standpoint that deconstructs the experiences of oppression and the asymmetrical relationship of power from the perspectives of the women who live such experiences. While the intercultural communication journal claimed to provide a voice for scholars not always available in other places, it became clear that my voice needed to toe a new color line where race, as it intersects gender, is concerned. When that intersection suggests some flaws within African American culture, the author must be reprimanded and silenced. As I attempted to illustrate how complicity un-

---

Culture Concepts

Conditions for Favorable Group Contact

The naïve view of intercultural contact—that any intercultural contact is likely to be beneficial—has been proven repeatedly to be incorrect. Research suggests four conditions that may lead to positive attitudes as a result of intercultural communication. First, support must be available from the top; if those who are in charge, or who are recognized as authority figures, support the intercultural contact, it is more likely to lead to a positive outcome. Second, those involved must have a personal stake in the outcome. Third, the actual intercultural contacts need to be viewed as pleasing and constructive. Fourth, all parties must perceive the outcome of the interaction as having the potential to be effective; that is, the members of both cultures must either have common goals or view the interaction as allowing them to achieve their own individual goals.

---

dermines intracultural understanding, I encountered an interesting double jeopardy. Indeed, I received the same message that Desiree Washington had received: "To be black is to unite at all cost; you are expendable for the greater cause."

This double jeopardy places African American women and all women of color in the impossible position of having to choose between race or gender. My refusal to make the choice in a manner that satisfied the reviewer of my work offers important insights about how the intersection between race and gender can disrupt our rigid notions of identity. The message I received from my "brothers" was that to be authentically "black" meant to be silent, while my "sisters" heard the authenticity of my voice in their own experiences with gender domination. Like me, they seemed to be more willing to explore how race, culture, and gender might be seen as entwined with each other, and not simply in conflict with one another. Rejected as a "race traitor" by some within the race, I was well received on the other side of the color line and encouraged to contribute my voice to a conversation that continues to challenge our understanding of difference and domination. This is a challenge that I believe intercultural communication students and scholars will increasingly face as we struggle to address the problems and possibilities of gender, race, and ethnicity in communication theory and practice.

▶ Mark Lawrence McPhail: Afrocentricity and Complicity

I first encountered Afrocentric thought while in graduate school, and I found that it offered a powerful commentary on the dominating or "hegemonic" character of traditional Western thought. As I delved deeper into the theories and philosophies associated with Afrocentricity, I began to notice how much of the scholarship associated with it tended to establish and sustain divisions between Afrocentric and Western or "Eurocentric" ways of knowing and being. At the same time, Afrocentric scholarship claimed to be inclusive and integrative, qualities allegedly missing in Eurocentric theories and perspectives. There seemed to be a basic contradiction at work here, and I began to look for connections between Afrocentricity and Eurocentricity. The result was an essay presented at the National Communication Association Convention titled "Afrocentricity and Complicity: An Ethnophilosophical Analysis."

The basic position that I took in the essay was that distinguishing between Afrocentric and Eurocentric thought as essentially different was neither useful nor justifiable. The distinction is not useful because it tends to perpetuate the very tendencies for which Afrocentric theorists criticize Eurocentricity: it creates rigid and sometimes false divisions, and it tends to privilege one position at the expense of the other. The distinction could not be justified because much of the research that influenced the Afrocentric perspective in communication was conducted by Europeans, thereby making distinctions based on racial or ethnic heritage somewhat suspect. I suggested that intercultural communication researchers might instead focus on the points of similarity between the two perspectives, and integrate these points of commonality, so that each position might strengthen or support the other. The individual scheduled to respond to my paper and those of the other members of the panel was an internationally recognized scholar on Afrocentricity, and I expected that whether or not my position was affirmed, it would certainly receive an engaged and insightful critique.

Unfortunately, my expectations were not met, as the scheduled respondent did not appear, and the individual who did respond to my essay basically dismissed it with the statement "everyone knows that Afrocentricity is not hegemonic." He went on, however, to make a much more telling comment that was both troubling and enlightening: troubling because it revealed a peculiarly "Eurocentric" type of racial reasoning, and enlightening because it further supported my thesis. In responding to a critique of Afrocentricity by the African philosopher Anthony Appiah, he remarked that Appiah was "a very troubled man": "I think," the respondent continued, "that one of his parents is white." Here was an Afrocentric scholar rejecting the scholarship of a respected African philosopher on the basis of a subjective and irrational argument: on the basis of racial classification. This is the same basis upon which Afrocentric scholarship was once rejected: it reflects the same type of racial reasoning that would deny any individual or group a legitimate intellectual voice because of gender or ethnic identity. It was invoked to silence Appiah and, in the process, to silence me.

I continued to work on the essay, however, and submitted it to a scholarly publication in intercultural communication. Almost a year later I received a letter from the editor rejecting the essay, accompanied by a single half-page review recommending major revisions and resubmission. "The irony here is the fact that Afrocentricity seems under attack for its failure to realize an unspecified goal," explained the reviewer, "when, in fact, Afrocentricity, admittedly, more closely reaches the implied goal that (sic) does Eurocentric hegemony." The reviewer went on to suggest that I might be "unfairly ascribing to Afrocentrists" a "deliberateness of motive" by suggesting their complicity in sustaining the "Eurocentric hegemony" they call into question. The reviewer, like the respondent at the convention, accepted the claims of Afrocentric thinkers as axiomatic, that is, as "givens." My critique of those claims, though having some "merit," showed "unclarity of purpose" and failed "to usher in the subtle prescription within the essay, arrived at in its end." Everyone knows that Afrocentricity is not hegemonic. Everyone, evidently, but me.

My lack of knowledge led me to submit the essay again, unrevised, to a "mainstream" journal of communication. My efforts resulted in an "enthusiastic" recommendation that I revise the essay as described by the responses of the editor and two reviewers, one of whom remarked that it was "an important essay that has the potential to transform not only how we think of Afrocentricity and multiculturalism, but also how we conceive of cultural relations." It was an essay, the reviewer wrote, "that should be read by many." Perhaps it will, since the essay has since been published.[6] Regardless of whether the essay is read by many, however, the concerns that motivated me to write it continue to be a focus of my intellectual energies, and in my opinion pose an important challenge to students and scholars of intercultural communication. If the expressed values of Afrocentricity are inclusivity and openness, then those values must be translated into tangible practices. The same is true for the discipline of communication in general, and for intercultural communication inquiry in particular, which can only benefit from increasing the number of our voices that we invite to participate in conversations and dialogues that challenge static notions of difference, identity, and diversity.

▶ Disciplining Blackness: Oppositionality and the "Embrace of Whiteness"

One of the values intercultural communication scholarship promotes is the importance of inclusivity and the valuing of diverse voices. Our story continues through an examination of how the narratives that we presented illustrate how difficult it can be to translate principles into practice, even for communication scholars whose research has emerged as a response to the exclusivity of traditional social science approaches to the study of identity and culture and who emphasize the importance of self-reflexivity in an understanding of difference. Because we believed that the respondent to our panel was one such scholar, we hoped that our essay would be seen as an opportunity to have a public conversation about the tension between inclusivity and exclusivity in intercultural communication research. Although we did not mention the essay that the respondent had rejected earlier, it did come back to haunt us in a very personal and public way. In the response to the essay presented on the panel, Mark was singled out and admonished to "come back to [your] black masculinity," and not to "embrace whiteness." Both of these statements seemed to be coded personal attacks directed at Mark because his wife is European American. This belief was confirmed by another participant on the panel, who said that the respondent had told him that the comments were meant to be "double edged."

When Mark confronted the respondent with the accusation that her critique was a veiled attack on him that was based on her inability to deal with his relationship with his wife, however, he was told that this was a conflict of "intellectual perspectives" that had nothing to do with his personal life. Shortly afterward, an email message was sent out to a public list to which both Mark and Karen are members that explained the respondent's position. In response to Mark's accusation that the comments were directed at his personal life, the respondent wrote:

> Is that true? Is that the "bottom line" of my criticism that, unlike [the other members of the panel], Mark appeared in his paper not as a "live black man" but only as a "disembodied intellectual"—raceless and genderless? Is that all that lies behind my caution to Mark and Karen not to get so lost in the "white embrace" of work that was not well received, or not universally well received by Black scholars, that they forget that such "white embraces" can be motivated by anti-black intellectual politics?

While the respondent noted that "in a sense [Mark was] correct," the response to the paper was ultimately defined as a conflict of intellectual visions.

That conflict was related back to our earlier essay, and an apparently new issue was raised: why had Mark not, when given the opportunity, written about his relationship with his wife? As the respondent recalls,

> I simply asked if you'd write about a positive, close personal relationship with someone of another race or culture, hoping that you would CHOOSE to write about your marriage. Imagine my surprise when you chose to write about the positive influence on your intellectual development of Robert Penn Warren (a long-dead white male poet!).

Somehow the conversations about the essay that occurred before it was submitted, in which Mark clearly explained what was intended (an earlier version of the essay had been presented publicly at a communication conference, and the respondent was aware of it), and the first email that we had received in which the respondent wrote "I love it," had been erased from memory. Mark was guilty of "the erasure of race" because he had chosen to write about something other than his marriage, and his silence was viewed as an indication of his wife's undue influence, his unwillingness to embrace his own "blackness," and Karen's unwillingness to do the same! The respondent continued:

Culture Concepts

Are Cultural Values Relative or Universal?

An ethical issue confronting intercultural communicators is whether it is ever acceptable to judge the people of a culture when their behaviors are based on a radically different set of beliefs, values, norms, and social practices. A culturally relativistic point of view suggests that every culture has its own set of values, and therefore judgments can be made only within the context of the particular culture. Most people do not completely subscribe to this view, partly because it would lead to a lack of any firm beliefs and values on which to build a sense of self-identity. Are there any values, then, that transcend the cultural boundaries and can be regarded as universal? Scholars suggest that at least two values transcend all cultures. The first is that each culture should be able to maintain a sense of dignity, pride, and respect. The second is that we ought to strive for a world in which people can live at peace with themselves and with one another.

After reading that essay, I said to myself, "Mark simply prefers to keep his private life private." Yet I think I read into the fact that you were silent about your marriage in a space where there was the opportunity to speak about it positively, the influence of one of those black man-white woman relationships that I "can't deal with." This was exacerbated by your (and Karen's preference, in both the proposed chapter and the NCA paper,) for intercultural perspectives that emphasize "empathy" and "understanding" over those that deconstruct "oppression," "power asymmetry" and "difference." Surely, this was the influence of a guilt avoidant white woman!

The attack on Mark's wife continues, despite the respondent's acknowledgement that "I don't know your wife—or ANYTHING about her except her race," and concludes that the critique of our paper "was not centrally about the 'black man-white woman thang' (not ee-ven close.)" The respondent acknowledges having read into Mark's silence

the presence of an imagined white woman with attitudes that I "can't deal with." Shame on me for doing that! I apologize to you for doing that (although for nothing else I said or did!). AND shame on you for leaving that space— among so many others that would locate you as black and male as well as intellectual—as a gaping void.

Because of the public character of these criticisms, we do not feel that it is improper to repeat them here. In responding to them we attempted to move the discussion beyond antagonism and debate and toward dialogue. Although both Karen and Mark were indicted by these public accusations, it was clear that they were largely directed at Mark, so he alone responded publicly, acknowledging his own role in sustaining the argumentative character of the interaction and apologizing for attributing to the respondent motives that may or may not have been the basis for the critique of our work. Mark suggested that the work that Karen and he have done together illustrates their commitment to including diverse voices, while at the same time being "critical of the notions of authenticity that have circumscribed what we define as 'real' blackness, or maleness."[7] Further, Mark explained that he would "continue to embrace whatever forms and perspectives that help us better understand that character of human antagonism and how we might be able to transform it for the better of all people. If that means embracing whiteness, as well as blackness, then I am guilty as charged."

In response to the accusations of guilt and "shame," however, we felt that something more needed to be said. Mark concluded the response with the following statement that, though phrased in the first person, reflects the position of both of us:

> But I hope that we can get beyond guilt, and shame. While we may not always agree, I believe that we can continue to be friends and colleagues, and to support and nurture each other in ways that advance our common goals and aspirations. I believe now, and always will, that it will be people who are willing to question our most basic assumptions about domination, identity, and difference who will set the example for creating the moral and spiritual knowledge that will guide us in the future as we cross the color line into the next millenium. I have always admired your willingness to be one of those people. Thank you.

This conflict was eventually resolved in a civil and professional manner, but the issues it raised, and those that we have attempted to address in this and other essays, will continue to confront students and scholars of intercultural communication.

▶ Black, White, or Brown as We Wanna Be: From Identity Politics to Intercultural Competence

Our story ends with some important lessons that our experience can offer students and scholars of intercultural communication. We believe that the most significant lesson is that we need to address the problems of "identity politics" if we are truly committed to the possibility of achieving intercultural competence. Identity politics assume that some voices are more authentic than others, and they speak to issues such as oppression, power asymmetry, and difference in ways that are more useful and acceptable than others. Intercultural competence helps us to understand that to deal effectively with the historical and social realities of cultural divisions and antagonisms, and with the problems of oppression and inequality, we must be willing to listen to those voices that are different from our own and that do not necessarily fit our personal and cultural beliefs and biases.[8] The irony of the conflict issues described above is that we have always addressed them in our work, which has been accepted by scholars and students of diverse backgrounds, although perhaps not in ways that all of our colleagues believe are legitimate.

Nonetheless, we believe that our voices, and the insights they offer, are just as important as those perspectives that define intercultural and interracial communication in oppositional terms. Indeed, we believe that the challenge we face as intercultural communication scholars and students is that of moving beyond oppositional stances and facilitating inclusivity in intercultural communication in practice as well as theory, and thereby establishing an enlarged understanding of difference and identity. One way of doing this is envisioned in what Dolores Tanno describes as "dialogue," an approach to communication that goes beyond debate and accusations, as it works toward inclusivity and reconciliation. "If we are truly going to address the issues of intolerance and stereotyping and discrimination," she writes, "we have to develop a history together (really we have to acknowledge we already have a history together!), commit ourselves through time, be inclusive of all voices, and invest both our minds and our souls to the dialogue for solutions."[9] The need to include all voices, we believe, is one of the most important challenges that intercultural communication theory and practice will encounter as we enter the next century.

The notion that our race, or gender, or intellectual perspective defines us in some essential way inhibits our ability to communicate not only across cultures, but within cultures as well. The experiences we recount in this essay have reinforced this belief, but we recognize that our understanding of the complexity of cultural difference and diversity will always be limited by our own peculiar personal and professional agendas. Still, we remain confident that the challenge that our discipline faces today is one that has defined it from the beginning: the challenge of communicating competently across and within our differences, and celebrating the diversity of all of our voices, regardless of race, culture, or beliefs. We have tried in this essay to tell our own story of this struggle and the impact it has had on our lives. We believe that these experiences, despite being uncomfortable and at times discouraging, have also helped us to understand better both the problems and the possibilities of intercultural inquiry.

As students and practitioners of intercultural communication, we all must come to grips with the implications of how we choose to understand our identities and our differences. We must also confront in ourselves the willingness to accept the differences of others despite the fact that they may not always conform to our own preconceived agendas. This, in intercultural interaction, is the difference between communication and competence. If we simply view "blackness," or "maleness," or "intellectualness" as fixed, static, and unchanging markers of who we are, we may miss one of the most important lessons that the study of intercultural communication can teach us: regardless of what others wish to impose on us, we already are the right color. Intercultural communication can help us understand that we have the right to be as black, or white, or brown, as we wanna be, as long as we are willing to extend that same courtesy to others. It is at this point, we believe, that we are able to erase the divisions between empathy and oppositionality, understanding and deconstruction, and move beyond intercultural communication toward intercultural competence.

Notes

1. Dennis Rodman with Tim Keown, *Bad as I Wanna Be* (New York: Dell Publishing, 1996), p. 178.

2. Our essay, entitled "Crossing the Color Line: From Empathy to Implicature in Intercultural Communication," appears in *Readings in Cultural Contexts,* ed. Judith Martin, Thomas Nakayama, and Lisa Flores (Mountain View, Calif.: Mayfield Publishing, 1998).

3. Carole Blair, Julie Brown, and Leslie Baxter, "Disciplining the Feminine," *Quarterly Journal of Speech 80* (1994), 383.

4. bell hooks, *Killing Rage: Ending Racism* (New York: Holt, 1995), p. 62.

5. hooks, 1995, p. 88.

6. The essay appears as "From Complicity to Coherence: Rereading the Rhetoric of Afrocentricity," *Western Journal of Communication 62* (1998), 1–18.

7. Karen L. Dace and Mark L.M. Phail, "Complicity and Coherence in Intra/Intercultural Communication: A Dialogue," in *Politics, Communication, and Culture,* ed. Alberto González and Dolores V. Ianno (Thousand Oaks, CA: Sage, 1997), 27–47.

8. See Myron W. Lustig and Jolene Koester, *Intercultural Competence: Interpersonal Communication Across Cultures* (New York: Longman, 1999).

9. Dolores Tanno outlined her position in "A Characterization of Dialogue," presented at the Western States Communication Association Convention, Portland, OR, 1995, p. 5.

▶ ▶ ▶ Learning AmongUS

1. Apply the concept of uncertainty and anxiety management to the interactions that McPhail and Dace describe.

2. If a cultural group has experienced oppression from members of a dominant group, what constraints should there be on the individual members of the oppressed culture to act in concert with other members of their group?

3. Use the ethical question/issue titled "Are cultural values relative or universal?" to explain the criticism Dace received for her scholarly work on Mike Tyson.

4. How important is it for members of a culture to critique and evaluate publicly the practices and values of their own cultural group? Does such criticism undermine the strength and vitality of the culture, particularly if that culture is surrounded by members of other cultural groups?

Can men and women work together effectively? Can an African American man and a European American woman sustain both a friendship and a business partnership? Why are others so fascinated and curious about competent intercultural communication that crosses both race and gender? What personal characteristics and communication practices support the development of competent task and social relationships for a man and a woman who come from different racial and cultural backgrounds? Business partners and friends Ann Bohara and Patrick McLaurin offer their answers to these questions.

22 Friends and Partners

Ann M. Bohara and Patrick McLaurin

Eight years ago, against the advice of almost everyone with whom we talked, we decided to form a business partnership. The main theme of the advice we received was that such partnerships are notorious for ending friendships. Even worse, most of the business consultants we talked to about forming a partnership recounted horror stories of financial ruin and business failure. In spite of those dire warnings, however, we decided to challenge conventional wisdom by forming a partnership to do consulting and training in organizational change and management development.

After eight years, we can say the experts were right; remaining friends and partners has been much harder than we ever imagined. Everything they said about a business partnership was true; it pushes the limits of friendship and trust. At the same time, however, they were wrong; we are still here, as friends and partners. We found that by putting the friendship before the partnership, we have been able to withstand the many challenges we encountered as a small consulting business. What's more, we found that, in surviving the partnership, the friendship became stronger and more secure. We would like to talk about that friendship, not only because it has survived the partnership ordeal, but because the other unique aspect of the partnership, and perhaps another reason we were so counseled against working together, is that one of us is a white female and the other is a black male.

The intersection of race and gender in American society has always been a source of interest, if not a cause of uneasiness. From the country's earliest days, the fact that America was made up of men and women of different races has presented a dilemma: how would the "melting pot" ideal address racial and ethnic diversity when it came to gender? As a culture, our fascination with cross-race relationships has been explored in books, movies, and plays. Same-sex friendships across racial lines can be problematic enough, as Jim and Huck Finn might attest. But given people's responses to the relationship's romantic or sexual overtones, black males and white females are a particularly troublesome combination in U.S. social thinking. In our case, even as professional business partners we found that our racial and gender identities seemed to fascinate people.

▶ The Business

We had known each other about three years and had done quite a bit of consulting together when we decided to form the business partnership. At the time, we were both teaching at an Ivy League university, and our offices were a few doors apart. In fact, Ann had been instrumental in Patrick's coming to the university, but the idea of working together in a business partnership was the farthest thing from either of our minds. We were teachers and researchers, struggling to meet teaching demands and publish articles.

As we found we had very similar research and teaching interests, we also began working outside the university, doing consulting and training for businesses. Most of this work we did as a team, and we found we liked working together outside the classroom. After a year or so of consulting as academic colleagues, we decided to formalize the association, despite those strong warnings from business consultants against forming a partnership.

Perhaps not surprisingly, much of our work both when we started and even today has to do with issues of race, gender, and other social dynamics as they relate to identity in organizations and communities. Some of this work focuses on organizational development to help organizations meet the demands of remaining competitive as workforce demographics change. Our consulting practice has been responsible for assessments that have led to substantial organizational changes and transformations. We have also worked with thousands of managers to give them the skills needed to manage today's changing workforce more effectively. Another aspect of our business has included work with international populations, focusing on issues of intercultural communication and management practices.

As a result of the business, we have traveled extensively throughout the United States and the world. We have worked with both Fortune 100 companies and small nonprofit organizations. No matter what the assignment or the location, however, we have always been fascinated by how people react to our partnership and our identities. At times surprise is visible on the face of a client who meets us for the first time. On other occasions it is clear the client finds our relationship intriguing by the way he or she keeps asking us about our partnership, rather than the business we have come to conduct. Sometimes the curiosity is more frank; we have been told by contacts inside organizations that "everyone is trying to figure out what it is with you two." When we ask what this means, the reply is usually that people assume we must be married or a couple in some form. On these occasions, we are reminded what an oddity our relationship is, as it seems to be hard to imagine a white woman and a black man working in a partnership for any other reason.

Culture Concepts

Intercultural Interpersonal Relationships

People in an intercultural relationship may define their experiences very differently. The diversity of cultural norms that govern romantic relationships is an excellent example of the wide range of cultural expectations; there are enormous differences in cultural beliefs, values, norms, and social practices about love, romance, dating, and marriage. Family or kinship relationships are also characterized by large cultural variations. Particularly important to these intercultural relationships are the following factors: how the family is defined, or who is considered to be a member of the family; the formality of roles and behavioral expectations for particular family members; and the importance of the family in social relationships and personal decisions.

Often people with whom we work begin by assuming that one of us must be in the lead or controlling role and, therefore, that the other is the (less competent) assistant. But the usual labels cannot immediately be applied to this partnership, and people sometimes react with confusion. Is it the woman who is in the subordinate role, making the minority the leader, or vice versa, making the woman the "boss"? To whom should they be directing their conversation, and who is it safe to ignore? More confusing for those hoping to detect a power imbalance, we are, we believe, both very competent and well matched in our professional strengths. In business negotiations, as we became aware of how our relationship can put some people off balance, we learned to use this dynamic to our strategic advantage.

In less competitive business dealings, we have found that after the initial surprise, many of our clients and some of our coworkers begin to feel as if this cross-race, cross-gender relationship is a source of optimism for them as well. They often seem to want to be part of this relationship and to see it succeed. The partnership seems to become a kind of symbol of the potential for collaboration across racial and gender differences. It is as if we are "beating the odds" and are "lucky" in a curious kind of way. Of course, we can also use this dynamic to our advantage; often clients will bring extra energy and involvement to their work with us, which usually improves the outcome of the consultation all around. For us, these optimistic responses to the partnership can be amusing and sometimes disconcerting; we have learned that they have little to do with us and our work and more to do with the hopes and preconceptions of those around us.

▶ The Friendship

When meeting us, most people immediately notice our obvious racial and gender differences. In our society, these social markers should indicate that we have very little in common. What most people don't realize, even after getting to know us, is just how similar we are despite our physical differences. As is often the case, what is not visible or noticeable is what really matters.

First, we are the same age, born the same year. One of us was raised on the East Coast and the other on the West Coast, but our upbringings were similar. Although we are of different races, both our families had about the same economic level, what could best be described as lower middle class. We both grew up in the suburbs in similar neighborhoods, only 3,000 miles apart. Although our families had their distinct, individual characters, we were raised in a time when most of America shared a common set of values and beliefs.

The shared American culture we grew up with was much less fragmented than in today's multichanneled cable world. We watched the same TV shows, saw the same movies, and listened to the same music on our transistor radios. Even more significant than our upbringings is that today we both enjoy similar interests. We are voracious readers, and we discovered that we read many of the same books for enjoyment when we were young.

This is not to say that the friendship has been easy or without problems. In fact, we have had major fights concerning the business and how we relate to each other. Interestingly, most of our conflicts have not been as a result of the differences caused by our race and gender. Rather, our need to fulfill the responsibilities of our other social identities as "spouses" and "parents" has sometimes led to choices that have interfered with our work, and our work has sometimes interfered with our family responsibilities. Balancing these needs takes time and is a matter of trial and error, requiring the other partner (and our spouses) to be understanding and patient. Again, carrying us through these difficulties has been our trust in the value of our friendship, a friendship we both experience from a unique perspective.

▶ Patrick's Perspective

Ann has been instrumental in my development as a professional and a person. When we started our partnership five years ago, it was difficult for me to talk to white people as a professional. I was insecure in thinking that they were noticing my race more than anything I had to say. Ironically, part of my professional work is in helping others overcome just this hurdle, so I know it is a fairly common problem for minority professionals. As a result of my insecurity, our early business practice usually consisted of Ann doing most of the talking whenever we met clients. I would chime in later, when I felt safer. Since then I have gained confidence and have become much more self-assured when talking, even to the most senior executives in corporate boardrooms. In the beginning, however, I was grateful to have Ann take the lead whenever we met new clients.

Much of our corporate work has been for very conservative organizations. I think that for me, our success in the very heart of white corporate America has a different significance than it does for Ann. Although I know she is proud of our accomplishments, she can't realize how meaningful it is for me to have had such success in these places where I probably would never have been

---

Culture Concepts

Describing Intercultural Friendships

The language people use to describe their interpersonal relationships often reflects the underlying cultural values about their meaning and importance. Thus friendships among European Americans are expressed by terms such as friends, allies, *and* neighbors, *all of which reflect an individualistic cultural value. However, among African Americans and some southern whites, closeness between friends is expressed by such terms as* brother, sister, *or* cousin, *suggesting a collectivist cultural value. Mexican terms for relationships, like the cultural values they represent, are similar to those of African Americans. Thus when European Americans and Mexicans speak of close friendships, the former may use a word such as* partner, *which suggests a voluntary association, whereas Mexicans may use a word such as* brother *or* sister, *which suggests a lasting bond that is beyond the control of any one person.*

---

hired. She might not understand what it feels like, as I work with the most conservative corporate types imaginable, to get to the point at which my race is not the issue.

Ann has also helped to fill the gaps in my understanding of mainstream culture. Like every school child in the fifties and sixties, I was educated by reading the classics, learning the history of the world from a Eurocentric perspective, and viewing mainstream European American culture as the norm. I was also very aware of my African American heritage and went through a period of discovery that left me with a sense of pride in and identity with my own ethnic culture. But that is not to say I rejected mainstream culture. On the contrary, as someone who studies cultures, I have always been fascinated with mainstream American culture, although I have not always understood it. One aspect of our friendship is that I use Ann as my cultural "guide" to make sense of Anglo-Saxon culture. In many ways, Ann has "explained" European and American literary culture and history to me.

I think that, to some extent, I serve the same role for her, helping her to understand African American culture. Unfortunately, I have trouble bringing her into my African American networks, primarily because I am not sure she would understand them or they her. I know this is an unfounded anxiety, and more my problem than hers, but I feel it nonetheless. In fact, she has always impressed me with her sensitivity and understanding of ethnic and minority issues and with her apparent comfort when she is the minority in a group of minorities. We do not talk about race or gender issues that much as part of the friendship, but when we do, I have always found Ann to be open, honest, and sincere.

Part of my unease comes from the realization that although our racial differences do not matter within our friendship, when we are around other African American professionals Ann's race and cultural background are more relevant and noticeable. African Americans are sometimes quick to label whites. I am afraid they will not understand her in the way I do, as a unique individual, and will not be able to get beyond her white skin and identity. This labeling is, in fact, a type of "reverse racism" not usually directed at an individual white person but aimed at some part of white culture in general.

Professionally, I know there are issues relating to race on which Ann defers to me when I am sure she would like to comment. Our work often concerns issues of race and culture. Like most majority people, there is much Ann does not know about minority or ethnic culture and experience. As a researcher, however, there is much she does know about multiculturalism and issues relating to social identity in a pluralistic society; still, on issues concerning race, she usually defers to my perspective.

Socially, I think Ann still does not quite feel comfortable admitting to me she dislikes some African Americans we meet, not because of race but simply because she does not like them as people. I think she is afraid I would take offense. I think she is also hesitant to comment on many of the social issues plaguing the black community, such as crime, drugs, and teen pregnancy. While we talk at great length about most social issues, these particular problems as they relate to the black community we often discuss at an abstract, distant level, not as if one of the people involved in the discussion was a part of that community.

There are times we both forget our major differences, race and gender, and are insensitive to each other. I can remember more than one occasion when Ann has been the only woman at the table when we have been out to dinner with colleagues or clients. On some of these occasions the talk becomes sexist, and I do nothing to support her, even though I know this kind of talk offends her. In fact, when she confronts me later and I apologize, I realize I had been thinking of her as "one of the boys" and not accounting for what it cost her as a woman to fit in socially with an all-male group. On another occasion, however, we traveled to Warsaw, Poland, together soon after the fall of communism as some of the first American educators to enter the country to teach Western business practices. In the week we were there, we never saw another person of color. But it was only toward the end of our stay that Ann became aware that people had been staring at me since our arrival, something I had noticed as soon as we got off the plane. After that, for the rest of our visit, while she could do nothing to change other people's behavior, she did her best to be supportive of me.

I think Ann struggles, as many majority members do, when trying to understand minority experience. Hard as she might try, there is a part of my identity that she can never truly know or experience. Although she understands, and can be empathetic, she cannot be in my skin or experience life as I do. What makes it worse is that I cannot explain it to her. I told her once that I had to raise my children as "black children," not just as children, as she was raising hers. She wanted to know what that meant and I couldn't explain it. I could not explain a 24-hour, seven-day-a-week process that takes a lifetime to learn and deals with both the most trivial and significant nuances of being a minority in this culture. Over the years, as her children and my children have grown, we have compared the different challenges we face as parents, and she has come to see what I meant; at the time, however, I could not put it into words.

I think for majority people who are sincere in their friendships with minorities, their friend's minority identity poses a dilemma. While wanting to become close friends, they are not sure how to share in that unique part of the identity of their friend. If the relationship is to be reciprocal, it is hard to find a comparable part of their identity to share. What I appreciate about Ann is that she is careful never to assume that she has access to that part of my identity simply because we are friends. I appreciate her understanding that my experience is a part of me that is uniquely mine. If she were to say she understood what it was like for me to be a minority because she understood minority experience in the larger sense or because we have been friends, I would be very disappointed. This is not to say that she doesn't understand my experience; in fact, she probably does to a large degree. But as part of our friendship, she never assumes or implies to me that she does.

▶ Ann's Perspective

When Patrick and I first began working together, I had a relatively naive perspective about the impact of race, gender, and ethnicity on people's personal and professional lives. In fact, my ideas were unformed and untested; they were based on incidents of prejudice and favoritism viewed from a distance. For me, working as one half of a cross-gender, mixed-race team has been an unexpected and startling education in the nature and intensity of race and gender bias. Moreover, working alongside Patrick has taught me many ways of responding to that bias with grace and with the determination to learn and to succeed.

Initially what brought us together intellectually were shared research and teaching interests. Emotionally what mattered was that we both saw ourselves as outsiders in the almost wholly white, mostly male Ivy League school where we were teaching. We were nontraditional types in a very traditional, conservative environment. Almost from the start, we recognized a commonality of interests and found that we could help each other, whether facing challenges in the classroom or navigating through the shoals of departmental politics. We discovered that the two of us working together made a strong combination: those who would tend to discount me because of my gender still needed to deal with Patrick; those who would discount Patrick because of his race still had to deal with me; and those who would try to discount us both found it harder to do so with two of us to account for.

Historically and on a larger political scale, alliances between dispossessed minority groups often founder at this point: when despite this initial commonality of interests, joint progress toward recognition and growth reveals the many political and social issues on which these groups differ. They recognize many issues in which the stakes they hold are radically different or even in competition. Patrick and I have come up against our own small-scale versions of these challenges. I believe that what has kept us together as a team is Patrick's ability to see both his side of the issue and mine—and his willingness to persist in explaining these insights to me so that ultimately we are both able to see and respect each other's issues. When needed, we have put one person's interest ahead of the other's. We can do this only because we trust each other and believe in the long-term fairness and growth of our partnership.

Professionally, Patrick opened up a whole new discipline for me to understand and study. In addition, watching him teach has helped me improve my classroom persona and shape an open, interactive environment for my students. But it has been our consulting work together that has taught me the most about presenting myself as a woman and as a professional person in mainstream corporate and academic America. Patrick credits me with helping him understand white, mainstream high (literary) culture, but my parents were blue-collar, union, and lower middle class; neither had a college education, and both worked full-time. The ways and mores of the upper middle class, especially of corporate or business-centered America, were things I knew about only from books and movies.

So when we first walked into the offices of conservative corporate America to market our consulting services, it was foreign ground for both of us. Neither of us would have been there without the other.

Personally, I feel fortunate that our relationship has allowed me to understand something of what it is like to be the focus of racial bias. Traveling together on business, Patrick and I have often been stared at, asked to wait a long while to be seated for a restaurant table and then given the worst table in the house, and ignored by receptionists and secretaries. Even more telling are the smaller missteps: the airline check-in clerks who hesitate for a long moment before accepting that, yes, we are traveling together and would like adjacent seats; or the flight attendant on a client's private jet who greeted me cordially but stopped Patrick (in full corporate three-piece suit and tie) on his way into the cabin and began to ask him to put the luggage outside before realizing her mistake. While neither constant nor particularly problematic, such events reveal to me something of the frustration and fatigue that people of color often need to manage when they work in mainstream white environments. In our case, the bias encountered is not always white against black; it also comes from people of both races who resent us as a cross-race couple.

More fortunately, through our consulting I have met and worked closely with other African Americans, several of whom I now count as friends. My partnership with Patrick and these friendships have allowed me to feel, in a concrete way, how inextricably connected we all are. These people are not foreign to me, and they are neither exotic nor sinister. I have a stake in their future and they in mine. Through my relationship with Patrick I am learning to see people of color as *people,* not as "them" but as individuals, and I am learning to recognize at the same time that a significant piece of their unique, individual identity is embodied in their race. Holding these two perceptions simul-

---

Culture Concepts

Intercultural Friendships

Intercultural friendships can vary in many ways: whom a person selects as a friend, how long a friendship lasts, the prerogatives and responsibilities of being a friend, the number of friends a person prefers to have, and even how long a relationship must develop before it becomes a friendship. For intercultural friendships to be successful, therefore, they may require an informal agreement between individuals about each of these aspects, so the people involved will have shared expectations about appropriate behaviors.

---

taneously is a challenging mental and emotional balancing act for me as an observer; I can only imagine the challenge it is for the participants.

Earlier this year, Patrick's teen-age daughter Clairissa came to visit me for a day. I was supposed to advise her about some of her schoolwork. I did this, but we spent most of the afternoon going to lunch and browsing in the shops along the main street of the small town where I live. Like the curiosity that Patrick and I experience in our travels together, this combination of middle-aged white woman and young black girl caused a few stares, despite the racially mixed nature of the community. The fact that we were together was hard for some people to grasp. I found myself wanting to let shop clerks know that the girl was with me—was mine, at least for the day—and they didn't need to watch her so closely when we entered a store and separated to look at different things, as often happens with my own daughters. I felt a little angry and a little embarrassed. I wanted to protect her from the suspicious and even the casually curious stares. Yet I was helpless to do so. I am not sure that Clairissa even noticed. But for me the day represented two things: the growth of my own understanding since I first started working with Patrick, and the growth of his trust in me, to share his child with me for the day.

▶ Conclusion

Writing this article about our partnership has given us a chance to reexamine what it is about this relationship that has made it "work" across the obstacles usually presented by race and gender. At heart, we respect and trust one another, a trust that has become stronger the more we have worked together. We hesitate, however, to draw any universal conclusions from our experiences. Clients and coworkers, observing how well we seem to work together, sometimes ask us for recommendations about building diverse teams, based on our own experiences. Yet we have always been reluctant to present our friendship as an example for anyone to follow. While it seems clear to us now that we have many commonalties in our backgrounds and views on many professional and personal issues, we are at a loss to explain what, initially, enabled us to see these similarities through the visible and real differences of race and gender. We are left with the realization that part of our success was the ability to focus on our commonalities and not let the potential divisiveness in racial and gender differences prevent us from seeing the other person.

▶ ▶ ▶ Learning AmongUS

1. Given the multicultural nature of the United States today, how important is it to establish friendships with people from other cultures?
2. What lessons do Bohara and McLaurin provide that can help us improve intercultural friendships?
3. As Bohara and McLaurin describe the development of their friendship over time, what is the most important obstacle or constraint they had to overcome: race, gender, or something else?
4. Using the ideas in the Culture Concepts box that describe the various ways in which cultures differentiate the characteristics of friendships, analyze the development of the friendship between Bohara and McLaurin.
5. Select one of your intercultural friendships and apply these ideas to it.

Using remembered and sometimes painful events from her own life, Gale Young examines the unacknowledged, uncontested, and unmentioned privilege of being white in the United States today. Her stories challenge those with white privilege to recognize and become uncomfortable with such unfair and unearned power over others. Gale also summons us to think about the difficult and complicated consequences of race in the United States. Through an analysis of our family stories, we can understand our taken-for-granted beliefs and actions, thus making connections between our personal experiences and the larger political and social world.

23 Leonard's Yard: Pulling at the Roots and Responsibilities of My Whiteness

Gale Young

I sat on the stone ledge surrounding my parents' garden, which contained the 50 roses my father had planted nearly 50 years earlier. They were the roses he liked to prune and pamper while I tagged along with a willing ear, first as a child listening to his tales of garden gnomes and later to his gentle suggestions for coping with my adolescent gyrations. This was the rose garden that bloomed on my wedding day, out of season, and that brought my mother so much pleasure in the years after my father's death. This was the rose garden that looked out over the San Francisco Bay, Mt. Tamalpais, and what had years ago been "Leonard's yard." In those moments by the garden, myriad memories flashed before me, rearranging themselves like pieces in a kaleidoscope, offering multiple views of my middle-aged life.

The memory pieces I want to share with you expose an emerging awareness of my whiteness. They are intentionally personal and presented as isolated instances. After 19 years of teaching intercultural communication to students and faculty from many ethnicities, I've come to believe that the way we learn about the differences that race/color and culture make is through gathering what may at first appear to be unrelated stories that we can then examine through the lenses of race and culture.[1]

The difference between a personal story and an ethnic story is not so much the pieces that are chosen but the expanse of the context. A personal story emphasizes the particulars of individuals and families. An ethnic story places the memory pieces in a racial and ethnic context that highlights the impact the social-political and cultural power structures have on individuals and their families.

> ## **Culture** Concepts
>
> ### Consequences of Living in an Intercultural World
>
> *Living in an intercultural world will inevitably introduce doubts about others' ex-pectations and reduce the certainty that specific behaviors, routines, and rituals mean the same things to everyone. Cultural mixing implies that people may feel threatened when challenged by the actions of those with an alternative cultural framework. Examples abound that underscore how difficult it is for groups of cul-turally different individuals to live, work, and play together harmoniously. The con-sequences of failing to create a harmonious intercultural society are obvious—hu-man suffering, hatred passed on from one generation to another, disruptions in people's lives, and unnecessary conflicts that sap people's creative talents and en-ergies and siphon off scarce resources from other important societal needs.*

Most white, Anglo, western European Americans in the United States don't feel their color or culture each moment, because they are not in contrast to it. So it is not uncommon for European Americans to say, "I don't have a cul-ture," "When I look in the mirror I see a human being or just a man or a woman," and "I don't have any white privilege; I work just as hard as the next guy." These statements are true in the sense that they mirror the emphasis that European Americans put on their experience. But what is left out of these statements is also true: that they reflect the unconscious and unearned privi-lege that comes with being racially similar to other members of the dominant group (Bowser & Hunt, 1997; Wildman, 1996). Conversely, people of color in the United States are forced, at an early age, to experience the contrast be-tween the dominant racial domain and their own. Herein lies the foundation of the racial divide and, paradoxically, the ability to envision a bridge across it.

In the act of recalling, collecting, and inquiring into what may initially ap-pear as fragments of memory about what was said, seen, and unspoken, we can understand how our race and ethnicity weave into our identity. As you read my memory pieces, look for the personal feelings of being different and in contrast to others. Notice the recurring theme of wanting to belong, and varia-tions such as feeling left out, favored or rejected, or feeling tolerated but not fully accepted juxtaposed with my lack of awareness about being part of the in-group. Notice the growing self-consciousness and confusion about being white and the sense of feeling responsible for and embarrassed by other whites.

Each person's experiences, when focused through the lens of power, cul-ture, race, and social institutions, provide the landscape for perceiving the in-group/out-group dynamics that drive sociopolitical policies and practices. In our families, we respond in various ways to the rules of politeness, protocol, secrets, and silence that are perpetuated across generations. By so doing we engage in the personal version of the social power to dominate, deny, respond, resist, rebel, and assimilate. When we learn to see and situate our place within these patterns, we can then acknowledge our feelings (such as how

> ## **Culture** Concepts
>
> ### Dimensions of Interpersonal Relationships
>
> *People use at least three primary dimensions to interpret interpersonal communi-*
> *cation messages: control, affiliation, and activation.* Control *involves status or so-*
> *cial dominance. We have control to the extent that we have the power and prestige*
> *to influence the events around us.* Affiliation *refers to the degree of friendliness,*
> *liking, social warmth, or immediacy that is being communicated. Affiliation is an*
> *evaluative component that indicates a person's willingness to approach or avoid*
> *others. Affiliation can be expressed through eye contact, open body stances, lean-*
> *ing forward, physical proximity, touching, smiling, a friendly tone of voice, and*
> *other communication behaviors. Cultures that display a high degree of affiliation*
> *are high-contact cultures; those that display a low level are called low-contact cul-*
> *tures.* Activation *refers to the ways people react to the world around them. Some*
> *people seem very quick, excitable, energetic, and lively; others value calmness,*
> *peacefulness, and a sense of inner control. Activation is determined by how fast or*
> *slow, active or inactive, swift or sluggish, relaxed or tense, and spirited or deliber-*
> *ate a person is.*

frustrated, sad, angry, hurt, and/or overwhelmed we feel) about our own circumstances. Paradoxically, being able to view and respond to our situation as
personal provides the possibility of comprehending that the collective version
of these dynamics has an exponential effect on the members of racial groups
who are different from the dominant culture. Furthermore, that exponential
effect varies in relation to the ways in which the dominant culture categorizes
each ethnic group.

The memory pieces that follow represent many others that touch the ten-
derness and vulnerability behind the dilemmas, dissensions, and tensions surrounding diversity—my own and those of others. They remind me that experiencing our ethnicity occurs moment by moment, and those of us who are
members of the dominant group can choose when to conceal and when to reveal our racial roots.

▶ Powdered Milk and Silver Pitchers: Learning about Socioeconomic Class

Living on the periphery of a blended family, I am seven when I ask my
mother, "Why do we kids drink powdered milk?" What I really want to ask is
why she gets whole milk and we don't. She declares it nutritionally superior
and prompts me to serve it in a silver pitcher. I am left wondering if whole
milk is bad for her or just bad for kids, or only good in silver pitchers, or if
something is left unsaid. My mother—English, French, and Scot—can trace
her U.S. ancestors back to the 1600s. She was raised and educated in the upper-class traditions of the East Coast establishment. Her father was tax com-

missioner for then Governor Franklin Roosevelt; as a young woman she and her father often dined at the White House once Roosevelt became president. Now, however, she lived in Northern California and was married to an under-employed artist who brought four children from two previous marriages with him into the household. She was unwilling to tell me that, though our lower-middle economic class meant that we couldn't afford "whole" milk for the children, we could serve our "poor" milk in the silver pitcher of her higher social class. Further, as an adult, she could treat herself to the enriched milk.

This experience marks the beginning of my wondering about what I would come to understand as the nature and consequences of who has power and privilege and who does not. Whole milk, store-bought (not hand-me-down) clothes, and gentle attention were scarce resources in my childhood. Much later I would learn about other scarce resources such as money, education, position, and housing. The split between my mother's upper-class social values and our lower middle class economic condition meant that I wasn't accepted by the "rich kids" and my mother wouldn't let me play with the "poor kids." Spending much of my free time feeling left out, I would often hang out with the available adults: playground directors, community-based leaders, and Leonard.

▶ Leonard: My First Mentor of Color

While I might have seen other African Americans in the integrated Richmond-Berkeley area where I lived, Leonard, as it turns out, becomes my first mentor of color, but that's not why I began talking with him. He would come to mow the neighbors' lawn each Wednesday afternoon, and I would look forward to his kindly ways. My baby brother was clearly "the family favorite" and my older stepbrothers were getting into so much trouble that my parents were just relieved to have me "out of their hair," as they would say. So they began paying Leonard to watch me, a weekly arrangement that continued for several years.

Leonard did not raise the topic of race when I complained that the kids at school teased me because of my dark eyes, hair, and freckles. Nor was race mentioned when I pined to be blond and blue-eyed like Daun Stone, because she was popular and everyone said she was pretty. Nor, in fact, did he mention race when I told him that my favorite older brother was sent away to live with another mother, and no one wanted to hear what I had to say about it. But somewhere along the way, Leonard did tell me that his relatives were working in the Civil Rights movement down south. I probably asked the dear man so many questions that he finally decided to try to explain a bit of U.S. racial history to this little white girl, all the while hoping that he wouldn't get into trouble with her parents. I can't now recall most of my questions or many of his responses. But I do remember that he used my self-consciousness about not looking like the other kids, and the experience of having my brother sent away without my wishes being heard, to introduce me to what life was like for lots of people "whose faces were brown all over, not just in freckles." In that moment, I remember viewing him simultaneously as more and less like me than I had before, when his being older and more attentive than my parents, peers, and siblings was all that had mattered. I knew his skin color was darker but I hadn't attached any particular meaning to it.

One hot summer day, I invited Leonard into my house for lemonade. My mother fluttered with too much friendliness, and my grandmother told tales of "how much she loved her colored cook and chauffeur." Leonard smiled but got really stiff. I didn't know why and didn't ask any questions; thereafter, I just brought the lemonade outside. It was the first instance of a feeling that now often reappears: being embarrassed by how my own kind acts when they are with or talking about people of color. To this day, in certain situations I tighten and wait for a white friend or stranger to say or do something that is racially insensitive. Like Wendell Berry (1989),

> I am trying to establish the outlines of an understanding of myself in regard to what was fated to be the continuing crisis of my life, the crisis of racial aware-ness—the sense of being doomed by my history to be, if not always a racist, then a man [or woman] always limited by the inheritance of racism, con-demned to be always conscious of the necessity *not* to be a racist, to be always dealing deliberately with the reflexes of racism that are embedded in my mind as deeply at least as the language I speak. (pp. 48–49)

A few years later, Leonard listened as I learned a family secret: I had a bi-ological father of Eastern European gypsy and Jewish descent who had re-turned "to get to know me." Leonard told me a story of similar happenings in his family. Then he added, "It happens a lot to blacks." I don't remember what happened after that, except that I wanted to ask him a slew of questions but didn't: Did blacks have gypsy-Jew fathers who showed up halfway through their childhood, or was there something else Leonard meant? Of course it was the latter, but I don't remember ever seeing Leonard again. It has taken me years to acknowledge that I never got to say goodbye to my first adult friend, nor told or asked for his last name, though I knew and usually referred to all the white adults in my life by their last names.

Looking back, I see the ways in which my parents kept Leonard at the margins of my life, which mirrored the social-political borders for blacks. Al-though Leonard and my family shared the same economic class, we were sepa-rated by the color line—a line that separated his caring for me from his becom-ing a family friend. It was a separation not of overt racism but of what Merton (1957) terms "nonprejudiced discriminators" or "fair-weather liberals."[2]

▶ Family Secrets: Silence, Power, and Politeness

By the time I was 13, I had been molested by my birth father and an adult neighbor, and sexually harassed almost nightly by an older stepbrother. I be-lieved that to tell about these events would create a mess that could bring punishment. I also feared that it was my fault and that if others found out I'd be sent away from the family. So I never directly told my parents or anyone, choosing instead to imply again and again that "I just wasn't comfortable with. . . ." I can now see how my parents were raised to be blind and deaf to the clues I persistently gave them.

It has taken me years to uncover and heal from the wounds inflicted by my parents' inability to acknowledge the sexual abuse, let alone protect me from it. But I now appreciate the connection between family secrets of sexual and physical abuse and the national secret of racial abuse. Secrets have a way of stealing and profaning personal power and memory. Only when I descended into my own awareness, pain, and rage could I imagine what it must be like to feel the daily onslaught of racial harassment and abuse—to feel unsafe in your own home country. I understand now that the subtle rules for silence and politeness that help to maintain family secrets are the same rules as those that perpetuate the national secret: "Don't talk about messy situations that might make you look bad and get you into trouble," and "Don't make the parents—whites—feel uncomfortable." The insidiousness of this dynamic is that those with the power to enforce the rules create the context for the rules to be internalized by the victims. Further, the inability of white America to acknowledge fully the racial abuse of the past and the present is disabling for all Americans. Stephanie Wildman (1996) and Benjamin Bowser and Raymond Hunt (1997) develop further this thesis.

▶ "Big D" and "Big G": Learning Personal and Institutional Rules

Raised in integrated Berkeley, in the San Francisco Bay area, I knew I was white long before I was in high school. But one experience initiated my life-long inquiry into the written and unwritten racial rules, the formal and informal bases of power, and the institutional and personal consequences of one's behaviors. I can't remember exactly when or where I met Danny, an African American classmate, only that we felt like we had been best friends forever. We nicknamed each other "Big D" and "Big G," though neither of us cleared 5'5". We were in high school classes together, he as a star football player and student body president, and I as the vice president. We talked often about such topics as our classes, homework, his girlfriend, my boyfriend, and ideas for class activities. The yearbook included pictures of us handcuffed together, participating in a "slave auction" to raise money for senior activities. At the time I remember feeling weird and strange, but I didn't question or examine the situation, choosing instead just to go along with the show.

"Big D" had a white girlfriend and, being nosy, I asked him why he never held hands with her. He said that he did, but only in private. I queried, "Why not around school like the other couples?" He said, "Because she is white." I asked him if there was a written rule about that; he said "No," but he just knew that he and his girlfriend would get into trouble if they held hands in public. In a spontaneous act I took "Big D's" hand and kissed him on the cheek in front of the oldest, whitest, and most prudish English teacher around. She hauled us off to the dean's office, where "Big D" sat and said, "What did you have to go and do that for?" and the dean warned us of consequences for "our inappropriate behavior."

With a rebel's confidence that I hadn't known before, I told the dean that I wanted my mother—a popular English and journalism teacher at the school—to witness whatever came next. I didn't know how my mother would react. She could easily turn me over to the wolves; after all, I had created quite a scene. But I guess I wanted to give her a chance, this time, to defend us, or at least Danny. She walked in with her blue-blood Anglo disdain for messes written all over her face and listened politely while the dean and I explained what had happened. I didn't know which way her sword-swift tongue would fall. With a strength and dignity I had only feared in her before, she told the dean that "in no way was interracial hand-holding and kissing legally, morally, or socially wrong." Her dramatic exit suggested legal and journalistic action if the dean intended to do anything other than let us go. Perhaps at that moment she recalled that she had been disowned temporarily by her family when she married my birth father, a Jew. Whatever the reason this time, she chose to use her informal organizational power to expose an unwritten racist rule.

Danny and I sighed and didn't speak of the incident until much later, when he said that all he remembers is hearing his mother's voice inside his head repeating, "You know better than to be holding hands with a white girl."

The Color Line: Feeling White

In college I was part of an interracial group of friends who were studying race in sociology classes. I remember feeling as if "I was part of something that mattered" and "I could help." As the Civil Rights movement intensified and the differences between Malcolm X and Martin Luther King, Jr., became sharper, the interpersonal tensions in our group mounted. I began to "feel white." Darcy and I spent a lot of time together, inviting each other to go places or to just hang out. And then she became less available. The friends she chose over me were all black, and I noticed. When the pressure between us finally surfaced, all I remember is the agony, shame, and harshness I felt when she said, "Take your condescending ways and go help your own kind." We never talked again.

Looking back, this was the first of what I would come to know as an opportunity for a difficult interracial dialogue. While I wish I could have maintained a friendship with Darcy, her challenge to me to understand the what, where, and why of her message has stayed under my skin to this day, and I thank her for it.

Who's the Teacher Here? Intersecting Differences

It is my first teaching experience, a course in public speaking that is included in a special program at UCLA for recently returned Vietnam veterans, mostly African American or Latino men, all older than me. On the first day a student calls out, "You don't look old enough to be my baby sister, let alone my teach." There I was, a 23-year-old European American female hippie doctoral candidate, away from my nursing baby for the first time, trying to conceal the leaking breast milk and my stand against the War, in a room full of men who had just returned from it. Their experiences and views of the world were radically different from my own. I realized that if I was to contribute in any way to their learning, I had to learn about them from their perspective. But how?

I can still smell the sharpness of feeling so white, so female, and so underprepared to teach. To this day, I can't recall how I got through that first class period. But I went on to learn that, as W. E. B. Du Bois (1973) contends, for education to be relevant it must grow out of the experiences of the students being educated. I went into class the next day and said, "I know a lot about what the authors of your textbook have to say about communication. And I know how it relates to my life. But in order for you to learn from this course we need to figure out how it is relevant to your world." That I taught in the program for three years remains the brightest star in my learning career, because I learned far more than I taught. I am also struck by how I stuck to the "concepts" discussed in the texts and steered the discussions toward the personal and gender dynamics but away from the racial domain. I was perpetuating the racial rule of silence.

▶ A White Woman Mentor

When I was in graduate school at UCLA I was fortunate to serve as a research assistant for Andrea Rich, a young European American professor, the author of the first communication text on interracial communication, the author of the "Interracial and Intercultural Communication Model" (Rich, 1973), and the first female professor in the department. She chose to work interracially with scholars of color and was not afraid to study, discuss, and teach about race relations in the United States. Her lectures and models cracked open my cognitive understanding of the difference that whiteness and color make in the United States. Working with Dr. Rich marked the birth of my passion for inquiring into the issues surrounding race relations. When Dr. Rich left the department there was no longer anyone with expertise in that area, so I pursued another topic for my doctoral dissertation. However, her knowledge, courage, and honesty in confronting these difficult issues served as a model for me of the work that white people could do to understand and improve race relations.

▶ Cultivating Allies

With my doctorate in hand, I moved back to the San Francisco Bay area. A single parent, I left behind a group of friends and colleagues, the majority of whom are white. I needed a rest and wanted to spend time with my daughter and my dying stepfather. But soon after arriving I was offered and accepted a temporary position at Cal State University, Hayward, with the specific charge to develop the area of intercultural communication.

I did not have the confidence of my role model, Andrea Rich, and I wasn't sure where to find it. Although I had read and thought about the theories, perceptions, and stereotypes regarding whites and people of color and the dynamics of interracial communication, I had not dealt consciously with my own emotional connection to the issues, nor did I have a clue how to facilitate others' feelings. I was terrified of anger—my own and others'—and I knew that the issue of race relations was a lightning rod to an emotional ocean. Furthermore, teaching this course to a diverse group of students brought up all my fears and vulnerabilities about making messes and being told I didn't belong.

Something told me there might be some truth in my fear; maybe I really didn't know enough and I couldn't get it from books. I sought out the student service staff who worked with racially and culturally diverse students and the faculty who taught race- and culture-related courses. I asked them what they would like to see taught in a course focused on interracial and intercultural communication. These conversations, as grace would have it, allowed me to meet other colleagues who shared my interests, to hear their concerns and perceptions about the racial climate on the campus, to learn their perspectives on advising and teaching, and to plant seeds for cultivating allies.

Somewhere along the line, Terry Jones—an African American professor, sociologist, and political activist who was the associate dean at the time of our meeting—ended up on the commuter train with me. To pass the time we chatted, discovering that we lived near each other, our kids went to the same schools, our fathers had worked at the same shipyard, and we taught similar classes.

Soon thereafter, the dean asked Dr. Jones and me to attend a conference on "mainstreaming the multicultural curriculum," after which we cowrote a grant proposal, which was funded. Along with the chair of Ethnic Studies, I subsequently codirected the funded program, along with the chair of the ethnic studies program, which was designed to help faculty integrate multicultural perspectives into their general education courses. These experiences marked the beginning of what would become my professional path: working in multicultural teams for multicultural issues. It was during this time that Dr. Jones mentored me in the politics of race in the university. By 1984 we had established the Center for the Study of Intercultural Relations (CSIR) as a means of institutionalizing the gains made by our first grant. CSIR's accomplishments are quite impressive, and the roots of my whiteness continue to be pruned and its responsibility nurtured by the richly intellectual and multicultural faculty at the center.

▶ Mom and Derrick Bell

Shortly after my mother's death, I am leading a one-day seminar for a multiracial and multicultural group of business folks on ways to engage in difficult dialogues about race, culture, and gender. It is the first time I am teaching this particular course without a cofacilitator of color. I feel confident in my knowledge of the material but tender and bit uneasy about being "just white." This feeling, while never fully welcomed on first appearance, has been around so often that I no longer shrink from or defend myself against it. I know it is here to stay for the day, and I hope I can befriend it and use it as my W. E. B.

Culture Concepts
_____

Self-Disclosure

The human tendency to reveal personal information about ourselves, and to ex-plain our inner experiences and private thoughts, is called self-disclosure. *Self-dis-closure occurs among people of all cultures, but there are tremendous cultural dif-ferences in the breadth, depth, valence, timing, and targets of self-disclosing events. The* breadth *of self-disclosing information refers to the range of topics that are revealed. The* depth *of the self-disclosing information refers to the degree of personalness about oneself that is revealed.* Valence *refers to whether the self-dis-closure is positive or negative, and thus favorable or unfavorable.* Timing *refers to when the self-disclosure occurs in the course of the relationship. Finally,* target *refers to the person to whom self-disclosing information is given.*

Du Bois reminder that we are all in the world in different ways and that that in-ness affects everything.

While the participants work in small groups, I look over the books I hastily pulled from my shelf for examples and potential resources that the students can pursue. Amid the stack is the paperback edition of Derrick Bell's (1992) *Faces at the Bottom of the Well: The Permanence of Racism*. I reach for it, one of my favorites, thinking to myself, "I own the hardback. Where did the paperback come from?" I open it up and see a note written to my mother from David, an African American and one of her former students. As I read the note, my hands began to tremble:

> Thought you would need both of his books to get the complete picture. *And we are not saved* [Bell, 1987] is a little more dense to read—need to keep a finger in the back with the references. They are both written in the same allegorical style. *Faces* moves quicker and is easier reading. Hope my relaying of the "story" about Dominican shows how much you taught me about being respect-ful—yet maintaining the desired "edge" to the conversation. Enjoy it! Politics! Yum, Yum! See you soon, David.

With tears welling in my eyes, I struggle to maintain my public compo-sure. I am filled with empathy for my mother who, both despite and because of her upbringing and experiences, was willing, at least in moments, to stay open-minded up until the end of her 80-year life. I saw her spend many after-noons talking with and listening to David. And when Irene, a recent Chinese immigrant she tutored, encountered difficulty understanding the assigned Cornel West's (1992) *Race Matters,* my mother asked me many questions about race relations in the United States. I was surprised at how quickly she caught on and without being defensive. We even discussed ways to explain to

Irene enough of the history of race relations for her to be able to critique the text.

Like most whites in the United States, my mother could choose when and where to be aware of her racial place, yet I know that she had been more willing to see and learn about race, power, and privilege than *her* mother. In turn, I hope that my daughters will be more conscious, knowledgeable, and responsible than I am. I realize that each of our stories and insights is always incomplete.

▶ Returning to the Rose Garden

The rose garden, and with it the family home in which my brothers and I were raised, was "on the market"—empty of all the objects that carried the Gale Graves Young stories. I felt blessed, though a bit overwhelmed, to inherit so many items, not because of their material worth, which was minimal, but because they evoked the stories I didn't want to forget. But what would arouse the stories of Leonard's yard? I sat on the ledge wondering whether to continue pulling at the entangled and deeply embedded roots so I could transplant, in my own garden, the "first rose bush" and my parents' favorite, "Mr. Lincoln."

In the end, I left the rose bush there, knowing that I couldn't really rip out the history and roots of my upbringing. The reminders of my heritage, and with them my whiteness, my blindness, my perceptiveness, my mentors, my unearned and earned privileges, and my institutional power, are everywhere. It is up to me, each day, to remain conscious and committed, so that I can contribute to the dismantling of unearned white privileges.

Notes

1. The distinction I am making here is between *race* as the complexion that is a socially constructed marker to group and divide people and *culture* or *ethnicity* as the values, attitudes, beliefs, and behavior styles that are shared by groups of people and are transmitted from generation to generation. Clearly the intersection of color and culture includes the values, attitudes, beliefs, and behavior styles that are transmitted intergenerationally and that evolve when groups of people share similar experiences of living in a society that values or devalues their skin color.

2. Gudykunst and Kim (1997) characterize this type of prejudice and communication as being dominated by expediency. "When people around them discriminate or talk in a prejudicial manner, fair-weather liberals will take the expedient course of action and keep quiet. The major reason for the inconsistency between attitudes and behavior is the social norms of the situation" (p. 128).

References

Bell, D. (1992). *Faces at the bottom of the well: The permanence of racism.* New York: Basic Books.

Bell, D. (1987). *And we are not saved: The elusive quest for racial justice.* New York: Basic Books.

Berry, W. (1989). *The hidden wound.* San Francisco: North Point Press.

Bowser, B. P., & Hunt, R. (1997). *Impacts of racism on white Americans* (2nd ed.). Newbury Park, CA: Sage.

Du Bois, W.E.B. (1973). *The education of black people: Ten critiques,* 1906–1960. H. Aptheker, ed. New York: Monthly Review Press.

Gudykunst, W. B. and Kim, Y.Y. (1997). *Communicating with strangers: An approach to intercultural communication* (3rd ed.). New York: McGraw-Hill.

Merton, R. K. (1957). *Social theory and social structure.* New York: Free Press.

Rich, A. L. (1973). *Interracial communication.* New York: Harper & Row.

West, C. (1992). *Race matters.* Boston: Beacon Press.

Wildman, S. M. (1996). *Privilege revealed: How invisible preference undermines America.* New York: New York University Press.

▶ ▶ ▶ Learning AmongUS

1. Is there a relationship between the "silence" Young describes about the privilege of being white, the silence of the "color line," and the ways that people are taught the cultural norms of self-disclosure?

2. Young describes the privilege of being white in the United States, even if the white person does not have economic means. Do you accept or reject this description of privilege for those from European American cultures? Explain the reasons for your point of view.

3. How does race, and a person's awareness of race, affect the development of an interracial friendship? Should people from different races acknowledge the impact of race and culture explicitly as they begin to develop a friendship?

4. A Culture Concepts box describes the dimensions of interpersonal relationships as control, affiliation, and activation. Using these dimensions, analyze the intercultural communication messages and relationships that Young describes.

S. Lily Mendoza provides a very powerful personal story of a woman on a quest to understand her Filipino culture, and she explores the consequences to her culture as a result of the colonial relationship between the United States and the Philippines. In examining each aspect of her identity—from language to religion to educational aspirations—Lily shows us how she has become the person she is. Her essay also describes the negative consequences to self-esteem and cultural identities when people are forced to learn and use the language of a more dominant group.

24 Tears in the Archive: Creating Memory to Survive and to Contest Empire

S. Lily Mendoza

I had never cried so hard, and certainly not in so strange a place as a library aisle. While doing library research for a graduate seminar paper, I chanced upon this immense shelf containing nothing but U.S. colonial discourse. I was not prepared for what rudely greeted my eyes; slumped on the floor, feverishly turning page after page of the volumes on that shelf, as I came face-to-face with a side of the United States I had never before encountered in the raw.

With angry tears burning my cheeks like live coals, I read the most rabid and racist discourse I had ever encountered; it was spoken and written by a people I had previously called my/our friends, and it was aimed directly at me! This is me, I thought—my people—being talked about in the third person as though we were not human beings but mere objects for others' disposition. Here were the actual records of the U.S. Congressional hearings from the debate at the turn of the 20th century, about "what to do with the Philippines." We Filipinos were the subject of the debate, but we were nowhere present in the deliberations, nor were we speaking; we were only being *talked about*.

It is one thing to read, in narrative form, about the fateful events of the U.S. invasion and forcible annexation of the tiny Republic of the Philippines shortly after it had fought (and won) a fierce battle of independence against Spain (thereby ending more than 300 years of Spanish occupation); it is quite another to read what was actually said about your people (and you), which was said to justify the most dastardly acts of murder, insult, and crime in the name of "civilizing" you. That debate culminated in the infamous speech of President William McKinley to a visiting Methodist delegation, as he justified the U.S. decision to annex the Philippines forcibly, even if it meant the massacre of thousands:[1]

┌───┐

Culture Concepts

Intercultural Contact

The assumption that opportunities for intercultural contacts will foster positive atti-
tudes toward members of other groups has been the rationale for numerous inter-
national exchange programs. Sometimes, of course, intercultural contact does lead
to positive attitudes between those involved. Unfortunately, contact between mem-
bers of different cultures does not always lead to good feelings. Sometimes, there-
fore, the outcomes of intercultural contacts are favorable; at other times, unfortu-
nately, they are not.

└───┘

I would like to say just a word about the Philippine business. I have been criticized a good deal about the Philippines, but don't deserve it. The truth is I
didn't want the Philippines, and when they came to us, as a gift from the gods,
I did not know what to do with them. . . . I thought at first we would take only
Manila; then Luzon; then the other islands perhaps also. I walked the floor of
the White House night after night until midnight; and I am not ashamed to
tell you, gentlemen, that I went down on my knees and prayed Almighty God
for light and guidance more than one night. And one night late it came to me
this way—I don't know how it was, but it came: (1) that we could not give
them back to Spain—that would be cowardly and dishonorable; (2) that we
could not turn them over to France and Germany—our commercial rivals in
the Orient—that would be bad business and discreditable; (3) that we could
not leave them to themselves—they were unfit for self-government—and they
would soon have anarchy and misrule over there worse than Spain's was; and
(4) that there was nothing left for us to do but to take them all, and to educate
the Filipinos, and uplift and civilize and Christianize them, and by God's
grace do the very best we could by them. . . . And then I went to bed, and went
to sleep, and slept soundly, and the next morning I sent for the chief engineer
of the War Department, and I told him to put the Philippines on the map of
the United States, and there they are, and there they will stay while I am
President![2]

I had come to the United States as a Filipino international student to pursue a Ph.D. degree. It was at a time in my life when the entire history of the
Philippine-U.S. relations was just beginning to unfold starkly before my eyes.
I had heard of the Philippine-American War before, but always it was obscured by all the good things that America is presumed to have brought to Filipinos in the course of colonizing them: notably, the blessings of progress,
democracy, and "civilization" in general. In the United States, official historiography so far has only admitted to a diplomatic history, not to an imperialist
one. Indeed, the picture painted of the U.S.'s occupation of the Philippines has
always been that of a "peaceful civilizing mission," not the violent invasion
and conquest that it actually was and which is only now grudgingly beginning
to be acknowledged as, in fact, "the U.S.'s first Vietnam."

Although I had gotten my undergraduate degree at the University of the Philippines—which is known as the hotbed of student activism and nationalist studies—my childhood upbringing in a Protestant Methodist church (founded by American missionaries who came to our shores as part of the U.S.'s "civilizing mission" at the beginning of the twentieth century), along with my subsequent conversion to evangelical "born again" Christianity in college, led me to embrace universalism as a worldview. For a long time, I was a Filipino by sheer geographic accident; in terms of worldview, I took pride in being non-culture-bound, allied with the universal Truth of God-in-Christ that was supposed to be unchanging and true for all time, peoples, and places. Within this universalistic frame, any documenting of the brutality of the Philippine-American war—the massacre by the U.S. of over half a million Filipinos; the total cultural deracination that attended the U.S.'s doctrine of "Benevolent Assimilation"; the wholesale destruction of the nation's social institutions; along with the rapacious exploitation of its economy and natural resources – ended up being soft-pedaled if not altogether denied or chalked up to being "expedient" within God's sovereign plan in the world for the Philippines.[3]

Shortly before I left for the United States, a hybrid course in *Sikolohiyang Pilipino* (Filipino psychology) and *Histograpiyang Pilipino* (Philippine historiography) shattered the imperial smokescreen for me. Much as I had wanted to hold on to the image of an innocent and benevolent America (having had genuine friendships with the American missionaries and Peace Corps volunteers I had known growing up), I was beginning to hate the lies and denials that now sat like a giant white elephant in the halls of our two nations' intertwined histories.

The year I came to the United States was a crucial one for me. My marriage of eight years had just broken down irreparably. The faith that had been my life's foundation to that point was unraveling fast and irreversibly.[4] A series of life-threatening surgeries left my immune system compromised. I needed to get out of the Philippines quickly, if only to save my sanity. Although the "belly of the beast" was the last place on Earth I wanted to be at that critical juncture, a standing invitation to apply to her school's Ph.D. program, from a U.S. professor I had met years ago, was my primary beacon. There was simply no time to search for other alternatives. As fate would have it, I was to face Empire no longer from a distance, but up close and personal.

My first year of encounter, like round one in a boxing match, left me pretty much reeling and bloodied. When one has grown up under a U.S.-oriented colonial education, with one's imagination completely shaped by the rhetoric of Empire, one does not expect to experience culture shock. After all, had I not been prepared all my life to know America? Has not my tongue spoken its language from childhood? Have my eyes not perused only texts by its authors? Yet what does it mean not only to survive the place of your debasement as a colonized subject but to live justly, with healing and forgiveness for the sins of the past? What kind of rapprochement is possible between peoples on opposite sides of the imperial-subject divide? How does a colonized subject make a life for herself in the heart of empire? Where does one find the resources to do so?

There are things you never question. Growing up in a small barrio in the Philippines, I remember always being inquisitive, but often I was stumped when pointed to the taken-for-grantedness of things. My world as a child was full of contradictions; yet nobody seemed bothered by them nor had a need (as I sometimes did) to resolve them. Throughout my years of formal schooling, for example—from the elementary grades all the way through college—the language in which we were required to speak, write, and communicate was English, yet no one cared to explain to us why; it just was. In grade school, infraction of that linguistic norm cost us five centavos apiece for every instance we were caught speaking in our native tongue.

Native tongue for me was Pampango *(or* Kapampangan*)—a regional language in the Philippines that is regarded as "the language of the angels" by the old folks who still know how to break into a spontaneous poetic rendition when toasting a celebrant at a community gathering, or are able to display their linguistic prowess in verbal joustings called* balagtasan, *wherein the contending parties battle wits by arguing in impromptu verse. Growing up, I scarcely knew and had very little exposure to those traditions of my home province,* Pampanga. *That's because "community" for my family and me primarily meant church—the local Methodist Protestant Church, specifically—where other kinds of traditions were taught to us—a legacy of years of tutelage by the American missionaries who came to save us from our "pagan, idolatrous" ways. Suffice it to say that in church and in the schools one learned all about this strange other world—one "far more advanced," "more developed," and in every way "better" than the world where we Filipinos lived. That world, unsurprisingly, spoke English.*

Indeed, our entire educational system was oriented toward that other world. Our textbooks, not to mention our history books, were written mostly by American scholars. As pundits often say, the winners get to write the history books. Conscious self-knowledge therefore came to us Filipinos primarily via the view from the outside. We were told who we were, and what we were like, by outsiders who presumed to know us better than we knew ourselves. And because their views were authoritatively inscribed in theories—the very instruments of knowing—we unsuspectingly took that knowledge as accurate descriptions of us. That internalization (of the colonial view) proved to be our debasement. "Never rely on others; it's a sign of weakness." "Learn to stand on your own two feet." "Let your 'yes' be a 'yes' and your 'no' be a 'no'; don't be a liar." "Filipinos can never be leaders; they're never on time." "This is a duplicitous culture; people never mean what they say and say what they mean." "Filipinos are lazy; they don't value time." And yet embedded in those claims about us is the looming figure of the taken-for-granted reference point, cunningly made invisible through omission of its explicit mention: the United States with its white Anglo-Saxon Protestant values and culture universalized as the default measure of what it means to be human. The implicit message was, to become fully human, you must become like *us*.

I remember, for example, being taught in grade school that there are three types of human dwellings: the "makeshift," the "temporary," and the "perma-

nent." The example often given of the makeshift one is the nipa *hut commonly found among indigenous Filipinos who make use of local materials such as the dried fronds of a palm tree; the temporary one is that which is built from lumber logged and supplied by the timber companies; and finally, the permanent one, which is made of concrete, brick, or cement. Each of these types of houses had varying durability, so we were told, with the makeshift one not lasting very long,[5] the temporary one lasting a very long time, and the permanent one lasting "forever." Indeed, were the big bad wolf to come and "huff and puff and blow your house down" as the tale goes, you had better not be caught in one of those flimsy little* nipa *huts; your house had better be permanent, or in the least a temporary one.*

And so growing up I became acutely aware of this other world that, although not present in my immediate environment, harped constantly on my conscious imagination and commanded attention. When I learned my alphabet, for example, I learned that "A is for apple" even when I scarcely knew what an "apple" was, being more familiar with our local home-grown *atis.* In church, the hymns we sang extolled God's eternal faithfulness all through summer, winter, springtime, and autumn, making one wonder whether having only "dry" and "wet" seasons somehow took away from God's watchfulness over these tropical islands. In science class, we were taught not to believe in ghosts—and, dutifully, we didn't; we were just afraid of them. It is as though we Filipinos were born "wrong" and the task of education, along with religious instruction and all the other institutions of government, was to set us "right," to make us into the "correct" kind of human beings, speaking the "correct" language, taking on the "correct" worldview, and imbibing only the "correct" knowledge. With Philippine institutional life thus saturated with such an alien(ating) body of knowledge, one wonders whether there was any space of autonomy left for Filipino subjects to chart their own course or write their own history. For that matter, I, too, wondered whether my incorporation into that other world had been so thoroughgoing and complete that that other world eventually became the only world I knew.

My family lived for many years in the basement of a ("temporary") house owned by distant relatives (an uncle, an aunt, and two cousins) on a street called High School Boulevard, right across from the provincial high school where all six of us siblings went. Prior to formal schooling, I had no notion that we were poor. I remember us girls inventing most of our toys—paper doll cutouts with corresponding cut-out kits to make different characters out of them, cupped gumamela *leaves serving as teacups, soft drink* tansan *bottle caps as miniature* batya *or washbasins, empty sardine cans that we fashioned into toy wagons or carts using four flattened-out* tansans *as wheels. A favorite pastime we girls had was climbing the* saresa *tree not only to pick its ripe sweet little red cherries but to curl each other's hair using its soft pliant twigs as improvised curlers. At night, when the stars were bright and the moon cast shadows, we liked to play* kulam *(witching game) with the neighborhood kids. With a tubful of water we would draw a huge circle halved in the middle on the dirt ground and we would run all bunched up and shrieking around the circular perimeter making sure we weren't tagged by the center "it" or caught isolated on one side of the circle, thus making us susceptible to the bewitching spell of the lord of the game. That was the time when there weren't any television sets yet, or if there were, we couldn't afford one.*

Then there were the rainy seasons to look forward to when High School Boulevard would get flooded an inch or two and we competed to see who could catch the most gurami *(little fish) that seemed to appear mysteriously from nowhere, carried along by the current. I don't remember now if we actually brought the squirming little creatures home to add to our dinner or simply let them go free after catching them, but always it was sheer delight if we spotted even just one or two performing acrobatic acts as they made quick jumps and disappeared again beneath the shallow waters.*

It is also during this time that the normally quiet creek by the house swelled and overflowed its banks and frightened us kids with its ominous rumbling, as if it was threatening to swallow us if we ever got too near. During particularly strong typhoons that carried heavy rains, the basement we were renting would often get about a foot or two of water and we would then temporarily relocate upstairs to stay with our landlord-relatives until the flood subsided. There, camped out in a small room, we improvised our living, dining, and sleeping quarters. Sometimes the flood would stay long enough for us to run out of food, thereby taxing my mom's culinary creativity. I recall at least once having a dish of kamaru, *brown soft-bellied field crickets that would be in abundance, especially in the late afternoons, tastily cooked* adobo-style using *vinegar, garlic, and soy sauce. And then there was that other memorable time when a particularly scrumptious dinner of duck* asado *turned out to be a "stolen" fowl from our cousin's stock generously gifted to us by a visiting relative of our relatives. He must have taken pity on my mom for having nothing to serve on the table, but he made sure he happily partook of the dish as well! It was to be our little family secret until much later, when we felt our cousins and aunt and uncle could laugh with us about that "desperate" time.*

Such fragments of childhood memories now serve as repositories of feelings, thoughts, and experiences that make up my world as a Filipina. Indeed, despite the determined imposition of that strange other world, there seems to be those parts of me that yet retain some remembrance of our own separate world as a separate people: the simple childhood delight in the gifts of nature, the pleasures of the technologically unaided imagination, the joy of bringing things into being with one's own hands, and the sheer fun of collective play. There was, too, the deep comfort and security of not fearing want, where scarcity was but an occasion for inventive resourcefulness and communal sharing but never self-pity. Well and quite often while growing up did our *Ima* and *Tang* model for us that we were neither poor nor deprived but always sufficiently provided and cared for.

Eventually we managed to make a down payment on a small nipa *hut that was up for sale a couple of blocks down High School Boulevard, mainly through my mom's boldness and initiative. It was about time we had our own*

Culture Concepts

Dominant Groups

A cultural group that has primary access to institutional and economic power can be characterized as dominant. *Scholars have given considerable attention to the influence of dominant and subordinate group membership on interpersonal and intercultural communication processes. For instance, members of dominant cultures often devalue the language styles of subordinate cultural members and judge the "correctness" of their use of preferred speech patterns. In some cases, members of subordinate cultures try to accommodate or adapt their speech to that of the dominant culture. In other circumstances, they very deliberately emphasize their group's unique speech characteristics when they are in the presence of people from the dominant culture.*

---

place, she thought, what with all six kids growing so fast. The house was a typical nipa *hut, with thatched roof and flooring of bamboo slats with spaces in between. It had a* lalam bale *(literally, "space under the house") that allowed for cool air to rise from the damp earth below and circulate through the house when it made its way in through the slatted bamboo floor. I will never forget the excitement that attended that move, no matter if the house we were moving to was only "makeshift"—supposedly the lowliest and least durable of all the types of houses—instead of "temporary" or "permanent." It felt good just to have our own place and our own little piece of land for the first time.*

The house was in a neighborhood composed mostly of kutseros *and their families, drivers of horse-drawn* karitelas *or* kalesas *that were the primary mode of transportation around town during those days. I miss those days of the* kalesa, *when one could stand on a street corner for a ride and not be assaulted by the deadly smoke-belch of diesel-run World War II surplus vehicles converted into passenger jeepneys. Indeed, in those days the* kalesa *was about the only form of public transportation that didn't make me dizzy or nauseous from the smell of gasoline. I particularly loved listening to the click-clacking rhythm of the horse's trot on the asphalt pavement as it made its way through narrow streets and alleys. Of course, living in a neighborhood where horse stables abounded, one had to get used to the strong earthy smell of horse manure, especially at the height of the summer months when it became particularly pungent. But give me the horse manure smell and a languid* kalesa *ride anytime; I would gladly take it over any motorized vehicle.*

My father in those days did not earn a lot. To augment his modest income selling bibles, he raised pigs in our backyard to pay for our school tuition. Each year, he would buy a piglet or two and grow it until it was big enough for slaughter. He would then sell its meat and earmark whatever money he made from the sale for our tuition. All of us siblings had our regular assignment to feed the pigs. In the afternoons, we took turns going around the neighborhood, pail in hand, to collect food leftovers door-to-door to mix in with the usual darak *or slops that was the pigs' daily fare (this way we saved some on the commercial feeds). I didn't mind it at all—and the neighbors were always ready for us—for it gave me my chance to stop by a nearby local* komiks *stand en route to the neighbors' houses. There I'd rent my favorite serialized* komiks *for no more than a cent or two, stealing ten to fifteen minutes from my pig food collection schedule to read and read quickly. You see, at home we weren't allowed to read these locally illustrated* komiks *magazines that were written in Tagalog. For some reason they were supposed to be "bad for you." Instead, our cousins from the old house would loan us the illustrated fairy tales of Hans Christian Andersen and The Brothers Grimm, which we read in English. I knew all about the long-haired Rapunzel trapped in a tower, the legend of Sleeping Beauty awakened only by the kiss of a prince, the poor abused stepsister Cinderella turned princess, and the fair Snow White with her seven dwarves, along with many others. It was an enchanted world populated by princes and princesses, all with shining radiant white skin, blond hair, and blue eyes. What my* Ima *and* Tang *didn't know is that I actually knew much more than that imported fairy tale world. I knew, for example, about the* taong tuod, *the adventures of that wooden figure that came alive at night, the long-legged giant* tikbalang *that went stalking in desolate places, the humongous hairy* kapre *that inhabited the forest and sometimes showed its face through the branches of giant trees, the naughty* dwendes *that played pranks on unsuspecting trespassers, and the host of other earth creatures or* lamang lupa *that relished playing tricks on the cocksure and the clueless.*

Looking back now, I always felt guilty "sneaking out" that way. One mustn't dirty one's mind with those "low class," "vulgar," and "pagan" magazines, I could almost hear the reprimand, but I couldn't help myself. The imported fairy tales were fine, but somehow I found more pleasure and suspense in the native fantasy world of the local *komiks*. Suffice it to say that I didn't mind paying for the pleasure with a little bad conscience.

Feeding the pigs wasn't always easy, especially when you fall a bit behind schedule and the poor creatures get really famished. Then you had to make sure you held the pail of slop mixture really steady; one false move and you would spill everything on the ground or on the pigs' heads, making them go even crazier. Somehow, the daily feeding routine had a way of bonding you to the squealing creatures, making it the saddest thing when the time for slaughter came. Perhaps it is the thought that another living being has had to sacrifice its life to allow you to go to school that one never quite took the privilege lightly.

Like church, school was a different world altogether. Because you had to learn English before you could acquire knowledge, you always felt dumb and faulted yourself for not learning fast or well enough. You also learned quickly, and at a very early age, that your native tongue wasn't good enough, at least not for acquiring an education; that prerogative is reserved only for English.

But no matter the strict imposition, I never could quite make my peace with the mandated language as the others apparently could.

In the elementary grades, we learned proper pronunciation from the American Peace Corps volunteers that we had as teachers. We were taught how to aspirate our t's and p's by holding a piece of paper close to our mouths and watching the paper move as we blew a bit of air when making the sound. We giggled and felt ashamed and embarrassed trying to imitate the foreign sounds our teachers made in an exaggerated way. I learned English grammar well enough but never to the point of being able to un-self-consciously speak it. In college especially, I hardly recited in class. That's because before I could complete the rehearsal in my head about what I should say in English, making sure I said it correctly, the discussion would already have moved to something else. I was unlike Annette and Portia, who spoke quite easily as native English speakers—"collegiala English" is what we called it, which is how girls from the wealthy exclusive schools in the city learned to speak it. Once, I recall huddling with another probinsiyano *(literally, "from the province") classmate right after a comparative literature class and having a very animated discussion—in Tagalog—about issues in literary theory that we had just finished covering in class but on which neither of us dared comment orally. I remember thinking then, what a pity not to have such brilliance be expressed in class!—and all because our tongues were tied, disallowed from expressing ourselves in the language we knew best. To this day, I wonder what it's like to be able to learn in your native tongue, to acquire knowledge about the world using your own categories of thought. What would that world look like with my very own—no longer borrowed—eyes?*

But foreign language learning need not always be so psychologically wrenching. In college, for example, where I decided to take basic French, Spanish, Japanese, and Bahasa Malay as language electives, I felt no shame or inferiority associated with not being able to learn the language quickly or well. English was different in that it was positioned vis-à-vis all other languages as superior in every way. Not only was it *the* language of currency, but in the way it was mandated and exclusively required in our school systems it was also the language of "class," education, upward mobility, and privilege. To speak English was to bear the mark of intelligence, good breeding, and belonging, so much so that one felt shame for not being able to master it. Little did I realize the massive implications of that linguistic imposition until much later.

There was a time when I thought the encounter of cultures was primarily only about the effective exchange of meanings, or a matter of arriving at common understandings about words and their referents. What happens when two cultures come into contact and attempt to arrive at mutual understanding? How might messages be translated accurately from one linguistic context to the next? How are meanings "preserved" and kept from "distortions" in the course of translation? These were the kinds of questions that preoccupied me then. At the back of my mind was the notion that perhaps the dissonance we

---

Culture Concepts

Muted Group Theory

Members of the dominant group have much greater access to public and mass communication channels. They may be excessively influential in determining the conversational topics regarded as socially relevant, the societal issues deemed important enough to be worthy of public attention, and the "proper" language for expressing their views in social discussions. Muted group theory *suggests that individuals who do not belong to the dominant group are often silenced by a lack of opportunities to express their experiences, perceptions, and worldviews. Essentially, the power of the dominant group's communication may function to silence, or mute, the voices of subordinate group members. To have their concerns recognized publicly, subordinate group members may be obliged to use the language and communication styles of the dominant group.*

Filipinos experience in our everyday life, from having had to constantly navigate two clashing worlds (with one violently imposed), had more to do with distortions in the way that we had understood America's "civilizing message" and not so much with faults in the message itself. Is it possible, I wondered, that the message about the benefits of "progress," "liberty," "autonomy," "aggressive pursuit of material wealth," and "modern civilization" was basically sound; that what was needed was simply proper "contextualization," a discerning of the objective, universal principles and *meanings* being communicated, but employing them using more culturally appropriate (Filipino) *forms* and expressions? My master's thesis was an exercise in this neutral framing of the colonial encounter with insights from linguistic translation and cross-cultural communication theories derived mostly from literature on Christian missions.

I tried; I did try. Lord knows I gave all the benefit of the doubt to the colonial project, especially in those days when I was still a "true believer" and sincerely believed in my heart that God sent America to the Philippines for a reason. From what I now know, for a long time Filipino immigrants in the United States tried as well. They tried to lose their accents, bleach their skins, think white, dress white, act white, talk white, and have their kids associate only with kids who were white. They called that mode of survival *assimilation.* Alas, it never worked; indeed, it failed miserably. As far as melting pot politics went, Filipino Americans remained among the "unassimilable others," with an otherness that simply remained "too other" to melt into the otherwise bland, white stew.

It never worked for me either. Years of trying to learn by heart the lessons about God's universal and unconditional love for all, as preached by the missionaries, somehow never cured me of a psychological malaise that I suffered as far back as I can remember. Call it low self-esteem, negative self-image, self-rejection, self-deprecation—name it, I suffered it. And yet there seemed to be no apparent reason for it. In school, I was a star performer. In church, I was a leader. Among my friends, I was the hub that kept the group together. The mystery of that affliction led me to suspect something else was going on— something that required more than just the routine spiritual(ized) answers. It was in a graduate class in the humanities that I unexpectedly found an unlikely explanation.

The title of the course was "The Image of the Filipino in the Arts," and it was taught at the University of the Philippines by a professor of ethnomusicology who conducted firsthand research on the cultures of our various indigenous communities. The professor was excellent. He wasn't being political at all. All he did was describe to us the various arts of the Filipino indigenous communities that had managed to keep their way of life despite centuries of colonization—their dances, music, weaving, basketry, sculpture, etc.—and what these signified in terms not only of aesthetic sensibility but of a different mode of being, including a different sense of the body and its relationship both to the natural environment and to the community. I was not prepared for the impact that the professor's innocent aesthetic descriptions would have on me. As I wrote elsewhere:

> *Suddenly, something very powerful ignited in the depths of my being. For the first time, I gained a recognition of a self separate from the self that was always wanting to be other than itself . . . like a self recognizing itself for the first time, or like looking into a mirror and finding not a degraded creature staring back but someone human. I was like a fool, bawling my heart out as I walked out of every class session, not knowing what it was that hit me from all the innocent aesthetic descriptions of the indigenous communities' art forms and what they expressed in terms of a different way of being.*
>
> *Now I know that that different way of being was the way of being I had always instinctively shared but had repressed; hence, the intense internal contradiction. For the first time, here was an entire people I felt I could belong to and identify with, a legitimate human community not necessarily degraded because different (different from the invisible White colonial norm).*[6]

Thus began the journey that would take me (back) to a very different trajectory from the assimilationist one I had earlier tried to track zealously. I realized that in order to survive my sojourn in the "belly of the beast" I first had to have a ground on which to stand that was separate from that set out by imperial power. And that meant needing to understand what happens in a relationship of colonial domination, when our past—our history—gets distorted or destroyed.

Overcoming colonialism's long-lasting effects invariably entails a massive archaeological project whose object it is to uncover the history (or histories) of an oppressed people that had been buried under the avalanche of lies and denials. Such a project involves a passionate search for one's culture, even though it is fraught with pitfalls, dangers, and illusions. Indeed, in today's "global" and "transnational" world, where unbridled cultural mixing, hybridity, and border-crossing is said to be the norm, such an archaic nationalist project may seem laughable. But to live in the heart of Empire without confronting its (and our own) historic denials and distortions of the past is to live in complicity with the lies that perpetuate its power.

Intercultural encounters among people who have opposing histories of colonial domination (such as those from the United States and the Philippines) can never be entered into innocently, no matter the level of goodwill on the interpersonal level. As Kenyan nationalist writer Ngugi wa Thiong'o warns, "Any study of cultures which ignores structures of domination and control and resistance within nations and between nations and races over the last four hundred years is in danger of giving a distorted picture."[7] Postcolonial scholar Gayatri Spivak likewise categorically asserts: "The idea of neutral dialogue is an idea which denies history, denies structure, [and] denies the positioning of subjects."[8]

It has been nearly nine years since my bout with culture shock during the first year of my sojourn in the United States. I spoke of being bloodied and close to being knocked down, and that's because my speaking of the newly excavated history of my people's relations with America often forced a head-on confrontation with that denial. To speak of pain, betrayal, and profound wounding doesn't always win friends or a cheerful audience. As Mark, a (white, male, American) well-meaning classmate, asked me after a graduate seminar one evening, "Why is it that each time you speak in class, I feel guilty?" I haven't found many ways to respond to his question that would invite an honest dialogue. Fortunately for both of us, what started out as a defensive reproach turned out to be one of the most remarkable intercultural friendships I have ever had. That's because Mark—courageously, and to his credit—was willing to wrestle with his own relationship to that painful history with awareness, with deep regret, and without flinching. For me, the ongoing confrontation with that history does not depend on the responses I receive from people like Mark, but his response does provide a small measure of comfort to the woman with the burning tears who is slumped in the aisle of the library. And inside that woman is a people.

Notes

1. Historians suggest that over half a million Filipinos were massacred in the Philippine-American war.

2. Daniel B. Schirmer and Stephen Rosskamm Shalom (eds.), *The Philippines Reader: A History of Colonialism, Neocolonialism, Dictatorship, and Resistance* (Boston: South End Press, 1987) 22–23.

3. To this day, the Philippines is touted as "the only Christian nation in Asia." During the 1960s and 1970s, evangelical rhetoric often mirrored that of the Cold War. Operating on the doctrine of the "domino theory," both missionary and Cold War rhetoric feared the impending danger that the Philippines would fall into Communist hands, which justified the need to contain and evangelize the nation.

4. Initially, Christianity was not imperialistic. But coupled with power and ambition, it became an

instrument of oppression and domination. It is with these latter propensities that I became totally disillusioned.

5. As I was to find out later, a well-made *nipa* hut can last 50 years.

6. S. Lily Mendoza, *Between Homeland and the Diaspora: The Politics of Theorizing Filipino American Identities: A Second Look at the* *Poststructuralism-Indigenization Debates* (New York: Routledge, 2001) xvi–xvii.

7. Ngugi wa Thiong'o, *Moving the Centre: The Struggle for Cultural Freedoms* (London: James Currey, 1993) 28.

8. Gayatri Chakravorty Spivak, *The Post-Colonial Critic: Interviews, Strategies, Dialogues* (Sarah Harasym, ed.; New York: Routledge, 1990) 72.

▶ ▶ ▶ Learning AmongUS

1. How important is it for U.S. Americans to acknowledge the colonial relationship with the Philippines?

2. Can you identify personal experiences in which power was used to oppress you and to achieve the ends of others? Analyze these experiences using the concepts in Mendoza's essay.

3. Apply the three ethical dilemmas described in Part II to the U.S. role in the Philippines. Apply them, as well, to Mendoza's choices in her own life.

4. Mendoza describes English as a language that created fear and psychological trauma for her because it was linked to political, economic, and social power. Can the disagreements about bilingualism in the United States be understood in the context of Mendoza's reactions?

5. Using the research on intercultural contact as a framework, explain the consequences of the U.S. presence in, and the consequences of, the colonization of the Philippines.

PART FOUR

Inside/Outside

Belonging to Multiple Cultures

25 On Becoming Intercultural

Young Yun Kim

Issues of "cultural identity" produce some of the most volatile responses in many societies.[1] Hardly a day passes without reports of some new incidents of identity conflict. The politics of cultural identity have been played out throughout the world, from Northern Ireland to Bosnia, from the Middle East to Russia, from Africa to North, Central, and South America. Questions are still being raised concerning the autonomy of French-speaking Quebec in Canada, while issues involving aborigines and new immigrants persist in Australia. In the United States, wide-ranging views are voiced on the historically embedded intergroup relations—from the pronouncement of Louis Farrakhan during his visit to Iran: "You can quote me: God will destroy America at the hands of the Muslims" (*Time,* February 26, 1996, p. 12), to former President Clinton's call for reconciliation and unity: "Long before we were so diverse, our nation's motto was *E Pluribus Unum*—out of many, we are one. We must be one—as neighbors; as fellow citizens; not separate camps, but family" (*Weekly,* 1995, p. 1851).

Against this contemporary milieu of identity politics, some basic questions need to be posed concerning the meanings that each of us holds about cultural identity. Is rigid adherence to the culture of our youth feasible or desirable? Is cultural identity in its pure form more a nostalgic notion than a reality? Can the desire for some form of collective uniqueness be satisfied without resulting in divisions and conflicts among groups? At what point do we cross the line from rightful and constructive claims for group identity to disastrous collisions and undue prejudice directed against one another? How can a society of multiple cultural identities such as that of the United States support and give confidence to all groups while upholding the communal values and responsibilities that transcend allegiance to each group? Can a society achieve this goal despite the increasing trend of disunity and "unbounded and unwholesome pluralism" (Etzioni, 1993, p. 217)?

Sam Rayburn, former speaker of the United States House of Representatives, used to say that "any jackass can kick a barn door down, but it takes a carpenter to build one." Today more than ever we need carpenters among us who can help bridge the chasms created by contentious identity politics. Ultimately our answers to the above questions have to be found, not in public policies but in the willingness and ability of each of us to get out of the conventional habit of solely defining ourselves in terms of a single cultural identity. In so doing, we may strive for a mental outlook that integrates, rather than separates, humanity. We need an outlook on self and others that is not locked in the provincial interests of our own group membership, where we can see ourselves as part of a larger whole that includes other groups.

▶ Identity as an Evolving Entity

Let me call this integrative self-other orientation an "intercultural identity"—identity that conjoins rather than divides. As Adler (1982) described it, the identity of an intercultural person is based "not on belongingness, which implies either owning or being owned by culture, but on a style of self consciousness that is capable of negotiating ever new formations of reality. He [She] is neither totally *a part of* nor totally *apart from* his [her] culture; he [she] lives, instead, on the boundary" (p. 391). The idea of intercultural identity is grounded in the premise that an individual's identity can be *achieved* as much as it is *ascribed* by birth or by society. This emphasis on what we can achieve with respect to our identity counters, as well as complements, the conventional ascription-based view of cultural identity. The conventional view tends to treat cultural identity as an immutable, *a priori* human condition that profoundly affects the experience of an individual. Erikson's (1950, 1969) early framework placed group identity at the "core" of the individual and yet also in the core of his or her "common culture." Erikson further viewed the process of identity development as one in which the two identities—of the individual and of the group—are merged and integrated into one. Many other investigators have echoed Erikson's conception of cultural identity as integral to an individual's identity, because it offers a sense of historical continuity and embeds one in a "larger" collectivity composed of one's group. As such, cultural identity is seen as a "genuine culture" (Yinger, 1986) and thus an inherent moral force that, when denied or compromised, results in a debasement of the individual or the group. An array of studies have, in fact, linked negative cultural identity to a variety of undesirable psychological and social consequences, including poor self-image (e.g., Tajfel, 1978) and alienation (e.g., Blackwell & Hart, 1982). Individuals who fail to develop a healthy cultural identity have been reported to be more prone to think of themselves as misperceived by others, more likely to view chance as a major determinant of events, more influenced by peer conformity pressure, and more likely to fall into substance abuse and other self-destructive behaviors.

Even though theoretical and research insights have served us well in promoting a social-political consciousness that calls for a greater equity and respect among cultural groups, they have also contributed to a general downplaying of the rich variation in the way individuals experience their identity at any given time. The notion that cultural identity is unchangeable has led to the unfortunate consequence of exaggerating its uniformity, permanence, and deterministic influence on individuals who happen to be affiliated with a particular ethnic group by ascription. Too often, a person is viewed as "belonging to" one and only one cultural identity, glossing over the multifaceted and varied nature of identity experienced by those whose lives crisscross multiple sets of boundaries. It is not surprising, then, that the viability of the ascription-based conception of cultural identity is increasingly challenged in recent years by scholars who argue for the need to understand the complexity of the way cultural identity is enacted across psychological, relational, and situational contexts (e.g., Brewer & Gardner, 1996; Hecht, Collier, and Ribeau, 1993; Thornton, 1996).

To this growing voice I add my own emphasis on the dynamic and evolving nature of cultural identity. I argue that cultural identity is not only an ascriptive entity; it is also subject to change through life experiences. In a series of works that examine the process of cross-cultural adaptation of immigrants and sojourners I have theorized that prolonged and cumulative experiences of communication between individuals of differing cultural backgrounds bring about systemic, adaptive changes in the individual's psyche. One such change is the gradual transformation of identity, from the original ascribed cultural identity to one that is increasingly intercultural in nature (Kim, 1988, 1995a, 1995b, 2001).[2] I explain this phenomenon of identity transformation in terms of a "stress-adaptation-growth dynamic," a psychological movement that is rooted in conflict between the natural inertia of old mental habits and the inherent drive to maximize life chances by adapting to new ways of dealing with unfamiliar challenges. The stress-adaptation-growth dynamic plays out not in a smooth, arrow-like linear progression, but in a cyclic "draw-back-to-leap" pattern, similar to the movement of a wheel. Each stressful event is responded to with a "draw back," which, in turn, activates adaptive energy to help reorganize one's psyche and "leap forward." Because growth of some parts always occurs at the expense of others, the movement follows a pattern that juxtaposes novelty and confirmation, attachment and detachment, progression and regression, integration and disintegration, construction and destruction. The state of misfit, stress, and heightened awareness serves as the very force that propels us to strive to overcome the predicament and partake in active learning of the new cultural elements. This is possible as we engage in forward-looking moves, striving to meet the challenge by making adjustments in our existing internal structure. In this adaptive struggle, some aspects of the new life conditions are incorporated into our psyches, thereby increasing psychic growth—our overall fitness to adapt to external realities. As the creative forces of "self-reflexivity" lead us to develop new ways of handling problems, the periods of stress subside (Jantsch, 1980).

Note that the stress, adaptation, and growth experiences are not unique to immigrants or sojourners who relocate to a different society. The same experience is broadly shared by anyone living in a multicultural society who is willing to confront and manage the challenges of intercultural encounters across ethnic, racial, and cultural lines. Whether we are at home or abroad, the same three-pronged dynamic of stress-adaptation-growth helps us move in the direction of increased chances of success in meeting the demands of intercultural contacts.

▶ Correlates of Identity Development

One of the long-term consequences of undergoing the intercultural transformation process is an *individualization* of identity, which is a self-conception and a conception of others that transcends conventional social categories such as race, ethnicity, and culture. Individualization allows a life that is lived without rigid constraint due to the grip of conventional social categories. Such an orientation generates a heightened self-awareness, a sense of authenticity, a feeling of certainty about one's place in the world, and a sense of personal power to fix one's sights and chart a course. An individualized identity further allows the enactment and pursuit of socially constructive ends, such as the attitudes of tolerance, mutuality, and cooperation in search of meaningful relationships across group boundaries (Waterman, 1992). Capturing some of these elements of individualized identity are the words of Muruddin Farah, a Somali novelist who traveled widely in Africa, Europe, and North America: "One of the pleasures of living away from home is that you become the master of your destiny, you avoid the constraints and limitations of your past and, if need be, create an alternative life for yourself. That way everybody else becomes *the other,* and you the center of the universe" (in Glad, 1990, p. 65).

Accompanying the individualization of identity is a parallel psychological development, *universalization,* which is "a new consciousness, born out of an awareness of the relative nature of values and of the universal aspect of human nature" (Yoshikawa, 1978, p. 220). As we reach an advanced level of identity development, we become better able to see, with clarity, the oneness and unity of humanity. We are better able to feel compassion and sensitivity for people who are different. It becomes easier for us to locate the points of difference and contention as well as the points of commonality, complementarity, and consent. In so doing, cultural parochialism can be overcome and a wider circle of inclusion can be reached. Like hikers climbing a mountain who finally see that all paths below present unique scenery but ultimately lead to the same summit, we are able to attain a perspective of a larger whole. With such an outlook we can experience the humanity in all people beyond apparent polarities and opposites. We can rise above the hidden grips of the culture of our childhood and discover that there are many ways to be "good," "true," and "beautiful" without being blinded by what is called the "paradigmatic barrier" (Bennett, 1986).

In a subtle manner, the individualization and universalization of identity present us with a special kind of *freedom*—freedom to make deliberate choices for actions, to exercise spontaneous empathy, to "imaginatively participate in the other's world view" (J. Bennett, 1977, p. 49) and to appreciate "outsidedness" through the ability to view the other from the perspective of a disinterested outsider (Harris, 1993, p. 93). Even though such a sense of personhood must be hard won through many moments of inner crisis, it represents an uncommon achievement of personal and social integration through the successful resolution of a process in which we struggle and triumph over the constraints of rigid social categorization. In this self-liberating process, our identity is transformed into something that will always contain the old and the new, side by side, forming "a third kind." In a sense, the development of an intercultural personhood is a continuous struggle of searching for the authenticity in self and others across group boundaries. Consistent with Erikson's (1969) notion of "transcendence" in describing "self-actualizing" people and with Ricoeur's (1992) idea of a "transcendental ego," intercultural personhood is a way of life that embraces and incorporates seemingly divergent cultural elements into one's own unique worldview. This conception of identity development is very much in agreement with what has been described as the development of "double perspective" and "stereoscopic vision" (Rushdie, 1992), "cultural reflexibility" or "cultural relativistic insight" (Roosens, 1989), and "moral inclusiveness" (Opotow, 1990). All of these concepts characteristically show an increased self-knowledge that is less encumbered by the hidden grips of culture and allows broader and less categorical perceptions.

▶ Intercultural Persons

The contemporary world of a tightly knit intercultural communication web offers ample cases of individuals who have attained a significant level of intercultural personhood. Numerous firsthand accounts witnessing the reality of intercultural identity transformation can be found in the form of case histories, memoirs, biographical stories, and essays of self-reflection and self-analysis available in popular books and newspaper and magazine articles and on radio and television programs. Among the more widely known are such prominent figures as Seiji Ozawa (the former director-conductor of the Boston Symphony Orchestra and a Japanese American), Colin Powell (the former U.S. secretary of state and the son of immigrants from the Dominican Republic), and Kofi Annan (the United Nations secretary-general and a native of Ghana). There are many more lesser known individuals whose life experiences span multitudes of cultural domains—Peace Corps volunteers, missionaries, exchange students, and immigrants and refugees, as well as those ordinary citizens of multicultural societies such as the United States who have embraced a truly inclusive and integrated life that crosses various ethnic boundaries.

The stories of "intercultural persons" bear witness to our theoretical understanding of intercultural identity development and offer a special insight into the ebb and flow of psychic transformation and the eventual emergence of a personhood beyond the confines of a particular cultural identity. Even though no two individuals travel an identical path in becoming intercultural, the intensity of experiences in crossing cultures offers everyone opportunities for full blossoming of the uniquely human capacity to face challenges, to learn from them, and thereby to grow into a greater self-integration. We learn that experiences requiring adaptive challenges bring about a special privilege to think, feel, and act beyond the boundaries of a single culture and beyond "either-or" categorization. Russian exile Edward (in Glad, 1990) noted, "having lived now in three countries—USSR, the USA, and France—I really am able to answer the question: 'Which is best?' All of them have become part and parcel of my own personal history" (p. 50). Equally instructive is the final story in Salman Rushdie's book of short stories, *East, West* (1996). The story ends with the narrator's declaration: "I . . . have ropes around my neck, I have them to this day, pulling me this way and that, East and West, the nooses tightening, commanding, *choose, choose*. I buck, I snort, I whinny, I rear, I kick. Ropes, I do not choose between you. . . . I choose neither of you, and both. Do you hear? I refuse to choose" (p. 211).

Stories such as these remind us that becoming an intercultural person does not necessarily entail a "surrendering" of our personal and cultural integrity. Muneo Yoshikawa (1978) offered a particularly pointed and thoughtful testimonial to this point. Born in Japan, Yoshikawa taught at a university in the United States for many years and examined his own intercultural evolution as follows:

> I am now able to look at both cultures with objectivity as well as subjectivity; I am able to move in both cultures, back and forth without any apparent conflict. . . . I think that something beyond the sum of each [cultural] identification took place, and that it became something akin to the concept of "synergy"—when one adds 1 and 1, one gets three, or a little more. This something extra is not culture-specific but something unique of its own, probably the emergence of a new attribute or a new self-awareness, born out of an awareness of the relative nature of values and of the universal aspect of human nature. . . . I really am not concerned whether others take me as a Japanese or an American; I can accept myself as I am. I feel I am much freer than ever before, not only in the cognitive domain (perception, thoughts, etc.), but also in the affective (feeling, attitudes, etc.) and behavioral domains. (p. 220)

Yoshikawa's thoughts are echoed in an essay by Glenn Loury (1993), whose reflection on his own life experiences as a black American eloquently depicts the true meaning of a universalized and individualized identity orientation:

> I have had to confront the problem of balancing my desire not to disappoint the expectations of others . . . with my conviction that one should strive to live life with integrity. . . . I no longer believe that the camaraderie engendered among blacks by our collective experience of racism constitutes an adequate basis for any person's self-definition. . . . The most important challenges and opportunities that confront me derive not from my racial condition, but rather from my human condition. I am a husband, a father, a son, a teacher, an intellectual, a Christian, a citizen. In none of these roles is my race irrelevant, but neither can racial identity alone provide much guidance for my quest to adequately discharge these responsibilities. The particular features of my social condition, the external givens, merely set the stage of my life, they do not provide a script. That script must be internally generated, it must be a product of a reflective deliberation about the meaning of this existence for which no political or ethnic program could ever substitute. . . . In my view, a personal iden-

tity wholly dependent on racial contingency falls tragically short of its potential because it embraces too parochial a conception of what is possible, and of what is desirable. . . . Of course there is the constraint of racism also holding us back. But the trick . . . is to turn such "nets" into wings, and thus to fly by them. One cannot do that if one refuses to see that ultimately, it is neither external constraints nor expanded opportunity but rather an indwelling spirit that makes this flight possible. (pp. 7–10)

▶ Forging an Intercultural Path

To the extent that intercultural identity is of value both to us individually and to the integration of a multicultural society such as the United States, we may accept and appreciate the real possibility that a part of who we are and what we are may be changed as we engage ourselves with those who are different from us. To be willing to undergo personal transformation, in turn, means that we recognize the necessity to be open to new experiences that may transform us. It further means that we accept that we cannot realistically choose between keeping the original identity intact and adapting to the increasingly intercultural milieu in which we live. We need to be mindful that embracing new cultural elements means not "throwing away" or "being disloyal to" our original cultural heritage but subjecting it to numerous intercultural tests and ultimately enriching it. We need to be guided by a foresight that there is a larger, reconstituted self at the end of our struggle to cross cultural boundaries. This foresight helps us to replace some of our short-term anxieties and reservations with optimism and resolve—a realization that most of us in most circumstances are capable of finding ways to face and overcome the challenges of intercultural interactions, including the most contentious of identity politics.

As members of an intercultural society, our true strength no longer lies in insisting on who we were in the past and who we are at the moment. Instead, our true strength resides in affirming and challenging our "uncommitted potentiality for change" (Bateson, 1951/1972, p. 49). In moments of inner calm, we must let our victorious personality spring forward with flashes of creative insights beyond exclusive cultural loyalty. This very idea was pointed out by Vaclav Havel, former president of the Czech Republic, in his remarks on the occasion of his receiving the Philadelphia Liberty Medal.

It logically follows that, in today's multicultural world, the truly reliable path to coexistence, to peaceful coexistence and creative cooperation, must start from what is at the root of all cultures and what lies infinitely deeper in human hearts and minds than political opinion. It must be rooted in self-transcendence. Transcendence as a hand reached out to those close to us, to foreigners, to the human community, to all living creatures, to nature, to the universe, transcendence as a deeply and joyously experienced need to be in harmony even with what we ourselves are not, what we do not understand, what seems distant from us in time and space, but with which we are nevertheless mysteriously linked because, together with us, all this constitutes a single world. Transcendence is the only real alternative to extinction. (Havel, 1995, p. 113)

The process of becoming intercultural, of course, is never easy or complete. Yet each step taken on this path is a new formation of life—a true reward for having withstood the test of continual tides of self-doubt and cynicism that are rooted in the habitual mental posturing of "us and them." This personal accomplishment is not an extraordinary phenomenon that only exceptional individuals achieve. It is simply an incident of the normal human mutability that all of us possess, manifesting itself as we stretch ourselves out of the old and familiar. The experiences of those who have already achieved a great deal of intercultural identity transformation bear witness to the human capacity for self-renewal. Even under extreme conditions of cultural estrangement, they have been able to revise their original cultural constitution and construct a life of their own that embraces a broad spectrum of human conditions. My own intercultural journey in the United States, which began in 1970 when I was a graduate student from Korea, gives me a sense of assurance and gratitude in joining them in the often arduous but ultimately rewarding path of becoming intercultural.

Notes

1. The term "cultural identity" is employed broadly as a generic term that is interchangeable with other commonly used terms including "national," "ethnic," "ethnolinguistic," and "racial" identity, and more generic concepts such as "social" and "group" identity. In this sense, the present use of the term "culture" includes common ethnic, linguistic, racial, and historical backgrounds. Correspondingly, the term "intercultural identity" is employed throughout this essay interchangeably with "interethnic," "interracial," and "intergroup" identity, as well as with other terms such as "meta-identity," "multicultural identity," or "transcultural identity"—all of which indicate a nondualistic, metacontextual definition of self/others rather than rigid boundedness within any particular group category.

2. The theoretical ideas and case illustrations presented in this essay are based on the author's previous writings, including *Communication and Cross-Cultural Adaptation: An Integrative Theory* (1988) and *Becoming Intercultural: An Integrative Theory of Communication and Cross-Cultural Adaptation* (2001). For a more condensed presentation of her theory see Kim (1995a, 1995b).

References

Adler, P. (1982). Beyond cultural identity: Reflections on cultural and multicultural men. In L. A. Samovar & R. A. Porter (Eds.), *Intercultural communication: A reader* (3rd ed.) (pp. 389–408). Belmont, CA: Wadsworth.

Bateson, G. (1951/1972). *Steps to an ecology of mind: Collected essays in anthropology, psychiatry, evolution, and epistemology.* New York: Ballantine.

Bennett, J. (1977, December). Transition shock: Putting culture shock in perspective. In N. C. Jain (Ed.), *International and intercultural communication annual* (Vol. 4, pp. 45–52). Falls Church, VA: Speech Communication Association.

Bennett, M. (1986). A developmental approach to training for intercultural sensitivity. *International Journal of Intercultural Relations, 10,* 179–196.

Blackwell, J. E., & Hart, P. S. (1982). *Cities, suburbs, and blacks: A study of concerns, distrust, and alienation.* Bayside, NY: General Hall.

Brewer, M., & Gardner, W. (1996). Who is this "we"? Levels of collective identity and self-representations. *Journal of Personality and Social Psychology, 71*, 83–93.

Erikson, E. H. (1950). *Childhood and society.* New York: W. W. Norton.

Erikson, E. H. (1969). Growth and crises of the healthy personality: Readings. In H. Chiang & A. H. Maslow (Eds.), *The healthy personality* (pp. 30–34). New York: Van Nostrand Reinhold.

Etzioni, A. (1993). *The spirit of community: Rights, responsibilities, and the communitarian agenda.* New York: Crown.

Glad, J. (Ed.). (1990). *Literature in exile.* Durham, NC: Duke University Press.

Harris, M. (1993, April). Performing the other's text: Bakhtin and the art of cross-cultural understanding. *Mind & Human Interaction, 4*, 92–97.

Havel, V. (1995, January/February). A time for transcendence. *Utne Reader, 53*, pp. 112–113.

Hecht, M. L., Collier, M. J., & Ribeau, S. L. (1993). *African American communication: Ethnic identity and cultural interpretation.* Newbury Park, CA: Sage.

Jantsch, E. (1980). *The self-organizing universe: Scientific and human implications of the emerging paradigm of evolution.* New York: Pergamon.

Kim, Y. Y. (1988). *Communication and cross-cultural adaptation: An integrative theory.* Clevedon, England: Multilingual Matters.

Kim, Y. Y. (1995a). Cross-cultural adaptation: An integrative theory. In R. L. Wiseman (Ed.), *Intercultural communication theory* (pp. 170–193). Newbury Park, CA: Sage.

Kim, Y. Y. (1995b). Identity development: From cultural to intercultural. In H. Mokros (Ed.), *Interaction & identity* (pp. 347–369). New Brunswick, NJ: Transaction.

Kim, Y. Y. (2001). *Becoming intercultural: An integrative theory of communication and cross-cultural adaptation.* Thousand Oaks, CA: Sage.

Loury, G. C. (1993). Free at last? A personal perspective on race and identity in America. In G. Early (Ed.), *Lure and loathing: Essays on race, identity, and the ambivalence of assimilation* (pp. 1–12). New York: Allen Lane/Penguin.

Opotow, S. (1990). Moral exclusion and inclusion. *Journal of Social Issues, 46*, 1–20.

Ricoeur, P. (1992). *Oneself as another* (K. Blamey, Trans.). Chicago: University of Chicago Press.

Roosens, E. E. (1989). *Creating ethnicity: The process of ethnogenesis.* Newbury Park, CA: Sage.

Rushdie, S. (1992). *Imaginary homelands: Essays and criticism 1981–1991.* New York: Penguin Books.

Rushdie, S. (1996). *East, West: Stories.* New York: Vintage Books.

Tajfel, H. (Ed.). (1978). *Differentiation between social groups: Studies in the social psychology of intergroup relations.* London: Academic Press.

Thornton, M. (1996). Hidden agendas, identity theories, and multiracial people. In Maria P. P. Root (Ed.), *The multiracial experience: Racial borders as the new frontiers* (pp. 101–120). Thousand Oaks, CA: Sage.

Waterman, A. S. (1992). Identity as an aspect of optimal psychological functioning. In G. R. Adams, T. P. Gullotta, & R. Montemayor (Eds.), *Adolescent identity formation* (pp. 50–72). Newbury Park, CA: Sage.

Yinger, J. (1986). Intersecting strands in the theorisation of race and ethnic relations. In J. Rex & D. Mason (Eds.), *Theories of race and ethnic relations* (pp. 20–41). New York: Cambridge University Press.

Yoshikawa, M. (1978). Some Japanese and American cultural characteristics. In M. H. Prosser, *The cultural dialogue: An introduction to intercultural communication* (pp. 220–239). Boston: Houghton Mifflin.

Tadasu "Todd" Imahori's essay illustrates, in very concrete terms, Young Yun
Kim's argument that extensive intercultural communication experiences can be
the catalyst for an individual's adaptive changes. Todd's journey from Japan to
the midwestern United States to San Francisco and back to Japan is a case study
in cultural adaptation and change. Through all the stages of change and con-
stancy, Todd shows how individuals seek to fit in, as well as to maintain core elements of their identities.

26   On Becoming "American"

Tadasu "Todd" Imahori

I was born in Japan as Tadasu Imahori. In the fall of 1978, at a college campus in the U.S. Midwest, I was ordering pizza on the phone. Though I attempted to say "Tad," a shortened version of my first name, the person taking
my order heard "Todd." That's when I decided that I would become "Todd
Imahori." In that instant, as I readily accepted a familiar "American" name as
my own, my cultural adaptation process started. I was content if people remembered my "American" nickname, even if they mispronounced my last
name, made fun of it, or didn't even try to remember it. Such an attitude toward my own name truly reflected my earnest desire to "fit in," to become
"American."

In those early days of my cultural adaptation to the United States, I
wanted to *adapt myself* to the "American" culture. Twenty years later, I see
my adaptation process as much more complex. A few years ago I had the following phone conversation with a hotel reservation clerk:

"May I please have your name sir?"
"Yes. It's Todd Imahori, and the last name is spelled I-M-A-H-O-R-I."
"Oh, come on, is this a crank call?"
"What?"
"I'm saying, are you pulling my leg?"
"Why do you think I am joking?"
"Well, a name spelled like that . . ."

At that moment, I surmised that the reservationist thought my last name
was spelled "I-M-A-H-O-R-E," which could be read "I'm a whore." I had previously encountered others who had made fun of my last name in this way.

"Oh, so you wouldn't think this is a crank call if I had a name like Johnson, or
Smith?"

ON BECOMING "AMERICAN"   259

Culture Concepts

Culture and Nation

In everyday language, people commonly treat culture *and* nation *as equivalent terms. They are not.* Nation *is a political term referring to a government and a set of formal and legal mechanisms that regulate the political behavior of its people. The culture, or cultures, that exist within the boundaries of a nation-state certainly influence the regulations that a nation develops, but the term* culture *is not synonymous with* nation. *Although one cultural group predominates in some nations, most nations contain multiple cultures within their boundaries. The United States, for example, is a nation that contains many cultures.*

"No, not that, but we get a lot of crank calls, and your name just . . ."

"My name is just what, not white? Not American? You've offended me, and I would like to speak to your supervisor right now."

After many years of trying to become "American" I had acquired a very different attitude toward my own name. I had developed a keen awareness of what *my* being "American" was supposed to look and sound like: I was forever to be an "other American," no matter how much I adapted. Madrid (1988) best described that awareness of and frustration with being an "other" in the United States:

> There was a myth, a pervasive myth, that said if we only learned to speak English well—and particularly without an accent—we would be welcomed into the American fellowship.
>
> Senator Sam Hayakawa notwithstanding, the true text was not our speech, but rather our names and our appearance, for we would always have an accent, however perfect our pronunciation, however excellent our enunciation, however divine our diction. That accent would be heard in our pigmentation, our physiognomy, our names. We were, in short, *the other.* (p. 56)

Today, as my cultural adaptation continues, I am simultaneously torn and excited by my multiple cultural identities. I am also frustrated with my never-ending status as the "other." Let me, then, present the tale of my journey through four stages of the cultural adaptation experience: (a) trying to become "American" and dealing with the "Japanese" or "American" choice; (b) becoming an "other American" and acquiring a "minority" identity; (c) becoming an "other Japanese" and being aware of a "majority" perspective; and (d) becoming "intercultural" and moving among the multiple identities of "other Japanese," "other American," "majority," and "minority."

Throughout this essay I will use quotation marks around terms that categorize people to indicate that such categories are overgeneralizations and need to be considered cautiously. I will use the term "American" to designate the culture and the people of the United States of America because that is the term "mainstream America" uses to refer to itself, and that was what I and others expected me to acquire and become in my adaptation process. Although the term should include other cultures and people located in all American (North, Central, and South) regions, I elect to use it because it best represents my own consciousness about "who and what" I tried to be in my adaptation processes. I will also use the terms "majority" and "minority" to refer to the two cultures defined by the relative differences in membership size, economic wealth, access to resources, and overall social power as defined by the larger culture.

▶ Becoming "American"

To describe my adaptation to "American" culture, it would be helpful to describe myself before my journey to the United States. I grew up as the first son of a middle-class family. I am a "third-generation" sojourner in the United States. Both my grandfather and my father lived in the United States for a few years. I accompanied my father as a newborn baby and lived for one year in the United States. My grandfather didn't talk much about his life in New York, where he lived in the 1930s, but he once told me how hard it was for him to find a place to live because of racism. This was the only "negative" thing about the United States that I heard growing up in Japan. My father, mother, and older sister spoke mostly positively about the United States. In school I was taught that the United States was a country to be followed and modeled after, and my generation was supposed to learn from it. I grew up thinking of the United States as a kind of utopia and I yearned to go there.

One direct effect this desire had on me was that I focused more on English than on other academic subjects and sought "American" cultural icons. During the 1970s I listened to "American" rock music, grew my hair long, and wore bell-bottom blue jeans. I intently watched "American" TV shows that were available in Japan. I felt very ready to come to the United States when I first arrived in 1978.

In my early stages of cultural adaptation I was mostly concerned with my English proficiency. Speaking English like an "American" was my criterion for successful cultural adaptation (or "assimilation"). I didn't know about the myth Madrid (1988) pointed out, but I knew my ability to speak English would facilitate my adaptation. I surrounded myself with "Americans" and for at least a year tried not to use the Japanese language or interact with other "Japanese." Within a year I mastered conversational English pretty well. Along with language skills, I also acquired the "American" lifestyle. I now had a mustache and a fashionable hair style. I had become almost "American." My "American" friends had accepted me as one of them; at least that's what I thought. One friend said, "Todd, you're more American than most Americans"—whatever that meant. I was happy, for a while, with my accomplishment: my amazing transformation from a "Japanese" to an "American."

My cultural adaptation, however, was subconsciously targeted to a specific sector of the United States. I was culturally immersed in the "white" youth culture of the late 1970s. I studied at a university in the Midwest, where nearly all of the students were "white." My "American" friends were mostly "whites." The English I acquired had a standard Midwestern "white" accent. The college lifestyle I maintained was that of "white men." In my consciousness at that time, that was "America." The subconscious belief that "white America" was "America" started early. I can't recall learning English in Japan from "nonwhite" native speakers. "Americans" I knew in Japan—in person, on TV, or in the movies—were almost exclusively whites.

Looking back, with the academic and personal sense-making frameworks I have since developed, I believe that my status in Japan before coming to the United States contributed to my subconscious adaptation to "mainstream America." I was a "mainstream Japanese": "male," "young," "middle-class," and "well-educated." Those who are in the "dominant" group, as I was, tend to have less awareness of their power and group identity. Thus, as a person who stood at the top of the "Japanese" social hierarchy without much awareness of doing so, it was easy for me to adapt to those who shared the same lack of awareness about their "mainstream" status in the United States. I took for granted that what I represented was "Japanese." My "mainstream American" counterparts also assumed that they represented the "American" culture and readily taught me what they regarded as "American." In the beginning phase, my cultural adaptation was thus focused on assimilating to a new national culture.

Although I was subconsciously adapting only to "white America" and thinking it was "America," it didn't take long for me to realize that most of my associations were with "white America." I had lost touch with others, particularly "people of color" and "women." Consequently, I denied a part of myself as a "person of color" as I developed into "almost white," or more specifically, an "almost white male." I remember a conversation with one of my "white" college classmates:

> "Todd, you're okay, you are like honored white."
> "What does that mean, 'honored white'?"
> "Well, it means that you are like 'white,' you are like many of your people who have become doctors, teachers, and earned your status."

These types of statements, made by those who supposedly had accepted me, created dissonance in my sense of identity. I began to feel a need to be even more "American" to be accepted fully. However, the more "American" I tried to be, the greater the hindrance in my background. I was not even sure whether my background was a barrier because I was a "foreigner" (i.e., "non-U.S. born") or because I was a "Japanese" (i.e., someone who was "nonwhite").

The following incident illustrates my uncertainty. I was once traveling on a motorcycle with a "Japanese" friend. As we rode through the Appalachian Mountains, it started snowing. We found a strip mall to shelter ourselves from the snow and were drinking hot coffee on a bench inside the mall when a sheriff's deputy approached us. The following conversation ensued.

Deputy: Where are you from, boy?
Todd: We're traveling from Ohio, sir.
Deputy: No, I mean, where are you really from?
Todd: Well, I guess, then, we are originally from Japan, and now we are both studying at XXX university.
Deputy: I thought so. It's dangerous for your kind to be here.

He then ordered us to follow his squad car as he "escorted" us to a rundown motel outside of town. In his mind he was probably doing us a "favor" by protecting the "outsiders." That made me angry. But I wasn't sure whether I was being treated as an "outsider" because I was "Japanese" or because I was a "foreigner" (that is, I didn't speak English well enough).

Even though these kinds of incidents gave me the sense that I might never be accepted as an "American," I spent nearly 14 years struggling to become one. During the period from 1978 to 1991, I was often confronted with the question of "American or Japanese." My "American" students enjoyed asking me, "Do you now consider yourself an American or a Japanese?" I was bewildered by their question almost every time. I usually answered "I'm both: I'm still Japanese, but not quite fully Japanese, and at the same time I'm almost American. I'm culturally schizophrenic, like Jekyll and Hyde." I often asked myself a similar question: "How much do I want to be an American? How Japanese do I want to remain?"

In answering these questions I constantly experienced a paradox: The more I tried to become "American," the more different I felt because of my "Japanese" background; the more I tried to stay "Japanese," the more I realized how much I had changed since coming to the United States. I was torn between "American" and "Japanese." The torment was hard on me. In retrospect, it was a relatively simple set of choices, because I was dealing with only two possibilities.

▶ Becoming an "Other American"

Carrying the dissonance with my identities as "American" and "Japanese," I moved from the Midwest to California in 1992. There I met many others who shared a similar sense of identity dissonance. They were also "Asian Americans," mostly second generation or later. Although they were born in the United States and grew up in a way that I thought of as "American," they expressed frequently the sense that they were never quite "at home."

Ronald Takaki (1993), a sansei (third-generation) "Japanese American" professor, relates the following story:

I had flown from San Francisco to Norfolk and was riding in a taxi to my hotel. . . . My driver and I chatted about the weather and the tourists. . . . The rearview mirror reflected a white man in his forties. "How long have you been in this country?" he asked. "All my life," I replied, wincing. . . . With a strong southern drawl, he remarked: "I was wondering because your English is excellent!". . . Somehow I did not look "American" to him; my eyes and complexion looked foreign. (p. 1)

Thomas Nakayama (1997), a yonsei (fourth-generation) "Japanese American" scholar, writes:

"Do you speak English?" This question always dis/orients me; I am lost when asked this question. Why wouldn't I speak the language of my parents, the language of my country? The simple response "Of course I do" does not usually dis/orient the questioner's assumption that one needs European ancestors to be "American." (p. 17)

I, too, am used to strangers complimenting my English or questioning me about whether I speak English. At times compliments or questions come after they learn that I grew up speaking Japanese, not English. At other times, they *assume*—as they did with Takaki and Nakayama—that I am a "foreigner." When I found this daunting similarity between my experiences and those of Takaki and Nakayama, I was no longer uncertain about the reason why I wasn't fully accepted as "American." I knew that my culture and my "foreign" status are the same to the "racist American" society.

As a result of this realization, I have come to appreciate my "Japanese American" experiences. What I share with the "Japanese American" experience is the assumption on the part of strangers that I am a "Japanese born Japanese." What I also share with them is the alienated feeling I experience when I encounter people who assume that I am not an "American." However, my experience is different from theirs because the strangers' assumption about me *happens* to be correct; for most "Japanese Americans" (and many other "nonwhite Americans"), it is grossly wrong. To the extent that this difference exists between my experience and theirs, the sense of denial that "Japanese (nonwhite) Americans" experience may be greater than what I have encountered. Nevertheless, it is clear that I am going to be an "other American" no matter how much I adapt to the "American" culture unless there is a change in the society that sees me as a "foreigner" because of my appearance.

Upon this somber realization, I then attempted to make sense out of my own "minority" experience as an "other American." My sensemaking process largely depended on learning the "Japanese (Asian) American" culture and its history. Because of my appearance I am perceived in the United States as either a "Japanese (Asian)" or a "Japanese (Asian) American." It was therefore sensible for me to examine the group of people with whom I was lumped together. It also meant claiming my own identity in the United States. As Kimoto (1997) asserted, cultural knowledge empowers one's identity by providing a basis to question, modify, and create a label for one's own identity.

As I began my studies of "Japanese American" history and culture, I realized that my experiences with prejudice in the United States are similar to

---

Culture Concepts

Individualism-Collectivism

For most European Americans, the emphasis on the individual self is so strong and so pervasive, it is almost impossible for them to comprehend a different point of view. The belief in individualism *means that many European Americans regard the self as located solely within the individual, and each individual is completely separate from all others. Alternatively, cultures may define who people are only through their associations with others, and an individual's self-definition may not be separate from that of the larger group. Cultures that believe in* collectivism *have a heightened sense of interdependence, so what happens to the group (family, work group, or social group) happens to the person.*

---

what other people of Japanese origin have experienced throughout their history there. The more I learned about the prejudices and discrimination committed against "Japanese Americans," the more determined I became to do something about racism as an intercultural communication scholar. I conducted a research study about the "Japanese American" internment experience during World War II (Imahori, 2001) and began preparing myself to teach a course on intracultural communication.

In 1995 I encountered a film called *The Color of Fear* (Mun Wah, 1994). I went to see the film partly to decide whether I could use it as a teaching tool, and also to find confirmations for my own experiences with racism. In the film, eight men of different racial backgrounds discussed their views about racism. One "European American" man kept denying that racism is a problem in the United States. He exhibited a complete lack of awareness about how "people of color" are treated and made to feel because of racism. I could easily identify with the seven other men, who were trying to convince this "white man" of the seriousness of racism. I had had experiences similar to theirs. While viewing the film, however, I realized that I was also the equivalent of the "white man" in Japan, as I was the "mainstream." Curiously, I found that I had two contradictory cultures living inside of me: a "majority" (as a "Japanese" in Japan) and a "minority" (as a "Japanese" in the United States).

In my earlier phase of cultural adaptation I struggled with the paradox of being at the same time "American" and "Japanese." Now I was also struggling with simultaneously being a "majority" and a "minority." What helped me understand the consequences of being a majority or a minority was the concept of "white privilege."

McIntosh (1995) offers a list of privileges whites in the United States enjoy. The list includes assumptions or conditions that apply (or do not apply) in daily life. Examples include: "I can turn on the television or open to the front page of the paper and see people of my race widely and positively represented" (p. 79); "If my day, week, or year is going badly, I need not ask of each negative episode or situation whether it has racial overtones" (p. 81). If I considered these two examples as an "other American," as a "minority" in the United States, I would answer "false" to both of them. If I responded to them as a "Japanese male," a "majority" in Japan, I would answer "true" to both of them.

McIntosh lists 46 such privileges. As an "other American" in the United States I answered "false" to 42 of them. The four conditions I could answer "true" were largely due to my "model minority" status[1] in the United States. As a "Japanese" in Japan I responded "true" to 43 of the 46 privileges. The three "false" responses were due to global-level racism and the relative status of the "Japanese" in the world's racial hierarchy.

When I looked at my answers to McIntosh's list, I was saddened by how far I was from the privileges of the "white American" in the United States. Conversely, I became unsettled as I realized how much privilege I am granted in Japan as a "majority Japanese male" and how much and how long I had taken such privileges for granted. I have also generalized McIntosh's list to include gender preferences, sexual identity, and physical disabilities. Every time I examined the privileges I did or did not have, it crystallized in me an understanding of the prejudices that exist in the society around me. I also understood more clearly the suffocating power of prejudice. My own prejudices kept me from interacting competently with others. The prejudices around me suffocated me by keeping me outside and oppressed. When I acquired this awareness about what it meant to be a "majority" and a "minority," I was able to see my world from multiple perspectives: "Japanese," "U.S. American," "majority," and "minority."

▶ Becoming an "Other Japanese"

As much as I have become an "other American," I have also become an "other Japanese" who can now examine the prejudices and privileges of the "mainstream Japanese" as an "outsider" with a "minority" consciousness. I am still a member of the "mainstream Japanese" in appearance. I would still be a member of the "mainstream" if I hadn't come to terms with my own prejudices and hadn't committed myself to changing the prejudices that lift the "mainstream" unjustly while oppressing racial, gender, and other "minority" groups. My values concerning diversity (e.g., gay marriage rights) further make me a "minority" in Japan.

I am also an "other Japanese" because I have transformed culturally. My "Japanese" family, friends, and colleagues in Japan expect me to be different from them as a result of my cultural transformations. Some of the cultural transformations resulted from consciously choosing an acquired value (e.g., an individual's right to choose) over my original "Japanese" cultural value (a duty to maintain group harmony), whereas other transformations were mostly unconscious (e.g., my initial instinct to avoid public confrontations with others). Not only have I changed some of my cultural beliefs and values, but I have also acquired an ability to examine "Japanese" culture from an "outsider's" view by taking the "American" perspective.

Culture Concepts

Conflict in Intercultural Relationships

People in collectivistic and individualistic cultures typically define and respond to conflict differently. In collectivistic cultures, people are more likely to merge task and instrumental concerns, and conflict is therefore likely to be seen as personal. To shout and scream publicly, thus displaying the conflict to others, threatens everyone's face to such an extreme degree that such behavior is usually avoided at all costs. Instead, members of collectivistic cultures are likely to deal with face threats such as conflicts by selecting strategies that smooth over their disagreements and allow them to maintain the face of both parties, that is, mutual face-saving.

In contrast, people from individualistic cultures are more likely to separate the task and the instrumental dimensions. They are able to express their agitation and anger (perhaps including shouting and strong nonverbal actions) about an issue and then joke and socialize with the other person once the disagreement is over. It is almost as if once the conflict is resolved, it is completely forgotten. Members of individualistic cultures are also likely to approach conflict in a verbal, action-oriented way. That is, the conflict precipitates overt responses, and the conflict is explicitly revealed and named.

My identity as an "other Japanese" mirrors my identity as an "other American." Although I am not accepted fully as a "mainstream American," I can no longer be accepted fully as a "mainstream Japanese." As much as I am "foreign" and looked on suspiciously in U.S. society, I am perceived as "strange" and treated with polite caution by the "Japanese." Although I hold an outsider's view of "American" culture, I am able to see "Japanese" culture from the outside as well. The difference, however, is that I am an "other American" because of my race and I am an "other Japanese" because of cultural transformations and my growth as an intercultural being.

As the "other" I am in a unique position to provide different perspectives as a "minority" in both the "Japanese" and the "American" "mainstream" cultures. In explaining the "minority" perspective I can also take on the "majority" perspective. In essence, by becoming both an "other Japanese" and an "other American," by having both "majority" and "minority" perspectives, I have become "intercultural."

▶ On Being "Intercultural"

More than 20 years ago I came to the United States to become "American." Today I seek to be "intercultural." I say "intercultural" rather than "multicultural" because the latter term suggests to me that I am merely the sum of my multiple identities. However, although I can take on only one perspective at any given moment, I can move from that perspective into another instantaneously. I am "intercultural" in that I can shift easily between my different cultural perspectives. In looking back, Kim (1997) best summarized my personal adaptation experiences:

> Communicating across cultural identity boundaries is often full of challenges as it provokes questions about our taken-for-granted cultural premises, habits. . . . Yet it is precisely such challenges that offer us openings for new cultural learning, self-awareness, and personal growth. (p. 443)

I agree with Kim that I have grown personally, and in ways that are consistent with her model of adaptation (Kim, 1988). However, my adaptation was even more complex than what her theory suggests. It was directed to both my home and my host cultures. It also occurred between the cultures of "majority" and "minority."

The literature on intercultural adaptation suggests that I may yet attain an ability to transcend my perspectives, achieving what is referred to as the "third culture" (Gudykunst, Wiseman, & Hammer, 1977). For example, Yoshikawa (1978), a scholar who has a cultural background similar to mine, wrote: "I really am not concerned whether others take me as a Japanese or as an American" (p. 220). I cannot yet quite echo his sentiment. I care that others perceive me as "American," "Japanese," "Asian," "foreigner," "dominant," or "nondominant," because how others see me affects my perspective taking. I may or may not choose to agree with the identity they ascribe to me. I may loudly announce a different identity and "correct" their assumptions. Depending on my interactional situation, I have to decide constantly "who" I am going to be.

This identity shifting is highly stressful, but my ability to move across these multiple identities also allows me to become a change facilitator. I hope to be "close" enough to communicate appropriately and effectively with the "Japanese" or the "Americans" but be able to pull back far enough to be "other Japanese" or "other American" when an alternative perspective is needed. If I succeed in providing different perspectives in this manner, I can at least convince some individuals to examine their values and prejudices from contrasting points of view.

I now realize that my internal cultural stress, born out of my complex set of identities, is my resource as an intercultural person, scholar, and change facilitator. When I deal with my own prejudices and fears of cultural differences, I am able to be comfortable with my own identities. I am not sure if I have yet developed the "third culture" perspective, but what carries across my various cultural identities are both my attitudes toward cultural differences as a source of enjoyment and personal growth and my commitment to keep learning and providing different cultural perspectives. I hope that you will be able to share the same joy of learning about cultural differences by studying intercultural communication.

▶ Postscript

Six months after I began writing the first draft of this essay, I find myself living and teaching in Japan. It was a drastic and "unbelievable" (as many of my friends said) decision to leave the United States and go to Japan after 19 years of absence (not "back to" because this is really a new adaptation and not a simple "reentry" process for me). I am adding this note to clarify that my move to Japan was not motivated by my dissonance of being an "other American" in the United States. Actually, I am now experiencing a great deal of dissonance with being an "other Japanese." For example, people often give me a sympathetic look when I play with my daughter at 10 o'clock on a weekday morning at a neighborhood park. Here in Japan, fathers are expected to work hard on weekdays. It's unusual to see a man in a park on a weekday. So perhaps the onlookers are thinking: "Look, he has no job. Poor man, poor girl." My days are now filled with these kinds of surprises and culture shocks.

I made the decision to move to Japan willingly, to experience being an "other Japanese" and to enrich my intercultural experience. I need to experience the feeling of otherness on this side of the Pacific Ocean so that I can make better sense of being a "Japanese," an "American," a "majority," a "minority," and above all an "other." So the tale of my intercultural journey continues (see next chapter).

Notes

1. "Model minority" is a term often used for "Asian Americans." Because some "Asian Americans" have earned economic success and upward mobility in the United States, they are perceived as models for other "minority" cultures to "follow." The racist assumption in this term suggests that "Asian Americans" will forever be a "minority," and thus it maintains and accentuates the distance between "Asian Americans" and "mainstream America." At the same time, by elevating "Asian Americans" from other "minority" cultures, it also encourages a sense of distance and discord among the "minority" cultures.

References

Gudykunst, W. B., Wiseman, R., & Hammer, M. (1977). Determinants of a sojourner's attitudinal satisfaction. In B. Ruben (Ed.), *Communication yearbook 1* (pp. 415–425). New Brunswick, NJ: Transaction.

Imahori, T. T. (2001). Identity management of Japanese Americans between "yes-yes" and "no-no". *Studies in English Language and Literature, Seinan Gakuin University, 41(3)*, 82–120.

Kim, Y. Y. (1988). Intercultural adaptation. In M. K. Asante and W. B. Gudykunst (Eds.), *Handbook of international and intercultural communication* (pp. 275–294). Newbury Park, CA: Sage.

Kim, Y. Y. (1997). Intercultural personhood: An integration of Eastern and Western perspectives. In L. A. Samovar and R. E. Porter (Eds.), *Intercultural communication: A reader* (8th ed.) (pp. 434–447). Belmont, CA: Wadsworth.

Kimoto, D. M. (1997). Being Hapa: A choice for cultural empowerment. In A. González, M. Houston, and V. Chen (Eds.), *Our voices: Essays in culture, ethnicity and communication* (2nd ed.) (pp. 157–162). Los Angeles, CA: Roxbury.

Madrid, A. (1988, May/June). Missing people and others: Joining together to expand the circle. *Change, 20*, 55–59.

McIntosh, P. (1995). White privilege and male privilege: A personal account of coming to see correspondences through work in women's studies. In

M. L. Andersen and P. H. Collins (Eds.), *Race, class, and gender* (pp. 76–87). Belmont, CA: Wadsworth.

Mun Wah, L. (Director), & Stir Fry Productions (Producer). (1994). *The Color of Fear* [Film]. (Available from Stir Fry Productions, 1222 Preservation Park Way, Oakland, CA 94612).

Nakayama, T. (1997). Dis/orienting identities: Asian Americans, history, and intercultural communication. In A. González, M. Houston, and V. Chen (Eds.), *Our voices: Essays in culture, ethnicity and communication* (2nd ed.) (pp. 14–20). Los Angeles, CA: Roxbury.

Takaki, R. T. (1993). *A different mirror: A history of multicultural America*. Boston: Little, Brown.

Yoshikawa, M. (1978). Some Japanese and American characteristics. In M. Prosser (Ed.), *The cultural dialogue: An introduction to intercultural communication* (pp. 220–239). Boston: Houghton Mifflin.

▶ ▶ ▶ Learning AmongUS

1. Do you agree with Imahori's decision to change his name from Tadusu to Todd? Why or why not?
2. What are the four stages of adaptation that Imahori describes?
3. Imahori chose to avoid speaking Japanese or interacting with other Japanese during his early time in the United States. Was this a wise choice? Why?
4. What does Imahori mean when he says that he is a "majority" and a "minority" simultaneously?
5. Analyze a conflict situation that Imahori presents, using the ideas about conflicts in intercultural relationships.

In this continuation of his earlier essay, Tadasu "Todd" Imahori now resides in Japan, visits the United States frequently, and lives in between these two cultural worlds. His story describes how his U.S. experiences have created alternative possibilities for him in terms of behavior, which is regarded as different and unsettling by his Japanese colleagues. His essay provides insights into the ongoing roles we assume, and the negotiations that inevitably occur as we adapt to another culture. His ability to find a comfortable role as a change facilitator in Japan is indicative of the journey he has traveled.

27 On Living In Between

Tadasu "Todd" Imahori

For most of my life, I have lived in between Japan and the United States. I was born in Japan in 1956, and my parents immediately moved us to the U.S. for a year. Returning to Japan, I was schooled and raised there through adolescence. In 1978, I went to the U.S. to study for a year, moved back to Japan for a year, then relocated once again to the U.S., where I lived for 17 years as a student and then as a professor of communication. In 1997, I moved back to Japan for four years, relocated to the U.S. for a year, and now am living in Japan again.

Among these numerous relocations, my 17-year sojourn in the U.S. was particularly influential in shaping my intercultural identities. In my earlier essay (see *On Becoming "American"*), I wrote about my intercultural experiences in the U.S. during this period. I concluded that I was not totally comfortable with being "American"[1] or "Japanese," and that I identified myself with being "other American" and "other Japanese." In other words, I was an outsider in both cultures.

My intercultural experiences in Japan and in the U.S. in these past years have also been very influential in the emergence of my intercultural identities. From my relocations back and forth between the "Japanese" and the "American" cultures, two new intercultural identities have emerged for me: as a cultural "maverick" in Japan and as a "foreigner" in the U.S. These two new intercultural identities are not separate from my "other Japanese" and "other American" identities. Rather, my cultural "maverick" identity is a variant of my "other Japanese" identity, and my "foreigner" identity is a metamorphic transformation of my "other American" identity. Therefore, I continue to also identify as being "other American" and "other Japanese." I am neither "Japanese" nor "American."

In addition to having two new identities, I have become keenly aware of the cultural boundaries that define me. Some of these cultural boundaries are marked explicitly and rigidly, such as in the form of my citizenship. There are other cultural boundaries that are implicitly determined by the prevailing beliefs, values, norms, and cultural practices for my behaviors. These implicit boundaries are not predetermined; they are negotiated in each of my intercultural interactions with others.

The negotiation of implicit cultural boundaries is very complex and sometimes paradoxical. I bring to my intercultural interactions my own sensibilities about where the cultural boundaries are—how "Japanese" or "American" cultural patterns ought to guide my behaviors. However, my assessment of the boundaries is not always correct, because I may be projecting my stereotypes of how "Japanese" or "Americans" expect me to act. Thus, I may unintentionally violate the cultural patterns and expectations held by others. Paradoxically, such unintentional violations help me to understand where the boundaries actually exist around me.

When my judgment of the cultural boundaries happens to be correct, I may either stay within them or push the limits by intentionally breaching the prevailing beliefs, values, norms, and cultural practices. If I stay within the cultural boundaries to show that I can "adapt" and act appropriately (according to the standards expected by others), I may be sacrificing my avowed identity as "other Japanese" or "other American." Moreover, despite my effort to follow the cultural patterns and expectations, my partners may still perceive me as a cultural "other" and may even be surprised by my ability to follow their standards for actions.

Conversely, if I push the cultural boundaries by intentional violations, I may be able to expand the space available to me. As long as such violations are moderate, people may come to accept me as "other Japanese" or "other American," thus allowing me to behave more freely. However, excessive intentional violations may lead to a perception of me as an "outcast," pushing me further away from "Japanese" or "American" cultures and cornering me into an even smaller space.

Through these complex processes, I negotiate the cultural boundaries that define my world. In this essay, which is a sequel to *On Becoming "American,"* I would like to uncover the complex dynamics of cultural boundary negotiations and describe how my two new identities as a cultural "maverick" in Japan and a "foreigner" in the U.S have emerged. I will primarily focus on my professional interactions with others, even though my day-to-day experiences include private and public lives.

▶ Coming to Japan as an "Other Japanese"

When I returned to Japan in 1997, I was widely regarded as "other Japanese." For 17 years prior to that, I had lived in the U.S., had internalized "American" values, and had acquired "American" behavioral patterns. Furthermore, when I was hired by my university in Japan, people there knew that I had lived in the U.S. for a long time, and therefore I was already perceived as "Americanized." As an informed intercultural communication scholar, I thought that I would not fit into the "Japanese" cultural boundaries. I was correct in this anticipation. In the beginning of my return to Japan, I experienced three types of difficulties in negotiating the "Japanese" cultural boundaries.

One of my first difficulties had to do with my attire. When I first began working, I noticed that most of the other professors wore suits and carried professional briefcases to class. I quickly surmised that, at least at my university, the faculty norm for attire was quite formal. However, after living in the U.S. for a long time, I was used to comfortable and functional attire. I also felt that formal attire would create too much interpersonal distance between my students and me. Thus, to this day, I wear a pair of khaki pants and a polo shirt, and I carry a backpack to my classes. I also wear sunglasses most of the time, since bright sunlight hurts my eyes. In this way, from the beginning of my life on campus, I decided to look different.

Because of my casual appearance, I anticipated comments from others that I looked atypical of a professor. However, most of the comments I received were that I looked "American." What is intriguing is that one of my "American" colleagues sometimes wears shorts to his classes, but people rarely comment about him. Because my colleague is European American, his "American" casual attire is perceived as natural and does not attract any special comments. In contrast, since my culture is "Japanese," and therefore I am expected to look like a "Japanese" professor (that is, wear a suit), I am regarded as being "Americanized."

In the early days of my cultural boundary negotiations, I experienced a second difficulty, because I had overadapted to the prevailing beliefs, values, norms, and cultural practices for communicating with elder professors. Although I was rusty at first, I tried to communicate with my distinguished colleagues in a polite and respectful manner, using the honorific style of communication available in the Japanese language. However, this polite and respectful manner surprised some people, because I came to my university with the reputation of having lived in the U.S. for a very long time. One professor told me, "You are not as bad as I thought. You are more Japanese than I expected." This comment illustrated that I was already given leeway as an "Americanized" "other Japanese." I was expected to act differently. Since then, I have made my communication with senior professors less formal, even though in public settings (that is, in the presence of others), I retain the honorific style.

My final difficulty in the beginning of my boundary negotiations was experienced in communicating with my students. My students and young-genera-

---

Culture Concepts

Cultural Differences in Conveying Status

Some cultures emphasize status differences between individuals. They view such differences as desirable, appropriate, and important. Other cultures may prefer equality and evenness in their interpersonal relationships. They may prefer to minimize status or class differences based on such features as age, gender, role, or occupation.

Culture Concepts

Formality-Informality

In cultures that emphasize formality, *people address others by appropriate titles, and highly prescriptive rules or politeness govern the interaction. Conversely, in cultures that stress* informality, *people believe that human relationships develop best when those involved can relate as equals, so casual language and behaviors are the norms.*

tion "Japanese" in general have developed a different set of cultural patterns. Even though they are silent and polite in the classrooms, I found that their behavior outside of the classroom setting is much less formal than when I was a college student in Japan. They were much quicker to say what they thought, and they stated their ideas more directly. At a class party, for instance, I was shocked when a female student said to me, "You know, what a waste you are! You are so good looking above your shoulders!" Hopefully she only meant to say that my face was attractive, but indirectly she was referring to my being overweight. When I was a college student in Japan almost 30 years ago, I would never have dared to comment to my professors on their physical features. From these types of informal interactions with my students, I realized that "Japanese" cultural practices for communicating with my students are much less formal than I had anticipated. Therefore, despite my initial culture shock at the behavior of the younger generation, I found myself comfortably interacting with my students, as their informality was closer to what I was used to with "American" students.

▶ Emergence of a Maverick Identity

Compared to my interactions with my students, with whom I felt comfortable, I was not entirely sure how to behave with my faculty colleagues. In particular, I did not know how to act appropriately in General Faculty Meetings, when all tenured instructors (approximately 180 of us) convene to decide on important issues. For four months after I began working, I kept my mouth shut during these meetings; as a newcomer, I thought that I should not readily voice my opinions but rather observe and learn the ropes. I knew that was usually expected of a new person in "Japanese" organizations. Hence I decided to stay within the cultural boundaries for these formal meetings.

About four months after I started working, I was at a General Faculty Meeting and felt a strong dissonance between keeping my mouth shut and speaking out. On that particular day, a proposal was discussed to expel a student who had committed a petty theft. The student was arrested by the police but was released, since it was his first criminal offense. He also apologized to the university, and consequently he was not given any punishment by the university. Then he was arrested for repeating the same crime and was prosecuted. At that point, the university could no longer tolerate his behavior and was proposing to expel him.

Although I did not necessarily agree that expulsion was the only choice of punishment, I mostly questioned the reasons for expelling this student. According to the stated reasons, the student had to be expelled because he had committed a crime not only once but twice, and he may have committed more thefts. Further, it was stated that when he perpetrated his crime for the second time, he betrayed the university's benevolence in forgiving him for his first offense. I was particularly troubled by this reason, because it sounded as if the university was concerned with losing its face for forgiving a criminal once, and therefore was reacting emotionally to the student's so-called betrayal.

I felt that such an emotional reason should not be weighed in deciding to expel a student. My internalized "American" values and thinking patterns for decision-making were loudly speaking that the reasons should remain rational. At the same time, as an intercultural communication scholar who was familiar with "Japanese" norms for decision-making, I could easily anticipate that face issues as well as emotional reactions surrounding face loss would be factored into "Japanese" decision-making. Thus, I found two voices coexisting that day in my mind: one "American" and one "Japanese."

After several minutes of debate between these two internal voices, I decided to articulate an opinion for the first time in the General Faculty Meeting. I asked the group if it might not be better to stick to rational reasons and to delete from the formal proposal the reason related to the student betraying the university, because it sounded emotional. My question was met by a response from a dean that there was nothing wrong with including emotional reasons. After that, no one else in the meeting objected to the reasons or to the proposal itself.

I left the meeting feeling hammered by the realization that my values, thinking patterns, and decision-making strategies were so different from those of my colleagues. I was questioning if my opinions could have any significance to the "Japanese," or at least to those at my university. Then a senior professor approached me to ask a question.

Professor: *Sensei* (professor), when exactly did you join our university?
Me: (using honorific language and a respectful tone of voice) "It was last October."
Professor: Last October? Well, you must be the first newcomer to make a comment in a General Faculty Meeting within the first year. . . .

This snide comment loudly announced that I was considered a "maverick," and it also reminded me of an important "Japanese" cultural boundary: A new person in an organization was supposed to keep quiet in the meetings. I knew of this cultural expectation, anticipated it, and thus tried to lay low. The first time that I spoke up, I was immediately criticized for doing so.

Since that day, I have constantly questioned whether it would be appropriate for me to voice my opinions in faculty meetings, wondering how much participation would be regarded as exceeding the cultural expectations. As I have swayed between following the "Japanese" cultural expectations to keep quiet and the "American" values for participating in meetings, my colleagues have gradually tagged me as an "Americanized maverick." For example, one of

---

Culture Concepts

Cultural Variations in Logic

Much of the tradition of persuasion and rhetoric among U.S. Americans is influenced by the rhetoric of Aristotle, who emphasized the separation of logic and reason from emotion. This separation is antithetical to good rhetorical practices in Chinese discourse, for example, as well as in Hindu rhetoric and philosophy. These Asian rhetorical traditions emphasize the importance of emotion in learning the truthfulness of a situation. The word logical *is often used to describe the preferred persuasive style of a culture. Logic and rationality seem to be invoked as though there were some firm truth somewhere that simply has to be discovered and used in order to be convincing.*

---

my colleagues usually introduces me to strangers by saying, "He has lived in the U.S. for a long time, and he is more American than Americans."

I seem to be labeled as a "maverick" by my faculty colleagues for two reasons. First, I tend to state my opinions in faculty meetings more frequently than they expect. Most of my colleagues do not say anything throughout an entire meeting, which sometimes lasts for three or four hours; I, however, might make three to five comments in a typical faculty meeting. Even though my colleagues believe that I participate quite often, I do so less frequently than I did during faculty meetings in the U.S. Moreover, in my attempts to follow the cultural norms regarding meeting participation, I try to think through what I am going to say and to voice opinions only when they are important. Nevertheless, there seems to be a gap between what I would prefer for my meeting participation and what my "Japanese" colleagues expect.

In addition to the quantity of my participation, my colleagues often comment that it seems "Americanized," though I try not to state "American" ideas. Nevertheless, my ideas are regarded as "American" because of my communication style in faculty meetings, which is more direct and low-context than is the typical style used in "Japanese" formal meetings. I tend to state the conclusion of my point first, followed by rational explanations that support my point. My "Japanese" colleagues, however, tend to start with background information such as how long they have worked in the university and precedents related to the issue at hand, and they often fail to mention the exact conclusion they want others to reach. That is the typical "Japanese" style of stating one's opinion. Since my "American" communication style deviates from their style, my colleagues view my actions as "Americanized."

My students also see me as a "maverick," but for different reasons. At my university, I teach English and communication courses. Because I want my students to learn to communicate effectively in an English-speaking cultural environment, I conduct my classes as close to the "American" style as possible. I try to talk with my students and encourage their participation in discussions, exercises, simulations, and role-plays. I also walk among students as I talk with them, and I use a lot of nonverbal gestures as I talk. My students, of course, are used to their professors giving straight lectures with no gestures while sitting still behind a desk for the entire class period. The students expect to take notes quietly and to say nothing. My students have not had a professor who teaches a class as I do. A frequent comment that I hear from them is, "You are a professor who is least like a professor."

A year or so after working in my university, I had emerged in the minds of my colleagues and students as a cultural "maverick," a person outside of their cultural boundaries. Since my image is etched in stone now, my negotiations with the "Japanese" boundaries today are conducted as a "maverick," not as someone who is expected to stay within the cultural norms. This newly acquired identity has thus given me a certain degree of freedom.

▶ Freedom as a Cultural "Maverick" and a Change Facilitator

As I have become known as a "maverick" in my university, greater space is permitted for me to operate outside of the "Japanese" cultural boundaries. Being a "maverick," I can knowingly violate some cultural patterns expected in Japan generally and certainly in my university. For example, my casual attire with sunglasses has become my trademark on campus. The way I communicate my conclusions first in faculty meetings is now better received; as a faculty colleague recently commented: "I realize that you always state your conclusion first. That's good because it's more efficient to understand what you want to say."

Nevertheless, the freer space I am given is not totally a blessing. It is born out of my being "other Japanese" and "other American." Since I do not fit the ethnocentric images, expectations, and stereotypes for how middle-aged "Japanese" male university professors are supposed to look and act, I am confined to this "other" space. To break through the cultural boundaries and be accepted as "Japanese," I would have to fit into their image, expectation, and stereotypes of who the "Japanese" are. Consequently, I would have to throw away my "other Japanese" and "other American" identities.

Living in Japan, I often need to test out the "Japanese" cultural boundaries so that I know where they lie and how my constraints are defined in a particular situation. Thus my cultural boundary negotiation is a never-ending trial-and-error process. At times I intentionally look and act "American," bringing in "American" ideas and expressing some of my "American" values, to learn the extent to which I can still operate without being totally forced out of the "Japanese" cultural boundaries. However, when I do so, I am bound to exceed the cultural boundary limits and be rejected. Then I retreat for a while and try to follow the cultural patterns of the "Japanese" culture and my university. Only through such continuous patterns of pushing and retreating can I find where the limits are and expand my boundaries.

It is tiring to negotiate the boundaries in this way. Yet the freedom that comes with doing so has given me a greater capacity to facilitate changes in Japan. This allows me to focus on one of my life-long goals: to be an intercultural change facilitator. I am particularly interested in facilitating social justice against various ethnocentrisms, stereotypes, prejudices, and other -isms. I give presentations regarding racism, sexism, sexual harassment, classism, and able-bodyism to my students and "Japanese" people in general. For example, in my intercultural communication course, I help students to become aware of the privileges they have as mainstream "Japanese" rather than as minority ethnic groups in Japan (for example, "Chinese" and "Korean Japanese" immigrants). Because I have experienced the prejudice and discrimination that go with being an "ethnic minority" in the U.S., I can present views that are not typical of the "Japanese" mainstream experience. People accept my ideas because, as a "Japanese," I have the same privileges as they do. The difference, of course, is that I am aware of many of the privileges that stem from my cultural and social status, and most of my students have been unaware that they have similar privileges. I then apply the idea of cultural and racial privileges to the advantages available to the able-bodied, to men, and to the economically advantaged in "Japanese" society.

My years in Japan have been productive as a change facilitator. Many of my students, and others who have attended my presentations, have learned to question the privileges they have and to identify the stereotypes and prejudices they might have. Some have started intervening on social -isms that exist around them. The success so far has given me a hope that one day every "Japanese" person will value social justice and will also be an intercultural change facilitator.

▶ Back at "Home" in the U.S.A. as a "Foreigner"

In 2001–2002, I returned to San Francisco to engage in a research sabbatical. Although I was going to be there just for one year, I didn't feel like a sojourner, because I had lived and worked in San Francisco from 1992 to 1997. When I arrived at the San Francisco International Airport in the summer of 2001, I could not contain my excitement to be returning "home."

Even though I considered San Francisco and the U.S. as my home, I have always felt "foreign" and "other American" while there. My physical appearance as non-white has been a barrier to my being regarded as "American." To cite just one small example, on a recent trip to the U.S., as I was heading to the "U.S. Citizens/Residents" line at immigration control, an officer stopped me and told me to go to the "Visitors" line. I had to show my green card (resident alien registration) to let her know that I am a permanent resident in the U.S. None of the people on my flight who were white—regardless of their cultures of origin—received similar treatment.

Though I have always felt "foreign" in the U.S., I did not identify myself as a "foreigner" when I lived there. I was made to feel "foreign" by the implicit cultural boundary that does not fully include people of color. Other people of color in the U.S., including U.S. citizens, share similar experiences.

However, during my one-year return to San Francisco, I was quickly made to realize that I have become a "foreigner" by the explicit cultural boundaries

---

Culture Concepts

Re-entry Shock

Often associated with culture shock are the U-curve and W-curve hypotheses of cultural adaptation. In the U-curve hypothesis, the initial intercultural contacts are characterized by a positive, almost euphoric, emotional response. As fatigue mounts and culture shock sets in, however, the individual's responses are more and more negative, until finally a low point is reached. Then, gradually, the individual develops a more positive attitude and the new culture seems less foreign, until a positive emotional response once again occurs. The U-curve hypothesis has been extended to the W-curve, which includes the person's responses to her or his own culture upon return. It posits that a second wave of culture shock, which is similar to the first and has been called re-entry shock, *may occur when the individual returns home and must readapt to the once taken-for-granted practices that can no longer be followed without question.*

---

of residence and citizenship. The first sign of these explicit boundaries came when my wife, my young daughter, and I were frantically trying to find an apartment. Though I still had my bank accounts in the city and had numerous references, we were treated as "foreigners" by potential landlords. After discovering that we had come from Japan only for a year, and my employer was some unknown university in a city they never heard of, some landlords were unwilling to rent to us and others demanded proof of my residence in San Francisco four years previously.

These landlords gave me a hard time, but they did not really hurt my feelings. It was rather my friends who made me feel that I had "gone" to Japan. This came as a shock to me. I thought that I was simply "absent" for four years in Japan and had kept up my friendships by visiting them on my countless short trips back to San Francisco.

One of the first things I did during short trips to San Francisco was to visit the university where I used to teach, to meet my former colleagues. In addition, I visited the department office very frequently during the year of my sabbatical, as I was conducting a research study at my former university. We chatted like old times and occasionally went out for happy hours like old times. Nevertheless, I was treated as a "guest," not as "one of them." To my former colleagues, I was no longer living and working with them because I had quit the university and moved my residence. Therefore, to them I was a person of the "past," not someone who had been "absent." To adjust, I had to redefine our relationships from those of university colleagues to a larger sense of collegial relationships in the academic discipline.

Every time I traveled to San Francisco, I also visited shops, restaurants, and a church where many of my friends worked or convened. Since I had made trips to visit them at least twice a year, I thought I could get back into our friendships as if I had never left. After finding a small apartment in the summer of 2001, I visited one of the Japanese restaurants I used to frequent. Upon entering, I greeted my friends who are all "Japanese" and who had immigrated to the U.S., "Hey, I'm back! My family and I are going to be living here again for a year." They replied almost in unison, "Yeah, great! But you are going back to Japan, aren't you?" Later that night, one of them who was (and still is) my closest friend said, "You know, we are Japanese in the U.S. You used to be one of us. But after going back to Japan, you are Japanese in Japan. You are different now." He added, "Now, I still like you, and you are still my best friend. The fact that you moved to Japan does not change a thing in our friendship. But you should be aware that you are now thought of as different from us." To them, I was not "absent." I was as good as gone.

After settling back in San Francisco, I also went to the church where I still keep my membership. My family and I used to go there almost every Sunday when we lived in San Francisco. The church consists of mostly "Japanese Americans" and other "Asian Americans." I used to be one of them when I was also considered a "Japanese immigrant" and as someone who lived and worked in San Francisco. My old friends at the church were happy to see my family and me again, but when they discovered that we would be leaving in a year, they were disappointed. Some of them seemed more distant than they used to be when we lived there.

I would like to emphasize, however, that my former colleagues and my friends are nice people, and they did not treat me badly. In fact, we enjoyed renewing our friendships through numerous gatherings during my one-year stay. However, I recognized ambivalence in some of them. It seemed as if they were afraid to get too close to me because I would eventually be leaving. I don't blame them for feeling afraid, however, because I could have been equally afraid of leaving in a year. It may be that they were trying to treat me as they did when I lived there, but perhaps I gave off a sense of distance to them out of my fear of having to leave them in a year. One way or another, my shift of "residence" from San Francisco to Japan outlined a cultural boundary that identified me as a "foreigner."

Then another explicit cultural boundary of citizenship faced me. I was born in Japan, hence I have Japanese citizenship. However, I considered the U.S. my "home." I had applied for U.S. citizenship in 2000, but after a long bureaucratic wait my application was denied during my one-year stay in San Francisco. The Immigration and Naturalization Service (now called the U.S. Citizenship and Immigration Services) determined that I had lived away from the U.S. for too long and my intent was to live and work in Japan, not in the U.S.

I was devastated by this denial, because my heart belonged to the U.S. even though I was working in Japan. I thought that I shared the same love of the country as did other "Americans." While I was in San Francisco in 2001–2002, the horrific 9/11 attacks occurred. I was as shocked, scared, and confused as were other "Americans." I cried as much as they did. I frantically called my friend who worked near the World Trade Center in New York City to find out if he was safe, just like many other "Americans" who did the same to find out the fate of their friends and loved ones. But to the bureaucratic process involving immigration and citizenship, my feelings did not count.

This incident made me aware that I cannot negotiate with the explicit cultural boundaries of citizenship in the U.S. like I can with the implicit cultural boundaries in Japan. My citizenship is a fact, written in law, and cannot be easily "negotiated." Hence, I am somberly reminded that my identity is partly defined helplessly by the explicit cultural boundaries based on the hard facts of my citizenship and residence. Because I have Japanese citizenship, I have no choice but to be a "foreigner" in the U.S., but I am an "other Japanese" and a cultural "maverick" in the country of my citizenship. This explicit bureaucratic definition of who I can and can not be has pushed me further in between.

▶ My Continual Role as a Change Facilitator

After my research sabbatical in San Francisco, I returned to Japan in 2002 to resume my job at my university in Fukuoka. There I saw some changes that I seem to have facilitated as a "maverick" in Japan. For example, more professors in my university, especially the junior faculty, have started wearing casual attire. Coupled with a keener awareness of energy conservation, even senior professors who used to wear suits have shown up in casual attire during the hot summer months. My "maverick" attire has gradually become the norm in my university. I have also noticed that other faculty members seem to expect me to speak out in faculty meetings. One of my colleagues often whispers to me during faculty meetings, "I bet you are going to say something about this issue."

These are signs of my being more accepted or "tolerated" as a "maverick" in my university culture. This gained latitude has consequently empowered me more as a change facilitator. Because my world is defined by the cultural boundaries, the more changes I facilitate, the more I can push the limits. In turn, the more I expand the space, the more changes I can facilitate. Thus, my resources as a change facilitator lie at the heart of my experiences.

▶ Who Am I?: A Tentative Conclusion

In *On Becoming "American"* I confided that I had not yet developed a "third-culture" identity, a comfortable zone where my identity was neither "Japanese" nor "American." To this day, I have not yet established such a third-culture identity. Instead, I have acquired two new identities: as a cultural "maverick" in Japan and as a "foreigner" in the U.S.

So who am I now? I am a "Japanese" in terms of my citizenship and culture. But I am an "other Japanese" and a cultural "maverick" because I am significantly different from mainstream "Japanese." In the U.S., I am an "other American" and a "foreigner." Because these identities are always situated in my intercultural interactions with others, I shift among these identities, depending on how the explicit and implicit cultural boundaries define my space and how I negotiate the boundaries. It seems that my life will continue drifting in the waves of my cultural boundary negotiations. But don't throw a lifesaver. I am happy drifting because, though the water may not be calm, the energy from the turbulence provides me with new insights into intercultural transactions. It is the destiny of my intercultural life.

Notes

1. As in my earlier essay, I place quotation marks around ethnic categories to remind readers that they are overgeneralizations.

▶ ▶ ▶ Learning AmongUS

1. When Imahori returned to Japan, did he experience re-entry shock? When he came back with his family to live in the United States, did he experience re-entry shock?
2. Review Imahori's description of his behaviors when he spoke for the first time at the Japanese faculty meeting. Do his behaviors collide more with typical Japanese expectations for conveying status, with the use of formality/informality, or with variations in what is considered logical for a persuasive argument?
3. Imahori describes himself as being an "other"—both an "other Japanese" and an "other American." Identify the positive and negative aspects of living between two cultures, as Imahori has chosen to do.
4. Do you agree with Imahori's assessment that, because he is willing to live on the cultural margins in Japan, he can become a facilitator of change there? Is the goal of being a change agent a good thing, or is Imahori simply imposing his U.S. American values on his Japanese colleagues and students?
5. Using the concepts of race, culture, ethnicity, and nation, describe who Tadasu "Todd" Imahori is.

Belonging to multiple cultures can sometimes lead to an odd sense of juxtaposition. Keturah A. Dunne describes how it feels to be bilingual and bicultural, simultaneously European American and Latina. Her poem expresses the poignancy and precariousness of living in two cultural worlds.

28   La Güera

Keturah A. Dunne

> ¿Quién soy?
> Me dicen La Americana
> La güera
> Is the color of my skin
> Lo más importante?

What is most important in determining the culture to which one belongs? Is it the genetic influence of one's skin color? One's learned patterns of behavior? The categories into which people are placed by a seemingly omniscient society? The issue of culture is a delicate one, especially for those of us on the border between two cultures. To come to terms with my life as a cultural anomaly, I composed a poem to express and define—at least to myself—who I am and how my perceptions were formed.

In simple terms, I, Keturah Alegra Dunne, appear to be of European American descent. In other words, I'm *güera,* or light skinned. My ancestors came to the United States from Ireland, Scotland, Germany, Australia, England, and Norway. Add to this heritage a great-great grandmother from the Blackfoot tribe. Such are the genetic facets creating my outward appearance. Yet culture is not genetics. To complete my cultural "profile," I must accurately state that I am a European American Latina.

How is it that I am a Latina when I have no such ancestors? Why is it that both Spanish and English can be considered my native tongues? Allow my poem to explain:

> Desde la infancia
> Spanish was the language
> de mis amigas
> mi comida
> mis hermanos
> y bailes folklóricos
> "La Raspa," "Jesusita En Chihuahua,"

"La Bamba"
With energy I danced
of places I never knew.

My parents were missionaries in El Salvador when I was conceived. Sociopolitical events prevented them from obtaining an extended visa, and I was born shortly after they returned to the United States. Because all of my family's religious activities have been centered in the Latino community, I was raised in a Latino environment from infancy.

When people discover that I speak Spanish, I tend to get various reactions. If European Americans find out that I speak Spanish, they often react with astonishment: "Oh, how do *you* know Spanish so well?" or "I was sure you were an American." In contrast, Latinos generally ask, "Where are you from?" or "You certainly don't speak Spanish like an American. How is it that you know Spanish?" I've even been told, "Why, you speak the language better than we do." To most inquisitive people of both cultures it seems incredible, almost implausible, that I've always spoken Spanish and that I can't remember ever "learning" the language.

Of course language, by itself, is not culture. This I discovered painfully in fifth grade, when I was uprooted from my bilingual classes and transferred into an advanced GATE (gifted and talented education) class populated solely by upper-class European American students.

And then
my reality was distorted
5th grade
        al pozo de los leones fui
to a class of cliquish "smart" rich kids
Entré
  They stared
        and
  looked me up
        and
  down,
You're not one of us they silently whispered
¿Cómo soy diferente?
I was white wasn't I
just like them
No entendí
Me trataban como si fuera invisible
¿Quién soy?

My rude awakening to the fact that I was no longer a "typical" European American girl shocked me. I was perplexed; I could not understand why my classmates so despised me. I cried a lot that school year. Now that I look back, I can see that the first nine years of my life had created such an indelible imprint on me that I was having serious trouble communicating with individuals outside my culture. Of course, I didn't realize this at that tender age. All I knew was that I was somehow different from my new classmates and that it hurt a great deal to be ostracized.

Although I felt isolated at school, I was confident that I still had my Latina friends and nothing could change or alter our friendship—or so I thought.

> Pero Hey!
> tengo mis amigas hispanas
>   right?
> Y de repente
>   vino el junior high
>   and you were too cool for me

Junior high school created more chaos. Unbeknownst to me, there is a secret transformation that occurs in almost all Latina girls as they enter junior high. In sixth grade we were free to jump, skip, or play tag, but with junior high the game plan changed. We were now expected to begin practicing to become full-fledged women. Thus I was no longer accepted as a part of my Latina group because I had no interest in makeup, boyfriends, or other culturally acceptable activities for my age group.

So where am I presently? The good news is that I wasn't permanently expelled from the Latino community. Although many of my childhood friends are now married, we've somehow come to terms with one another. I still enjoy doing many hours a month of volunteer work in the Latino community. As for my relationship and communication with my university peers, most of them don't realize that I speak Spanish or was brought up in a Latino community. Since I am used to being different, I find that I am now rarely bothered by negative or insensitive comments regarding my biculturalism:

> My skin betrays my culture
>   No soy Americana
>   ni Mexicana
> I stand precariously between
> 2 peoples
> A cultural anomaly

Here is the complete poem, as I originally composed it.

"La Güera"

> ¿Quién soy?
> Me dicen La Americana
>   La güera
> Is the color of my skin
>   Lo más importante?
>
> Desde la infancia

```
┌─────────────────────────────────────────────────────────────────────┐
│                                                                       │
│  Culture Concepts                                                     │
│  ─────────────────────────────────────────────────────────────────   │
│  Code Switching                                                       │
│  Because of the many languages spoken in the United States, code      │
│  switching is an important form of language use. Code switching       │
│  refers to the selection of the language to be used in a particular   │
│  interaction by individuals who can speak multiple languages. The     │
│  decision to use one language over another is often related to the    │
│  setting in which the interaction occurs—a social, public, and formal │
│  setting versus a personal, private, and informal one.                │
│                                                                       │
└─────────────────────────────────────────────────────────────────────┘
```

Culture Concepts

Code Switching

Because of the many languages spoken in the United States, code switching is an important form of language use. Code switching *refers to the selection of the language to be used in a particular interaction by individuals who can speak multiple languages. The decision to use one language over another is often related to the setting in which the interaction occurs—a social, public, and formal setting versus a personal, private, and informal one.*

> Spanish was the language
>   de mis amigas
>   mi comida
>   mis hermanos
>   y bailes folklóricos
>   "La Raspa," "Jesusita En Chihuahua,"
>   "La Bamba"
> With energy I danced
> of places I never knew.
>
> And then
> my reality was distorted
> 5th grade
>   al pozo de los leones fuí
> to a class of cliquish "smart" rich kids
> Entré
>   They stared
>   and
>   looked me up
>   and
>   down,
> You're not one of us they silently whispered
> ¿Cómo soy diferente?
> I was white wasn't I
> just like them
> No entendí
> Me trataban como si fuera invisible
> Quién soy?
> La poderosa niña
>   transformada
>   crying wet salty tears
>   lágrimas . . .
> Pero Hey!
> tengo mis amigas hispanas
>   right?

Y de repente
   vino el junior high
   and you were too cool for me

Ana M.
compartimos
   tap dancing lessons
   sleepovers
   quesadillas
   "Sabado Gigante"
Now you want nothing to do with me
No soy
      tú type
      I was not mature
"¿Por qué no te gustan los chicos?"
      she repeatedly asked,
"¡Yo nunca me casaré!"
      I defiantly stated;
"Mijita, tú cambiarás,"
      Ana's mom chided when I was 12,
"y un dia iré a tu boda."
Pero fuí terca
   and instead of me
Tú, Ana, a los diecinueve
   ya eres en verdad mujer
   y tienes esposo
   que te cuida
   'til death do you part

Y yo me he quedado atras
      Or have I?
Y tú, Elizabeth M.
   con tu copete
   varnizado con hairspray
   y tu chola stance
You told me
      in my face
   I wasn't one of you
"¿Porque no te pintas?"
      you asked
Are you a baby
   a mama's girl
   a schoolie
Why can't you be normal?
¿Pero qué era ser normal?
Were you normal Elizabeth?

I didn't understand
would make-up
a boyfriend
copetes
tight dresses
make me one of you?
Why couldn't I wear
my long skirts
and bobby socks
and skip

My mother said:
"Sticks and stones
will break your bones
but
words will never
hurt you"
But these words
did

10 años han pasado
Y un viaje a México he realizado
Could it be so?
Was I truly discovering my roots?
Now I listen to
Radio Latina
with confidence
Speak Hebrew
Cook Equadorian Llapingachos
and smile

My skin betrays my culture
No soy Americana
ni Mexicana
I stand precariously between
2 peoples
A cultural anomaly.

Culture Concepts

Tolerance for Ambiguity

Tolerance for ambiguity *concerns a person's responses to new, uncertain, and un-predictable intercultural encounters. Some people react to new situations with greater comfort than do others. Competent intercultural communicators are able to cope with the nervousness and frustrations that accompany new or unclear situations, and they are able to adapt quickly to changing demands.*

▶ ▶ ▶ Learning AmongUS

1. Is Dunne a Latina or is she a European American? Explain.
2. Recall an interaction you had with individuals who switched between two languages. How did you react to the code switching? Were you comfortable? Did you feel included or excluded?

3. If you speak more than one language fluently, describe how you feel when you speak each of them. Are there differences in your communication and your sense of comfort with the different languages?

Amy Liu's essay displays the "work" of creating a professional and personal life that draws on the cultural traditions of her Chinese culture-of-origin and those of the U.S. American cultural environment in which she now lives. Her essay describes the stark contrasts she has experienced and the choices she has made in parenting her son, in adapting to U.S. educational institutions as a student and a faculty member, and in negotiating appropriate gender-role behaviors in her marriage.

29 The Search for Cultural Identity by a Chinese American Professional Woman

Amy Qiaoming Liu

I was born and raised in the People's Republic of China (PRC) and immigrated to the United States in my twenties. My experiences in America and in the PRC have made me realize that people from different cultures want to be happy and successful, but they often use quite different approaches to achieve these goals. What is taken for granted and considered desirable in one culture may be regarded as strange and undesirable in another. In the following sections, I will discuss in detail several differences between the Chinese and the European American cultures. My objective is to show how I have integrated diverse cultural dimensions in my life and work to form a multicultural identity.

▶ Which Matters More: Self-Esteem or Vigorous Discipline?

My nine-year-old son dashed into my study one day and asked, "Mom, what do you think about my story? I did it at school today."

I stopped my writing and looked at it. He had received an A for his writing. The story was interesting, but there were some obvious grammatical mistakes. Since my mind was still on my work, I said, without too much thought, "It is good."

"Good? What do you mean good? It's not just good. It is EXCELLENT! I've spent a lot of time working on it, and my teacher said several times to me that it is excellent!"

I thought: *I might have been too harsh on him. I should have been more positive about his story. After all, he was born and raised in the U.S. and is used to receiving a lot of positive reinforcement.*

"Let me look at it again," I said immediately. After glancing at it briefly, I said, "You are right. It is one of the BEST stories you have written. Thank you

---

Culture Concepts

Role of Families in Interpersonal Relationships

In some cultures, the family is the primary means through which a person's social life is maintained. In others, families are almost peripheral to the social networks that are established. In the more collectivist cultures of Japan, Korea, and China, families play a pivotal role in making decisions for children, including the choice of university, profession, and even marital partner. In contrast, in individualistic cultures, where children are taught from their earliest years to make their own decisions, a characteristic of "good parenting" is to allow children to "learn for themselves" the consequences of their own actions.

---

so much for sharing it with me. I am so proud that you can stand up for yourself and fight for your recognition." After a brief pause I added, "Can I make a copy and take it to school? I'll keep it there." I hoped this would maintain his high level of interest in writing. I did not want to give him the wrong impression that nothing he had done was good enough for me. I really wanted him to learn how to write, but I also hoped he could make mistakes, speak out, and dare to fight for himself. Even more importantly, I wanted him to enjoy the process of writing.

"OF COURSE!" he said, and started jumping up and down. Then he added: "I will correct all the grammatical mistakes and then give it to you, Mom."

I could see he was excited again. He seemed to realize that learning was a lifelong process, and that he could always do better. I also felt better about how I had handled the situation.

When I shared this story with one of my European American colleagues, he was amazed. He has two sons, an eleven-year-old and a seven-year-old. He told me that he would say to his sons, "Honey, it is excellent. I am so proud of you. You are an excellent writer." As he explained: "You know, their self-esteem is very important. Strong positive reinforcement is good for their self-esteem and their success in school."

This was quite different from what I experienced as I grew up in the People's Republic of China. Parents and teachers wanted children to be successful at school, but they seldom worried about young children's self-esteem. On the contrary, many Chinese believe that youngsters should be treated very strictly. Rather than receiving constant praise, children should have their mistakes pointed out directly. Moreover, children were expected to correct their errors quickly. This would help them to pass the countless vigorous tests that are given as they go from elementary school through college. In short, an old Chinese saying indicates, only teachers and parents with high demands and expectations can raise successful kids.

I still remember the last day of eighth grade, when I brought my school report card home. I received an A in math, English, physics, chemistry, music, physical education, and political studies, and an A- in Chinese language studies. My teacher handed me the report card and simply said, "You are number one in the class. You did a good job."

I was very happy to be number one in the class. I went home and immediately showed my report card to my mom. She stopped her cooking, glanced at it quickly, and immediately focused on the only A- I had received. She asked me about my Chinese language class, and I had to explain to her in detail what mistakes I made and what I needed to do to make sure that I would not make the same mistakes again.

"I hope you will get an A in Chinese next time," she said, with a very serious tone in her voice. Then she started cooking again.

At that moment, I really hoped she had noticed all the A's I received. However, I was not supposed to challenge my parents. I knew my mom wanted me to do better so I could pass the college entrance exams. I dreamed about that, too.

National exams have been very important in China's long history, and people often assume that everyone has an equal opportunity to do well on the tests. For the Chinese, being tops in those tests has traditionally been one of the most legitimate means to success. For example, for several thousand years, Chinese civil-service exams had been used to select government officials at all levels. No matter whether you were the sons of prime ministers or the sons of prostitutes, you had to take the same set of tests and were graded by the same standards. If you passed the tests, you were eligible to be appointed as a government official such as a mayor, a governor, or a prime minister. Such individuals became the elite ruling class in Chinese society. Moreover, except for the royal families, most of these positions were not inherited. Therefore, passing the tests and getting official appointments often brought honors and fortunes not only to the individuals but also to their entire families.

I was born in China in the 1960s and lived in a large city there. People in the cities often enjoyed a much higher quality of life than did those living on farms. However, due to government's policies at that time, young adults essentially had only two choices when they graduated from high school: go to college or go to the countryside to work on the farms. Like millions of young people then living in the cities, I did not want to go to the countryside because it was very rough working in the fields and there was no future in doing it. However, the college entrance tests were very competitive. All those who wanted to go to college had to take exams in seven subjects, which were spread out over three days, and only about five percent of those who scored well on the exams would be admitted to colleges and universities.

Because of my hard work, I was able to obtain high scores and was admitted to a university after I graduated from high school. I knew my teachers and parents were very proud of me, but they seldom complimented me on my intelligence. This never bothered my self-esteem. In fact, I was really grateful to my parents and teachers at that time. Without their strict discipline and high expectations I would not have been able to make it to college.

Several years later, I had a chance to come to the United States to pursue my master's degree and, subsequently, my Ph.D. I did extremely well in these graduate programs, and my professors and fellow students often told me that I was smart and intelligent. Although graduate work was hard, I felt good about myself and gained a sense of great accomplishment and satisfaction. Moreover, I really enjoyed graduate school and learning. I wish my high school years had been as enjoyable as my graduate studies were.

Living in the U.S., I was really shocked to learn that many parents and teachers, from elementary school through high school, do not like giving tests to students. Though some college students have very poor math, reading, and writing skills, many think standardized tests are unfair. Some want to get rid of them because they think that bad test scores may hurt a child's self-esteem. However, I think that tests in elementary school through high school could be used as important assessment tools to help parents and teachers understand how the children are learning. Similarly, I think that an overemphasis on children's self-esteem may prevent some parents and teachers from telling children what they need to do to master the basic skills that are essential for success in college and beyond.

▶ Which Matters More: To Speak Up or to Be Humble?

To be successful in China, I had to do my best and sacrifice a lot so I would not miss the available opportunities. This required that I be very disciplined and focused on my studies. Over time, I became quite cautious about taking on other responsibilities. When I first came to the United States, these tendencies often prevented me from willingly volunteering my talents, from speaking up, from taking risks, and from seeking opportunities in my life and career.

In graduate school, I was an excellent student in all of my classes. Even though I knew the course materials, I seldom spoke up or joined the class discussions. I was not used to such behaviors as talking in the class, arguing with other students, and challenging my professors publicly.

While in school, this reticence did not affect my image as an outstanding student. I did not have to tell my professors and fellow students how well I was doing; I took tests and wrote papers throughout semester, and those served that purpose. However, things started to change dramatically once I graduated. There were no more tests and papers. If I wanted people to know about me, I had to inform them directly. Many other Chinese immigrants to the United States also had to learn this lesson, often the hard way. In discussing this issue with a friend, she told me the following story:

> I had been working hard for a company for six years, but I seldom went to my boss's office and chatted with him about what I had done and what my aspirations for my career were. I assumed that my boss would know. Each year, when the annual review came, I just wrote down my major contributions. As an ordinary engineer, I did not make many big contributions. Since I started there six years ago, the company has hired a few more people. They did not work nearly as hard or as well as I did, but the others got promoted much faster. When I found out that their promotion was based on a performance review, I decided to

> *write down many of the obvious things that I previously thought were not worth reporting. I was amazed when I finished the report. It was quite long. A few days later, my boss called me to his office and congratulated me. He was really impressed with my work that year. He said he was not aware, until now, of how much good work I had done.*

I can still remember the plaintive question she asked me, again and again, "Why did it take me six years to figure this out?"

I, too, took a long time to learn to express my desires and opinions openly and directly. For example, when I was a Ph.D. student in the early 1990s, I really wanted to be the student representative on a major departmental committee. However, when on several occasions my fellow students asked me to serve, I refused. I often regretted these decisions right after I declined. What I really wanted was for them to urge me to do it several more times, and then I would consent to do it. This is the way it often happens in China. Since I wanted to give the impression that I was modest and not aggressive, by Chinese standards I was "required" to refuse the opportunity the first time it was offered. However, my U.S. American colleagues thought I simply did not want the job, so they elected someone else who was eager to take the challenge. I lost out on several great opportunities as a consequence.

When I first came to the United States, I was strict not only with myself but also with others. I seldom opened my mouth in public, but whenever I did I tended to criticize more often than to praise. As I pushed both myself and others to become better, I was constantly critical of our performances and ideas. This did not hurt my self-esteem, since I was used to the Chinese belief that high expectations and strict discipline would make one better and more successful. However, this often gave those who were not familiar with the Chinese culture the impression that I was either a faultfinder or very difficult to please. This was especially true in my early days in the United States, because I did not feel comfortable saying big and positive words to others frequently, directly, and publicly.

▶ Which Matters More: Overt Bias against Women or Subtle Discrimination?

Compared to teaching and learning, talking about women's issues openly and effectively are much more complicated and harder for me. I still remember a conversation I had with a colleague several years ago:

"How long does it take you to get to the university from your home?" a fellow professor asked me while we were having lunch together.

"About an hour and half," I replied.

"What?" his eyes were wide open.

"Do you go home every day?"

"Not always. Sometimes I stay here."

"Do you have any kids?"

"A five-year-old son."

"Do you miss him?"

"Of course. But he enjoys playing with Dad," I emphasized.

"Really?" he asked. Somehow, I could sense that he did not believe I would leave my five-year-old son at home with his dad while staying on campus, working. This reminded me of a story my husband tells to show how good a husband he is.

"How many children do you have?" a colleague asked my husband.

"One."

"That is too few. You should have more," he urged seriously.

"My wife is working far away from home, and I have to take care of my son several days a week," my husband replied.

"In that case, one is enough," he laughed. My husband could not help but laugh with him, too.

My husband has asked me many times whether we should have another child. I hesitate to have another one, and he supports the decision to have only one child. Like me, he originally came from the People's Republic of China and is familiar with women's employment and the one-child family policy.

For several thousand years, Confucianism and its deference to male supremacy defined women's roles and status in China. A woman's place was at home as a virtuous wife and good mother ('xian qi liang mu'). Women were expected to obey their father before marriage, their husband once married, and their oldest son if widowed. When the Chinese Communist Party took power in 1949, the country began to adopt significant legal, economic, and political policies to liberate women. By the late 1950s, approximately 90 percent of women were employed. Since then, the PRC continues to be a country with one of the highest female employment rates in the world. Thus, the overwhelming majority of Chinese women from the PRC enjoy the many benefits of employment outside their homes.

Many people in America think that Chinese Americans are one people, with shared values and experiences. This is not the case at all. Some Chinese Americans have immigrated to the U.S. from different regions of the world, and at different stages of their lives. Others, like my son, have been born and raised in the U.S. Since Chinese people have lived through quite different social and historical times, there are significant differences among them.

For many Chinese in the PRC or for Chinese Americans who recently immigrated from the PRC, women's liberation was equal to women's work outside the home. This has made some of my female Chinese American friends from Taiwan very envious. One day, seven Chinese American women from my church Bible study group were having tea together. Three of us originally came from the People's Republic of China. We were all employed. Four were from Taiwan; two were working outside the home and the other two were staying at home. One of my friends from Taiwan said to the three of us from the PRC that we were really lucky, because we often have parents or in-laws who come to help us when we have children, so we do not have to quit our jobs. She indicated that she had to stop working so she could take care of her three

Culture Concepts

Confucian Values

Key principles of Confucian teaching include the following:

1. Social order and stability are based on unequal relationships between people. Each relationship, including those among friends (who differ, however slightly, in age and in other indicants of status), presumes the existence and legitimacy of a social hierarchy and the reciprocal, complementary obligations that each position in the hierarchy requires. The higher-status person in each pair must provide protection and consideration; the lower-status person owes respect and obedience.
2. The family is the prototype for all social relationships. The virtues learned within family relationships form the central core that specifies how to interact with others in the widening circle of social relationships. Similarly, the roles regulating family relationships can be extended to include the whole town, organization, or country.
3. Proper social behavior consists of not treating others as you would not like to be treated yourself. This negatively phrased Golden Rule emphasizes benevolence toward others. It exists in the context of reciprocal relationships, where there are shared expectations about social obligations and responsibilities.
4. People should be skilled, educated, hardworking, thrifty, modest, patient, and persevering. Teaching and learning are highly valued, moderation in all things is preferred, conspicuous consumption is frowned on, losing one's temper is unacceptable, and persistence in solving difficult problems is widely valued. Because human nature is assumed to be inherently good, it is the responsibility of each individual to train his or her moral character in these standards of behavior.

children. She regretted that circumstance, and she really wished her in-laws, parents, or husband would have encouraged her to remain employed.

What she did not recognize was that many Chinese women from the PRC are still the primary bearers of family responsibilities such as childcare and housework, even though they work outside the home. Thus, employment outside the home can only be regarded as the first phase of an unfinished process of liberation for many women.

Sons are traditionally very important to many Chinese. The one-child policy gave women a socially accepted "excuse" to have only one child, because it was very difficult for a Chinese woman to resist enormous social and family pressures to have a son. At home, many Chinese women were not used to speaking out for themselves or for their daughters. This policy gave many women without sons the help they needed from the government to resist the pressure from family and friends to have a son, or to protect them or their daughter from family violence and abuse. Essentially, this policy liberated many women from heavy child care burdens and family responsibilities, and it enhanced the status of girls who were the only child in the family. Many women have taken advantage of those opportunities to pursue their dreams and to develop their careers. In this sense, the one-child policy can be regarded as the second liberation for many Chinese women, even though many others consider this as a very coercive policy, as its implementation has gone to unfortunate extremes in some cases.

However, the economic reform since the late 1970s has also brought about tremendous surplus labor in China, and unemployment has been a big problem since then. Many workplaces have dealt with this problem through overt gender discrimination in hiring and promotion and through an emphasis on the traditional roles of women as being good wives, mothers, and daughters-in-law. Although many Chinese women wanted to take care of their only child, neither working-class women nor highly educated female Chinese students studying in the United States were willing to give up their employment.

Gender and racial discrimination is prohibited now in the United States, but very subtle biases against both women and Chinese Americans often exist in many work places. For example, our campus needed to elect a new chairperson for an important university committee. A few colleagues were talking about the potential candidates for this position in a lunch meeting. Peter, a full professor and a respected faculty leader on campus, suggested that Jack should run for the position. Jack politely declined, because he preferred to pursue other opportunities. Peter was disappointed about Jack's decision, as he thought Jack would be a great candidate. Then he turned around and asked me, "Do you want to be the chairperson?"

"Maybe," I replied.

Peter was happy to hear that. He said to me, "It is not a good idea to be a chairperson for this committee before you become a full professor. Besides, you have to take care of your child and your family. That takes a lot of time too."

I was very grateful for his advice at that time. Promotion to full professor and spending more time with my son were both very important to me. Moreover, this was not the first time several respected senior colleagues gave me such advice. However, after some reflection, I wondered whether he would have given the same advice to Jack. I had been an associate professor for two years, and Jack was still an assistant professor. In addition, I have only one child and Jack has two.

Like millions of European American women, Chinese American women have great leadership potential and abilities. For many of them, women's liberation is not just women's work outside the home. They hope to be treated equally both at home and at work.

▶ Integrating Eastern and Western Traditions

Chinese and U.S. Americans have quite different approaches to achieve success and happiness. Chinese tend to work hard to make sure they will ultimately be successful, even if they have to sacrifice individual interests along the way. U.S. Americans think the process is at least as important as the outcome, as they value happiness and want frequent positive feedback. Therefore, while the Chinese tend to be more humble, strict, and cautious, U.S. Americans often put more emphasis on self-esteem, positive communication, and risk-taking. When these two approaches are taken to an extreme, there are many unintended negative consequences. If used complimentarily, however, a unique style can be created to benefit teaching and learning. It took me a few years to realize this.

In my teaching, I try to incorporate Eastern (Chinese) and Western (American) traditions into a unique teaching style. I want my students to learn something from my classes while enjoying the learning process. Starting on the first day of my classes, I make sure students know that whatever their backgrounds might be, if they work hard I will be there for them. I take attendance and have homework assignments due almost daily. To keep track of each student's progress, I often talk with them individually, particularly if they miss classes or labs.

I try to create many opportunities to give my students positive feedback and encouragement. Rather than focusing on traditional tests and lectures, I emphasize learning by hands-on experience. In my research methods class, students must develop a research topic that is feasible, socially important, and scientifically relevant. They have to conduct a thorough literature review and develop hypotheses. They also need to review critically the advantages and disadvantages of their study. Finally, they must analyze the data, prove or disprove the hypotheses, discuss the results, and draw appropriate conclusions.

I spend a lot of time working with students. I meet with them individually before they decide on a research topic. I ask them to rewrite each chapter at least once. Each time, I give them detailed criticism and a lot of positive feedback. Although rewriting often doubles or triples my workload, it gives students a great opportunity to reflect on their learning and observe the progress they have made. Students' confidence grows as they finish each chapter. By the end, many students are really amazed at what they have accomplished.

What is more important, students in my classes can get involved in my own research projects. Through participation in real research projects, many students acquire useful tools to understand society, and they learn that their efforts can affect communities and social policies in the region and in the state.

Attending and presenting research at national and regional academic conferences has also boosted many students' interest and confidence as professional researchers. I have organized sessions at professional conferences so my students can present their research. I have also encouraged students to submit their papers to other professional conferences, and many of their papers have been selected for presentation. Those presentations have opened many eyes and minds and significantly boosted their self-esteem.

Many students enter my research methods courses with anxiety, but they leave with a heightened sense of confidence in their own ability to carry out

---

Culture Concepts

Face Needs

Face *involves people's sense of dignity, self-re-spect, and prestige. There are three kinds of* face needs: *the need for control, the need for approval, and the need for admiration.*

social research and with a deepened understanding and appreciation for the conduct of empirical research. All of this reflects my consistent effort to make sure my students are learning what I expect them to and enjoy the experience. This is rarely an outcome of required typical research methods courses.

▶ Summary

It has been almost twenty years since I came to the United States to pursue my American dream. Since then, I have lived and worked in many diverse cultural communities that have no clear national, racial, or gender borders. As I am searching for success and happiness in my new home, America, I have incorporated Western and Eastern traditions to live in this new multicultural world. I have also learned to fight for equal rights and equal opportunities, to speak up, and to promote my beliefs and my work. In sum, I have profoundly changed my own cultural identity. Now I am neither totally a part of nor totally apart from my Chinese culture. My new cultural identity is truly intercultural in nature, because it has integrated divergent cultural elements from both cultural traditions.

▶ ▶ ▶ Learning AmongUS

1. Based on Liu's essay about her search for cultural identity, how influential do you think Confucian values have been in shaping what she believes?

2. Do you think Liu should use the expectations and practices of the wider U.S. American cultural groups in praising, criticizing, and raising her son? Or should she rely on the same set of values that her parents used when raising her? That is, which cultural values should Liu use to raise her son?

3. At the beginning of her classes in the United States, Liu indicates that she rarely talked, and she felt awkward when

she had to participate. Reflect on the expectations for student participation in the typical U.S. college classroom. Can you identify the rules for how these classes are typically conducted?

4. How did Liu maintain her face needs in the interactions described?

5. Apply Hofstede's taxonomy of cultural patterns to Liu's essay. How would you describe her? Has she changed by living and working in the United States and at a U.S. university?

6. How has Liu's cultural background influenced her approach to being a professor?

Mohammad Qayoumi describes a lifelong journey from Afghanistan, where he was born, to Los Angeles, where he now lives. Mo's story is that of a person who was forced from his native country because of its brutal occupation by others. Yet he manages to receive a professional education, build an outstanding career in higher education, and develop into a person who can live competently, and almost seamlessly, in multiple cultures. Combining a knowledge of Afghani history with the influence of his parents' values, Mo provides insights into Islam and the place of Muslims in the United States after September 11, 2001.

30   From Silk Route to Route 66: My American Journey

Mohammad H. Qayoumi

I was born in Kabul, Afghanistan. For my first sixteen years, I was raised there. Afghanistan is roughly the size of Texas; despite its relatively small physical size, the country is ethnically very diverse, consisting of Pathans, Tajiks, Uzbecks, Turkmens, Hazaras, and others. Similarly, several languages are spoken there, including the two official ones, Dari and Pashtu, which are derived from Germanic languages.

For centuries, Afghanistan had been at the crossroads of many cultures. When travel by land was the primary means of moving from one place to the next, Afghanistan's location along the Silk Route, which was the main thoroughfare between China, the Middle East, and Europe, was a blessing as well as a curse. While it gave the region exposure to many peoples and cultures, it also was a prime target for invading armies—Alexander the Great, the Arabs, the Mongols, and others—that overran the region and in each instance caused major carnage and human suffering for the local inhabitants.

With the advent of sea transportation, the dependence on land routes decreased quite significantly. Since Afghanistan was a landlocked nation, it was no longer along the main thoroughfares; over time, it became a very remote location. Ironically, however, during the past few centuries the country became important in other ways. In the 1800s, when it was the buffer state that separated the Russian and British empires, the local people were subjected to brutal military campaigns by these two nineteenth-century superpowers. In the twentieth century, it was perhaps the only nation that was bombed by both superpowers: the former Soviet Union as an occupying force and the United States as a liberating one.

Culture Concepts

Why Do Cultures Differ?

Cultures look, think, and communicate as they do because they have had to accommodate and adapt to the pressures and forces upon them. Among the many types of forces affecting cultural changes, the following six are key: history, ecology, technology, biology, institutional networks, and interpersonal communication patterns. History refers to the unique experiences that have become part of the cultures' collective wisdom. Ecology includes the climate and other physical forces in the culture's external environment. Technology refers to the inventions that a culture has invented or borrowed. Biology refers to genetic or hereditary differences that arise as a long-term consequence of environmental adaptations. Institutional networks are the formal organizations that structure activities for large numbers of people. Finally, interpersonal communication patterns refer to the ways the culture's code systems create and sustain relationships.

My father was a carpenter with a grade-school education; my mother did not have the opportunity to go to school or to learn how to read or write. My father had an insatiable thirst for education. He did his best to help my siblings and me get a good education. Despite very limited formal schooling, he deeply believed in lifelong learning. One of his preoccupations was following world events and listening to the radio for the news. For him, the evening news was like listening to a sermon; that was not the time for anyone to have a conversation. He always wanted to know what was happening in the world, and he instilled in me a deep sense of curiosity about other lands and cultures.

My family was somewhat religious, but my father and many Afghans of his generation were very suspicious of the clergy. As a child, I heard many stories about British spies impersonating Muslim clergy in many parts of Afghanistan. My father always viewed most clergy as people who were opposed to the nation's progress and modernization. As I grew up, I learned the reasons for his views. In the 1920s Afghanistan had a benevolent monarch, King Amanullah, who had played a pivotal role in securing independence from the British. He had a deep passion for modernizing the country and had begun implementing a very ambitious and fast-paced program to Westernize the nation. Unfortunately, the clergy declared these reforms blasphemous, and King Amanullah was forced to abdicate in 1930. Subsequent regimes, which were very regressive and Draconian, assured that the country would remain a traditional society with limited opportunities for development. The succession of many suppressive regimes and the lack of progress led to several coups and ultimately the Soviet invasion of 1979. Then followed two decades of civil war and political unrest, until the U.S. Army liberated Afghanistan in late 2001.

Years later, when I read more of the regional history of the area, I learned that in the late 1800s the British Empire used its social scientists to assist the government in perpetuating its colonial rule. Based on their recommendations, the British started a number of fundamentalist Diwbandi Islamic religious schools in the Western frontiers of the Indian subcontinent (now Pakistan). Through these schools, the British were able to train many of its agents, disguised as the Muslim clergy, who were then dispersed as informants. The irony is that after India and Pakistan gained their independence, these religious schools not only survived but thrived and multiplied. By the 1980s, at the time of the Soviet invasion of Afghanistan, they had become the cradle that produced the Taliban and the menace of Islamic fundamentalism. That is why many Afghans of my father's generation blame the clergy and the British for the nation's lost opportunities for progress and modernization.

In contrast to the clergy, my father had a deep respect for scientists and inventors like Thomas Edison, Albert Einstein, and the Wright brothers, who contributed to the world's progress and quality of life for humankind. Similarly, there were two old French nuns who lived in our neighborhood and who worked as volunteers at a local hospital. My father had a deep admiration for them, since they were only in Afghanistan to assist their fellow human beings regardless of faith, color, or creed. My father used to recite a Persian poem that roughly translates as follows:

Prayer is nothing but serving humankind
It is not in holding the rosary, or kneeling at the altar.

At my birth, I became the first child of our extended family. Growing up, I interacted with elders far more than with children my own age. As the center of attention, I was quite self-conscious and was required to measure up to the high expectations of my elders. Over time, I developed a strong inner drive to excel.

My full legal name is Mohammad Humayon Qayoumi. In the Islamic world, one's first name is actually just a prefix. Nobody in Afghanistan, and certainly no one in my family, ever called me Mohammad. Growing up in Kabul I was called Humayon, which in Persian means "fortunate" and comes from the Emperor Humayon, the great grandson of Genghis Khan, who ruled most of India in the 1530s.

In formal settings in college, I was called by my last name, Qayoumi. Concurrently, some classmates called me Mohammad while others used Humayon. This pattern continued when, after college, I was working in the Arabian Peninsula. When I began working in the United States, on my first day on the job, my boss took me around and introduced me as "Mo." That name stuck as my *de facto* identity and, with the exception of my Afghan acquaintances, for the past 25 years practically everyone has referred to me as Mo. Sometimes I have found it quite amusing and comical when I have introduced myself as "Mo" and immediately have had to respond when someone else has called me "Humayon." I sometimes reflect upon my names and consider how each of them represents the "real" me.

Although our family's economic status was quite modest, it was one of those accidents of history that our home was in a relatively affluent part of Kabul, where the majority of the foreigners lived. From early childhood I interacted with people from all over the world. About a block from our house, for example, there was a huge mosque. I enjoyed going there for Islamic feasts and for prayers, since the diplomatic corps from the other Muslim countries would also come to pray. I was fascinated by the differences in clothing styles and yearned to experience the cultures they represented.

As I began attending elementary school, two subjects—history and religious studies—particularly aroused my curiosity. I remember many history lessons that explained how gallantly the Afghan armies fought on the battlefields and how they were constantly defeating their enemies. I was curious about what was being covered in the history books of the nations that Afghans had defeated. I wondered how embarrassed the students in those communities were to learn that their people had been defeated in battle. Later, as I began to read history books from neighboring countries, I realized that they all made similar claims of victory.

In the religious courses that I took as a young child, the readings argued very explicitly for the supremacy of Islam over all other religions. I was curious about why people of other faiths did not see these clear arguments and embrace Islam, until I began studying other religions and became painfully aware that almost every religion claims to be the one and only true path to salvation.

Experiences such as these had a profound impact on my thinking and cultural outlook. I realized that practically every society perpetuates similar fables to glorify their history and justify their view of the world. This realization not only shattered the myths of my childhood, but it also created an insatiable curiosity to learn more about the cultures, peoples, and beliefs that differed from my own. I also realized that I could learn more about my own culture by learning about others.

After finishing high school, I received a scholarship to attend the American University of Beirut (AUB), in Lebanon. In the early seventies, Beirut was a very fast-paced, modern, and exciting city. As a teenager, I was fascinated by the natural beauty of Beirut as well as by its dynamic business environment. AUB was a very diverse community of roughly 4,000 students from about 100 countries. Moreover, the faculty came from almost every corner of the world and from more than 40 countries. Every day, walking on campus, it was common to hear more than a half-dozen languages. In fact, just among the Arab speakers, one would typically hear more than a dozen Arabic dialects.

Since at that time Beirut had the most open and free press in the Middle East, it was the hotbed of the region's politics as well. The early 1970s were a time of student unrest in the United States and in many other parts of the world; naturally, AUB was affected by these events. No matter where individual students stood in the wide political spectrum, it was hard for any to remain indifferent to world events. For me, the learning environment outside the classroom was at least as important as the encounters in class. My undergraduate experiences at AUB not only provided me with excellent technical knowledge, but they also gave me a uniquely valuable learning environment in a genuinely multicultural context. As a young man, I was able to develop a global perspective in such an environment, and it challenged my remaining traditional and parochial biases.

During my last semester at AUB, the Lebanese civil war broke out. This fundamentally shattered the existing way of life for the people of Lebanon, and it resulted in many tragedies and much human carnage. In the summer of 1975, sniper attacks became very common. One had to listen to the radio every morning to know which roads to avoid and which were likely to be safe. It took more than a decade for things to quiet down and a sense of normalcy to return. Even today, when I listen for the traffic alerts on the radio, I think of Beirut in the summer of 1975.

After graduating in the mid-seventies, I began working on the Arabian Peninsula, first in Saudi Arabia for a year, then for almost two years in Abu Dhabi, which is in the United Arab Emirates (UAE). The most fascinating aspect of these experiences was again the multicultural environment that both places offered. In my office in Riyadh, Saudi Arabia, no more than three of my coworkers were from the same country. Business was conducted in a combination of English and Arabic. Since my work took me all over the Kingdom, I had a unique opportunity to see all its major cities as well as many remote areas.

The work environment in the UAE was even more interesting. For instance, in Abu Dhabi only 20 percent of the population were UAE nationals; the rest were expatriates from every continent. The staff that I managed came from ten countries, spoke seven languages, and practiced various religions. At times, operating round-the-clock shifts for the power generation plant and keeping track of religious holidays for all of the staff had its challenges, but the lessons these experiences taught me, and the sensitivities that I acquired, were invaluable and have assisted me in many ways.

I recall one incident that I still cherish. One evening, as I was checking a construction site generation plant, I ran into one of the plant operators who seemed quite tired and sleepy but was pulling double duty by working two consecutive shifts. Looking at the frail and tired condition of this man, I asked why he had to do this. He responded that since tomorrow was Good Friday, he wanted the other operator, who was a Christian, to enjoy the time off; he was a Muslim, he said, and the next day did not have any particular significance for him, so he did not mind. Though most of the plant operators had very limited education, I was deeply touched by the cultural sensitivity they had developed for one other.

After working for three years in the Arabian Peninsula, I grew quite restless and was very anxious to continue my education and start graduate school. I started graduate studies in a major city in the Midwest. One of the first

---

Culture Concepts

Competent Intercultural Communication

Interculturally competent communicators integrate a wide array of culture-general knowledge into their behavioral repertoires, and they are able to apply that knowledge to the specific cultures with which they interact. They are also able to respond emotionally and behaviorally with a wide range of choices in order to act appropriately and effectively within the constraints of each situation. They have typically had extensive intercultural communication experiences, and they have learned to adjust to alternative patterns of thinking and behaving.

---

things that I experienced in the Midwest was hearing only English as I walked around the campus and in the streets. Since I had lived in more diverse environments before I moved to the Midwest, it felt strange and surreal, both initially and for several months thereafter, until I grew accustomed to hearing only English. I spent close to eight years in the Midwest. Over time, I developed deep and lasting friendships that I still cherish and maintain, although I left the area about twenty years ago.

In 1979, while I was in the Midwest, the Soviets invaded my native land, which resulted in more than two decades of chaos, bloodshed, and political instability. During this period, there was hardly an Afghan family that did not lose loved ones. My family had to leave all its worldly possessions behind and flee to Pakistan as refugees. Because we did not lose any immediate family members in the fighting, my Afghan family might be considered as one of the fortunate ones. But like every family there, we lost cousins and other extended members. The fighting continued for two decades, until late 2001,

---

Culture Concepts

Language, Knowledge, and Intercultural Competence

Getting along in another language can be exhilarating and a very positive experience, but it can also be fatiguing and frustrating. Speaking and understanding a new language requires energy and perseverance. Therefore, functioning in a culture that speaks a language different from your own is often tiring and exasperating. Making yourself understood, getting around, obtaining food, and making purchases all require a great deal of effort. Recognizing the possibility of irritability and fatigue when functioning in an unfamiliar linguistic environment is an important prerequisite to intercultural competence. Without such knowledge, the communicator may well blame his or her personal feelings of discomfort on the cultures being experienced.

---

when the United States invaded Afghanistan as part of Operation Enduring Freedom. Only then, for the first time in twenty-six years, was I able to go back for a visit.

My first trip back to Afghanistan was a bittersweet experience. I was very excited to be able to go, since for so many years I could not. I recalled two earlier trips I had taken. On the first one, in 1986, I went from Europe to Pakistan to visit my parents, and the flight path was over Kabul. I had a strange set of emotions as I watched from a commercial airliner at 35,000 feet and knew that an actual trip there was impossible. While looking out the window I saw several flashes of light; living in the Midwest then, I associated the light bursts with lightning. By the next day, in Pakistan, I realized that it was not the season for lightning in Afghanistan, and the light flashes I had seen from the aircraft were skirmishes between the Soviet occupation forces and the resistance forces. A decade later, I was on a similar flight from Nepal to Europe. Again, part of the flight path was over Afghanistan. By then, after so much time away and with such continuous fighting there, the hope of ever being able to return to my birthplace felt quite remote.

Therefore, when I arrived in Kabul in early 2002, I was filled with intense and intensely mixed emotions. After such a long absence, I was finally visiting the place where I grew up, and I met many people that I knew from long ago, which was very exciting. Though a lot of Afghanistan's destruction had been in the news for the past two decades, experiencing it firsthand while keeping one's eyes dry was a difficult challenge. The western part of Kabul was practically a ghost town. Because of land mines, it was not advisable for anyone to venture in a car or on foot beyond the main roads. As I was seeing the physical destruction, I was imagining the level of carnage, death, and human suffering that must have accompanied each fallen structure, and I was thinking of hundreds of thousands of innocent men, women, and children who lost their lives in vain.

In the midst of this tremendous destruction, however, there was still a sense of optimism, as many smiling faces projected a feeling of hope for a better future. One of my cousins told her story of being beaten by the Taliban's vice police because she had not covered herself fully with the *burqa*. Before the Taliban took over Kabul, she had never worn a *burqa* and didn't know how to wear one properly. In telling her story, she was able to laugh rather than feel victimized by the atrocities. This showed me that, though the Afghan people suffered tremendously from the savagery of the Soviets and the tyranny of the Taliban, their spirit had not been broken. Experiencing this firsthand was a source of tremendous inspiration and optimism.

As I walked around the streets of Kabul, in the areas where I spent the first sixteen years of my life, I experienced both nostalgic familiarity and a sense that everything had changed: the way the place looked, the way it felt, and the people who lived and worked there, compared to what I remembered of them.

Since 2002, with the liberation from the Taliban, I have traveled to Afghanistan several times. Many there refer to me as "Doctor Sahib," which literally translates as "Dear Doctor" and is used both as a sign of respect and as a term of endearment.

During the past twenty years, one of the significant opportunities to explore differences in values, culture, and Islamic fundamentalism occurred with the publication in 1989 of Salman Rushdie's *The Satanic Verses*. That book drew strong reactions from certain Muslim fundamentalists, including the Ayatollah Khomeini in Iran. Unfortunately, many in the Western media merely jumped in to support Rushdie, defending his right to free speech. They did not seize the opportunity to understand the issues that had resulted in such sharp criticisms. Such a dialogue between the followers of Islam and those who hold Western values would have been very fruitful in understanding the cultural differences. We lost a tremendous opportunity to learn better why some in the Muslim world were having such a strong reaction to some of the ideas raised in the book. With the exception of a few meaningful discussions, the book has been largely forgotten.

One of the turning points in our recent U.S. history was the horrific events of September 11, 2001, which dramatically changed everyone's lives. After the 9/11 tragedy there was a renewed sense of curiosity about Islam and the rise of Islamic fundamentalism. In America, non-Muslims were learning about Islam, and most Muslims were speaking out against the 9/11 travesties. When some Muslims were attacked by thugs in various U.S. cities, many Americans spoke out against such travesties. As a Muslim American, it was heartwarming to feel the overwhelming support and solidarity of the people for these victims, for their families, and for those who died in the initial assaults on September 11. However, there were those who questioned whether Muslims like me could be true to their religion and be patriotic Americans as well. Let me briefly examine this issue.

Migration has perhaps a stronger symbolism in Islam than it does in other major world religions. The Islamic calendar is not based on Mohammad's birth or death; rather, it is based on his migration from Mecca to Medina. When Mohammad migrated to Medina, and the people of that city accepted him as one of their own, he adopted Medina as his home. During the rest of his life, Mohammad went to Mecca only once, for a pilgrimage. He lived the rest of his life in Medina, where he is buried. The people of Medina take great pride that Mohammad adopted their city as his home, and most Muslims view his behavior as an exemplar that they should emulate. So in addition to the many secular reasons why Muslim-Americans take their duties to the flag and the nation seriously and defend their country, they also feel a religious duty, following Mohammad's example, to maintain a deep loyalty to the country they have adopted.

Now, as a middle-aged man residing at the end of Route 66, I find it natural to reflect upon my cultural experiences of the past half-century. The rich cultural mosaic of southern California is exciting and is a source of great pride and satisfaction for me. To live in a city with such a rich tradition of ethnic, cultural, and religious diversity is something that I cherish and enjoy every day. The tolerance and artistic creativity make Los Angeles a world-class city despite all of the challenges that it faces.

From my beginnings along the Silk Route in Afghanistan to my current home in Los Angeles, at the end of Route 66, I have been blessed with many opportunities to explore diverse cultures. Each experience has had positive effects on me. Each has helped to form my cultural identity, to make me a better person, and to appreciate being a citizen of the United States and of the world.

▶ ▶ ▶ Learning AmongUS

1. Qayoumi's several names become a critical part of his intercultural experiences. Compare and contrast Qayoumi's experiences with those of Covarrubias, Kroll, and Imahori.

2. Qayoumi says that most religions "claim to be the one and only true path to salvation." Do you agree with him? If so, how do you think this tendency has shaped the course of history? If not, why not?

3. Qayoumi has lived in many countries and different cultural settings since he left Afghanistan. What are some of the conse-

quences of such cultural experiences on his identity?

4. Would you regard Qayoumi as interculturally competent? Why or why not?

5. Does the information on the history and current circumstances in Afghanistan provide any insights into Afghani culture? Explain.

6. What were your experiences on September 11, 2001? What are the insights that Qayoumi provides into the Muslim communities in the United States?

The consequences—both positive and negative—of living in multiple cultures is the central theme of this essay by Ringo Ma. Belonging, comfort, predictability, and fitting in are all emotional states that can be rare for those who live extensively within cultures other than their own. While Ringo acknowledges the hazards of multicultural living, he also makes a passionate argument for the benefits that result from an ability to function within multiple cultures.

31 "Both-And" and "Neither-Nor": My Intercultural Experiences

Ringo Ma

A question that I have been asked repeatedly and do not know how to answer is "Where is your home?" When asked, my answer is that "home" is the place where I currently live and work. To those who ask, however, "home" refers to the place where I was born and raised. The question also implies that one's place of birth and residence remain the same for most of one's life. Because I have lived in many places and among several cultures, my response is not the one that most people expect. My multicultural experiences have blurred my sense of "home," as well as my cultural identity, in many ways.

Born and raised in Taiwan, I spent my childhood in three different cities and completed my undergraduate studies there. I came to the United States for graduate studies; taught in Canada and the United States; lectured in the People's Republic of China (PRC); and visited numerous countries in Africa, Asia, and Europe. I did miss my "home" in Taipei, Taiwan, at the beginning of my intercultural experiences, but my attachment and belonging have gradually faded as my stay outside Taiwan has been prolonged. The process of becoming familiar with new cultures has also moved me away from my "home" culture.

People describe the consequences of their intercultural experiences differently. Some describe them as "broadening their horizons" and "enlightening." Others associate their intercultural experiences with being "marginalized," "disfranchised," and "muted." Still others view their experiences with greater complexity, with their intercultural experience initially exciting but later frustrating as the novelty and curiosity wear off. All three views explain my experiences over the past two decades, and all are necessary to understand my evolving sense of belonging to multiple cultures.

I believe I will never be fully accepted as a community member in Canada or the United States because of my appearance, accent, and cultural naiveté. During the first year of my graduate studies in the United States, a European

American told me how he feels about Asians: "Although blacks look different from us, I know how to deal with them. But I don't know how to handle Asians. Asians are so different and can be more threatening to me."

I was not offended by the remark, because I thought it was more genuine than an insincere and patronizing statement. Instead, I tried to understand the meaning of his words from his perspective. I understood him to be saying that because African Americans had lived in the United States for centuries, many European Americans were more familiar, and thus more comfortable, with African Americans' behavioral patterns; the two groups also share many cultural values and behaviors. I also heard him say that because I was Chinese, I was too different and too unpredictable for him to feel comfortable around me. Certainly, Chinese value systems and the resultant communication behaviors are at odds with the prescriptions of the European American culture. For example, I was trained as a child to be considerate and to refrain from expressing my preferences directly. I was encouraged *not* to stand out in a group and *not* to tell others what I really wanted. In the United States, however, children are encouraged to express their own desires. When I was in graduate school, this cultural difference frustrated me because, whereas my fellow graduate students would directly tell me what they wanted from me, I never could tell them what I wanted from them. This put me in an ever-giving and never-taking position.

When I lived in Canada, I felt I had to insist on being treated with respect in many situations. For example, in a department newsletter article to introduce new faculty members, I was the only one referred to by first name, while all the others were presented as "Doctor." Occasionally people in the community showed the same lack of respect, addressing my colleagues as "Doctor" and me as just "Ringo." I experienced similar unequal treatment in nonprofessional contexts. In a store one day, my request for a rain check was ignored, despite a note posted in the store to encourage customers to take a rain check for on-sale merchandise that was out of stock. I had to raise my voice and show displeasure on my face in order to get the clerk's attention. Of course, what was annoying to me in each of these instances was not the absence of the title "Doctor" or being ignored. It was, instead, the unequal and inconsistent treatment that I received in comparison to others; usually the "offender" didn't even notice that something was "wrong."

It has been very difficult to handle situations such as these. First, I am not accustomed to and do not feel comfortable requesting "respect" or equal treatment from others. Second, if I complain about unequal treatment, I risk being accused of "making too much of it." However, if I avoid dealing with the offense, the situation may repeat itself in the future. So what am I supposed to do? Hint? Sometimes that works and sometimes it does not. Ignore what happened? I can do that occasionally, but not always.

Barriers to communication between people from different cultures can be related to race or cultural differences or both. I have found that prejudice, hostility, and unequal treatment are often race related, whereas misinterpretations of verbal and nonverbal behaviors and inappropriate responses are related to differences in culture. Prejudice and cultural misunderstandings are

---

Culture Concepts

Face

A very important concept for understanding interpersonal communication among people from different cultures is that of face, or the public expression of the inner self. Face is the favorable social impression that a person wants others to have of him or her. Face, therefore, involves a claim for respect and dignity from others. There are three important characteristics of face. First, it is social. This means that face always occurs in a relational setting; because it is social, one can only gain or lose face through actions that are known to others. Second, face is an impression, which may or may not be shared by all, that may differ from a person's self-image. To maintain face, people want others to act toward them with respect, regardless of their "real" thoughts and impressions. Third, face refers only to the favorable social attributes that people want others to acknowledge. Unfavorable attributes, of course, are not what others are expected to admire.

---

not mutually exclusive but interact with each other. Prejudice, for instance, can develop from frustrations due to an inability to understand what someone is trying to communicate—a combination of both race-related and culture-related problems. Many of the problems I experienced could be related both to my physical appearance and to my communication behaviors. The situations I face tend to be different from what American-born Chinese (Chinese Americans) face. European Americans and Chinese Americans are less likely to misinterpret each other's behaviors because they share a common educational system and speak the same language. Similarly, Chinese Americans are familiar with such icons of popular culture in the United States as professional sports, television, radio, and other media. Taiwanese-born Chinese, like me, suffer not only from our Chinese appearances but also from our naiveté about appropriate cultural behaviors. There is less tolerance and acceptance of my inability to perform cultural rituals perfectly, yet there are so many cultural rules that I fear it is impossible for me to learn them all! A simple ritual like kissing the hostess's cheek at the end of a dinner party, for example, is done so intuitively by members of the culture but can never be performed competently and comfortably by me.

Did my sense of belonging return when I paid a return visit to Taiwan, the place where I was born and raised? Yes, but only to a limited degree. After spending so many years in North America, I am no longer completely Chinese or Taiwanese, and this change sometimes makes me a stranger in many social situations in Taiwan. Whenever I phone old friends and express my desire to see them, they almost always begin to arrange a dinner for me. I enjoyed their dinner invitations at the beginning, but gradually they have become a burden. In my daily life in the United States I eat very little for lunch and do not eat out often, because I try to avoid eating MSG and high-sodium foods. In Tai-

---

Culture Concepts

High- and Low-Context Cultures

Cultures differ on a continuum that ranges from high to low context. High-context cultures prefer to use high-context messages, in which most of the meaning is either implied by the physical setting or presumed to be common knowledge; very little specific information is provided in the coded, explicit, transmitted part of the message. Low-context cultures prefer to use low-context messages, in which the majority of the information is vested in the explicit code. A simple example of high-context communication is interactions that take place in a long-term relationship between two people who are often able to interpret even the slightest gesture or the briefest comment. The message does not need to be stated explicitly because it is carried in the shared understandings about the relationship.

---

wan, however, if one turns down a dinner offer for no "legitimate" reason, he or she is perceived as unfriendly or socially inept. A time conflict because of another social obligation is a "legitimate" reason, but simply not wanting to eat out is not an acceptable excuse. The dilemma I face is that I want to see my friends but do not want to eat with them. Sometimes I was dragged to a restaurant even though I had told my friends, "No, I do not want to eat." They didn't believe me. Instead they thought I was trying to be polite. After living in North America for many years, I did mean "No" when I said "No." I had to repeat my "No" message to them many times and use facial expressions to validate my "No" message before they finally accepted that I really did not want to eat.

I had the same communication problem with my mother—she did not accept my "No" messages when food was to be served. She would ask me, "Do you want to eat anything now?" Whether I said "Yes" or "No" didn't make any difference to her. She would just go ahead and prepare some food for me, even though I told her I was not hungry and didn't want to eat anything at that moment. She thought I was just trying to be considerate, because I would have given her "trouble" had I said "Yes."

When I visited friends' houses, I tended to stay for a relatively short period of time. My friends would expect me to stay for dinner and would feel guilty if they could not persuade me to stay. Having adjusted to the United States, where social engagements are planned and time and purpose are negotiated ahead of time, I was not comfortable acting spontaneously and "staying for dinner."

I found I could no longer tolerate the complexity of many Taiwanese social rituals, though I am still familiar with them. I have discussed this cultural reentry problem with other Taiwanese-born people who decided to work in Taiwan after studying and working in the United States for many years. They all identified similar disruptions and discontinuities in displaying appropriate social behaviors. One man mentioned that he had spent six months learning to drive in Taiwan, though he had driven in the San Francisco area for almost 20 years. He said that driving in Taiwan was quite different in terms of the distance one is expected to maintain between cars, the right of way, and how to cope with parking problems. Because my return visits to Taiwan were for relatively brief stays, my ability to regain a level of comfort there has been severely constrained.

In the summer of 1995 I was invited to lecture at eight universities and colleges in Hubei and Sichuan Provinces in Central China. This was my second trip to the People's Republic of China (PRC), or "mainland China." Because my first visit in 1991 was brief and I did not have a chance to visit any academic institutions, I was quite excited. This visit also constituted a valuable and exciting experience in my life for other reasons. First, my parents were born and raised in mainland China and moved to Taiwan before the Communist government was established in the late 1940s. Ever since I was a little child, I have heard numerous stories about this "big" China. I also have many relatives there. Until the 1980s, however, Taiwanese were unable to visit mainland China because of the military confrontation between the Communist government in Beijing and the Nationalist (Kuomintang) government in Taipei. Yet Taiwan and mainland China share a common cultural heritage, in spite of their different political ideologies and systems. Mandarin is the official dialect in both Taiwan and mainland China. Furthermore, people on both sides are familiar with each other's history and customs. In other words, we are familiar with each other, yet we are distant because of the political situation.

In addition to different political ideologies and systems, the characteristics of mainland Chinese social life are different from the Taiwanese social life in many important ways. After living in North America for years I was unprepared for the treatment I received in the PRC. For example, due to the lack of privacy in the PRC, I felt a little uncomfortable at the beginning of my visit. When I stayed in a university hostel for international teachers, I was not given a key to my room. The service people, however, could enter my room at any time. One day a service person entered my room without even knocking on the door, and then she said without apology, "Oh, I thought you were already gone." My phone calls were often monitored, and the operator sometimes interrupted my conversation. On a few campuses, the door to my room was expected to be open for most of the evening because those coordinating my lectures were continually shuttling between the rooms. On almost every campus, my year of birth was included in my visiting schedule. Furthermore, in most rural areas, using a public squat toilet is a group-oriented activity; people of the same sex squat next to each other and are separated only by waist-high walls.

I quickly learned, however, that there was a more benign explanation for these differences than I had originally thought. The lack of concern for privacy, for instance, is not necessarily associated with unfriendliness. In the PRC, hotel rooms are monitored and all tenants are required to register with official identification. A man and a woman are not allowed to sleep in the same room unless they are married. In most university hostels, the main en-

trance is closed at 11:00 P.M. The purpose of this policy is to prevent prostitution and crime. In other words, it is a way to protect tourists. Monitoring phone calls was not necessarily for the purpose of spying. In at least one of my hotels in the Hubei Province, my coordinators made an effort to ensure that my phone connections were trouble free. They asked the operator to pay special attention to my phone connections. Thus, they monitored my phone to ensure that there would be no breaks in the service. By the same token, shuttling between my room and theirs was a gesture by my hosts to indicate that "my services are at your disposal." I also learned that a special guest's year of birth in the PRC is treated with reverence, which is why it is usually announced at the beginning of a reception. Obviously, hiding one's age is a learned behavior that is not found in every culture! There are several other things that made me uncomfortable in the PRC. While I was expected to share a lot of information, including facts about life in the United States, details of U.S. society, and how I felt about issues of international relations, my Chinese hosts did not tell me much about themselves and their lives. I also found that although I was treated as a fellow Chinese on the surface level, I was actually viewed as an outsider—"Mr. Ma"—instead of as "Comrade Ma," the insider. The "unequal" treatment, I realized afterward, was largely due to the unique political and social situation in the PRC, rather than a reflection of their attitude toward me personally.

From the frustration and alienation I experienced in Canada, the People's Republic of China, the United States, and even Taiwan, it is not difficult to understand my "homeless" feeling. Although I am associated with the four countries and cultures in various ways, there is no place that gives me a strong sense of belonging. Nowhere am I an insider. In the United States I am an "Asian faculty member" on campus, a "resident alien" to the U.S. Immigration and Naturalization Service, and an "Oriental" to the community. In Taiwan, I am an "overseas Chinese" (that is, someone who does not reside in Taiwan) or an Americanized Chinese. Others expect my behavior to differ from theirs, and it does.

So, you might ask, have my intercultural experiences produced only liabilities with no rewards? The answer is an emphatic "No." My multicultural identity and bilingual skills are a valuable asset in all facets of my life. After experiencing diverse lifestyles in different cultures, I believe that I have a broader and deeper understanding of life and its circumstances than those who have not been exposed to "other" cultures.

In North America, for example, my Chinese cultural background, with its emphasis on subtle, nonverbal cues, sometimes allows me to see and understand what many others do not. I can also provide alternative evaluations of right and wrong, and good and bad, and can provide stories and examples that illustrate multiple interpretations of a single event. I think that when I teach, my intercultural experiences enrich my lectures, and students regard them favorably. For example, when I describe for my students that different cultures have different attitudes about the importance of verbal communication, I tell them the following story from an ancient Chinese book:

> ## **Culture** Concepts
>
> ### Relationship of Nonverbal Codes to Verbal Codes
> *The relationship of nonverbal communication systems to the verbal message systems can take a variety of forms. Nonverbal messages can be used to accent, complement, contradict, regulate, or substitute for the verbal message. Nonverbal messages are often used to* accent *the verbal message by emphasizing a particular word or phrase, in much the same way as* italics *add emphasis to written messages. Nonverbal messages that function to clarify, elaborate, explain, reinforce, and repeat the meaning of verbal messages* complement *the verbal message. Nonverbal messages can also* contradict *the verbal message. When nonverbal messages help maintain the back-and-forth sequencing of conversations, they function to* regulate *the interaction. Finally, nonverbal messages used in place of the verbal ones function as a* substitute *for the verbal channel.*

> A student asked his teacher whether it is good to talk a lot. The teacher replied by saying, "The toad in the field makes noise throughout the day and nobody cares to hear. The rooster crows only once a day but people are enlightened by it."

I then provide a contrasting story that was told to me by a colleague and is derived from the European American cultural framework:

> The codfish lays thousands of eggs and the hen lays only one egg each time. The hen is much more appreciated because she cackles whenever she lays an egg.

So the "moral" of the Chinese story is that "More talk just makes talk less valuable," while the European American story emphasizes that "It pays to advertise." Students tell me that they do not often hear such stories and that they appreciate them. From my perspective as a professor interested in having my students learn, I know that if they remember the two stories, they have learned important cultural differences in communication from me.

Having learned to adapt my teaching style to U.S. students who expect greater openness and less formality, I found my experiences in China to be more positive than they might otherwise have been. Certainly as a professor and scholar, I find continual benefits from my ability to draw on a deep knowledge of two different cultural traditions. My research has also been positively informed by my bicultural knowledge.

I would summarize the advantages and disadvantages of being an intercultural person in two phrases: "both-and" and "neither-nor." "Both-and" is the joy of functioning effectively in dual cultures. "Neither-nor," on the other

hand, is the agony of being rejected by both one's old original and one's new culture. There are also two Chinese idioms that can represent these contrary feelings: *zhu1 ba1 jie4 zhao4 jing4 zi3, li3 wai4 bu4 shi4 ren2* ("When the pig spirit [in the popular novel *Pilgrims to the West*] looks in the mirror, he found no humanity both in and outside the mirror") and *zuo3 you4 feng2 yuan2* ("Be able to achieve success one way or another" or "Gain advantage from both sides").[1] The abilities to see "no humanity both in and outside the mirror" and "gain advantage from both sides" are actually developed from two facets of the same process. When blue changes to purple, it is not as blue as before, but it is redder. The resulting color can relate to both blue and red, but it is neither pure blue nor pure red.

The process of moving toward a "purple" area through intercultural experiences is a mixed blessing for many people. To become a profoundly happy intercultural person requires the ability to maximize the "both-and" experience and to minimize the "neither-nor" feeling. It is my hope and professional goal through teaching intercultural communication that a multicultural world can be created in which "both-and" is the dominant experience and people from all cultures appreciate the cultures of others.

Notes

1. The *pinyin* system of Romanization is used to transliterate the Chinese terms. The number immediately following each transliterated word represents the tone of the word when pronounced in Mandarin Chinese.

▶ ▶ ▶ Learning AmongUS

1. Using the concept of face, explain Ma's experiences when he first came to Canada and was treated differently by the colleagues in his department.
2. Using the framework of high- and low-context cultures, explain Ma's initial reactions to communication in Canada.
3. Ma adapted to the prevailing social norms and cultural practices when living in North America, and he then had trouble adapting and communicating competently upon returning "home." To what extent should people adapt to another culture and risk not fitting in with their culture of origin?
4. Throughout Ma's essay are examples of and references to the relationship between verbal and nonverbal codes in communication. Analyze several of these examples using the framework provided.

While acknowledging that he speaks from the privileged position of the white U.S. American male, William Starosta describes his identity as one that draws on multiple cultural perspectives. Bill lives and interacts among multiple cultures: teaching at a predominantly black university, relating in an intercultural marriage, socializing with Asian Indians, and working as a scholar seeking (and sought out) to interpret and understand Chinese cultural patterns as they influence communication. Yet he recognizes that he is often, ultimately, the outsider in many of these intercultural interactions.

32 dual_consciousness@USAmerican.white.male

William J. Starosta

The domain "USAmerican.white.male" (UWM) receives hits almost daily from scholars investigating gender, culture, ethnicity, and nationality. Various visitors to this site carry away observations about power, patriarchy, resistance, hegemony, and ethnocentrism. (For many visitors, UWM is not a pretty site to see!) Remarkably, however, few UWMs enter their own domain to examine themselves as enculturated communicators.

Consequently, this analysis represents a visit to the UWM domain by one member of that domain. It relates the experience of one USAmerican.white.male who has spent most of his adult life amidst those of contrast cultures. Questions that occur to me concern the construction of identity, the consciousness of identity by those within and without that identity, and the search for a middle perspective from which to assess issues of identity.

▶ I

"Your brother teaches at Howard? You don't look black!"—Midwest coworker

I have been on many sides of the looking glass during more than 50 years spent as a white USAmerican male. My formative years indoctrinated me into the naturalness of being Anglophone, of speaking the "standard" form of U.S. English, of coming from the "first" world, and of internalizing the privilege of being a white male. In ways that I do not yet understand—since a culture is often the most invisible to one who lives in it—I am a profoundly US-American specimen, culturally baptized into the "original sin" of racism, sexism, and nationalism.

316

My middle years were spent learning of South and East Asia. Mine was the only doctoral minor in Asian studies at my graduate institution, as I prepared myself to understand India, Sri Lanka, and China in some depth. As a graduation requirement, I was tested on two Asian languages. From my time spent executing research in India and Sri Lanka, and as a byproduct of 30 years of a bicultural marriage to a north Indian, a side of me has become identifiably Indian. I have lectured and written on Indian philosophy, meditated, become completely vegetarian, recoiled from Indian regional and communal bias, and adopted the nonviolent philosophy of Mahatma Gandhi *(satyagraha)* that came to inspire many who sought redress from oppression globally. My social circle is mostly north Indian.

For the most recent two-fifths of my life I have taught at an historically black (college or) university (HBCU). Within and without the classroom I have negotiated or shared attitudes, worldviews, values, and assumptions with African American students and faculty. When I leave the classroom for home gatherings, I am met with incredulity that I left a famous white school to teach in a black university. "Um, how are the students there?"

Of still more recent vintage, I have rekindled an interest in Chinese culture(s). By some mechanism unknown to me, I became identified as a person who has an interest in things Chinese. Soon I was responding to, presenting on, or chairing conference panels dealing with conflict resolution, relationship formation, or linguistic practices among those of the Chinese diaspora.

This peculiar mixture of cultural elements led me to initiate a professional journal that deals with gender, culture, and ethnicity. The journal is probably too black for Asians, too Asian for African Americans, too Hispanic for Anglophone readers, and pleases Europeans little if at all. In this sense, the journal parallels my identity: it can be described in a few words, but those few words really describe too little.

As I reflect on my identity, I see that I am an anomaly. I appear, when or if I wish, or even if I do not wish, to be a white USAmerican male. But I chafe at racial and communal slights and have come to take them personally. I socialize with Asian Indians, but I feel their resentment that I have married into their community, though I am told that "I am more Indian than most Indians." To reduce the social gulf between Indians and me, I speak, sing, write, or listen to jokes in two Indian dialects. I recognize this is not enough—I am still the outsider who is treated only on the surface as an insider by the local Indian community. Similarly, I teach at an African American university, but I do not feel I should try to become an administrator there. ("Some people are born into a religion; others convert. Some are born black; some, I am beginning to think, convert.") I sit down to dinner with Chinese Americans and am told that a person cannot stay balanced or healthy by eating no meat. The body needs certain qualities only meat can provide.

Always, I am the outsider who is treated, from friendship or social duty, as a pseudo-insider. Yet, at unprotected moments, I see that I can socially penetrate into other communities only to a certain degree. I have worked hard at gender inclusiveness, and can be accepted as a friend, maybe even as a fellow

---

Culture Concepts

Intercultural Adaptation

In intercultural communication, the certainty of our own cultural framework is gone, and there can be a great deal of uncertainty about what other code systems mean. Individuals who engage in intercultural contacts for extended periods of time may respond to the stress in different ways. Most will find themselves incorporating at least some behaviors from the new culture into their own repertoire. Some take on the characteristics, the norms, and even the values and beliefs of another culture willingly and easily. Others resist the new culture and retain their old ways, sometimes choosing to spend time in enclaves populated only by others like themselves. Still others simply find the problems of adjusting to a new culture intolerable, and they leave if they can. People's reactions also change over time. That is, the initial reactions of acceptance or rejection often shift as increased intercultural contacts produce different kinds of outcomes. Such changes in the way people react to intercultural contacts are called adaptation.

---

traveler, but I see that a gulf stands between many feminist-leaning female white professionals and me. I see that I can do many things to project an interest in, and an identity with, other groups, but admission to these groups is priced beyond my means. No matter how I try to project an identity over and above my native UWM one, the other sees me only as a member of my "domain," USAmerican.white.male.

▶ II

The questions that occur to me following cultural introspection rest on identity. I have argued elsewhere (Chen & Starosta, 1996) that a major difference between intercultural communication competence and competence within a single culture is that interactants must make judgments about which cultural identities are in play and which are not. The best introduction to the question of the clash of cultural identities comes from W.E.B. Du Bois, who coined the term "double consciousness" in *The Souls of Black Folk* to describe the competing demands placed on African Americans who walk a fine, wavering, and perilous line between black and white. In a sense, what follows is a footnote to the thinking of the first detailed intercultural communication identity theorist, W.E.B. Du Bois:

> One ever feels his two-ness—an American, a Negro; two souls, two thoughts, two unreconciled strivings; two warring ideals in one dark body. . . . The history of the American Negro is the history of this strife, this longing to attain self-conscious manhood, to merge this double self into a better and truer self.

In this merging he wishes neither of the old selves to be lost. He would not Africanize America, for America has too much to teach the world and Africa. He would not bleach his Negro soul in a flood of white Americanism, for he knows that the Negro blood has a message for the world. He simply wishes to make it possible for a man to be both a Negro and an American.

Similarly, Frederick Douglass asserted a lack of common identity with white Americans in his address on the slave having little reason to celebrate the Fourth of July, while Sojourner Truth asserted a common identity with white women in her speech "Ain't I a Woman?" Intercultural identity issues ever punctuate the black experience in America.

It is relatively straightforward to pose the dilemma of culture for the African American. Should one try to aim for parity and success in the white world? If so, he or she succeeds only to the degree that mainstream society permits. One's destiny is placed in the hands of a sometimes unwilling other. But if this attempt to orient to the white world is perceived by the black community as assimilation, the person risks being taken as a "Tom" (based on *Uncle Tom's Cabin*). He or she can be viewed by some members of the black community as abandoning blacks, of trying to forget his or her blackness, and he or she will be called to return back to a black orbit. (Some in the community remark "Didn't I say so?" when they see the best efforts of white-oriented African Americans fail.) In short, neither the white nor the black community forgets black skin tone. Social forces pull and push from one side and the other, and they offer few convenient answers to the problem of dual consciousness. The double bind of dual identity stays with the person from birth to death.

The point to be explored is whether such a sense of dual consciousness is also the legacy of the USAmerican.white.male. Is he, too, destined to be stigmatized according to both gender and skin tone? If he asserts his Americanness and his whiteness, he claims unfair privilege; but if he disavows these personal characteristics, he is distrusted by other whites and foreign expatriots, and he is tested by those of color. White maleness is not something to be given away, since it and its meanings rest simultaneously in the mind of the beholder as well as in the man himself.

▶ III

Experience is individual, but its interpretation shows evidence of cultural patterning. In sifting through my own adult experience I hope to locate some sites where my training as an Indian, as an African American, as a Chinese, and as a white male have come to the fore. Indeed, these identities probably will be seen to supplement one another or to clash at times.

Sifting through personal data poses the question of objectivity. How can a person put the self into perspective? My answer comes from the lessons of other experience-close studies: what is lost in distortion should be gained in

verisimilitude, richness, and detail. What I make of my own experience cannot be "bias," since it is the only available measure of my own meaning. (It can, of course, suffer from deliberately selective reporting or from my inability to translate the subtleties of my experience into terms that others can comprehend.) I hold out the hope that others of the UWM domain and elsewhere will "see themselves" in some way in my personal data. I start my inventory with an attempt to uncover where, if at all, I have grown into an African American perspective.

I find myself believing, as do many—perhaps most—African Americans, that prejudice is "alive and well" and that racial equality in USAmerica is anything but accomplished. From my teaching perspective alone I have been told of three recent instances from Louisiana, California, and Montreal that support my perception: in two cases, African American students were told by a high school guidance counselor not to go on to college, to attend a two-year vocational program, and/or not even to attempt to enter the University of California system. ("Ha-ha! You aren't remotely qualified!") These students moved on to a 3.9 undergraduate average, in one instance, and to graduating with honors from the University of California system in the other. The third student had the chance to see a reference that was written for her only to find the words, "She isn't very capable, even for a black student." She is now a successfully published doctoral student. These are only a few of a multitude of pertinent cases gleaned from daily conversations with African American students.

A case reported by a sensitivity trainer makes a similar point. She and another trainer accepted an assignment to put on a workshop in a small city outside Philadelphia. After completing the morning session, one workshop participant came up to her and related, "Ma'am, that sure was pretty, what you said. But if I was you, I would be out of town before dark!" She found the threat credible, since the KKK had an active local chapter.

One more case is offered in support of my perception. A black Ph.D. took up a university teaching job in Kentucky. Her young son was at the head of his class before she moved there. Once settled there, though, she and the only other parent of a black child in that parochial school class received notices at home from one instructor that explained that the two children were unteachable and would not succeed in school. Turning the letters over, the parents found the letters were written on the back of KKK stationery. The school authorities issued an apology, but the teacher remained on the faculty to repress future students of color.

These instances and others are not firsthand, in that I did not live the original experiences. But they happened for persons who are for me very real and very important. Why else would I have felt personal anger when a panel of regional communication journal editors "looked right through" an African American woman in the front of the room, only to call repeatedly on white males of greater fame elsewhere in the room? And why did I feel a personal insult when a second such panel at a national convention related, "[We] would like to place more minorities on our editorial board, but we can't find enough who are qualified." As I looked at four white questioners who were charged

with asking the journal editors "tough questions," I asked if this same logic prevented the panel from locating qualified minority questioners?

Beyond attitudes and worldview, though, I find myself learning new habits and mannerisms. I perform frequent greetings (even of strangers), downplay parliamentary rules in meetings to seek consensus, state my personal opinion on topics that are under consideration, spend time getting to know my students personally, talk about a student's personal circumstances before talking business, become more attentive to nonverbal qualifiers in verbal messages, enjoy verbal interruptions in the classroom, "call on" students with facial gestures, rely heavily on friendship networks and brokers, raise the emotional level of my discourse, and accept the education of young African Americans almost more as a "mission" than as a salaried "job." These and other behaviors I would not have assimilated, were it not for my extended sojourn at an HBCU.

▶ IV

> I will open the windows of my house to breezes from all the directions, but I will not be blown from my feet by any of them. —Mahatma Gandhi

Every person who enjoys extensive contact and interaction with others of differing heritages and nationalities heightens his or her self-consciousness about identity. Although I could extend my analysis to recount in some detail how I have consciously and unconsciously refashioned myself as an Asian communicator, I would rather consider the juggling of various identities that are acquired through interethnic and intercultural interaction.

It is instructive to view the person who has engaged in extensive intercultural communication as someone who cooks from a recipe book. Early in life, we cook and eat what we were taught to cook and eat from childhood. We reproduce that cooking behavior, as best we are able, and we think of "eating" as that which is drawn from a familiar universe of cuisine. For a picnic, a party, a banquet, we come programmed with a set variety of responses. We can, of course, improvise with a touch of spice, or perhaps with a garnish. But food critics would recognize the result as the product of a certain culture—that is, as a product of our food identity.

Then we invite a person over to eat, but discover she is vegetarian. We rush to our cultural cookbook, only to find little beyond macaroni and cheese and grilled cheese sandwiches to serve the guest. Our cultural recipe book is revealed as lacking in its capacity to respond to a certain task. Indeed, the more suitable cookbook may be written in Hindi, Italian, or Arabic. If we go through with the task of preparing a meal from a new cookbook (though some would still serve steak, cancel the dinner, or "eat out") we raise our consciousness of new possibilities. Now we can cook from several books in several languages, and we have further ideas on how to improvise in the future. Indeed, we reach a point where we prepare food from various cuisines because it is

more interesting, because we are curious, or because we want to showcase our new cooking skills. The real test of our skills is when we are told by a native that they recognize our dish, that it is just as it used to be prepared at the guest's own home.

Earlier writers looked at a new identity as something that tramples an older one. If enough identities were learned, the person might become "multi-phrenic" and have no cultural base of operations to which to return. Perhaps these writers critiqued identity from a standpoint of ethnocentrism: each was comfortable with his or her own identity and was convinced of its "correct-ness." They feared a bad result cooking with an unfamiliar book. They felt that visitors, whether vegetarian or Jewish or Muslim, should "eat steak," or pork, or not visit. For every person who embraces new alternatives in identity, there is another who offers resistance. Further, issues of sampled new identi-ties create moments of misunderstanding and confusion: "Salmon is vegetar-ian" or "You eat onions and garlic, so do not say you are vegetarian." Our new identity may have a certain permanence, or it may be temporary. It may be re-inforced or rejected by persons who are significant for us. It may be practiced in places where it is not rewarded.

Resistance

In a multicultural society, eventually someone of a differing ethnicity or na-tionality or religion or sexual orientation enters our orbit. Such persons differ in socialization, and they practice different communication behaviors. They may have different notions of the roles of supervisors. They may "look over our shoulders" when we do our work, whereas we are accustomed to working on our own unless we encounter a problem. They may single out individuals for praise or blame, or credit an entire unit with achievements more traceable to individuals. They may be slow to ask for help or may seek help perpetually. They may associate mostly with others like themselves. They may want holi-days that we do not recognize, or wear a turban or facial covering at work. They may not be able to "take kidding." They may complain about things we take for granted. They may seem to "want special treatment."

Some percentage of those who formerly defined the "mainstream" may never want to "open a new cookbook." They may assert that it is the duty of those "who cook from a different cookbook" to "eat like us." They will see no reason—enhanced flexibility, provision of scarce skills, access to other mar-kets, the chance to compare different techniques, the gaining of fresh voices, the chance for synergy—that would justify making adjustments for the new entrants. ("Is this sensitivity effort at work going to be optional or required? If it's optional, I won't get anywhere near it!") What others may view as delica-cies will be for them "raw fish."

Confusion

For some amount of time cues are misinterpreted. A meeting "at 2:00" means literally 2:00. A majority vote may leave disgruntled losers as a consensus might not, but business moves on. Finding fault in the work of subordinates

> ## **Culture** Concepts
>
> ### Intercultural Transformation
>
> *Some individuals move easily among many cultures. Such people generally have a profound respect for varied points of view and are able to understand others and to communicate appropriately and effectively with people from a variety of cultures. They are able to project a sense of self that transcends any particular cultural group. The term* intercultural transformation *is sometimes used to describe the process by which individuals move beyond the thoughts, feelings, and behaviors of their initial cultural framework to incorporate other cultural realities.*

may, in the minds of some Greek, Chinese, or West Asian supervisors, make the unit look bad; but in the local context, it speaks to the evaluator's keen eye as a supervisor. Entering the conversation while another person is still talking may be considered rude, not enthusiastic. Being made to write frequent reports may be viewed as the company "keeping a suspicious eye" on the new worker. The arrival of a worker of color is viewed as "affirmative action," even when the new worker has comparable credentials. Other workers give the new worker extra space and deny him or her a needed sense of corporate belonging.

Especially for the new entrant into the context, the rules are unfamiliar. He or she may talk with a supervisor with whom smooth interpersonal relations have been established, only to be accused of "going behind someone's back" or "skipping levels." The question "Can you do this?" may sound patronizing. In a thousand ways, the new setting is unfamiliar just where it should be clear. Too many cues can be taken in multiple ways; indeed, this may be the sarcastic intent of an associate.

Permanence

Some sojourns are temporary, and the trainee or student expects to return "home." The incentive decreases for such persons to learn new recipes or ways of coping. For so long as misunderstandings and confusion do not prevent the acquisition of desired knowledge, life will be tolerable. Similarly, some workers are "loaned" to a branch elsewhere. Even though they may have a limited understanding of the new context, both parties may decide to "suffer through" a temporary assignment.

Life in a multicultural society is more permanent. Various projections see white and nonwhite workers in USAmerica reaching parity in about 50 years. In a seemingly permanent relationship, both parties are called on to make adjustments. My model of third culture building (Starosta & Olorunnisola, 1995; Chen & Starosta, 1997) moves from stages where impressions are fleeting through other stages where changes in communication become permanent. In the parlance of this essay, foreign cooking comes to taste better than the home cuisine. The new recipes are taught to the next generation as standard fare.

Reinforcement

Some companies in search of a new multicultural identity establish incentives and penalties for those who advance company policy. Similarly, some exclusionary choices are sanctionable in court. Fundamentally, however, the force behind an accepting attitude toward multiculturalism is largely individual. Mahatma Gandhi believed that each person must make him- or herself answerable for deeds that are committed against others. Scripture should never be used as an excuse to countenance the oppression of others; "I decline to be bound by any interpretation [of the Scriptures] if it is repugnant to [my individual] reason or moral sense. . . . I would rather be torn to pieces than to disown the suppressed classes" (Gandhi, 1929). Nor would Gandhi say the problem is "with them," and not his concern. Gandhi's goal in life was to free himself from rebirth, but "I prayed that if I have to be reborn . . . I should do so . . . as an [untouchable]" (1921).

The answer to those who repressed others was to act with "transparent morality," and to reflect the deeds of the other back to the perpetrator. The person who holds a spark of morality will not long be able to stand his or her reflection in the mirror if that reflection betrays a moral flaw. Gandhi's movement of "truth force" goes from a committed individual to commitment on the part of those surrounding that individual. Finally, a whole society is moved in the direction of greater virtue. The most potent reinforcement for a positive reception for culturally diverse individuals takes part in individual minds. The impulse for inclusion starts as an individual impulse. It continues even when courts and workplace evaluators are not looking. This outlook of individual accountability and its methodology, "transparent morality," alone can achieve and expand inclusive communication conduct.

Reward

In recognizing that the workplace, particularly in high-tech fields, must draw on the skills of workers from a variety of cultures, some computer firms put incentives in place to reward those in the firm who seek out, consider, hire, and promote nontraditional workers. Turning to the cultural natives of a region to avoid naming an auto (a Chevy Nova) with a word that means "no go" in the local language, or knowing not to tell people to "put a tiger in your tank" in areas where tigers are scorned produces economic outcomes that are visible to a savvy company. Latinos and African Americans make up a sizable section of the USAmerican market, and it would be wise to seek input from persons of these cultures and others to decide how best to tap this market. That is, some rewards for inclusiveness are tangible and self-evident.

Arguably, it is the nontangible reasons for including others that offer an individual his or her first real choice. "Synergy," "telling a better story," "knowledge," "new horizons," "alternatives," "adventure," "culture learning," "fair play," and the like are not, in themselves, totally convincing reasons to include others with parity in everyday interactions. They sound vague and remote. Medical studies have demonstrated that it is the innovations with less

tangible and visible benefits (boiling water, spacing children, getting a vaccination, quitting smoking) that are the hardest to introduce. The richest rewards for multicultural inclusion may be like those for preventive medicine: the innovative practice (cultural inclusion) must take place now to realize the harmony, synergy, liberation, and new possibilities of the future.

▶ **V**

Experiencing dual_consciousness@USAmerican.white.male, as is the case for the black and Asian and Native American domains, is neither a blessing nor a curse in itself. At most, it presents a host of expanded possibilities.

Dual consciousness is a fluid moment where identities flow and collide. Some of the consequences are delightfully fortuitous; others are bitter. Few are predictable with great fidelity. The same set of raw materials can be used to build towers or dungeons. Worse still, the materials may be returned unopened, their potential untapped and unrealized.

Dual consciousness is a vantage point from which new outcomes become thinkable and old possibilities appear outmoded and antiquated. It is a point of unsettled perspective, of shifting allegiance, of new linguistic possibilities, of racial antithesis, of sexism, of hegemony, of hope. Those who visit the USAmerican.white.male site, as well as every other contested site, will take away, in great measure, that which they bring to the site. The site can magnify intolerance and it can liberate. The difference between the two rests in the identity or identities of the individual beholder.

▶ ▶ ▶ Learning AmongUS

1. Starosta describes several ways to adapt to intercultural differences. He also describes the United States as a place where a multicultural society is relatively "permanent." What can you learn from Starosta's story about adapting to intercultural differences?

2. Starosta identifies some of the choices he has made as he interacts, works, and lives among cultural groups other than his own. Do you think Starosta has made the right choices? Why?

3. How would you describe Starosta's culture?

4. What makes it possible for Starosta to display such a high level of intercultural competence in his interactions with people from such varied cultures?

About the Authors

Ann M. Bohara is a senior manager at Booz Allen Hamilton, a global strategy and technology consulting firm.

Charles A. Braithwaite is the director of the International Studies Program at the University of Nebraska-Lincoln. His published research includes ethnographic studies of communication among Vietnam veterans, communication practices among the Navajo, and intercultural communication along the U.S.-Mexican border. He is the editor of the *Great Plains Quarterly*.

Donal Carbaugh is a professor of communication at the University of Massachusetts. He has explored various cultural philosophies of communication from an ethnographic perspective, including Popular American, Finnish, Russian, and Native American. He is the author of *Narrative Identity: Studies in Autobiography, Self & Culture, Situating Selves* and the editor of *Cultural Communication and Intercultural Contact*.

Patricia Covarrubias is an assistant professor of communication at the University of New Mexico. Her scholarly interests include the study of cultural and intercultural communication, language in social interaction, and ethnographic research methods. She is the author of *Culture, Communication, and Cooperation: Interpersonal Relations and Pronominal Address in a Mexican Organization* (2002). Born in Mexico, she has worked in the United States and abroad and is fluent in English, Spanish, French, and Italian.

Karen Lynette Dace is associate vice president for diversity and associate professor in the Department of Communication at the University of Utah. Her research interests include small group communication, organizational communication, and minority theory.

Keturah A. Dunne graduated from California Western School of Law and is an attorney in the public defender's office in San Diego, California.

Samuel M. Edelman is a professor of communication studies and of Jewish studies at California State University, Chico.

Elane Geller is one of the youngest survivors of the Holocaust. She lectures widely throughout the United States and regularly tells her story at the Museum of Tolerance in Los Angeles.

Juan C. Gonzalez is the vice president for student affairs at Arizona State University. He has also served as the vice president for student affairs at Georgetown University, California Polytechnic State University at San Luis Obispo, and at California State University, San Bernardino.

Alfred J. Guillaume, Jr., is vice chancellor for academic affairs and professor of French at Indiana University-South Bend. He previously served in similar academic administrative positions at Humboldt State University and Saint Louis University.

Rona Tamiko Halualani is associate professor of communication studies at San Jose State University. Her research focuses on issues related to cultural identity, power, and race, and she authored *In the Name of the Hawaiians: Native Identity and Cultural Politics.*

Tadasu "Todd" Imahori is a professor of communication studies in the Department of Foreign Languages at Seinan Gakuin University, Fukuoka, Japan. Before relocating to Japan in 1997, he had lived in the United States for almost twenty years and taught communication at San Francisco State University and at Illinois State University. His research interests include competent identity management in intercultural communication, and his scholarly writings have appeared widely.

Young Yun Kim was born and raised in Korea and now lives in Norman, Oklahoma, where she is a professor of communication at the University of Oklahoma. Her research has been primarily aimed at explaining the role of communication in the cross-cultural adjustment process of immigrants and sojourners, and native-born ethnic minorities.

Jolene Koester is president, as well as professor of communication studies, at California State University, Northridge. Despite her primarily administrative responsibilities, she is deeply committed to the importance of teaching and researching intercultural communication issues. She is a co-author of *Intercultural Competence: Interpersonal Communication across Cultures.*

Mei Lin Kroll graduated from the University of Minnesota and is now in Seoul, Korea, taking intensive Korean language classes, teaching business communication classes, and tutoring children in English.

Amy Qiaoming Liu is an associate professor of sociology at California State University, Sacramento. Born in the People's Republic of China, she loves traveling and talking with people. Her passion in life includes teaching and researching intercultural communication issues and conducting public opinion polls. She has completed more than twenty surveys in the past ten years.

Myron W. Lustig is a professor of communication at San Diego State University. He writes actively in the areas of intercultural and interpersonal communication and is the co-author of *Intercultural Competence: Interpersonal Communication across Cultures.* He likes talking with people, working with data, and eating Thai food.

Ringo Ma is an associate professor in the Department of Communication Studies at Hong Kong Baptist University. Born in Taiwan, he completed his B.A. there, and M.A. and Ph.D. degrees in the United States His major research area is communication and culture in East Asia and North America.

Patrick McLaurin is director of diversity at Booz Allen Hamilton, a global strategy and technology consulting firm. He is a co-founder of MEE Productions, a media research company.

Mark Lawrence McPhail is a professor in the Western College School of Interdisciplinary Studies at Miami University. His research focuses on relationships between discourse and difference, with an emphasis on the problems and possibilities of oppositional discourse. He is the author of three books, *The Rhetoric of Racism, Zen in the Art of Rhetoric: An Inquiry into Coherence*, and *The Rhetoric of Racism Revisited: Reparations or Separation?*

Vicki Marie teaches communication at San Joaquin Delta College and has taught at the College of Micronesia. Her passions in life are world travel, teaching intercultural communication, and serving as the U.S. mother to three Micronesian children.

S. Lily Mendoza is assistant professor in culture and communication at the University of Denver. She is the author of *Between the Homeland and the Diaspora: The Politics of Theorizing Filipino and Filipino American Identities.* Her current research interests include issues of identity and post/transnational contexts, discourses of indigenization, and cultural translation and resistance.

Chevelle Newsome is associate dean for graduate studies and professor of communication studies at California State University, Sacramento.

Peter O. Nwosu is chair of the Department of Communication Studies at California State University, Northridge. He is coauthor of *Communication and the Transformation of Society: A Developing Region Perspective.*

Saila Poutiainen is a doctoral candidate in communication at the University of Massachusetts and teaching at the University of Helsinki, Finland. Her research includes explorations of dating in cross-cultural perspective, as well as Finnish conceptions and uses of the cell phone in relationship development.

Mohammad H. Qayoumi is vice president for administration and finance at California State University, Northridge. Most of his professional writing is devoted to disaster preparedness, business continuity plans, and improving energy efficiency in higher educational institutions. Since 9/11 he has spent considerable time in Afghanistan helping that country reestablish the necessary infrastructure to govern itself.

Rui Shen received her doctorate in English and comparative literature from the University of Oregon. She has now returned to her home country, the People's Republic of China.

William J. Starosta teaches at Howard University in Washington, D.C. In 1973 he received the nation's first doctorate specifically designated as intercultural communication.

Thomas M. Steinfatt is a professor in the School of Communication, University of Miami.

Zhong Wang was born and raised in the People's Republic of China and received her doctorate in communication from the University of Miami. She now works in private industry.

Gale Young is professor of speech communication at California State University, East Bay, where she has held numerous administrative positions in support of her deep commitment to diversity and equity, as well as an institutional focus on documenting educational effectiveness.